𝕿𝕖𝕟 𝕭𝕺𝕠𝕜𝕤

THAT SHAPED THE

British

EMPIRE.

Ten Books

THAT SHAPED THE

British
EMPIRE.

Creating an Imperial Commons

ANTOINETTE BURTON

AND

ISABEL HOFMEYR,

EDITORS

Duke University Press • Durham and London • 2014

Library of Congress Cataloging-in-Publication Data
Ten books that shaped the British Empire : creating an imperial commons /
Antoinette Burton and Isabel Hofmeyr, editors.
pages cm
Includes bibliographical references and index.
ISBN 978-0-8223-5813-8 (cloth : alk. paper)
ISBN 978-0-8223-5827-5 (pbk. : alk. paper)
1. Books—Great Britain—History. 2. Imperialism—Historiography.
3. Great Britain—Colonies—Historiography. I. Burton, Antoinette M., 1961–
II. Hofmeyr, Isabel.
DA16.T45 2014
909.09'71241—dc23

Cover art: Collage based on vintage endpaper of red grosgrain silk. Spencer
Collection, The New York Public Library, Astor, Lenox and Tilden Foundations.

CONTENTS

ACKNOWLEDGMENTS

We would like to acknowledge the National Research Foundation and the Faculty of Humanities, University of the Witwatersrand, which provided funding that enabled a meeting of the contributors in Johannesburg. Our thanks as well to Merle Govind for her sterling administrative support, and to Miriam Angress for her skill and care in shepherding the manuscript through the many highways and byways of the process.

INTRODUCTION. THE SPINE OF EMPIRE?

Books and the Making of an Imperial Commons

ANTOINETTE BURTON AND

ISABEL HOFMEYR

Like the history of modern paperwork more generally, the career of the English-language book in the age of empire is full of surprises.[1] The embodiment of English manly authority, the book was not simply "a surrogate Englishman in his highest and most perfect state," it was the very emblem of imperial sovereignty—with the rigorous spine a testimony to its singularity, its probity, its titular power. Discussions of the colonial archive highlight the monumentality of imperial volumes—blue books, surveys, censuses, commissions, dictionaries—that embodied the apparent solidity of imperial rule.[2] The King James Bible is perhaps the best example of a book conscripted into an imperial role: a tome conferring the philanthropic gift of Christianity and civilization, it was imagined in some evangelical accounts to be capable of traveling by itself through different landscapes of "palm and pine" and creating a unified Christian empire in its wake.[3] Nor was the book's power contained merely within its covers. As studies of individual authors like Walter Scott and John Bunyan have shown, the characters and titles from their texts were memorialized across empire in the names of suburbs, streets, ships, and people.[4] Like the wide variety of goods and commodities that made their way through the circuitry of global market capitalism, books impressed themselves in the everyday lives of imperial subjects, manifesting the formal values of an elite or bourgeois self and modeling in their material form the coherence and commanding presence of British imperial power itself.

Yet for all their pretensions to coherence and stability, books in the age of empire were both less and more than they appeared to be. As the titles we have gathered here illustrate, the book was not always a prefabricated thing, ready-made and unified along a neat vertical axis. More often than not, what arrived between covers was the consequence of a variety of imperial trajectories: upcyclings from pamphlet material or recyclings from scissor-and-paste newspaper clippings—fragments remixed, in turn, through the "geographically disaggregated networks" that constituted the British Empire in its modernizing forms.[5] In this sense, the book as we imagine it may be said to be part of a global "paper empire."[6] We seek here to push that concept in two directions: first, *toward* the book as a material form and a geopolitical influence—a carrier of imperial opinion and authority and a provocation to imperial power as well—and second, *away* from the book as distinct from or superior to the varieties of imperial print cultures-in-common through which it circulated. Though this seems paradoxical, even contradictory, in fact it is indispensable to any study of books and empire that refuses to fetishize either object of inquiry. It is our collective contention that their entwined histories require otherwise. For the history of books and their imperial careers that contributors to this volume have built allows us to see with particular vividness how and why changes in and challenges to empire were always dispersed events, not dependent on singular, bounded origins or forms but produced by "multiple singularities" that congealed in and against specific historical circumstances.[7] If empire was not a coherent whole but an assemblage—a far-flung, reticulate, and vascular patchwork of spaces joined by mobile subjects of all kinds—the book itself was often also just such an assemblage. Indeed, the very category of the book is potentially a red herring. The presumptive spine that unified empire and fixed dissent, the book turns out to be a radical sign of the "chaotic pluralism" of imperial authority and legitimacy, and in the case of this book, times ten.[8]

Like all books, this book has a multifaceted genealogy. It started as a collaboration between a historian of imperialism and a scholar of transnational book history interested in thinking about how books shaped the modern British Empire, both through the ideas they articulated and the material forms those ideas took. In our quest for a commanding title ourselves, we fixed on the notion of "ten books that changed the British Empire"—not *the* ten most significant books, but a diverse set of titles whose influence on imperial discourse and power we could trace through the careers of the texts themselves. To our surprise, among the ten we chose, five had begun as pamphlets and one as a newspaper serial—embryonic book forms that became consolidated between permanent, formal covers as a result of their movement through various circuits of empire. We began to realize that books themselves were not necessarily as self-evident as we first thought: while some started with the purposeful spine their authors intended, others grew from the tumultuous realm of the periodical, the pamphlet, the manifesto, the broadsheet, the newsletter into something else altogether: the canonical—and as Hofmeyr has written elsewhere, the monumental— book form.[9] The influence of these books was both direct and indirect, depending on their form: depending, in other words, on their specific historical iterations in and through the imperial commons they helped to create. Taken together, the ten books in this collection reveal the workings of an imperial print culture-in-the-making that enabled such unlooked-for transformations: a species of mobile imperial commons that took various material forms, of which the book is surprisingly just one.

As surprising to us, in all the various conversations we had about this volume, none of our interlocutors questioned its basic premise: that books could change empire. People seemed quite ready and willing to envisage a series of big books that founded empires (Macaulay, Seeley, Dilke, Lugard) and a set of equally significant books that ended up dismantling them (Fanon, Cabral, Guevara). These authors and their books certainly mark out a historically familiar path from empire to nation. Yet despite our interest in the question of transformation, this collection resists a strictly developmentalist model of historical influence or change. Instead we've focused on how books in the age of empire imagined how imperialism worked, assessed how or why it didn't, and diagnosed what its successes and failures meant for the fate of global hegemony at a variety of historical junctures. So we revisit imperial classics, big books automatically associated with the British Empire dominant, if not ascendant: Charlotte Brontë's *Jane Eyre* (1847), Macaulay's *History of England* (1848 and following), Charles Pearson's *National Life and Character* (1893) and Robert Baden-Powell's *Scouting for Boys* (1908). We explore anticolonial blockbusters, texts that rocked the foundations of imperial authority, from their initial appearance

(C. L. R. James's work *The Black Jacobins*, 1938), or long afterward (Mohandas K. Gandhi's *Hind Swaraj*, 1909). And we look to texts that may be less well known, if at all, to students of empire: Edward Gibbon Wakefield's work *A Letter from Sydney* (1827), the jointly authored *Century of Wrong* (1899), Totaram Sanadhya's 1914 work *Fiji Mein Mere Ekkis Varsh* (My Twenty-One Years in Fiji), and Gakaara wa Wanjau's 1960 work *Mīhīrīga ya Agīkūyū* (The Clans of the Gikuyu). We do so not by way of bringing these works into some kind of literary canon, postcolonial or otherwise. We see them more as the portable property of an ever-evolving imperial commons: not the kind that moves "from space to space unchanged" but, more precisely, the kind whose mobility reshapes the very form and content of the "book" itself.[10]

Though we remain attached to our ten books as vehicles for this argument, we focus more purposefully here on the meanings of imperial commons as a site of deterritorialized sovereignty in the textual economy of the modern British Empire. Our use of the phrase "imperial commons" derives from an old term that has recently gained a new life in relation to digital communications (or "dot.commons," as one writer styles it[11]). A commons is normally understood as a resource "in joint use or possession; . . . held or enjoyed equally by a number of persons." The right to the resource is not contingent on obtaining the permission of anyone: "No one exercises a property right with respect to these resources."[12] To put the terms "rights," "enjoy," and "joint use" alongside the term "imperial" may seem shocking, since empire represents the very opposite—denial of rights, exclusive access for racialized elites, enclosure and dispossession.

Yet, when applied to textual resources, the term makes considerable sense. Most printed matter in empire functioned without reference to copyright: American reprints, Protestant evangelical publications, official publications, or the extensive network of periodicals that carpeted empire and generated most of their copy from each other, with or without formal exchange agreements.[13] Indeed this situation was in part abetted by imperial copyright legislation that protected the rights only of European metropolitan-based producers selling in the colonial market, although colony-specific regulations did attempt to fill the gap.[14] The tangle of national, colonial, imperial, and international intellectual property law created an uneven terrain.[15] Those agencies invested in copyright, such as large British publishing companies and their associated agencies, customs officials, or colonial states, had limited success enforcing these rights. This confusion created opportunities where colonized elites could strategically deploy or ignore copyright. As Karin

Barber has argued, elite Yoruba writers did at times make use of copyright legislation, generally in relation to books rather than newspapers.[16] Yet such attempts to seek copyright protection were limited, especially in existing intellectual systems and media (whether manuscript, performative, or oral) where the notion that words could be converted into private property made no sense.

The periodical exchange system was especially important in creating a mobile imperial commons. Initially a pretelegraph phenomenon, the system persisted among those who could not afford the steep wire service fees and/or objected to their imperial bias. These interwoven periodicals produce the textual format so familiar to anyone who has worked with imperial newspapers. Any one page will largely be composed of cuttings from elsewhere, each page convening its own miniature empire as snippets from the *Calcutta Herald*, the *Rangoon Times*, the *Johannesburg Star*, the *Manchester Guardian*, and the *Sydney Herald* rub shoulders. The juxtaposition of these pieces invited readers to construct their own empire without copyright. Such forms of reading depended on comparison and circulation, with readers juxtaposing different colonies or different imperial systems via a format that announced that it had come from a periodical elsewhere and was more than likely destined for another. This periodical format and its mode of reading constituted a widespread and homemade global idiom and needs to be understood as a demotic form of world literature. This description accords well with Emily Apter's argument for a lowercase world literature, one of whose characteristics (alongside untranslatability, the burden of her monograph) might be a "dispossessive ethics of reading that challenges the presumptive self-interest and self-having assumed to condition the reader's relation to cultural property. This dispossessive stance casts World Literature as an unownable estate, a literature over which no one exerts proprietary prerogative and which lends itself to a critical turn that puts the problem of property possession front and centre."[17] This twentieth-century rubric had underpinnings that were, indubitably, a global imperial commons: not simply a shared imperial space but a densely populated domain with "a miniature empire" convened on virtually every page.[18]

As with all commons, access would have been uneven and dependent on wealth, location, levels of literacy. Censorship and colonial state intervention would have constituted another hindrance. Yet, despite these factors, the principle remained that very few property rights existed with respect to these resources. They were textual resources over which one could exercise a common right. The implications of such an imperial commons are wide-ranging and call minimally for histories of copyright and intellectual property across empire that work from the textual practice up rather than the law down.[19] This collection deploys the idea of the imperial commons to grapple with ideas of both book and empire, an intersection that requires us to provincialize the book, the better to grasp its power.

Charismatic Books, Mobile Imperial Histories

Our ten books came in different shapes and sizes, from the slender tract to the multivolume tome. Some were artisanally crafted pamphlets; some started in periodicals or as ephemera, only to rise up into bookness before sinking back again. Working through the capillaries of imperial print culture and colonial politics, these charismatic texts speak broadly to the history of the book and its empire-building capacities from the start of the nineteenth century to decolonization and beyond. Elleke Boehmer's discussion of Baden-Powell's *Scouting for Boys*, for example, shows how its ideas of friendship, imagined initially in a racialized vein, were taken up across empire and beyond and turned into a model of international exchange and comradeship that echoed Rabindranath Tagore's famously cosmopolitan versions of Indian nationalism. Mrinalini Sinha, in contrast, considers a "humble book," namely a Hindi pamphlet (*Fiji Mein Mere Ekkis Varsh*) written by an indentured laborer returned from the plantations of Fiji. In its content, the booklet gave expression to a growing desire in India to put an end to the indenture system that humiliated "our countrymen overseas," as the parlance of the day put it. Having worked in South Africa, Gandhi understood these sentiments and was quick to capitalize on the anti-indenture movement for his own mobilization. An anti-imperial text like the multiauthored work *A Century of Wrong*, the hasty manifesto that set out the Boer cause on the eve of the Anglo-Boer war (South African war), also worked in unexpected ways. As André du Toit explains, the tract flared briefly, courtesy of the pro-Boer international solidarity movements, but then disappeared, its longer term effects only manifest via the slow violence of Afrikaner nationalism and apartheid more than half a century on and beyond, finding echoes in late twentieth-century discussions of nationalism. What came up and off the printed page in the age of empire not only traveled far, in other words; it illuminates, for us, a variety of pathways between texts and power rather than a singular, evolutionary, quantifiable or predictable one.

If each of our ten books tells a story, it does not do so just because it was published or made its way into readers' hands (or heads or hearts). There are deep histories of composition, circulation, suppression, and even disappearance that these essays track, shedding light on imperial processes not otherwise visible via either a pure history-of-ideas approach or a bottom-up social history approach. Appreciating the materiality of the book, its mobility and its storied career, is critical for the *communicative* history of empire it has the capacity to tell. The emphasis on the book as one particular, if not peculiar, embodiment of an imperial information system is crucial for challenging the "methodological fetishism" of the object itself; so as not to reify it, in other words, but to reinsert it into the series of imperial commodity chains and virtual public spheres whence it came and which it indubitably shaped.

And yet the book is hard to put down or set aside, especially in the age of the e-reader and the tail end of anglo-global empire in which we live. So while our texts are diverse, our method for thinking through the byways and the zones of encounter they sponsored is, quite simply, the book itself: an object and a category that this collection aims to right-size in the context of the imperial commons through which it exercised its power. Books, we argue, need to be placed against the sprawling media ecologies of empire that take shape as different circuits and systems of textual transmission intersected—manuscript, codex, oral genres, writing systems, print. As Tony Ballantyne reminds us in his account of Wakefield's *Letter from Sydney*, the public spheres of empire depended on avalanches of circulating words, whether lithographed, cyclostyled, scribbled, whispered, sung, declaimed from the hustings, printed in tomes, enacted on stage, or read aloud. By paying attention to these manifold material forms of the word, we can better grasp the big and small ways in which texts act as forces in an imperial world. For all that modern British imperial culture fetishized the book form—that "surrogate Englishman"—in the end it was an imperial commodity, subject to the laws of political economy and the vagaries of the global market, which flung it into often improbable hands with equally improbable consequences, some of which we can determine, some of which are not recuperable even through the kinds of materialist histories we aim for here.

Against all odds, there are some things we can know about the reception of some books.[20] We know that the joys and sorrows of transnational intimacies that an imperial book in transit could conjure were felt firsthand by readers of Brontë's *Jane Eyre*. As Charlotte Macdonald's essay shows, the novel's imperial "journey"—and the choices Jane's own colonial encounters pressed on her—was at the very heart of the reader's experience, whether she resided in the heart of England, stood at the docks of Wellington, or struggled to gain access to the classrooms of 1950s South Africa. There, a young Xhosa girl named "Lily" may or may not have read Brontë's novel. Indeed, the quest for the sovereignty of the gendered imperial self that it archives had a very long life in the global imagination and lived on through other books, most notably Jean Rhys's *Wide Sargasso Sea* (1966). This is likely what Woolf meant when she said that "books continue each other." Though she did not live to see it, she would have appreciated Rhys's extensions and reversals, even if Woolf's surprisingly obdurate imperialist views would have prevented her from appreciating what Firdous Azim calls "the colonial rise of the novel" itself.[21]

When books are charismatic, as *Jane Eyre* certainly is, they outlive their particular historical moment, making history and underwriting historical change beyond, perhaps, what their authors ever intended or imagined possible. This is certainly true of Gandhi's *Hind Swaraj*, which, though published in 1909, only exhibited the full force of its political influence decades later, its translation into English in 1910 being one precondition for this subsequent reach. James's work *The Black Jacobins*, too, moved powerfully through political time, bringing eighteenth-century Haiti and its revolutionary promise to the heart of postcolonial Third World politics via a form of ideological conscription that may have been sui generis, but that shaped the outcome of postcolonial Caribbean societies in myriad ways nonetheless. As for Pearson's *National Life and Character*, his argument about the rise of Asia in world history was nothing short of prophetic, a combination of his own imperial attitudes and his encounters with Chinese in Australia who modeled a decidedly entrepreneurial future for themselves as diasporic agents in an emergent new global order at the turn of the twentieth century. His anxiety about the fate of the "white man" traveled far and wide. Theodore Roosevelt was one of the book's earliest and most impressed readers, even as he undertook his "imperial turn," urging intervention in Cuba/Hawaii/Philippines to preempt the vanquishing of the "white man." Nor is a once and future impact the only way books exhibit mobility. As Derek Peterson's account of *Mĩhĩrĩga ya Agĩkũyũ* so effectively shows, some texts have huge influence but comparatively banal lives. As Gakaara's text moved from prison writing to a book-between-covers, it was incorporated into an educational system where it was read by thousands of Kenyan schoolchildren, who likely absorbed its moral lessons but scarcely noticed its author. A decidedly downwardly mobile book, it did its transformative work out of sight, in the wake of the violence of empire, in the pedagogical recesses of the newly postcolonial state.

In thinking about books not just as mobile objects but as themselves dispersed events, this introduction draws on the work of Carol Gluck and Anna Tsing. Their collection, *Words in Motion*, treats discrete words (secularism in Morocco, responsibility in Japan, custom in Southeast Asia, minority in Egypt) the way we treat our ten books: as intellectual and political configurations shaped by their movement in time and space even as they shape the historical conditions in which they operate, whether by affirmation of the status quo or dissent from it. What Gluck and Tsing have said about the dozen or so words they have nominated for study, we might say about the books we examine here. "If power pushed some words around," they write, "others moved by virtue of their own magnetism." Or: "One way to pay attention to both the cosmopolitan and the regional specificity of words in motion is to consider their materiality . . . [and] the materiality of communication."[22] As Michael Warner has suggested, this entails the recognition that books, like words, are not fictitious, or even simply material, objects. They are themselves material *agents*: path-makers for the circulation of ideas and discourses and, as such, makers of history in the bargain. Like Gluck and Tsing's words, we argue that books must be treated as social entities that, in our case, help to bring imperial publics and their critics into being.[23]

As usefully for our purposes, Gluck and Tsing argue that "words show us struggles over which scales . . . matter." Books in the age of the British imperialism function analogously here.[24] They contained the world of empire by shrinking it between covers, making it highly portable and even proprietary, as those who purchased *Jane Eyre* or owned *Scouting for Boys* might have felt. Books could also scale empire up to epic proportions, as Macaulay's monumental *History* and—for young men and women, at least—Baden-Powell's small but sturdy manual were wont to do. Books could also bring empire abruptly to ground, as *The Black Jacobins* did, or sow seeds of anxiety and doubt, as was the case with Pearson. Not incidentally, we are as interested in the plasticity of the book form, the bookish-ness of its becoming, as in the books themselves. In emphasizing its antecedent forms—the origins of Wakefield's *Letter from Sydney* as a prison scribbling or the beginnings of *Hind Swaraj* in the columns of a Durban newspaper—we resist the pull of the book as the incarnation of empire, preferring to find imperial power on offense or defense in the fits and starts of its multiple embodiments. We resist, too, a frankly vain search for literal connection (X read Y and then did Z). In these essays, the book form reveals the chaotically plural worlds of empire, where vertical grids certainly operated but where connections were as typically horizontal: "a crazy patchwork" that crosscut core and periphery and radiated influence rather than modeling an event chain of influence or consequence.[25]

This approach suggests itself in part because the books under consideration here were sites of deterritorialized subjectivity. Though produced in the context of empire, they were a refuge for those who did not necessarily think in conventionally imperialist or even nationalist idioms. As such, they were also a mechanism for deterritorialized *sovereignty*: a moving object that opened up spaces inside and outside the two covers—spaces that, in turn, allowed for questions about the character of imperial rule, the nature of good government, the urgency of resistance, the injustice of imperial narratives, the right and proper conditions of colonization and settlement. Though downwardly mobile and recessively influential, Gakaara's booklet encases a key question for the ten books we have brought together here: "Why am I fit to rule?" In his case, the question was endemic to the end of empire: as Peterson notes, "Africa's patriots sought to surpass their colonial rulers, to project an image of integrity and responsibility that testified to their fitness to govern themselves." Despite their particularities, the books featured here can be read as both raising and answering this question. They explore diverse ideals of sovereignty, of who should and should not rule, what rule should or should not be—a project that involved imagining the limits of empire, even and especially when the author's intention was to tout its providentiality or its endless futurity. That most writers strove to express these ideas in books (or the closest they could get to that form) is not an accident, since books themselves were a form of and claim on sovereignty in an imperial context.

Books and Sovereignty: The Single Volume and the Chaos of Empire

In the highbrow worlds of modern national-imperial culture, the English book betokens autonomy, authority, and sovereignty. It can exemplify an idea like nation and empire, making these monuments and exemplars of

English virtue, civility, and nation-ness. Macaulay's book is a model in every sense: it tells the biography of a model nation, it models good governance and nationhood, its portability models mobile Englishness, and as an object it stands as a miniature model of England itself. The *History* encompasses the scale of empire not only by the vast imperial spaces it maps between covers but by the distance it traveled as well. In a particularly performative instance of this kind of textual entwinement, an advertisement for Cole's Book Arcade in Melbourne in the Australian media in the 1910s showed a sea serpent stretching from England to Australia carrying packets of books on the curves of its back.[26]

Small wonder that those with anticolonial ambitions frequently expressed themselves in similarly monumental volumes designed to stand as the counter-current to empire's master narrative and to circulate among those who wished to curtail its persuasive power. Nehru's *Discovery of India* (1946) and *Toward Freedom* (1941) are suitably epic in both content and form. When C. L. R. James produced *The Black Jacobins* in 1938, it appeared in a handsome 328-page edition from Secker and Warburg. The back of the dust cover featured a series of companion volumes all in epic vein (examples include *The Tragedy of the Chinese Revolution*; *Green Banners: The Story of the Irish Struggle*; and *Stalin*). While not motivated by any straightforward anti-imperialism, Gakaara wa Wanjau aspired to have all his work published in one large volume, an ambition he never realized due to the expense. Today syllabi of postcolonial literature still show a bias toward "the book" in the form of the novel. More popular forms like the magazine or periodical tend to be studied in courses on popular culture. Like the bildungsroman, the book constitutes a proxy for autonomous selfhood.

Peter Stallybrass has traced out the long confessional history of the ideology of "the single volume," that avatar of universal knowledge that served as the legitimating basis of an immodestly evangelizing imperial mission.[27] In Christian pictorial traditions going back to the late Middle Ages, the four evangelists write their gospels in bound volumes rather than loose sheets of parchment, which would have been the extant medieval practice. What they inscribe is already gathered together, consolidated, and error free. The bound volume exuded permanence: it was designed to last and could stand on a shelf (when modern bookshelves finally took shape). The pamphlet by contrast was dog-eared, could not stand on its own, and apparently expressed ideas that were provisional and still in formation. In a more secular vein, Leah Price has thrown light on the affective power of the single volume.[28] Her route into this theme starts in the present. How is it, she asks, that our methods for studying books are so divided: literary studies for the inside and book history for the outside? Why is it so difficult to study the book as an integrated object? Her answer takes us back to Victorian Britain and its particular ideology of the bound volume. As she demonstrates, the novel becomes a singularly popular form: brought freely as a commodity and read pleasurably from beginning to end. The style of reading it entails is important: readers become possessed by the text, forgetting both themselves and the physical book that they hold.

As her ingenious interpretation of the Victorian novel itself demonstrates, these modes of reading sort good characters from bad (a theme Charlotte Macdonald takes up in her discussion of *Jane Eyre*). Virtuous characters are recognizable by the way they read, namely in an attentive and disembodied way. Feckless characters read only fitfully or use books as weapons to harm others, or demonstrate their superficiality by caring for books only as objects of interior decoration. As Price indicates further, the affective hold of the novel is reinforced by its implicit contrast with the tract. The former is actively chosen by a consumer and is read with pleasure. The latter is given away as an object of charity and involves reading as duty. The tract transaction underlines the relative social status of giver and receiver—mistress and servant; doctor and patient; Christian missionary and "heathen"; colonizer and colonized; husband and wife. As Price also makes clear, the glamour of the novel depends on the dowdiness of the tract. Stallybrass likewise calls for the printed book to be parochialized in relation to other print forms.[29] Bound books only ever constituted a small percentage of what was printed: forms, labels, handbills, letterheads, booklets, leaflets, tracts, chapbooks, newspapers made up the bulk of a printer's business. Yet, however much they may tower above these nether regions of print, hardcover volumes still accrue meaning in relation to them.

For those invested in the monumentality of the hardback volume, the printed book loomed above this landscape (especially in settings where hardback books were relatively rare and expensive). Yet, when we place it back in its habitat, we see that the book was not a self-starter but arose out of and sank back into these other forms. Books are rehearsed in newspapers, periodicals pamphlets, letters, and plays. They travel through reviews, polemical argument, and public debate. They channel and plagiarize each other. The book is always already a dispersed and a *dispersing* event: print sprawled across distance, time, language, and script, carving out pathways of interest and influence, creating and re-creating imperial events and, in the process, shaping an imperial commons that presumed shared values but also sponsored debate, doubt, critique. These collusions and collisions produced distinctive textual formations across empire that scholars are just beginning to investigate in qualitative and quantitative terms.[30] Meanwhile, it seems highly probable, if not likely, that the book, imagined as a text between covers, constitutes a smaller slice of the market share than the layperson and even the student of empire might anticipate.

Media ecologies—by which we mean the combination of textual and technological environments in which books circulated through empire—were crucial to these imperial textual formations, in which a book of the day made its career. As printing innovations spread across empire, they were taken up by existing institutions and brought new ones into being. Princely states acquired show presses; large metropolitan publishing companies sought to extend their reach in colonial markets, which in turn shaped them; evangelical organizations whether Hindu reformist, Protestant, or Muslim acquired presses that featured as protagonists in their reforming accounts of themselves; colonial states undertook large volumes of printing; private companies whether British or indigenous were a substantial sector: as Ulrike Stark's account of the Nawal Kishore Press in Lucknow demonstrates, the company employed 350 handpresses, a "considerable number" of steam presses, and nine hundred employees producing material in a range of languages.[31] Africans trained in Protestant evangelical settings established presses often in the teeth of racist opposition from white journeymen who saw printing as the preserve of the "white man."[32]

Printers moved in and between these settings, producing worlds of conflicted but cosmopolitan print activity. Port cities drew together diasporic printers, whether Indian, African, Chinese, or British, who might find themselves in evangelical presses, colonial state operations, private concerns large or small. Many started their own operations, generally tenuous jobbing presses. These not only undertook commercial work but also printed periodicals and pamphlets in various languages (and scripts) that gave expression to the new sets of transnational alignments that mass migration produced. As many scholars have demonstrated, movements like Sikh internationalism, imperial citizenship, theosophy, Sufism, pan-Buddhism, pan-Islam, African nationalism, Hindu reformism, and ideals of the "white working man" were fueled by small presses and printed matter that linked together far-flung constituents.[33]

At a minimum, this emerging configuration of the artisanal multilingual presses and the periodicals and pamphlets they produced redirects our attention to the themes of the imperial commons and requires us to rethink the proportional role of the single-authored book as the distinctive textual form in the age of empire. Discussing textual formations in Africa, Karin Barber has suggested that the term "printing cultures" may be more appropriate than "print culture" with its overtones of vast, monoglot, anonymous, and impersonal address.[34] By contrast, the phrase "printing cultures" captures the small-scale, artisanal, multilingual operations that produced texts rooted in personalized but transnational forms of address. Often depending on "home-made" or "home-spun" methods (to borrow a term from Derek Peterson's work), such printing cultures were common across much of empire.[35] Elsewhere in his work on colonial New Zealand, Tony Ballantyne has pointed to newspapers and periodicals as "material and semiotic" institutions that were involved not only in ideology and representation but also in forming a continuum of "materials, skills, technologies, financial arrangements and cultural conventions."[36] Where books were expensive and rare, newspapers and periodicals constituted a do-it-yourself medium for creating personalized collections and scrapbooks. The newspaper/periodical was a scissors-and-paste affair arising from the exchange system by which consenting publications agreed to clip material from each other.[37] Its cut-and-paste genres trained readers in ongoing comparative and transnational forms of interpretation; its lack of copyright normalized a routine disregard for intellectual property law across much of empire; and its endless circulation of portions of text encouraged a model of the author as editor rather than a creative genius producing sui generis texts.

One famous example of such an artisanal configuration was the International Printing Press set up by Gandhi and others in Durban in 1898, which was made up of personnel from South India, Gujarat, Mauritius, the Cape Colony, Natal, and England. The press offered printing services in ten languages involving seven different scripts (English, Gujarati, Tamil, Hindi, Urdu, Hebrew, Marathi, Sanskrit, Zulu, and Dutch).[38] The newspaper it produced from 1903, *Indian Opinion*, initially appeared in four languages and four scripts: English, Gujarati, Tamil, and Hindi. The newspaper itself was never run for profit and in its later years, Gandhi got rid of virtually all advertising (depending instead on subsidies from merchants and industrialists in both South Africa and India). Instead the paper was dedicated to furthering the ideals of satyagraha and the rights of British Indians across the world.

Mrinalini Sinha's account of the world of provincial Indian print and journalism shows a similar picture, with small-time reforming editors running multilingual papers, generally on a shoestring budget. These papers served as hubs for itinerant journalists, traveling revolutionaries, and would-be writers to meet either via the publication or in person in the newspaper offices. Sanadhya's text emerged from precisely such a setting, where he encountered Benarsidas Chaturvedi, a journalist who took up the cause of Indians overseas and to whom he dictated his story. Derek Peterson's essay likewise illuminates an African world of small artisanal presses in which Gakaara worked and which he helped establish. *Scouting for Boys*, too, even though it emerged from the heart of the metropolitan mass media machine, has its own patched-together book history, as Boehmer details in her essay. The comparative informality of printing operations, especially before the high noon of mechanical reproduction, relativizes existing ideas of global histories of print rooted in ideas of print capitalism, the novel, and the newspaper, which pivot on notions of commodity saturation, intellectual property, machine-driven nationalism, and vast monoglot publics. By contrast the small artisanal presses and their products raise themes of philanthropy, merchant patronage, personalized address in a transnational matrix, multilingualism, and variable notions of authorship and copyright.

In the history of print in empire, print-as-empire, all dimensions of the equation remain relevant: there can be no question of either print capitalism/or artisanal "homemade production," just as there can be no question of the supremacy of the book over other protean or embryonic casts. The material forms in which Gandhi's work appeared illustrate this point. His first public writing was published serially in 1889 in the *Vegetarian*; his first work between hard covers, in the 1920s. In between, he produced numerous pamphlets, generally culled from the periodicals he edited in South Africa and India. Hence it took some four decades for Gandhi's work to rise from the domain of the periodical and pamphlet to that of the hardbound book. This move was not one that he sought: it was rather thrust upon him as his own stature and that of his work gained international visibility. A lifelong critic of copyright, Gandhi resisted the commoditization of print and the attempts by the nation-state to claim rights over its reproduction. He had little interest in producing expensive volumes and across his life largely worked with the periodical and pamphlet.

Given the particularities of his biography, his charismatic politics, and the worlds of print from which his claims to sovereignty emerged, the heterogeneous forms in which Gandhi published may capture the chaotic plurality of printing cultures in empire, but they are not necessarily representative of the paper empire whose histories we are trying to nuance here. Yet if we understand the instability of the book form as representative of the historical conditions in which an imperial commons was imagined and operated, we can better appreciate the book itself as an illuminating dye—at once clearing space for and running through empire's pathways, consolidating notions of the imperial self in some places, challenging them in others. In light of recent work that throws the British national-imperial legal system into question as the self-directing autonomous export of the imperial center, it is tempting to range the book alongside the law, that inimitable index of English civilizational progress, political order, and self-government. Both the book and the law are exemplary English "goods" that map spaces of extraterritoriality, archive tests of colonial authority and legitimacy, and offer their users evidence of the thin "jurisdictional net" of imperial power on the ground.[39] In this sense, in form and function they each have the capacity to track "the spatial variations of imperial sovereignty" that underwrote global cultures of empire, offering us the opportunity to see its rifts and fissures, if not its cataclysmic challenges as well. As assemblages of a patchwork variety of "things," the book and the law both contain, in other words, the histories of rule and its undoing, the evidence of imperial legitimacy and its challenges to it. As for books and empire, neither was a coherent or self-contained thing. Each was, rather, the *effect* of a set of contingencies and collisions with history on the ground: a pair of moving subjects that, together, configure the history of each in new ways.

Recycling and Upcycling: Genre, Author, Owner

The periodical was a key textual institution of empire and furnished a set of intersections, an imperial commons from which new genres, modes of reading, authorship, and ownership could be fashioned. As Sinha shows, Indian-language papers were the first to give public expression to individual experiences of indentured labor by printing affidavits and sworn statements, a genre of personal testimony that Sanadhya in turn developed. In *Hind Swaraj* Gandhi mapped an old Indic genre of dialogue onto the templates of mass media by creating a series of exchanges between an Editor and a Reader that mirrored a newspaper encounter in which the Editor had to speak through the forms of that medium. *Scouting for Boys* exploited the cut-and-paste form of the periodical in a spectacular way, appearing in tandem with the stable of publications of the magnate C. Arthur Pearson, which included *Daily Express*, *Pearson's Weekly*, and *Tit-bits*. As Boehmer argues, the success of Baden-Powell's book pivoted on the way it enacted a networking of networks, a genre that the imperial periodical embodied in miniature.

This pick-and-mix format encouraged an idea of reading as shaped by circulation. Any periodical was a brief thickening of text from elsewhere, pausing briefly courtesy of a reader before moving on to another destination. Virtually all of our ten books are dominated by such genres of circulation: the letter, the clipping, the résumé, the extract, Q and A, the tract, the pamphlet. Reading formations likewise bear an imprint of circulation. Several texts in this collection depended on international reading circuits for their success. *A Century of Wrong* became a calling card and item of solidarity across boundaries. C. L. R. James's ideas percolated through cosmopolitan revolutionary networks, reading groups, debating societies, friendships, and feuds. The charisma of both text and author pulsed through these networks. *Scouting for Boys* created the illusion that all scouts, wherever they were in the world, participated in the same text, which circulated yet apparently remained unchanged.

These genres of circulation in turn implied ideals of authorship that were closer to that of the editor than the creative genius. Writing emerged as much from clippings and extracts as from original composition, as Ballantyne's account of Wakefield demonstrates so vividly. The figure of the editor is present elsewhere: *Jane Eyre* was edited by "Currer Bell"; *A Century of Wrong* was edited by several hands, most of whose owners subsequently disavowed their involvement; Gandhi chose to express himself through the persona of the Editor; *Scouting for Boys* was composed through an almost absentminded gathering of textual fragments.

This figure of the editor finds its analogue in the idea of the tin trunk as a form of demotic self-archiving and mode of composition, as Karin Barber and Derek Peterson have argued elsewhere.[40] Sanadhya and Gakaara carted trunks and boxes of documents with them, often having to practice subterfuge to keep them from the attentions of the colonial state (itself a conscientious and thorough, if paranoid reader). Gandhi was a great keeper of scrapbooks, which traveled with him. Baden-Powell used a metaphorical filing box as a way of generating text.

Editing likewise played a role in constructing ethnic identities. As Peterson shows, Gakaara spent his time in a Mau Mau detention camp doing ethnography on the Gikuyu, gathering information on clans and subsequently editing it into a series of pamphlets on Gikuyuness. In the case of *A Century of Wrong*, the history of Boers was radically edited, their Dutch origins being excised in favor of starting the story with the advent of British imperialism, thereby turning Afrikaners into an anticolonial and hence injured people. The role of editor is perhaps most interesting in *Hind Swaraj*, where Gandhi sets out his view in the foreword to his manifesto: "These views are mine, and yet not mine. They are mine because I hope to act according to them. They are part of my being. Yet, they are not mine, because I lay no claim to originality." As Suhrud points out, in making this claim, Gandhi draws on Indic ideas of composition in which the writer-composer articulates the existing state of knowledge. At the same time, Gandhi also draws on his work as a newspaper editor, wherein most of the text that passed through his hand came from other publications. Importantly, Gandhi equates authorship with conduct ("I hope to act according to them"). In this equation, the point of any text is that it can be applied to circumstances to help the reader to understand them better, and to act with more insight. We encounter this model of reading across the essays presented here: the point of all ten books was that they be applied to present and pressing circumstances.

Today, this mode of reading would be classified somewhat pejoratively as "didactic," a style that high literary modernism has marginalized by constructing it as the abject opposite of complexity and irony. Taken together, these essays remind us of how global this form of "didactic" reading in fact was (and indeed still is). By taking an empire-wide purview, this collection supports Leah Price's parochialization of hegemonic modes of reading that we inherit from the Victorians.[41] As she argues, today still, ideal reading is presumed to be continuous (from beginning to end), to be disembodied, and ideally to have involved book-buying. By contrast, the forms of reading discussed in this volume are discontinuous, are often embodied, and seldom entailed a book purchase. In empire, novel and tract did not always shun each other and entered alliances, producing demotic styles of reading that revise dominant assumptions about what reading is.

Such demotic styles of reading were further encouraged by ideas of ownership and copyright, in turn shaped by the model of author-as-editor. Strikingly, across these ten essays, there is no discussion of copyright.

While the "big books" were copyrighted and embodied an imperial order of intellectual property (itself a confused terrain where national models of copyright were awkwardly and ineffectually thrust upon transnational spaces),[42] most of the books discussed here embody an idea of common-right. If books were miscellanies composed of bits and pieces, then they were texts in which everyone could share and have a share.[43] There was no author who claimed prior ownership. The tracts and pamphlets discussed here were authorless, they were cheap or free, and their point was to be passed from hand to hand. Scouts literally shared their manuals. Gandhi, as noted, rejected copyright, and the first English edition of *Hind Swaraj* specifically indicated that there were "No Rights Reserved," a phrase inviting readers to reproduce their own copies and freely share in the book.

In terms of reading rhythms, these essays suggest a variety of tempos: the sedate and solemn pace of reading Macaulay; the urgency of Pearson and *A Century of Wrong*; the possession of *Jane Eyre*; the stop-and-start style of *Scouting for Boys*; the serialization of Wakefield's *Letter to Sydney*. Gandhi's dialogue required pausing and rereading, a mode that sought to turn the haste of discontinuous periodical reading against itself. These rhythms themselves carried implications about time and sovereignty, about who should own the future and how. To read *National Life and Character* was to become anxious about imminent loss. To read *Hind Swaraj* was to try and pause industrial time to create, however fleetingly, a miniature sovereignty in the self. To read *A Century of Wrong* was to participate in an urgent and potentially catastrophic present. To read *The Black Jacobins* was to anticipate allegorically the independence of Africa—not as a fait accompli but as a process unfolding in real time, in part by building on long histories of powerful, highly mobile ideas generated by and sustained in the imperial commons.

Taken together, these various modes of reading and writing today may strike us as unusual since like many imaginaries, they have been obscured in retrospect by the hegemony of the nation-state. This point is poignantly underlined by the number of tenuous or even imaginary textual sites that emerge from these essays. Gakaara dreamed of running "a big and popular bookshop, where while writing I can deal with selling of books from other countries, be an agent for books and periodicals, school materials, stationeries, sports equipment etc." The journalist Chaturvedi, whose connections with Sanadhya's work Sinha mentions, likewise had a daydream, this time about owning a press of his own, supported by a library and news agency that would serve the cause of "overseas Indians."[44] In both cases, these imagined scenes place their protagonists in the midst of transnational networks whose import today is no longer fully understood. Similarly in Suhrud's essay, Gandhi's ashram emerges as a fragile space in which to practice Gandhian ideas of sovereignty as rooted in the individual rather than an abstract territorialized nation-state. Gandhi's ashrams were also reading and writing communes, from some of which newspapers were produced. Both Sanadhya and Chaturvedi spent periods living on the ashram Sabarmati, which provided intellectual refuge for those whose projects did not inhere—or find traction—in the imperial nation-state.

Judging This Book by Its Cover

What, in the end, is the relationship between these ten books and historical change in the modern British Empire? The idea that books can shape empires is provocative, conjuring the kind of spectacular impact authors always, if secretly, seek when they write books. The rate at which books about empire, especially the British Empire, continue to be produced and to fly off the shelf—whether historical polemic (Niall Ferguson's *Empire: The Rise and Demise of the British World Order and the Lessons for Global Power*), creative nonfiction (William Dalrymple's *White Mughals*), or historical fiction (Amitav Ghosh's *Sea of Poppies*)—speaks to a long-standing reader desire, reanimated by the crisis of American imperialism before our eyes, to grapple with empire as a motor of history, if not as the engine of contemporary events and apprehensions as well.

Yet, as we have been arguing here, the ten books whose contributions to the kind of imperial commons we have investigated here are less an engine than a camera.[45] Rather than connecting the dots between a single spine and a cataclysmic imperial event or events, they capture a variety of kinds of historical change, typically over a long time, whether decades or more. Using them as a springboard, we ask how, why, and under what conditions such change happens, what its modalities and delivery systems are, and what the timing of impact is over the *longue durée*. To be sure, books can be preternaturally defiant, taking aim at powerful structures with the intention of fixing them as objects of critique and, with the kind of utopian energy perhaps uniquely propelled by the book form, with the hope of dismantling them in the process. This might be said of *Jane Eyre* or *Century of Wrong*. Each was motivated by a passionate sense of injustice—about the way imperial political economies shaped English women's choices and experiences, about how narratives of one violent event threw the whole system of imperial "justice" into question for a nationalist community like the Afrikaners, respectively. The prison writings of Wakefield and Gakaara that gave shape to *Letter from Sydney* and *Mīhīrīga ya Agīkūyū* were also acts of defiance, as was *Hind Swaraj*, albeit in a characteristically Gandhian way. Meanwhile, the impact of a text like *Scouting for Boys* can hardly be denied, though its publication was not a singular éclat but a tentacled, snaking pathway of influence on the adolescent psyche, both imperial and colonial. A primer for empire identification and the promise of transnational connection for all those who wanted to read it, its pedagogical career represents the transformation of the imperial ideal from a local metropolitan aspiration to a global phenomenon. As with Macaulay's *History*, a genealogy of Powell's primer shows us the technologies of historical change at work over broad reaches of space and time yet intimately as well, in the hearts and minds of readers who might have no direct encounter with empire otherwise but who became familiar with its plots and possibilities via these big, enduring books.

The same can and should be said of humbler, down-market publications like Sanadhya's *Fiji Mein Mere Ekkis Varsh*. But how, you might ask, can such an apparently microhistorical work make any claim on imperial history, let alone on the category of historical influence? In Sinha's reading, *Fiji Mein Mere Ekkis Varsh* is not the exception that makes the rule; quite the contrary. Her account compels us to rethink the direct-hit logic of challenge and influence that lingers even and especially in an age of poststructural and postcolonial assemblage, precisely because she recenters the motors of transformation at the heart of communities of print and politics that are frankly scarcely visible except through a materialist book history like this one. Sanadhya's book did not bring about the end of indenture. There was no éclat: its work was perpetually dispersed and dispersing. And it looks "subterranean"—below the sightline of empire proper—only with respect to dominant vectors of imperial power and authority, which were not in any case its exclusive or intended audiences. What is truly provocative about Sanadhya's book is that it gives readers of imperial history an opportunity to resuscitate one of the possibilities of a subaltern method: an approach that emphasizes not just resistance to imperial authority and its representatives but comparative indifference to them as well. That is to say, the efficacy of *Fiji Mein Mere Ekkis Varsh* lay not simply in its challenge to the vertical spine of imperial power but in its movement through the interstices of the imperial system. Its target was the unsupportable condition of imperial capital, and it operated horizontally against it, snaking—like Baden-Powell's *Scouting for Boys*—through the capillaries of that power, making lateral connections to do its work in the world and to achieve what minor success it had. Much the same could be said of Gakaara's pamphlet, a text indifferent to high anti-imperial registers and written instead in the moral idiom of slow reform.

Those who study, or who otherwise appreciate, the materiality of the book will tell you that titles, like covers, matter. They are like vestibules, staging the inner chambers of the space about to be entered and announcing the design, architectural and otherwise, of what is to come.[46] Like all staging devices, titles set expectations into motion, in this case on the very spine: that vertical axis that organizes the contents and directs the reader toward a horizon, an argument, a monographic set of claims. Echoing objectivist standards for historical change, a book's title bears the burden of showing, even proving, its accomplishments. For those seeking a literal reading of books + empire = impact, we have one smoking gun. As Marilyn Lake details in her essay on Pearson, the connection between his book and the White Australia policy is clear and direct, practically irrefutable. If it were needed, a case could equally be made for the causative effects of *The Black Jacobins*, that bible of global revolutionary realization that had material consequences for postcolonial Caribbean governmentality in personnel: Eric Williams was the first prime minister of Trinidad and Tobago, after all. If a post-Enlightenment preoccupation with authorship has distorted our view of the centrality of books (and vice versa),[47] the history of C. L. R. James's classic illustrates how one book rarely acts alone. As Kamugisha's essay so skillfully shows, *The Black Jacobins* was a camera *and* a catalyst, clashing and meshing with a variety of other books of its time to shape political outcomes in real time and over the long haul as well.

There are other twinnings among our ten books, pairings that suggest that the singularity of the book as an influence peddler should be further provincialized beyond the print culture upcyclings and recyclings we have materialized here. We have already spoken of the forward/backward motion of *Jane Eyre* and *Wide Sargasso Sea*; Boehmer discusses the relationship between Baden-Powell and Kipling; and the intellectual slanging matches between James and Williams were utterly consequential to the impact of their work, on each other and on haltingly, fitfully postimperial worlds they traveled in and helped to make. In this sense, reproportioning the book as a multiform commodity, whether via an appreciation of its hybrid textual histories or via its conjuncture with other spindled texts, both mirrors and maps the dispersed assemblage of imperial spaces and places—the communicative empire—that the itineraries of our ten books make visible. More precisely, the travels and travails of the book in/and empire allow us to see how and why the imperial commons we have evinced was both integrated intellectually *and* perpetually disintegrated by the myriad subjects and agents who constructed, lived inside, and sought to exceed its territorial and epistemological frames. In this sense, historical change can be sensational, but it is also always already immanent and ubiquitous; revolutionary and melodramatic *and* endemic to everyday writing and reading practices, as it is to quotidian experiences in all their imperial variety and contingency.

The rise-and-fall narrative of British imperialism, which has impressed itself on nearly every spine in the historiography of empire and continues to shape contemporary headlines about "the end of history" in politics and academia alike, does not necessarily allow for this kind of reading. Indeed, aided by the antecedent of Rome, it constitutes both a description of the British Empire's fate and a method, albeit a limiting one, for historicizing it as well. The tenacity of this arc makes the claims about books and change we are advancing here seem counterintuitive, when in fact they are commonsensical, given, at least, the particular book and empire histories this collection archives. What Kath Weston in another context has called "the long, slow burn" is a much more historically accurate account of how change happens than the drama of rise and fall that has been the explanatory framework for empire tout court.[48] It is no small irony that a study of books—those disappearing occasions for long-form thinking and slow reading—should be one of the most effective ways of dramatizing the limits of the climactic end of empire or the momentous challenge that ushers in revolutionary change. It's also a testimony to the resilience of books, and of empires, that for all the hype around their disappearance, they are, for the moment anyway, not quite yet in the rearview mirror of history.[49] As we have endeavored to show in what follows, thinking them together, as makers of an imperial assemblage always in process, still has relevance for understanding how change happens—and for choosing with vigilance and care the lenses through which we diagnose its symptoms and historicize its possibilities.

NOTES

1. Ben Kafka, *The Demon of Writing: Powers and Failures of Paperwork* (Cambridge, MA: Zone Books, 2012).

2. Javed Majeed, "What's in a (Proper) Name? Particulars, Individuals, and Authorship in the Linguistic Survey of India and Colonial Scholarship," in *Knowledge Production, Pedagogy, and Institutions in Colonial India*, ed. Daud Ali and Indra Sengupta (New York: Palgrave, 2011). More indirectly, see Ann Laura Stoler, *Along the Archival Grain: Epistemic Anxieties and Colonial Common Sense* (Princeton, NJ: Princeton University Press, 2010), 616–662.

3. Leslie Howsam, *Cheap Bibles: Nineteenth-Century Publishing and the British and Foreign Bible Society* (Cambridge: Cambridge University Press, 1991), 1–2.

4. Isabel Hofmeyr, *The Portable Bunyan: A Transnational History of "The Pilgrim's Progress"* (Princeton, NJ: Princeton University Press, 2003); Ann Rigney, *The Afterlives of Walter Scott: Memory on the Move* (Oxford: Oxford University Press, 2012), 17.

5. Jonathan Plotz, *Portable Property: Victorian Culture on the Move* (Princeton, NJ: Princeton University Press, 2009), xiii.

6. The literature on "paper empire" as well as "paper (and books) in empire" sprawls in several directions, as shown in the following categories, in each of which we list some key titles. Empire and information: C. A. Bayly, *Empire and Information: Intelligence Gathering and Social Communication in India, 1780–1870* (Cambridge: Cambridge University Press, 1996); Bernard S. Cohn, *Colonialism and Its Forms of Knowledge: The British in India* (Princeton, NJ: Princeton University Press, 1996). Writing and governance: Adam Ashforth, *The Politics of Discourse in Twentieth-Century South Africa* (Oxford: Clarendon Press, 1990); Stoler, *Archival Grain*; Thomas Richards, *The Imperial Archive: Knowledge and the Fantasy of Empire* (London: Verso, 1993); Mikes Ogborn, *Indian Ink: Script and Print in the Making of the English East India Company* (Chicago: University of Chicago Press, 2007). The precolonial book: Shamil Jeppie and Souleymane Bachir Diagne, eds., *The Meanings of Timbuktu* (Pretoria: Human Sciences Research Council Press, 2008). Manuscript cultures: Sheldon Pollock, *The Language of the Gods in the World of Men: Sanskrit, Culture, and Power in Premodern India* (Berkeley: University of California Press, 2006). Print technology in empire and beyond: Nile Green, "Persian Print and the Stanhope Revolution: Industrialization, Evangelicalism, and the Birth of Printing in Early Qajar Iran," *Comparative Studies of South Asia, Africa and the Middle East* 30, no. 3 (2010): 473–490; Sydney Shep, "Mapping the Migration of Paper: Historical Geography and New Zealand Print Culture," in *The Moving Market*, ed. Peter Isaac and Barry Mackay (New Castle, DE: Oak Knoll

Press, 2001), 179–192. Itinerant printers in empire: for research on British printers, see SAPPHIRE (Scottish Archive of Print and Publishing History Records), www.sapphire.ac.uk/, accessed 1 April 2014. Muslim print culture: Francis Robinson, "Technology and Religious Change: Islam and the Impact of Print," *Modern Asian Studies* 27, no. 1 (1993): 229–251; Nile Green, *Bombay Islam: The Religious Economy of the Western Indian Ocean* (New York: Cambridge University Press, 2011). Christian mission printing: Hofmeyr, *Portable Bunyan*; Howsam, *Cheap Bibles*. Ethnographies and histories of reading and writing: Sean Hawkins, *Writing and Colonialism in North Ghana: The Encounter between the LoDagaa and "the World on Paper," 1982–1992* (Toronto: University of Toronto Press, 2002); Archie Dick, *The Hidden History of South Africa's Book and Reading Culture* (Toronto: University of Toronto Press, 2012); Karin Barber, ed., *Africa's Hidden Histories: Everyday Literacy and the Making of the Self* (Bloomington: Indiana University Press, 2006); Derek Peterson, *Creative Writing: Translation, Bookkeeping and the Work of the Imagination in Colonial Kenya* (Portsmouth, NH: Heinemann, 2004). Orality and literacy: Ruth Finnegan, *Orality and Literacy: The Technologizing of the Word* (London: Routledge, 1982). Transnational history of the book: after being dominated by national histories of the book, this field has started to exploit the inherently transnational capacities of the book. Bill Bell, "Crusoe's Books: The Scottish Emigrant Reader in the Nineteenth Century," in *Across Boundaries: The Book in Culture and Commerce*, ed. Bill Bell, Philip Bennett, and Jonquil Bevan (New Castle, DE: Oak Knoll Press, 2000), 116–129; Rimi B. Chatterjee, *Empires of the Mind: A History of the Oxford University Press in India under the Raj* (New Delhi: Oxford University Press, 2006); Robert Fraser, *Book History through Postcolonial Eyes: Rewriting the Script* (London: Routledge, 2008); Priya Joshi, *In Another Country: Colonialism, Culture, and the English Novel in India* (New Delhi: Oxford University Press, 2002); Martyn Lyons and John Arnold, eds., *A History of the Book in Australia 1891–1945: A National Culture in a Colonised Market* (St. Lucia: University of Queensland Press, 2001); James Raven, *London Booksellers and American Customers: Transatlantic Literary Community and the Charleston Library Society, 1748–1811* (Columbia: University of South Carolina Press, 2002); Robert Fraser and Mary Hammond, eds., *Books without Borders*, vol. 1, *The Cross-National Dimension in Print Culture* (London: Palgrave Macmillan, 2008).

7. Jasbir Puar, *Terrorist Assemblages: Homonationalism in Queer Times* (Durham, NC: Duke University Press, 2007), 194.

8. The phrase is John Darwin's. See his "Imperialism and the Victorians: The Dynamics of Territorial Expansion," *English Historical Review* 112, no. 447 (1997): 614–642.

9. Isabel Hofmeyr, *Gandhi's Printing Press: Experiments in Slow Reading* (Cambridge, MA: Harvard University Press, 2013), 6.

10. Plotz, *Portable Property*, 21.

11. Lawrence Lessig, *The Future of Ideas: The Fate of the Commons in a Connected World* (New York: Random House, 2001), 17.

12. This discussion of the commons is drawn from Lessig, *The Future of Ideas*, 19–23 (quotes from pp. 19 and 20); Eva Hemmungs Wirtén, *Terms of Use: Negotiating the Jungle of the Intellectual Commons* (Toronto: University of Toronto Press, 2008).

13. On American reprints, see Meredith L. McGill, *American Literature and the Culture of Reprinting, 1834–1853* (Philadelphia: University of Pennsylvania Press, 2003); on evangelical printing see Howsam, *Cheap Bibles*; on imperial periodicals see Hofmeyr, *Gandhi's Printing Press*, ch. 3.

14. Alexander Peukert, "The Colonial Legacy of the International Copyright System," in *Staging the Immaterial: Rights, Style and Performance in Sub-Saharan Africa*, ed. Ute Röschenthaler and Mamadou Diawara (Oxford: Sean Kingston, forthcoming); Lionel Bently, "The 'Extraordinary Multiplicity' of Intellectual Property Law in the British Colonies in the Nineteenth Century," *Theoretical Inquiries in Law* 12, no. 1 (2011): 161–200.

15. For an account of this process, see Alison Rukavina, *The Development of the International Book Trade, 1870–1895* (Basingstoke, England: Palgrave Macmillan, 2010). For a more Whiggish account, see Catherine Seville, *The Internationalisation of Copyright Law: Books, Buccaneers and the Black Flag in the Nineteenth Century* (Cambridge: Cambridge University Press, 2006). Rosemary Coombe has made the point that the Protestant evangelical publishing endeavor fostered a view of texts, whatever their message, fostering one meaning and message, an idea she suggests feeds back into metropolitan ideas of copyright and its assumption that texts must be made equivalent and equitable. Rosemary J. Coombe, "Authorial Cartographies: Mapping Proprietary Borders in a Less-Than-Brave New World," *Stanford Law Review* 48, no. 1357 (1996): 2.

16. Karin Barber, "Authorship, Copyright and Quotation in Oral and Print Spheres in Early Colonial Yorubaland," in *Staging the Immaterial: Rights, Style and Performance in Sub-Saharan Africa*, ed. Ute Röschenthaler and Mamadou Diawara (Oxford: Sean Kingston, forthcoming).

17. Emily Apter, *Against World Literature: On the Politics of Untranslatability* (London: Verso, 2013), 329.

18. Hofmeyr, *Gandhi's Printing Press*, 13.

19. For one excellent "bottom-up" example, see Michael D. Birnhack, *Colonial Copyright: Intellectual Property in Mandate Palestine* (Oxford: Oxford University Press, 2012).

20. As Leslie Howsam has observed, Victorian readers remain "the 'shadowy accomplices' of authors and publishers." Leslie Howsam, *Kegan Paul and Victorian Imprint: Publishers, Books and Cultural History* (Toronto: KPI and University of Toronto Press, 1998), 11.

21. Firdous Azim, *The Colonial Rise of the Novel* (London: Routledge, 1994).

22. Carol Gluck and Anna Lowenhaupt Tsing, eds., *Words in Motion: Toward a Global Lexicon* (Durham, NC: Duke University Press, 2009), 5 and following.

23. Hofmeyr, *Portable Bunyan*, 25.

24. Gluck and Tsing, *Words in Motion*, 12; see also epilogue to C. L. Innes, *A History of Black and Asian Writing in Britain* (Cambridge: Cambridge University Press, 2008), 233–252.

25. For a superb rendering of the ad hoc origins and composition of the nineteenth-century empire, see Dane Kennedy, "The Great Arch of Empire," in *The Victorian World*, ed. Martin Hewett (London: Routledge, 2012), 57–72.

26. Martyn Lyons and Lucy Taksa, *Australian Readers Remember: An Oral History of Reading 1890–1930* (Melbourne: Oxford University Press, 1992), facing p. 120.

27. Peter Stallybrass, "What Is a Book?," lecture, Centre for the Study of the Book, Bodleian Library, University of Oxford, 13 April 2010.

28. Leah Price, *How to Do Things with Books in Victorian Britain* (Princeton, NJ: Princeton University Press, 2012).

29. Stallybrass, "What Is a Book?"

30. See note 2.

31. Ulrike Stark, *An Empire of Books: The Naval Kishore Press and the Diffusion of the Printed Word in Colonial India* (New Delhi: Permanent Black, 2007).

32. Chatterjee, *Empires of the Mind*; Joshi, *In Another Country*; Howsam, *Cheap Bibles* (which demonstrates how the demand for bound Bibles across the Christian mission empire transformed the bookbinding industry from an artisanal affair to a modern mass-production operation); Green, *Bombay Islam*; Graham Shaw, "Communications between Cultures: Difficulties in the Design and Distribution of Christian Literatures in Nineteenth-Century India," in *The Church and the Book*, ed. R. N. Swanson (Woodbridge, England: Boydell, 2004), 339–356; Lal Chand and Sons, *State-Owned Printing Presses and Their Competition with Private Trade* (Calcutta: Lal Chand and Sons, 1923).

33. On diasporic artisanal printers see Hofmeyr, *Gandhi's Printing Press*, ch. 1. On transnational movements, print culture, and port cities see Mark Ravinder Frost, "'Wider Opportunities': Religious Revival, Nationalist Awakening and the Global Dimension in Colombo, 1870–1920," *Modern Asian Studies* 36, no. 4 (2002): 937–967.

34. Karin Barber, "Audiences and the Book," *Current Writing* 13, no. 2 (2001): 9–19.

35. Derek R. Peterson and Giacomo Macola, "Introduction: Homespun Historiography and the Academic Profession," in *Recasting the Past: History Writing and Political Work in Modern Africa*, ed. Derek R. Peterson and Giacomo Macola (Athens: Ohio University Press, 2009), 1–30.

36. Tony Ballantyne, "Reading the Newspaper in Colonial Otago," *Journal of New Zealand Studies* 12 (2011): 49–50. Anna Johnston, *The Paper War: Morality, Print Culture, and Power in Colonial New South Wales* (Crawley: University of Western Australia Publishing, 2011). On newspapers and periodicals in empire, see Milton Israel, *Communications and Power: Propaganda and the Press in the Indian Nationalist Struggle, 1920–1947* (Cambridge: Cambridge University Press, 1994); Simon J. Potter, *News and the British World: The Emergence of an Imperial Press System* (Oxford: Oxford University Press, 2003); Chandrika Kaul, *Reporting the Raj: The British Press and India, 1880–1922* (Manchester: Manchester University Press, 2003); Chandrika Kaul, ed., *Media and the British Empire* (Basingstoke, England: Palgrave Macmillan, 2006); David Finkelstein and Douglas M. Peers, eds., *Negotiating India in the Nineteenth-Century Media* (London: Palgrave Macmillan, 2000); Julie F. Codell, "Introduction: The Nineteenth-Century News from India," *Victorian Periodicals Review* 37, no. 2 (2004): 106–123; Julie F. Codell, "Getting the Twain to Meet: Global Regionalism in 'East and West': A Monthly Review," *Victorian Periodicals Review* 37, no. 2 (2004): 214–232; Sukeshi Kamra, *The Indian Periodical Press and the Production of*

Nationalist Rhetoric (London: Palgrave Macmillan, 2011); J. Don Vann and Rosemary T. van Arsdel, eds., *Periodicals of Queen Victoria's Empire: An Exploration* (Toronto: University of Toronto Press, 1966). Also: Ellen Gruber Garvey, "Scissorizing and Scrapbooks: Nineteenth-Century Reading, Remaking and Recirculating," in *New Media, 1740–1915*, ed. Lisa Gitelman and Geoffrey B. Pingree (Cambridge, MA: MIT Press, 2003), 207–227.

37. On the exchange system, see Garvey, "Scissorizing"; Ross Harvey, "Bringing the News to New Zealand: The Supply and Control of Overseas News in the Nineteenth Century," *Media History* 8, no. 1 (2002): 21–34; Richard B. Kielbowicz, "Newsgathering by Printers' Exchanges before the Telegraph," *Journalism History* 9, no. 2 (1982): 42–48.

38. *Indian Opinion*, 4 June 1903.

39. Lauren Benton, *A Search for Sovereignty: Law and Geography in European Empires, 1400–1900* (Cambridge: Cambridge University Press, 2009), 101.

40. Karin Barber, "Introduction: Hidden Innovators in Africa," in Barber, *Hidden Histories*, 1–24; Peterson and Macola, *Recasting the Past*.

41. Price, *How to Do Things with Books*.

42. Seville, *The Internationalisation of Copyright Law*, 2–6.

43. This idea is drawn from Andrew Piper, *Dreaming in Books: The Making of the Bibliographic Imagination in the Romantic Age* (Chicago: University of Chicago Press, 2009).

44. Benarsidas Chaturvedi, "The Ashram of My Dreams," *Indians Overseas: Weekly Letter*, 14 November 1923, Benarsidas Chaturvedi Papers, National Archives of India, Delhi.

45. Significantly, this interpretive angle comes out of critiques of the empire of the free market. See Donald Mackenzie, *An Engine, Not a Camera: How Financial Models Shape Markets* (Cambridge, MA: MIT Press, 2008).

46. Nicole Matthews and Nickianne Moody, eds., *Judging a Book by Its Cover: Fans, Publishers, Designers and the Marketing of Fiction* (Aldershot, England: Ashgate, 2007), xi.

47. James Wald, "Periodicals and Periodicity," in *A Companion to the History of the Book*, ed. Simon Eliot and Jonathan Rose (Chichester, England: Wiley-Blackwell, 2009), 429.

48. Kath Weston, *Long Slow Burn: Sexuality and Social Science* (New York: Routledge, 1998).

49. Angus Philipps, "Does the Book Have a Future?," in Eliot and Rose, *Companion*, 547–559.

One

REMAKING THE
EMPIRE FROM NEWGATE

Wakefield's *A Letter from Sydney*

TONY BALLANTYNE

This essay explores *A Letter from Sydney*, an unusual and important text that articulated an influential new template for colonization within the British Empire. Its arguments laid the foundation for the establishment of South Australia; underwrote the establishment of "systematic" schemes for the settlement and governance of Otago, Canterbury, Nelson, Wellington, and Taranaki in New Zealand; and were significant in policies and debates relating to the colonization of Canada in the 1830s and 1840s. This text—which was highly mobile within the various forms of print (newspapers, pamphlets, periodicals, and reforming tracts) that were central to a burgeoning imperial commons—mobilized opinion in favor of colonization as a solution to Britain's demographic and political problems and encouraged Britons to see geographic mobility within the empire as a way to escape constrained social mobility at home.

Written by Edward Gibbon Wakefield while he was incarcerated in Newgate prison, *A Letter* was published anonymously as a book in 1829. This publication strategy allowed Wakefield to publicize his ideas while avoiding any moral controversies arising from his own stained reputation after the scandal and sensational trial that had led to his imprisonment for abducting a young woman. Wakefield's authorial sleight of hand also had the effect of encouraging many contemporary readers to believe that this work was the "genuine" product of a colonial writing at the distant edge of the empire. The conditions around the *Letter*'s production posed long-term difficulties for Wakefield, who was desperate to reestablish his "name": how to position himself as a serious commentator on "social problems," a political economist, and an architect of empire was a persistent conundrum that haunted him.

In addition to locating *A Letter*'s theory of colonization within several intellectual traditions, this essay recovers the production, circulation, and reception of what has long been recognized as a foundational text for British settler colonialism. In exploring *A Letter*'s textual history and its long afterlife in the imperial commons, here I develop an approach to intellectual history that is sensitive to the significance of different media, their quality, and the cultural work they carry out. It is underpinned by a desire to measure and understand what Peter Mandler has identified as the "relative throw" of texts—the social geography of their intellectual and political influence.[1] Thinking about the transformative power of texts requires us, I argue, not only to be attentive to language and how a text's arguments relate to both contemporary discourses and earlier texts but also to pay close attention to material form, the history of its production, dissemination, and reception, and its afterlife in subsequent debates and exchanges: we should strive for a more balanced appreciation of text and object.

In the specific case of Wakefield's *Letter*, it would be a mistake to try and measure the "throw" of this text simply as a "book"—the first edition of *A Letter from Sydney* published anonymously in 1829 with Robert Gouger as the "editor." Such a strategy would be misguided, not only because that work did not immediately establish Wakefield as the author of this new theory but also because the book was not the only print culture artifact or public articulation of Wakefield's theory of colonization. To trace the "throw" of these arguments, we need to reconstruct the development of an argumentative complex, made up of the initial newspaper articles that presented "A Letter from Sydney" to the public, its publication as a book and its subsequent life through newspaper and periodical commentaries and reviews, and its reworking in pamphlets, promotional literature, and Wakefield's later commentaries on empire and the practice of colonization. Taken together, these printed texts, as well as the verbal articulations of the *Letter*'s theory in evidence before parliamentary commissions, in speeches to potential emigrants, and the cut and thrust of both metropolitan and colonial debate, produced a kind of sedimented complex of social diagnosis and political argument. This essay attempts to trace how this complex took shape, the traditions it grew out of and reworked, its movement through the political domain, and its mobility across an extended imperial sphere of political conversation and argument. By the middle of the nineteenth century, the pathways of production, dissemination, and reuse were such that Darnton's communication circuit—which imagined a sequence of author-publisher-printers-shippers-booksellers-readers structuring the operation of print culture[2]—seems an uneasy fit for polymorphous outputs of a man like Wakefield and for the avalanche of words, spoken and written, that constituted the energetic and extended public sphere of the British Empire.

Manuscript

"A Letter from Sydney" was produced under unusual circumstances: like Gakaara's *Mīhīrīga ya Agīkūyū*, discussed by Derek Peterson, it was written in prison (see chapter 10). But where Gakaara was extolling moral reform within the context of decolonization, Wakefield's imprisonment encouraged him to see the empire as the solution to Britain's pressing social problems.

After the death of his first wife in 1820, the moderately successful career Wakefield fashioned came to an abrupt halt in 1826, when an elaborate plan to secure his political future misfired badly. He abducted Ellen Turner, the fifteen-year-old daughter of a rich manufacturer and county sheriff. Wakefield, who had never met Ellen, believed that marrying her would secure her father's support and enable him to launch a successful career in parliamentary politics. After deceiving Ellen, Wakefield married her at Gretna Green and then fled with his new wife to France, where agents of her family staged a rescue in Calais. The case became a public sensation. Wakefield was sentenced to three years in prison in May 1827, and the marriage was annulled though a special act of Parliament.

Wakefield's incarceration at Newgate was a trying, humbling, and at times terrifying experience. Because Newgate prisoners were able to purchase a range of resources, Wakefield largely escaped the prison's infamous conditions: he paid rent to secure a room to himself, retained a servant, and was supplied with books and newspapers by his family.[3] Nevertheless, he was curious about the prison's operation, his fellow inmates, and especially the experiences of those sentenced to death. His experiences and the interviews he conducted with fellow prisoners underpinned his *Facts Relating to the Punishment of Death in the Metropolis* (1831) and invested the evidence he gave the Select Committee on Secondary Punishments in 1831 with particular authority.

Imprisonment encouraged Wakefield to think about a set of problems he came to see as interrelated: population and emigration, poverty and crime, Britain's development and the status of its colonies. In addition to writing about the penal system, he also began to produce a series of reflections on the connections between colonial and metropolitan development. He did this through a series of fictional letters from a colonist in New South Wales: he had no firsthand knowledge of Australia but nevertheless saw that colony as a squandered opportunity for Britain.

The text he crafted in Newgate suggested that the colony had developed slowly because land policies had distorted the labor supply: the practice of making land grants, often of large tracts by British standards, made it possible for men to quickly become landowners rather than having to work to accumulate capital. Wakefield argued that colonial land needed to be sold, rather than granted. Land should be fed onto the market in such a way that settlement was restricted and concentrated, rather than dispersed: through this mechanism the government had the power to "civilise" the colonists by bringing them into regular contact, interdependence, and mutuality. Most important, the cost of the land had to be fixed at a level that would prevent workers from becoming landowners too quickly: this price, which he would later term the "sufficient price," would produce an equitable balance between the interests of capital and labor. Through a tax on rent, it would be possible to fund the further emigration of laborers from Britain, relieving population pressure at home: ideally, these new colonists would be young, and there would be an equitable ratio between men and women. Such measures were necessary because the lack of order in colonial economic and social life meant that cultural decline became characteristic of life in the new society: haplessly following their sheep across their large farms, colonists would swiftly become "a Tartar people." This would not just mean that British civilization would founder in the colonies; it would also make the colonists ungovernable by Britain, as they would be "uncouth, and ignorant, and violent as the great mass of North Americans." Ultimately this would sever the bonds of empire: "our grand-children will assert their independence," and they "will govern, or rather, misgovern themselves."

Thus the vision for colonial development that Wakefield developed in Newgate was not driven by a desire to create self-sufficient offshoots of Britain but reflected a wish to use these territories to solve British problems: to relieve the pressure of population that constrained opportunity, to create new fields for British capital, and to generate new markets for British goods. Under this system, the colonies "would no longer be new societies" but "so many extensions of an old society." Although he suggested that colonial life already offered greater happiness and opportunity than life in the metropole, properly ordered colonies would bring greater benefits, as they could help blunt "Want," the terrible desire for food, land, and security that blighted British life.

He decided that this text should be published anonymously. Even before his trial, Wakefield was deeply concerned with his reputation: before his capture by Ellen Turner's family, he worked furiously, preparing a text titled "Statement of Facts" in an attempt to defend his conduct, which was published in *John Bull*. That text, which was initially published anonymously, was designed to counter the salacious narratives that were circulating through sensational public prints, cheaply printed texts that carried the latest news and rumors to wide audiences.[4] This strategy failed. Newspaper editorials and reportage dismissed Wakefield as "malignant" and "infamous"; the *Times* condemned Wakefield as a "callous-hearted wretch," suggesting that "Nature does not often produce such a monster."[5]

Morning Chronicle

Between 21 August and 8 October 1829, the *Morning Chronicle* published Wakefield's letter in nine installments.[6] No author was credited. When the first letter was published on 21 August, it was prefaced with this editorial comment: "We are enabled to publish some valuable Correspondence respecting Australia. The following letter, which contains many interesting details, will be followed by others." Below this prefatory editorial gloss, the text of the first letter was set more closely and in a smaller font. The letter plunged the reader into what seemed like an exchange of letters, beginning: "I will not pretend to answer all the questions of your letter; but will endeavour to give you, in general terms, my opinion of this country, and of the prospects it affords to Emigrants."[7] This text offered readers a description of life in New South Wales that effectively critiqued imperial governance and the character of colonial society as well as reflecting on the development of empires in world history.

Historians have relied on the book version of *A Letter* and as a result have failed to recognize that *Morning Chronicle* readers encountered the serialized "Letter" alongside another anonymous Wakefield text.[8] On 27 August, under the heading "Sketch of a Proposal for Colonizing Australasia," the *Chronicle* informed its readers: "We have frequently alluded to a pamphlet, under the above title, containing views on the subject of colonization, of great importance to the interests of the country. . . . We have received permission from the author to print it in our columns."[9] As its title suggested, this was a schematic outline of a plan for colonization: it was programmatic, clear, concise, even clipped in tone, in stark contrast to the more descriptive, digressive, and discursive tone of the "Letter."

At least one reader drew a connection between the texts. On 2 November 1829, the *Chronicle* featured a long letter from a certain "CC," who suggested that the "author of the Sketch" and the "writer of the series of Letters" were "both probably the same person." The letter outlined the theories developed in both texts and offered some refinements of this model of colonization.[10] This letter writer may well have been Wakefield as well. Not only does this letter have a strongly Wakefieldian tone, but a crucial piece of internal evidence suggests that it was him. This letter forcefully made an argument about Canada that Wakefield would make in his later work. This argument suggested that controlling the land price would be an ineffective instrument for directing the colonization of Canada, where a large and open border with the United States allowed colonists to move there to take up large land grants.[11] On 3 November, "DD" responded with another letter to the editor, offering further criticisms, both of CC's letter and of the original scheme: the speed of this exchange, the very composed and argumentative sensibility of the letters, and their tone might suggest that "DD" was also Wakefield, who was intent on keeping his scheme and its ideas before the public. If Wakefield was indeed the author of one or both of these letters, they not only display his investment in publicizing his arguments through the press but also initiated his almost constant reworking of his key arguments.

Wakefield's "Letter," his "Sketch," and the subsequent exchanges were part of the *Morning Chronicle*'s treatment of social problems and its uncompromising critiques of the established order. The *Chronicle* was an ideal venue for Wakefield's criticisms of British life and his questioning of the orthodoxies of political economy. John Black, who was closely connected to Jeremy Bentham and James Mill, was the editor of the *Chronicle*. John Stuart Mill suggested that Black was the "first journalist who carried criticism & the spirit of reform into the details of English institutions."[12] The *Chronicle* played an important role in cementing the press as a political force, and its editorial commentary and detailed reportage were important in constituting the "social problems"—such as pauperism, vagrancy, overpopulation, and the limited franchise—that came to be a recurrent feature of Victorian public life. Charles Dickens wrote for the *Chronicle* from 1834, and it would later provide a forum for the articles by Henry Mayhew that were collected as *London Labour and the London Poor* (1861). Wakefield's 1829 texts were an important contribution to reformist writing; but his arguments were unusual in their identification of the reorganization of colonial economies and a new systematized form of colonization as cures for Britain's social ills.

Textual (and Familial) Relations

Wakefield's writings can be read against those of his contemporaries and within the context of debates over population, poor relief, and empire in the 1820s and 1830s. But the form of "A Letter," its sensibility and arguments, really only make sense when read against the much older traditions of writing that shaped it: imaginary voyages, diagnostic political economy, and Scottish Enlightenment discussions of social development. Much of Wakefield's reading, like that of most educated Britons (as William St Clair has reminded us), was drawn not from the newest or most fashionable works, even if he was an avid reader of the press; rather, he drew heavily on layers of older texts in a variety of editions and formats.[13] Unlike many of his peers, however, Wakefield's connections to some of these textual traditions were familial as well as intellectual.

Key here was his grandmother Priscilla Wakefield, who effectively functioned as his primary parent for much of his youth. An influential Quaker social reformer, she also became a prolific author. Her seventeen books blended moral didacticism with large amounts of information. They were designed as instruments for teaching as well as leisure, which she believed should be dedicated to improvement, rational recreation, and wholesome pleasures of the family. In her three-volume *Mental Improvement, or, The Beauties and Wonders of Nature and Art* (1794–1797), for example, a family with children aged between nine and sixteen spend their evenings in pleasant and instructive conversations with their parents.

Most of her work harnessed the conventions of travel writing for educative purposes. Although Priscilla traveled little, her reading and imagination enabled her to produce a sequence of travel narratives, most of which followed family groups on journeys within the United Kingdom, Europe, America, and Asia. In her work, the empire was less a realm over which Britain providentially exercised its military might or economic power than a space within which Britain and British individuals could exercise positive and benign moral influence, redeeming the nation.[14] These works contained significant criticisms of British society and colonial development. In her *Excursions in North America*, Priscilla Wakefield suggested that New World societies had regressed because of the dispersal of migrants and the resulting erosion of civilization. Among the American colonists, she suggested, were many who wanted to "retire to the uncultivated parts of the country, and obtain a grant of a certain portion of land." After building basic dwellings, beginning rudimentary cultivation, and seeking food through hunting, they "quit the spot on which they have bestowed some labour, before it is completely clean, and remove further into the forest, where they can live unrestrained by law or good manners." These qualities meant that these Europeans "are a kind of savages, hostile to the Indians, and to their more civilized countrymen, who succeed them."[15] These arguments anticipated many of the arguments that her grandson would make three decades later about the dangers of large land grants and the importance of "concentration" to the cultivation of "civilization" in the colonies.

Priscilla Wakefield herself also engaged with traditions of political economy. Her important if unpopular *Reflections on the Present Condition of the Female Sex* (1798) criticized Adam Smith's support for the dismantling of apprenticeship regulations. She highlighted the implications of his vision of the organization of work, which locked women into unskilled work without any training. She believed that Smith's theories impinged on the liberties of women.[16] While her grandson exhibited much less concern with the particularities of women's financial opportunities, he embarked on editing a serial edition of Adam Smith's *Wealth of Nations*, complete with commentary. Smith's arguments were an important touchstone for Wakefield, especially his concern with civilization and his insistence on regulating the cost of land.[17]

Edward Gibbon Wakefield's enthusiasm for the political economy tradition was probably also shaped by the work of his father, Edward Wakefield, who was a friend of Henry Brougham, Francis Place, and James Mill. He was best known as the author of *An Account of Ireland, Statistical and Political*, a work undertaken at the suggestion of John Foster, First Baron Oriel, formerly chancellor of the Irish exchequer. *An Account* offered a Malthusian reading of Ireland's development. It was deeply concerned with quantification, a preoccupation that undercut the usefulness of the "wild Irishman" as an analytical framework and demonstrated that Ireland was amenable to being "read" through the lens of political economy.[18] He was well respected for his understanding of economics, being called to give evidence to parliamentary committees on sugar imports (1808), bullion (1810), and agricultural depression (1821). He was also an influential land agent and an advocate for educational reform and the improvement of lunatic asylums. In the 1830s and 1840s he championed his son's theories, writing numerous letters to newspapers and using his political connections to lobby for the colonization cause.[19]

Just as Wakefield's father had been deeply concerned with the pressures of population in Ireland and his work was studded with references to Malthus, *A Letter* can be read as initiating an argument about population that rejected the claims of Malthus, who saw plans for emigration as at best a "slight palliative" for the pressures of population and who saw emigration as plagued with "dangers, difficulties, and hardships" that were not conducive to building civilized society.[20] Despite Malthus's skepticism of the power of migration to resolve Britain's population pressures, Gouger and other associates of Wakefield tried to press-gang Malthus into supporting their visions of colonization. After the provisional committee of the National Colonization Society was established in March 1830, Gouger, the Society's secretary, held meetings with Malthus, in which Malthus articulated his reservations about colonization and the Society's plans. He was subsequently surprised, therefore, to discover that the Society had represented him as a "decided approver" of its scheme. In August Malthus underlined his skepticism of the scheme again in a letter to Sir Robert Wilmot-Horton, the former undersecretary for war and the colonies, who had earlier championed the idea of assisting British pauper families to resettle in Upper Canada, reaffirming his misgivings about the plan to produce "artificial concentration" and his broader doubts about the value of colonies as a solution to population pressure.[21] This is an important reminder of the extent to which Wakefield's advocacy of colonization was pushing against powerful established ideas about demography, economics, and politics.

Wakefield's *Morning Chronicle* articles were anthologized in a single volume in 1829. This book was not a straight reprint of the newspaper letters; not only was the *Chronicle's* editorial gloss, which had helped initially frame "A Letter," removed, but also this volume offered readers a preface (drawn from a *Quarterly Review* essay) and an introduction. The introduction provided some basic geographical discussion of the Australian colonies for eight pages before the material drawn from the *Chronicle* began. This somewhat blunted the effect of reading a real letter that had been central to the version published in the *Chronicle*, as the colonist's first letter became subsumed into the introductory text, and there was no textual apparatus explaining who wrote the introduction: the "colonist" or the text's editor.[22]

Most important, *A Letter* did not appear under Wakefield's name. Gouger agreed to act as a fictional editor of the volume as well as seeing it through the press. Gouger, who felt his prospects were constrained in Britain, had planned to emigrate to the Swan River settlement to serve as manager for Thomas Macqueen, but when he met Wakefield at Newgate he had been dissuaded from this course of action. Caught up in Wakefield's vision, he circulated the pamphlet version of Wakefield's *Sketch* and put his name to the book version of Wakefield's *Letter*. This was published in London as *A Letter from Sydney: The Principal Town of Australasia: Together with the Outline of a System of Colonization* by Joseph Cross, Simpkin and Marshall, and Effingham Wilson, in 1829. It sold for 6 shillings, whereas a reader could have purchased the nine issues of the *Chronicle* in which Wakefield's original text appeared for 4s. 8d.: the book's cost meant it was unlikely to be purchased by the poor, but it was within the means of the "middling types" to whom Wakefield's theory was addressed. Gouger, unfortunately, carried the printing costs of *A Letter*, and when he was unable to discharge this debt he too ended up in prison.[23] Gouger's debt would suggest that *A Letter* did not sell well immediately; but there is some slight evidence to suggest that a second edition may have been published.[24]

Of course having the work "edited" by Gouger worked within an established conceit. A range of novels had used the device of a fictional editor: Scott, in particular, was fond of this device, and Carlyle later used it in his *Sartor Resartus* (1836), and in 1836–1837 the *Pickwick Papers* emerged under the editorship of "Boz." Charlotte Macdonald explores some of the consequences of this authorial strategy in her discussion of Charlotte Brontë's *Jane Eyre*, which was "edited" by Currer Bell when it appeared in 1847 (chapter 2, this volume).[25] While this strategy allowed Wakefield to float his new vision of the role of colonization in the public sphere, avoiding a clear declaration of his authorship caused him difficulties in the long term. Key figures in his circle knew that he was the author of these texts, and some influential officials knew too. For example, Gouger explained to the Colonial Office's T. F. Elliot in 1831 that Wakefield was the author of the *Letter from Sydney*: "you must remember to have heard of him in connection with the abduction of Miss Turner some years since."[26] But this knowledge remained quite restricted, and the authorship of *A Letter* remained unclear for some later historians until the 1960s.

Newspapers and Pamphlets

A Letter from Sydney was never an entirely self-contained book: its life as a commodity and a set of ideas was dependent on a broader apparatus of print and political culture. Its first appearance was made plausible by the imperial information flows that meant that readers of the *Chronicle* and other newspapers were accustomed not just to reading reportage from the colonies and editorial commentary on the politics of empire but also to regularly encountering extracts from letters from colonists.[27]

From the outset, of course, *A Letter*'s existence and value was advertised. Here newspapers were crucial, and the *Chronicle* took the lead. But advertisements appeared in a range of other newspapers as well, both as stand-alone insertions and as part of the holdings of booksellers. Newspapers could help to ensure Wakefield's connection to readers in unexpected ways, too. In 1837 an unfortunate reader advertised in the *Hereford Times* informing locals that he had lost his copy of *A Letter*, along with the first volume of his collected works of Edmund Burke, "about 20 numbers" of Harriet Martineau's *Illustrations of Political Economy*, and assorted other serious works.[28]

A Letter also entered the public sphere through a print culture where books were constantly recycled: their arguments were reviewed, excerpted, discussed, and alluded to, and as objects they were deployed for a bewildering array of ends.[29] Increasingly, it was newspapers that were central in establishing the significance of particular titles: they were pivotal in making authors' reputations, shaping the sales profile of works and propelling certain volumes to the status of bestsellers or "sensations."[30] Wakefield's *Letter* was not a bestseller; but its arguments became entangled within the increasingly diverse cultural apparatus of print in the 1830s and threaded through a series of debates on population, politics, and empire. Not all of these were conveyed through print: Robert Gouger himself became a vigorous exponent of the colonization of South Australia on Wakefieldian lines, using letter writing, verbal argument, and printed texts to push forward many of the principles first set out in the letters and sketch that made up the 1829 book. Wakefield worked with his brother Daniel on drafting a bill that would create South Australia as a "British province" and enable the colonization of the region by British emigrants. Alongside Gouger, Wakefield was at the forefront of the campaign that led to the successful passing of the resulting bill by Parliament in 1834, and his writings provided rich material for the advocates of the project. This provided him with another opportunity to restate his theories, producing a colonization manual despite his lack of firsthand experience of Australia: that volume, *The New British Province of South Australia,* was quite successful, quickly running through two editions.[31]

This venture indicates one domain of activity that continued to disseminate and publicize Wakefield's ideas in the 1830s: the political agitation for the creation of new colonies. Here Wakefieldian arguments entered the public sphere through a variety of vectors: some emanating directly from Wakefield himself, others through his associates and those who forwarded his vision through various colonization companies. Perhaps because of the evidence furnished by his father to parliamentary select committees, Wakefield recognized the importance of these forums in framing "social problems." He understood that they presented opportunities to exercise direct influence over key decision makers in the legislative process, and that they were constituted as political events by the flurries of pamphlet and press coverage that frequently accompanied their inquiries. In 1836 Wakefield provided evidence before a committee of the House of Commons on land disposal within the empire. He was a persuasive witness, and the committee recommended that the underlying principles of his scheme be enshrined in legislation and then widely applied to the empire.[32] He gave evidence on further occasions; most influentially, perhaps, to the select committee assembled in 1840 to investigate the "New Zealand crisis." This was a crisis Wakefield had played a pivotal role in creating: his New Zealand Company had dispatched its first cohort of colonists in advance of Lieutenant Governor Hobson, who was sent by Lord Normanby, secretary of state for the colonies, in August 1839 to direct any formal British intervention. Wakefield was the first to give evidence to this committee and spoke for two and a half days and then was recalled at the end of the hearings and spoke across further two days, while the other nine witnesses gave evidence across less than three days. The report of the committee was strongly imprinted by Wakefield, as it directed Parliament's attention away from the question of de jure sovereignty that was to have been the focus of its inquiries, arguing that "large numbers" of "British emigrants" were in New Zealand. Therefore, it suggested, "sovereign rights over the whole of the islands will shortly be ceded by the natives to the Queen," and accordingly recommended that the legal foundations of colonization were sound. Not surprisingly, one of the key mechanisms this report recommended to guide future colonial development was the sale of the land at a uniform and sufficient price.[33]

Newspapers also remained central to the dissemination of Wakefield's work in the 1830s. If it was the *Morning Chronicle* that first published his "Letter," over the next decade or so it was primarily through the *Spectator* that his ideas were championed. In April 1830, while Wakefield was still incarcerated, the *Spectator* published his essay "Cure and Prevention of Pauperism, by Means of Systematic Colonisation," which elaborated the theories set out in *A Letter from Sydney* but focused more narrowly on the question of pauperism, which stood at the heart of moral, economic, and political debate within Britain.

Under the editorship of the radical Robert Rintoul, the *Spectator* became a consistent advocate for reform, and its supplements directed particular attention to issues relating to war and its costs, the finances of the government, and the operation of the empire. Rintoul's investment in critiquing the establishment provided an ideal platform for Wakefield, and Wakefield emerged as the paper's most important and influential writer.[34] Rintoul himself was convinced, through discussion with Thomas Chalmers, that Adam Smith was mistaken in not valuing the colonies as "a profitable field for investment, labour and accumulated capital."[35] This perhaps helps explain Rintoul's willingness to found and edit from 1838 the *Colonial Gazette*, which functioned as an important mouthpiece for Wakefield and his supporters, enabling Wakefield to make the case for colonizing New Zealand and to criticize the administration of Canada.[36]

It is clear, then, that *A Letter* was influential because it was the first iteration of a set of ideas that were carried to a wide range of publics through speeches, parliamentary evidence and debate, and pamphlets and the press. Wakefield's writings on Newgate and the death penalty established him as an important commentator on "social problems" and helped rehabilitate his name.[37]

Yet the extended commentary on migration, colonization, and the state of England offered in his sprawling two-volume *England and America* (1833) once again appeared anonymously. It drew on his work on pauperism and punishment—the powerful second chapter was entitled "Misery of the Bulk of the People." But it also addressed the pressures confronting the middling types in the third chapter, "Uneasiness of the Middle Class," speaking for and to the community he saw as central to the effective development of colonies in the future. Perhaps he preferred anonymity because he was firmly entangled in the lobbying for the foundation of a colony in South Australia; whatever his motivation, it certainly allowed him to launch staunch attacks on those such as Malthus who were skeptical of colonization as well as to extend the case for the creation of new colonies.[38]

For Wakefield's texts on colonization in the 1830s, the anonymity of *A Letter* could be useful. Without Wakefield's name attached to it, it functioned as a text that could referred to, footnoted, and listed in bibliographies: a significant text that was seen to independently confirm the broader arguments he was making. *England and America*'s discussion of the National Colonization Society, in which Wakefield was a prime mover, included *A Letter from Sydney* in the list of materials that made the case for colonization.[39] *England and America* also footnoted *A Letter* as an authoritative text.[40] In a similar vein, readers of Wakefield's anonymous pamphlet *Plan of a Company to Be Established for the Purpose of Founding a Colony in South Australia* (1832) were also directed to *Letter from Sydney*.[41] A later work, written with some assistance from John Ward but again published with no author's name appended, *The British Colonization of New Zealand* (1837), also drew on *A Letter* in making a case for the application of Wakefield's theory as a framework for the operation of the procolonization New Zealand Association.[42]

Wakefield's final substantial work, *A View of the Art of Colonization* (1849), offered a further articulation of "systematic colonization," but not in the dispassionate and methodical way in which some, like John Stuart Mill, had hoped he would.[43] Mill wrote to Wakefield in 1848 stating that he was "glad to hear" of Wakefield's project, as he had "long regretted that there does not exist a systematic treatise . . . from your hand and with your name, in which the whole subject of colonization is treated. . . . At present people have to pick up your doctrines both theoretical and practical."[44] But *A View* was not an ordered treatise of thoughtful analysis, in the mode of political economy. It was a baggy, slightly shapeless work, built around a familiar device: letters. In this case, it was a book supposedly produced out of the exchange of letters and arguments between "Colonist" and "Statesman," an exchange "edited" by Wakefield. This dialogue format was mobilized as an effective didactic tool in later works such as Gandhi's *Hind Swaraj*. Yet the title page of *A View* also offered the acknowledgment that Wakefield was "one of the writers." While this epistolary dialogue may have reflected a desire to make political economy and debates on the nature of colonization accessible and easily comprehensible, it more immediately allowed Wakefield to launch a series of attacks on old adversaries, such as Lord Grey and James Stephen. But this strategy backfired: where a summative and scholarly work may have established a lasting reputation among the political economists, *A View* once again displayed Wakefield's passion for political brawling. It did not display the temper or careful measure that were the defining qualities of a Victorian "public man."

The arguments Wakefield first developed in his *Letter* also had an afterlife through ongoing debates between political economists. Although John Stuart Mill was critical of Wakefield's belief that his theories marked a clear break with the tradition of political economy, he was a firm supporter of Wakefield's core vision of "systematic colonization."[45] But perhaps the most significant treatment of Wakefield's work came from Karl Marx. While David Harvey's commentary on Marx's *Capital* suggests that Wakefield "hardly rates amongst the greatest political economists of all times," he also recognizes that Marx considered Wakefield's work of "great import because it amounted to a devastating rebuttal of Adam Smith."[46] Marx suggested that Wakefield's understanding of the importance of labor relations in shaping the pattern of colonial development was crucial because it "discovered that capital is not a thing, but a social relation between persons which is mediated through things."[47] Equally important, Wakefield's theory, Marx suggested, offered "not something new *about* the colonies, but, *in the* colonies, [it identified] the truth about capitalist relations in the mother country." Marx paraphrased Wakefield's argument (primarily drawing on *England and America*), suggesting that if capitalism was to flourish in the colonies of settlement, governments would have to "set an artificial price on the virgin soil, a price independent of the law of supply and demand, a price that compels the immigrant to work a long time for wages before he can earn enough money to buy land and turn himself into an independent farmer."[48] Marx used this line of thought to critique Smith's theory of primitive accumulation. Harvey suggests that Wakefield's argument also underwrote Marx's reformulation of the Hegelian dialectical model of capitalist economic development and Marx's conclusion that colonization simply extended and re-created the internal contradictions of the capitalist order on a global stage.[49]

Moving Words

Wakefield's concern with his metropolitan standing led him to underestimate the impact of his work. But he was looking in the wrong place, as the value he placed on British political and intellectual luminaries led him to discount the significance of the work in shaping colonial development. His arguments contributed to the Colonial Office's decision to curtail the making of free land grants in New South Wales in 1831.[50] And, as noted, they were central in plans for the colonization of South Australia. They also provided templates for the establishment of colonies in New Zealand. Wakefield had a hand in the schemes for the colonization of Wellington, Taranaki, and Nelson. And his later reworked vision, which accorded more prominence to religion as a safeguard of colonial civilization, also underpinned the foundation of the Otago and Canterbury settlements. Wakefield was also influential in Canada. His theories provided an important template for the Hudson Bay Company, he worked as an unofficial advisor to Lord Durham (who investigated the Canadian colonies from June to October 1838), and he acted as an agent for the North American Colonial Association of Ireland and remained entangled in Canadian politics until 1844.[51]

Wakefield's schemes turned out to be awkward and ineffectual templates for building functioning colonies, but it would be a mistake to dismiss the significance of his work for this reason.[52] In most cases, it quickly became clear that the controlling the price of land could not control the pattern of colonial development as easily as the Wakefield writing in Newgate believed. Nor did his vision for an ordered system of migration live up to its promises. Although a significant number of Britons did migrate, Wakefieldian schemes were much less of a safety valve than migration to the United

States, and in the settler colonies his model of a carefully balanced mix of colonists, in terms of gender and class, was rarely the reality.

Historians of the colonies have been consistently critical of Wakefield, not only because of character, but because his schemes never delivered what they promised. But they have not been sensitive to the way he shifted the British lexicon for discussing empire. Some concepts that were central to his thought, such as "civilization" and "improvement," were, in Carol Gluck's term, "big words." They embraced large, frequently abstract, and polyvalent concepts, and they were made by many texts and arguments over a long time frame.[53] Wakefield's work did not substantially recode the freight of these terms within Britain; but his theories certainly inflected understandings of these concepts in New Zealand and Australia, especially South Australia. These were "moving words" and tracked across the globe. They fed into debates over policy and practice connected to land and migration in France, Brazil, and the United States. This suggests that it would be an interesting project to track the global motion and localization of Wakefieldian ideas; that would be an especially valuable project, given that most recent work on British imperial political thought focuses narrowly on the attitudes of a small handful of English liberal thinkers, primarily concerned with India, in the later eighteenth and nineteenth centuries. Writing the history of ideas in their contexts beyond Britain, western Europe, and the United States remains a challenge.

But Wakefield's arguments—in their various iterations—primarily moved within Britain and its empire; through its newspapers and periodicals, through its book markets, through the pages of emigration prospectuses and guides to colonists, through the pages of periodicals and newspapers, and through spoken argument, in Parliament, in public meetings, on the hustings, and in lecture halls.[54] These words settled most heavily in South Australia and in New Zealand: in those spaces Wakefield's arguments were a key feature of the imperial commons. As his arguments were woven into debate and policy, they generated a new and quite durable lexicon for debating the structure of the economy and the role of the state. Even if his embrace of anonymity as a strategy created difficulties, we have seen that influential contemporaries recognized Wakefield as an important voice in British debates over social problems. But in the metropole, his words jostled with and pushed against the weight of established languages and more authoritative voices. His arguments did not move metropolitan opinion easily. Conversely, in the colonies, especially those established on "systematic" lines, his ideas about "concentration," "waste lands," and the "sufficient price" took root and formed a foundational element of the political lexicon. They formed an integral part of public debate and were a key strand of what I have called elsewhere a "folk political economy," which welded together biblical teaching, popularized understandings of the rights of powerful nations and civilizations (following Vattel), the primacy of labor and improvement in establishing property rights (after Locke), and Wakefield's stress on the centrality of land policy in shaping society.

Wakefield's influence in these locations was in part a result of his prominence in the very creation of these colonial settlements. But it also reflected the uneven transplantation of inherited political idioms and ideas to the colonies and the reality that Wakefield was much more preoccupied with the potential of emigration and these "extensions" of Britain than any other significant British thinker in the 1830s and 1840s.[55] The arguments and ideas he first fashioned in Newgate resonated for decades in the settler colonies, reminding us of the ways the constant recycling and repackaging that was central to the imperial commons continued to reanimate old ideas and texts. In part because his ideas never went away, he remains an awkward ancestral figure, not simply because of his early crimes but also because his vision was so deeply implicated in the economic, demographic, and geographic marginalization of indigenous communities.[56] His words remade the empire—perhaps not as he hoped, but in potent and abiding ways nonetheless.

NOTES

1. Peter Mandler, "The Problem with Cultural History," *Cultural and Social History* 1 (2004): 95–117.

2. Robert Darnton, "What Is the History of Books?," *Daedalus* 111, no. 3 (1982): 65–83.

3. Philip Temple, *A Sort of Conscience: The Wakefields* (Auckland: Auckland University Press, 2002), 118.

4. *Examiner*, 20 August 1826, 540.

5. *London Standard*, 22 May 1827, 1; *Lancaster Gazette*, 26 May 1827, 3; *Times*, 7 June 1827, 1.

6. Temple and the *Australian Dictionary of Biography* mistakenly suggest that the final letter was published on August 6. Temple, *Conscience*, 134.

7. *Morning Chronicle*, August 21, 1829, 2.

8. Temple overlooks this version of the "Sketch." Temple, *Conscience*, 134.

9. *Morning Chronicle*, 21 August 1829, 4.

10. *Morning Chronicle*, 2 November 1829, 2.

11. Temple, *Conscience*, 323.

12. Francis E. Mineka and Dwight N. Lindley, eds., *The Later Letters of John Stuart Mill, 1849–1873* (Toronto: University of Toronto Press, 1972), 978–980.

13. William St Clair, *The Reading Nation in the Romantic Period* (Cambridge: Cambridge University Press, 2004).

14. Cf. Paul Bloomfield, *Edward Gibbon Wakefield: Builder of the British Commonwealth* (London: Longmans, 1961), 21. Also see Ruth Graham, "Juvenile Travellers: Priscilla Wakefield's Excursions in Empire," *Journal of Imperial and Commonwealth History* 38 (2010): 374.

15. Priscilla Wakefield, *Excursions in North America*, 3rd ed. (London: Darton, Harvey and Darton, 1819), 83.

16. Kathryn Sutherland, introduction to *An Inquiry into the Nature and Causes of the Wealth of Nations: A Selected Edition*, by Adam Smith (Oxford: Oxford University Press, 1993), xxxiv, 496n.

17. Adam Smith, *An Inquiry into the Nature and Causes of the Wealth of Nations*, ed. Edward Gibbon Wakefield, 4 vols. (London: Charles Knight, 1835–1840), 3:290–291; [Edward Gibbon Wakefield], *England and America: A Comparison of the Social and Political State of Both Nations*, 2 vols. (London: Richard Bentley, 1833), 2:68–70.

18. Compare Roberto Romani, *National Character and Public Spirit in Britain and France, 1750–1914* (Cambridge: Cambridge University Press, 2002), 208–209.

19. David J. Moss, "Wakefield, Edward (1774–1854)," in *Oxford Dictionary of National Biography* (Oxford: Oxford University Press, 2004).

20. *An Account of Ireland, Statistical and Political*, 2 vols. (London: Longman, Hurst, Rees, Orme and Brown, 1812), 2:18, 78, 172, 185, 191, 403, 431–434, 561. Malthus, *An Essay on the Principle of Population*, 3 vols., 5th ed. (London: John Murray, 1817), 2:288.

21. Patricia James, *Population Malthus: His Life and Times* (London: Routledge and Kegan Paul, 1979), 397–398.

22. Robert Gouger, ed., *A Letter from Sydney, the Principal Town of Australasia. Together with the Outline of a System of Colonization* (London: Joseph Cross, 1829).

23. "Bacon, Anthony (1796–1864)," in *Australian Dictionary of Biography*, vol. 2 (Melbourne: Melbourne University Press, 1967).

24. *Journal of the Royal Australian Historical Society* 15 (1929): 125.

25. Jane Millgate, *Walter Scott: The Making of the Novelist* (Toronto: University of Toronto Press, 1984), 6, 10–13; Bradley Deane, *The Making of the Victorian Novelist: Anxieties of Authorship in the Mass Market* (London: Routledge, 2002), 33.

26. Richard Charles Mills, *The Colonization of Australia (1829–42): The Wakefield Experiment in Empire Building* (London: Sidgwick and Jackson, 1915), 78n.

27. E.g., *Bradford Observer*, 23 May 1839, 4; *Aberdeen Journal*, 8 April 1829, 2; *Hereford Journal*, March 1829, 2; *Sherborne Mercury*, 20 July 1829, 3; *Derby Mercury*, 25 March 1829, 2; *Newcastle Courant*, 28 March 1829, 2; *Hampshire Telegraph*, 30 March 1829, 4; *Leeds Mercury*, 4 April 1829, 2; *Leeds Intelligencer*, 16 April 1829, 4.

28. *Hereford Times*, 25 March 1837, 2.

29. Leah Price, *How to Do Things with Books in Victorian Britain* (Princeton, NJ: Princeton University Press, 2012).

30. James A. Secord, *Victorian Sensation: The Extraordinary Publication, Reception, and Secret Authorship of Vestiges of the Natural History of Creation* (Chicago: University of Chicago Press, 2000), 129.

31. Edward Gibbon Wakefield, *The New British Province of South Australia* (London: C. Knight, 1834); 2nd ed. (London: C. Knight, 1835). Graeme Pretty suggests that a further edition was published in Edinburgh in 1835. Graeme L. Pretty, "Wakefield, Edward Gibbon (1796–1862)," in *Australian Dictionary of Biography*, vol. 2 (Melbourne: Melbourne University Press, 1967), available at adb.anu.edu.au/biography/wakefield-edward-gibbon-2763.

32. *Report from the Select Committee on the Disposal of Lands in the British Colonies; Together with the minutes of evidence, and appendix* (1836) (512).

33. *Report from the Select Committee on New Zealand; Together with the minutes of evidence taken before them, and an appendix, and index* (1840) (582), vi.

34. *Spectator*, 1 May 1858, 464.

35. *Spectator*, 465.

36. Temple, *Conscience*, 204, 218; Peter Burroughs, ed., *The Colonial Reformers and Canada, 1830–1849* (Toronto: McClelland and Stewart, 1969), xv, xix.

37. Edward Gibbon Wakefield, *Facts Relating to the Punishment of Death in the Metropolis* (London: J. Ridgway, 1831); *Swing Unmasked, or, The Causes of Rural Incendiarism* (London: Effingham Wilson, 1831); *The Hangman and the Judge, or, A Letter from Jack Ketch to Mr. Justice Alderson: Revised by the Ordinary of Newgate and edited by Edward Gibbon Wakefield* (London: E. Wilson, 1833).

38. *England and America*, 1:78.

39. *England and America*, 2:161–162.

40. *England and America*, 2:187n.

41. [Edward Gibbon Wakefield], *Plan of a Company to be Established for the Purpose of Founding a Colony in Southern Australia* (London: Ridgway and Sons, 1832), 65.

42. *The British Colonization of New Zealand: Being an Account of the Principles, Objects, and Plans of the New Zealand Association* (London: John W. Parker, 1837), 25.

43. On "systematic colonization," see especially Edward Gibbon Wakefield, ed., *A View of the Art of Colonization: With Present Reference to the British Empire* (London: John W. Parker, 1849), 9–11.

44. Temple, *Conscience*, 424–425, emphasis original.

45. John Stuart Mill, *Principles of Political Economy: With Some of their Applications to Social Philosophy* (Boston: Charles C. Little and James Brown, 1848), 2:286–289; Temple, *Conscience*, 131, 216.

46. David Harvey, *Companion to Marx's "Capital"* (London: Verso, 2009), 301.

47. Karl Marx, *Capital: A Critique of Political Economy*, vol. 1, trans. Ben Fowkes (London: Penguin, 1990), 932.

48. Marx, *Capital*, 938.

49. Harvey, *Companion*, 303–304.

50. Miles Fairburn, "Wakefield, Edward Gibbon—Biography," in *Biography Dictionary of New Zealand. Te Ara—the Encyclopedia of New Zealand*, www.teara.govt.nz/en /biographies/1w4/wakefield-edward-gibbon.

51. H. J. M. Johnston, "Wakefield, Edward Gibbon," in *Dictionary of Canadian Biography Online*, www.biographi.ca/en/bio/wakefield_edward_gibbon_9E.html.

52. As John Weaver does. John C. Weaver, *The Great Land Rush and the Making of the Modern World, 1650–1900* (Montreal: McGill-Queen's University Press, 2003), 381n76.

53. Carol Gluck, "Words in Motion," in *Words in Motion: Toward a Global Lexicon*, ed. Carol Gluck and Anna Lowenhaupt Tsing (Durham, NC: Duke University Press, 2009), 4. Also see Carol Gluck, "*Sekinin*: Responsibility," in Gluck and Tsing, *Words in Motion*, 83.

54. Tsing gestures toward the ways in which language and religion shape the movement of words. "Words in Motion," 13.

55. On the uneven transplantation of political languages, see Tony Ballantyne, "The State, Politics, and Power, 1769–1893," in *The New Oxford History of New Zealand*, ed. Giselle Byrnes (Oxford: Oxford University Press, 2009), 99–125.

56. Patricia Burns, *Fatal Success: A History of the New Zealand Company* (Auckland: Heinemann Reed, 1989); *Edward Gibbon Wakefield and the Colonial Dream: A Reconsideration* (Wellington: Friends of the Turnbull Library / GP Publications, 1997).

Two

JANE EYRE AT HOME AND ABROAD

CHARLOTTE MACDONALD

Charlotte Brontë received her first six author's copies of *Jane Eyre* on 19 October 1847. From Haworth, Yorkshire, she wrote to her London publishers acknowledging the volumes she now held in her hand: "You have given the work every advantage which good paper, clear type and a seemly outside can supply—if it fails—the fault will lie with the author—you are exempt. I now await the judgment of the press and the public."[1] Far from failing, *Jane Eyre* was an instant success.[2] From its sensational debut as the first novel of the unknown "Currer Bell," *Jane Eyre* has remained in print, attracting critical acclaim and a lasting popularity with readers. The foundational coming-of-age tale (bildungsroman), the enduring women's emancipation text, *Jane Eyre* sits securely in the cultural canon. Simply to note a world before *Jane Eyre* existed in the hands, minds, and hearts of readers is to point to a vital transformation, a watershed in modern history.

By April 1848 *Jane Eyre* was into its third London edition. A first American edition appeared early in the same year. Smith, Elder paid Brontë £500 for the work and rights to a second novel; her first manuscript, "The Professor," they had rejected. Unlike Macaulay's *History of England* (1848), which Catherine Hall discusses as another publishing hit of the decade, *Jane Eyre* did not drop from view but has continued to attract fans.[3] "Victorian fiction" continues to be avidly consumed in the early twenty-first century, a phenomenon noted by John Sutherland and Antoinette Burton, among others.[4] *Jane Eyre* is unambiguously a charismatic work. Yet it is also an emblematic product of its mid-nineteenth-century making. What is it about Charlotte Brontë's narrator-protagonist, the small, put upon but rebellious ten-year-old child turned eighteen-year-old plain, passionate yet outspoken governess, that endures in the global imagination? In the hands of readers across the imperial commons, Jane Eyre has variously been a creature of empire, has taken aim at the foundations of power, and has become a target of empire "writing back." In her influential 1985 essay Gayatri Chakravorty Spivak set out an agenda linking nineteenth-century literature with the "social mission" of imperialism, feminist individualism, and that imperialist legacy, and a connection between Brontë's 1847 classic and Jean Rhys's 1966 *Wide Sargasso Sea*.[5] Here that agenda is pursued through a focus on the books as links in chains: chains that connect author to reader, buyer to seller, borrower to lender, and readers across time and space. Spivak's argument drew attention to the bondage underlying Jane's freedom; the ongoing life of both original and countertext testify to the entangled narration of empire and emancipation.

Jane Eyre is one of the archetypal spines of the British empire. In this discussion it is *Jane Eyre* as a material object, an agent within the communicative assemblage of empire, that is to the fore rather than *Jane Eyre* as a singular literary text. Mobile, portable, and talismanic, the book moved rapidly along circulation routes, finding paths through plural print cultures and divergent readerships. It tracked along colonial, metropolitan, commercial, recreational, and pedagogical capillaries, becoming a book in the hands (and minds) of many. Among them were readers in London and colonial Wellington in the 1840s–1850s, in the Antarctic in 1901, and in southern Africa in the 1940–1950s. As a defiant tale, Jane's narration of her own triumphant self-formation has pressed its claims on readers in intimate yet powerful form. In the pages of *Jane Eyre* lies the promise of an independent inner life. The potent sovereignty Jane achieves, and exemplifies, rests on relations of empire. Exposing those foundations in the later twentieth century served to reconfigure the imperial commons, with challengers writing back to Brontë's original. In *Wide Sargasso Sea* (1966), Jean Rhys's character Antoinette Cosway willfully burns down Thornfield Hall. Rhys repossesses rather than repudiates Brontë's story, reimagining Bertha Mason as Cosway and the Caribbean world from which she hails before entering the pages of *Jane Eyre*. More than this, Rhys takes aim at the paper underpinnings of imperial authority, dispatching the "manly spines" of bound volumes to destruction by vermin. The discussion falls into three sections: a consideration of *Jane Eyre*'s initial circulation routes and readers in the late 1840s–1850s; *Jane Eyre* as text of defiance and its promise of sovereignty of the gendered self; Jean Rhys's writing back through the *Wide Sargasso Sea* and her challenge to the spines of empire and "good reading."[6]

A Book in the Hand

Within months of *Jane Eyre*'s London publication in October 1847, the book was being read across England, and around the globe. As a commodity for sale it was carried along the market routes linking publisher's warehouse to book buyers. But it was also wordy traffic surrounding the book—gossip and speculation—that fired the arteries of circulation. *Jane Eyre*'s originality, and the mystery of its then unknown creator, "Currer Bell"—man or woman, one or several, "autobiography" or fiction—heightened the book's sensational debut. The original title page presented the work as *Jane Eyre. An Autobiography*, edited by Currer Bell. There was, thus, camouflage of title and pseudonym in the "seemly outside" of hard covers. The second edition's dedication to William Thackeray inflamed rumors that the author was the great writer's spurned mistress. As Mrs. Gaskell was soon to record, "smooth and polished" Londoners accustomed to "spending their time in nothing but" telling or hearing "some new thing" were among those at the forefront of conjecture over the book's authorship; it was gossip that "ran about like wild-fire."[7] Only nine months after *Jane Eyre*'s publication did Brontë's own publishers know, for sure, the identity of their author. Books and their makers were hot property, events in themselves, as much as the stories they told.[8]

Such sensation is not surprising given the very rapid expansion in the book and printing industry that was in full flood by the 1840s. Large sums of money were at stake in a highly competitive market. Alexis Weedon estimates that the "potential market for print in England and Wales" alone quadrupled between 1830 and 1901. By the 1850s an annual production of over five thousand titles (in increasingly long print runs) hugely surpassed the output of just a few decades earlier, while double that number of titles was being published by 1909. A mass reading public came into existence.[9] A particular feature of the British book industry was its capacity to tap large overseas markets through its imperial reach, and an even wider diaspora of English-language readers. By 1848 the total value of books exported to Britain's colonial possessions stood at £90,086, a threefold increase from 1828. In the single decade to 1858 it reached £273,281, and by the end of the century £1,088,940. By the late 1840s, the shift from India as the major market to Australasia was well advanced. Five times the quantity of books passing through Indian ports were reaching their Australasian equivalents by the early 1850s.[10] White settler colonialism provided a lucrative and geographically dispersed market for a British trade in book and print. A highly popular title such as *Jane Eyre* was a valuable commodity, expanding the market by extending the pool of readers, and *regular* readers, across boundaries of age, gender, and education. Smith, Elder's history illustrated the rapid growth and adaptation of the trade. Established in 1816 as a company to trade in publishing and as East India agents, by the mid-1840s the company was thriving in the hands of the second generation. The East India agency was only split off as a separate business in 1868.[11]

Books were beneficiaries, and agents, of the accelerating mobility of the mid-nineteenth century. Evidence of books literally "on the move" is abundant. If faster and more reliable shipping routes underpinned overseas trade and the development of colonial markets, it was the railways that opened up domestic markets and signaled the modernity of the 1840s. Within a year of *Jane Eyre*'s publication W. H. Smith had opened the first railway bookstall at London's Euston Station.[12] Reading on the train, and while waiting for trains, became part of the world moving to the rhythm of the rail timetable rather than the stagecoach.

News of *Jane Eyre*, and copies of the book, also spread across the world through the massive quantum of envelopes and packets sent by friends and relatives in private correspondence and goods exchange. Glimpses of specific readers of *Jane Eyre* provide a view of the book as words in motion, evidence of the book as a dispersing event.[13] Mary Taylor, Charlotte Brontë's school friend and fellow Yorkshirewoman (now living in New Zealand), read *Jane Eyre* in May 1848. Taylor received her copy through the post and shipping system that linked Smith, Elder's offices at 65 Cornhill, London, with the newly named Port Nicholson at Wellington, New Zealand. While it took around five months to reach her, Taylor was almost certainly the first person to read *Jane Eyre* knowing precisely the identity of its author. "After I read it," Mary wrote to Charlotte, "I went to the top of Mt. Victoria and looked for a ship to carry a letter to you. There was a little thing with one mast, and also H.M.S. *Fly*, and nothing else."[14] The letter she did send, not by that ship but by a later one, contains a wonderful response by one of Charlotte Brontë's most astute and, in the first year of the book's life, most geographically distant readers.[15] The significance of this correspondence has been discussed elsewhere in relation to the intimacy of friendship across imperial space.

Even by the time of this first letter to Charlotte Brontë, a month or so after she had read *Jane Eyre*, Taylor had lent it "a good deal." Informal borrowing was an important mode of secondary circulation. Taylor reported disdainfully to Brontë that these readers told her that *Jane Eyre* made them cry. But they gave no "opinion" of the book; if one ever did, Taylor promised Charlotte she would "embalm it for you."[16] Eager as Taylor's neighbors were to read the latest book, it was sentiment rather than passion, outrage, or critique that *Jane Eyre* produced among these colonial readers. Mary Taylor was characteristically astringent about the shortage of cultural capital in her immediate milieu. The presence of good books was not sufficient, in itself, to provide her with intellectual companions. But it was with the purpose of increasing her financial capital—and thereby her economic and social independence (freedom from governessing or marriage as options for middle-class women in England)—that Taylor had taken up colonial life. While Brontë created an imaginary world in which her character Jane Eyre overcame these limits to female autonomy, her friend had taken up life in a Wakefieldian settlement as a practical experiment to the same end. The Wellington in which Mary Taylor read *Jane Eyre* was less than ten years old: a raw, straggling, quarrelsome realization of what Edward Gibbon Wakefield had imagined of "systematic colonisation" in his *Letter from Sydney* (discussed in chapter 1). Already blood had been spilled in resistance to the British presence. Arthur Wakefield, Edward Gibbon's brother, was one of twenty-six Maori and European people who died in June 1843 in a conflict over land.

Just as new reading matter was prized in colonial Wellington, so too was it something to remark on in correspondence among the "reading classes" of London and its environs. At her home in Wimbledon, twenty-three-year-old Jane Maria Richmond read *Jane Eyre* one Saturday in May 1848 with her close friend Margaret Taylor. Soon after, her friend having returned to her home in the German spa town of Wiesbaden, Jane Maria recalled fondly the day in which they had "wickedly devoured 'Jane Eyre' in bed."[17] Correspondence between the two friends subsequently incorporated the imaginary world *Jane Eyre* had conjured up. Writing to Margaret in January 1850 Jane Maria referred to one of her former admirers, but one of whom her family did not approve, as "My French Mr Rochester."[18]

For a reading family such as the Richmonds, the years around 1846–1851 brought a wealth of new works. *Jane Eyre* appeared at what can be seen as a particularly productive spike in nineteenth-century publishing; a defining expansion of the textual commons and one that would contribute to the elevation of books to a higher station in the world of print culture. In the same year in which *Jane Eyre* appeared, William Thackeray's *Vanity Fair* was first published (in monthly parts from 1 January 1847). *Pendennis* followed in 1849–1850. The year 1848 brought to bookstands Macaulay's *History of England* (vols. 1–2); Mrs. Gaskell's first novel, *Mary Barton*; Charles Dickens's *Dombey and Son* (1846–1848); Charles Kingsley's *Yeast*; and Trollope's early work *The Kellys and O'Kellys*. Emily Brontë's *Wuthering Heights* (1847) and Anne Brontë's *Tenant of Wildfell Hall* (1848) were also part of this outpouring. Charlotte Brontë's two subsequent novels, *Shirley* and *Villette*, appeared in 1849 and 1851, respectively.

The Richmond household's reading diet over the two years surrounding *Jane Eyre's* publication provides a glimpse into a middle-class ecology of print. In March 1849 Jane Maria promised herself "some pleasure in reading Macaulay's 'History,'" impressed by "how people have been and are devouring it," and that Mudie (the largest circulating library) was supplied with one hundred copies. Her older brother William got the work from there. A couple of weeks later she told her friend Margie: "We like Macaulay very much, but get on slowly, as old James [in fact her younger brother] chooses to read it aloud to us, and we often have interruptions that prevent our all three assembling. It is certainly the lightest history I ever read, one gets along as glibly as with a novel, and it is very interesting; quite a Young Ladies' history in ease and cleanness; it leaves nothing for the poor female intellect to do; all the ideas are made smooth and easy of comprehension even to my rusty brain, and I believe I should stand a questioning on it better than on Godwin."[19] They were also reading Frederika Bremer's *Midnight Sun* ("weak stuff"), Newman's *Nemesis of Faith*, Longfellow's *Hyperion*, and work by Carlyle, and were looking forward to *Mary Barton*, which their friends, the Huttons, and others, "rave about."[20]

The pathways forged by *Jane Eyre* can be traced through reports of how readers described its press on their bodies and intimate routines. People complained about what the book did to them. George Smith was brought the manuscript on a Saturday by his colleague, W. S. Williams, with the suggestion that he read it at the earliest opportunity. In his memoir Smith recalled, "After breakfast on Sunday morning I took the MS. of 'Jane Eyre' to my little study, and began to read it. The story quickly took me captive. Before twelve o'clock my horse came to the door, but I could not put the book down. . . . Presently the servant came to tell me that luncheon was ready; I asked him to bring me a sandwich and a glass of wine, and still went on with 'Jane Eyre.' . . . Before I went to bed that night I had finished reading the manuscript."[21] In reply to the person who had sent him a copy, Thackeray wrote: "I wish you had not sent me 'Jane Eyre.' . . . It interested me so much that I have lost (or won if you like) a whole day in reading it. . . . Some of the love passages made me cry, to the astonishment of John who came in with the coals."[22] The skeptical reviewer of the book's third edition, William George Clark, set out his encounter with the novel to readers of *Fraser's*: "We took up *Jane Eyre* one winter's evening, somewhat piqued at the extravagant commendations we had heard, and sternly resolved to be as critical as Croker. But as we read on we forgot both commendations and criticism, identified ourselves with Jane in all her troubles, and finally married Mr. Rochester about four in the morning."[23] These readers were careful to record their reading in forms that could easily be produced as evidence if called to testify in court. Smith's manservant, Thackeray's "John" are witnesses to strange behavior, witnesses who could be trusted to think of uses for paper other than reading (wrapping rubbish, wiping clean, or setting a fire).

The tempo of reading, and the disembodied state in which readers forgot both themselves and the material object they held in their hands, distinguished the book and book readers in the imperial commons. Reading continuously, and pleasurably, from beginning to end, cover to cover, was a measure of worth. It was these features that denoted quality content from dross, good readers from poor skimmers, lasting impact from ephemerality. Reading as "possession" put time in the hands of those with books. To own property in books, or to have proprietary borrowing rights from Mudie's, was to be in the temporal space of the future—a future of confidence. The book that could command its reader in these ways spoke to the power that was imbued in the well-ordered page. The "possessed" book was also one in which owners held the world in their hands. In the case of the bildungs-roman, that world was one of the autonomous self. Reader, narrator, and author became one between the covers, creating a powerful motor force for the book as an agent. In the hands of readers, *Jane Eyre*'s impress was on individual hearts and minds. Readers describe the book's consumption, books being devoured, literally taken into themselves.

Jane Eyre contributed a particular spatial imagining to the wider 1840s–1850s appetite for stories of Englishness. Whether it was Dickens's extraordinarily popular tales of teeming contemporary London, Macaulay's *History of England*, or Brontë's story of a Yorkshire governess, the era of empire fed an appetite for tales of England. As Catherine Hall tells us, Macaulay's *History* provided a narrative of English success as the basis for western and white expansion. Firmly set in the remote provincial surrounds of a thinly veiled Yorkshire, Jane's fate was directly linked to events in the distant spaces of Britain's empire: the declining fortunes of the plantation Caribbean and the rising fortunes of India. In *Jane Eyre* the setting of an era just passed—of province, stagecoach, country property—provided a reassuring and confirming story of England at a moment of early nineteenth-century modernity. Readers inhabited a time beyond their own, one layered with meaning that linked a particular historical setting with the protagonist's success. Ruth Livesey has described this as a vision of the "Tory nation."[24] Jed Esty designates both *Jane Eyre* and *David Copperfield* as tales of "national historical time," their heroes underscoring the triumph of national culture. In these two canonical forms of the high Victorian bildungsroman, Esty notes "the protagonist's maturity interlocks with the reconsolidation of the national boundaries." *Jane Eyre* deals with empire, but ultimately the plot must banish these non-English, colonial elements in order to "pave the way for the ultimate insertion of Jane into a stabilized and socially sanctioned English container at Thornfield Hall."[25]

A Defiant Text: Sovereignty on the Small Scale

Jane Eyre proved to be an unusually defiant work. Long outliving its creator, and the mid-nineteenth century in which it first appeared, *Jane Eyre* continued to find its way into the hands of readers. Charlotte Brontë's death in 1855, aged thirty-nine, fed the expanding "Brontë legend," which almost immediately memorialized the author in book form with Mrs. Gaskell's *Life of Charlotte Bronte* (1857).[26] Defying the forces that rendered other print works obsolete, *Jane Eyre* continued to travel along circulation routes of global print capitalism as a commodity for sale, as an item in private collections and public libraries, as a work read, discussed, recommended, and remarked on well into the twentieth century. The book became part of the cultural bloodstream. Robert Falcon Scott's expedition to Antarctica in 1901 set off with a travel library in which *Jane Eyre* was one of the carefully selected volumes.[27] But it was the passionate, triumphant character of Jane that also gave the book its quality of defiance. Jane's passionate speaking out against injustice, as a governess to a master, subordinate to superior, galvanized its forcefulness. Sovereignty on the small scale, Jane's story of selfhood achieved against the odds, produced a remarkably long life in the global imagination.

Among the many places *Jane Eyre* can be traced in the twentieth century is in the schoolrooms of southern Africa. As a set text in the curriculum for matriculation students *Jane Eyre* had congealed in what might be termed the pedagogical commons. In this form the book was part of a wider colonial legacy in institutions of church and education, in the libraries and literacy associations of paper and print that lived alongside, and often outlasted, formal relations of empire. (C. L. R. James described a similar pattern in his education in Trinidad.)[28] For "Lily Moya," Mabel Palmer, and "Tambu," readers of *Jane Eyre* in southern Africa in the mid-twentieth century, the book was a medium of gendered colonial formation. It signified differently for each of these women.

Jane Eyre was one of the books requested by fifteen-year-old "Lily Moya" (a pseudonym) writing from the Transkei in 1949 to seventy-four-year-old Mabel Palmer, the Fabian socialist and feminist head of the Non-European section of the University of Natal in Durban. Moya, a young Xhosa woman, was desperate to continue her schooling. Without passing the matriculation exams she could not continue her studies, and without the books she could not prepare for the exams. Listing the books she needed, Lily Moya also asked Palmer to send her "their summaries" (published study guides), while also indicating that she would "tell you the other books later, which I would like to read for pleasure."[29] Palmer sent her a copy of *Jane Eyre* along with Shakespeare's *King Lear*, James Barry's *Admirable Crichton*, and several other works. As Shula Marks notes in her history of the correspondence between the two women, neither Moya nor Palmer commented on the suitability of what was the standard curriculum set for the Cape Senior Certificate across all schools, black and white, rural and urban.[30] A common commitment to education was a bridging ground for a small, largely mission-educated African elite and the progressive section of white society in the deeply divided South African society.

Moya was the only girl, and six years younger than her fellow students at St. John's School in the Transkei; across the whole of South Africa she was one of a tiny number to advance beyond elementary education. Over the course of their three-year correspondence, Moya went on to Adams College in Natal. Books continued to be part of the exchange between Moya, Palmer, and Sisbusiswe (Violet) Makhanya, a Zulu community leader who had been educated in America under mission sponsorship. A deep belief and shared desire for education spanned what were often huge gulfs and painful misunderstandings between the women. That commitment, Marks suggests, was reinforced by Lily, Mabel, and Sisbusiswe's shared, if very differing, attempts to forge independent paths in worlds largely determined by men. All three struggled with their aspirations as women: for autonomy, for choices around marriage, work, livelihood, and a life of the mind.[31] Moya told Palmer soon after she had started at Adams College that part of why she was so pleased to be there was because it enabled her to escape from a marriage her uncle was arranging for her. Marriage "to a man I hated so much" she termed an "awful bondage."[32] Tragically, Lily Moya's time at Adams did not live up to expectations; Palmer proved unable to understand Moya's difficulties or meet her need for more than formal support. The relationship broke down. In her final letter to Palmer, Lily Moya's pained and angry cry is that she had to leave Adams College "due to the fact that I was never meant to be a stone but a human being with feelings, not either an experimental doll."[33]

In Tsitsi Dangarembga's novel *Nervous Conditions* (1988), the protagonist, Tambu, is a fourteen-year-old girl in Zimbabwe's Umtali district at the time of the independence wars, 1968–1969. Tambu reads everything "from Blyton to Bronte" in the bedroom she shares with her cousin in the mission home of her schoolmaster uncle.[34] For Lily and Tambu, reading was not the path to the classic integrative bildungsroman. The impossibility of reconciling the conflicts of gender, colonial position, class, mobility, Christianity, imagination, village, and town with being an educated woman led to mental illness. Twentieth-century southern Africa is not the Caribbean of the 1830s, but Bertha Mason's shadow hovers. Lily Moya and Tambu are close proximates, in time and place, for the kind of independent women against whom Kenya's Wanjau was writing (see chapter 10, this volume).

If Wanjau's place for formulation of ideas was the detention camps of the 1950s Kenyan Emergency, Moya and Tambu's parallel was the late colonial mission classroom—also a place of confinement, rules, uniforms, sex segregation, and reading.

If Lily Moya and Tambu's experiences speak starkly of the constraints colonialism continued to exercise over gendered autonomy, the enduring popularity of *Jane Eyre* also underlines how remarkably long-lasting was the quest for sovereignty of the gendered imperial self. When *Jane Eyre* first appeared in 1847 readers were shocked, and thrilled, by Brontë's depiction of an impassioned, articulate heroine who spoke back to power as a subordinate. The anonymous reviewer of *Jane Eyre* in the April 1848 issue of the *Christian Remembrancer* accused Brontë of "moral Jacobinism." "Unjust, unjust" burned on every page.[35] At a moment when Chartist petitioners gathered en masse at Kennington Common and revolutionary insurrection ran through Paris streets, such an allegation carried a charge.[36] From the opening scene, where Jane's angry outburst against the taunting violence of John Reed gets her sent to the red room, Brontë's narrator-protagonist is engaged in resistance: speaking out, acting independently, remembering the cruelties, injustices, and deprivations that her lesser position entails.

Jane Eyre's angry indictment is a powerful critique of the system by which English women were destined to lives as chattels, decorative dependents, dutiful companions, or conduits for family reputations, names, and fortunes. Brontë's book might have physically resembled the bookish spine of manly authority, but it took direct aim at the exercise of such authority in political economy, law, and social convention. In this way we can see *Jane Eyre* as a text propelled into circulation, and sustained in circulation, long beyond the particular era and setting in which it originated. Sovereignty on the small scale, over an autonomous self, a reader in command of her self, was the utopian promise that *Jane Eyre* long illuminated in the global imagination. The book is one of resistance.

At Lowood School, where she is starved, at Thornfield, where she is humiliated, and at Moor House, where she is bound by obligation, Jane resists. As the narrator of her trials, Jane is at pains to explain that the position from which she writes (the Jane she is and has become), the Jane who "speaks" directly to her reader, is the work of an insistent inner self. The outer person, the unprepossessing appearance, the humble station, are unreliable guides to what lies within. "Do you think, because I am poor, obscure, plain, and little, I am soulless and heartless? You think wrong—I have as much soul as you—and full as much heart."[37] Jane speaks audaciously, dangerously, against her superiors. Her words are thrown at a man with power, property, age, money, family, station—her master. *Jane Eyre* turned the tables on power. It is this story of resistance, a resistance rooted in an autonomous self, that gives *Jane Eyre* enduring power as a tale against oppression. The "inside being," the individual who thinks, feels, and acts, is the book's promise to all. The book inspired a genre of self-formation narratives; works significant for telling of women's and other subordinate groups' struggles of becoming "the one" rather than "the other."

Jane Eyre's story of weak against strong takes place within the sovereign world conjured by the book. Jane Eyre's story, of a woman who challenges the powers ranged against her, overcoming them to tell her own story of survival and success, is one of remarkable longevity. The first-person tale provides the reader with a powerful and intimate experience of self-rule. In doing so the book and the self become one. In *Jane Eyre* there is a clear example of the book as a proxy for autonomous selfhood. In the portable, mobile, compact form of the book lay the promise of sovereignty of the self that Jane Eyre's coming-of-age tale relayed. That story was one that captured the global imagination, living on far beyond the mid-nineteenth-century world of its creation and initial circulation.

Wide Sargasso Sea *and the Repossession of* Jane Eyre

In Jean Rhys's *Wide Sargasso Sea* (1966) defiance was turned on *Jane Eyre*.[38] Rhys was a contemporary of C. L. R. James, born in Dominica but living much of her life in France and later in England.[39] Rhys's brilliant novel gives us the backstory to Brontë's classic. Antoinette Cosway, the main narrator, is Rhys's reimagining of Brontë's Bertha Mason, the madwoman in the attic. *Wide Sargasso Sea* takes us to the world before Brontë's book begins: the Caribbean port of Spanish Town, Jamaica, and the Windward Islands, in the postemancipation 1830s. In so doing Rhys reconfigures the commons *Jane Eyre* produces for late twentieth-century readers as imperial and historic rather than transcendent and literary. It is Antoinette who has life, agency, spirit and exercises it outside and against "the man who hates her" (her unnamed husband, the character we recognize as Rochester).

In this specific space of empire, Antoinette's narration tells of a past—her own, as the daughter of a Creole mother and a father who died too soon—and, through her traumatic childhood memories, of a place simmering with insecurity, threatened with violence, poverty, and hostility. Groomed as an heiress, Antoinette is pursued by an Englishman whose family's mercenary ambitions bring him to the unfamiliar place of the Caribbean in search of a marriage partner who will bring him capital. The Cosway and Rochester family fortunes link the wealth of the former slave colonies to provincial England at a time of political and economic crisis. In part 3 of *Wide Sargasso Sea* Antoinette is in the upper attic of what we recognize as Thornfield Hall, bringing Rhys's world directly into that of Brontë's Jane, connecting the two books.

Whereas Charlotte Brontë had resolved her protagonist's fate by banishing the non-English elements of Jane Eyre's ventures, Rhys reinserts the plot and character into an imperial setting. Spivak depicted the connection between the two works as a form of "mirroring"; the link might be considered a more dynamic and entangled one.[40]

Wide Sargasso Sea took direct aim at the textual monuments of empire and at an imperial commons in which the book reigned supreme. In place of veneration, Rhys's *Wide Sargasso Sea* throws the book (and pen, paper, and print culture generally) to the margins, where it decays, to be consumed by insects. The characters who have knowledge are those who do not read and write. By this means, Rhys not only provincialized the book but struck at the authority of the "paper empire." At Granbois, the family estate where she is to spend her honeymoon, Antoinette points her husband to the door that leads to his dressing-room. For the first time Rochester finds comfort in a space furnished in a familiar style. There is "a carpet, the only one I had seen, a press," and under the open window, "a small writing-desk with paper, pens, and ink." For a moment he thinks of it as a refuge.[41] Over the desk was "a crude bookshelf made of three shingles strung together." Moving closer, Rochester reads the spines of the volumes leaning on the shelf: "Byron's poems, novels by Sir Walter Scott, *Confessions of an Opium Eater*, some shabby brown volumes, and on the last shelf, *Life and Letters of* . . . The rest was eaten away."[42] The stature of the volumes, exemplars of the "surrogate Englishman in his highest and most perfect state," mirrors his own.[43] But on closer inspection his confidence dissolves. The books' physical state is one of neglect and decay. Now the bound books sitting on a shelf sound a warning: Byron, Scott, Thomas de Quincey's *Confessions* (1821), and most of all, the partial remains of a personified title (*Life and Letters*) whose very identity and body had been consumed "eaten away" rather than read. Rhys denies the book a complete title in the same way she denies Antoinette's husband a name. At the conclusion of the scene Rochester has no memory and no written words: "As for my confused impressions they will never be written. There are blanks in my mind that cannot be filled up."[44] Alongside Rochester's loss of memory and disorientation, the old woman Christophine, who has been Antoinette's faithful black nurse and attendant throughout her life, is the repository of knowledge. But as she tells him, her knowing does not rely on paper and writing: "Read and write I don't know. Other things I know."[45]

Rhys's titles are carefully selected. Scott's work features in Brontë's original when Rivers gives Jane a copy of Scott's *Marmion*; Thomas de Quincey's *Confessions of an Opium Eater* was published in 1821; *Life and Letters of . . .* points at the memorialization of lives preserved between covers. The passage offers further evidence of Woolf's observation that books continue each other, even as they exist as separate titles.[46] They live in each other's pages, or are sentenced to decay in such pages. The looping back and forth in time—from Rhys's publication in 1966 to Sir Walter Scott and Quincey (1821) to *Jane Eyre* first in 1847—illustrates the temporal fluidity of the imperial commons.

Rhys's depiction of books as unsettling signifiers of Rochester's vulnerability and confused state of mind extends Brontë's use of books as measures of value in her characters. The affective power of books that Leah Price describes is apparent in Brontë's original and at work in Rhys's reimagining. Brontë uses books as objects to tell us about characters and the moral world they inhabit. We know John Reed as bad—and someone our protagonist-narrator Jane will have to battle against—when he bursts in on her "double retirement" in the window seat with Berwick's *Birds*, throwing the book at her head in the opening scene of *Jane Eyre*. Similarly, St. John Rivers's cold, duty-centered, passive authoritarian character is indicated by his reading habits. He holds books rather than reads them; gives them to others rather than letting them chose their own; puts away Jane's books. Even in the company of his loved and loving sisters around the breakfast table, he sits with "a book in his hand—it was his unsocial custom to read at meals."[47] Nor do books, paper, or reading bring Jane and St. John Rivers together. Rather, these things set the terms on which they relate as unequals. Rivers requires Jane to join him in learning Hindustani as part of his preparation for mission work.[48] He sets her to work in the village schoolroom of his parish. He puts away her books, and his own, telling her she "shall take a walk" with him, alone.[49] He chooses the verses and reads the Bible at the household's evening prayers.[50] He reads the lawyer's letter telling Jane of her bequest, a letter that has come to him as a clergyman in the district "who knows things and people." It is all one-way traffic from higher to lower, man to woman, powerful to powerless, instilling obligation and requiring from the recipient a gesture of gratitude. We know the cozy drawing room at Moor House is furnished with books, but it is Jane, and St. John Rivers's sisters, Diana and Mary, who read together in loving companionship. Their brother declines to join the circle. St. John Rivers does not receive but distributes. Books are part of his world of obligation, of inequality, of superior to inferior. He is "implacable," someone who cannot be resisted.[51] Jane tells us "I could not resist him."[52] He is impervious.

Crucial to Price's argument for the nineteenth-century origins of the privileged style of reading associated with the bound novel is the distinction between novel and tract.[53] One is an object in the market, the exterior value (price for sale) denoting an interior value of absorbing and pleasurable reading experience (consumption). The other is a flimsier and duller thing, distributed rather than sold, and thereby signaling a reading of duty and effort rather than absorption. Rivers is the tract to the glamorous and more enticing Rochester-as-novel. Rivers, unlike Rochester (and Jane), has no "inside." He proposes marriage to Jane as a partnership of duty rather than love; he has virtue and principle in abundance, but he has no feelings; he has a vocation, but he cares little of what its pursuit might mean for those closest to him; he has many advantages in the world—he is loved, he is looked after, he is respected—yet he rarely shows any feelings. In the last we see of Rivers, and it is with his fate the novel closes, he is in India fulfilling his missionary vocation. "He entered on the path he had marked for himself; he pursues it still. A more resolute, indefatigable pioneer never wrought amidst rocks and dangers." Jane tells us that "St John is unmarried: he never will marry now." Rivers remained virginal, an unread text.[54]

In the end Jane chooses love and desire at home rather than duty and service abroad; the novel (Rochester) over the tract (Rivers). The hard cash of an inheritance that enables her to follow her heart is "an affair of the actual world," a material thing in both physical and economic senses.[55] So too was Charlotte Brontë's own book, for all that she played with the distinctions between outer covers and appearances and inner value. Her letter to Smith, Elder in October 1847 clearly separated "the good paper, clear type," and "seemly outside" of her own book from "the work" inside; herself as author (with whom the book's future failure or success would lie) from her publisher (whose responsibility for its material form was now complete).[56] But the separation was, as she knew, a compelling fiction. The material form and life of the book was inseparable from the tale it contained.

Jane Eyre's insistence on the possibility of the independent inner life makes Brontë's work significant as an inspirational coming-of-age story, a novel of self-formation. From the classic English form of mid-nineteenth-century social novels, the genre has developed and adapted, exploring relations between individuals and their societies across many contexts. For women, *Jane Eyre* has long been a reverberant text, speaking for a full personhood where gender remains a central axis for inequality. In colonies and former colonies, coming-of-age novels have been part of the struggle against subjection and toward autonomy. Yet *Jane Eyre*'s position in the imperial nexus is tangled. While Brontë's work has been central in providing a universal story of the individual overcoming social conditions, it is also a work that is highly specific. As Rhys's *Wide Sargasso Sea* and Dangarembga's *Nervous Conditions* attest, *Jane Eyre* is also part of an "Englishness," a culture of empire, that continues to imprison the mind, to limit subjectivity. This contradiction, the problem of whether there can be a postcolonial bildungsroman, remains.[57] In a related way, James Slaughter has pointed to the influence of coming-of-age narrative in the making of a twentieth-century culture, as well as of the international law, of human rights. The universal path to "self-development" is one with specific historical origins. *Jane Eyre* is a part of a cultural history that has created the notion of the fully realized individual, the textual inner self. "Human rights and the *Bildungsroman*," Slaughter argues, "are mutually enabling fictions: each projects an image of the other's vision of the ideal relations between individual and society."[58] His message is: beware what we read!

Conclusion

Jane Eyre has had a remarkably long life in the shifting assemblage of empire. Commercial capillaries that first propelled the book into a mid-nineteenth-century global market have accreted other motors of circulation. In the process the work has gathered its own history, evident in the multiple lives of Brontë's characters, in the experiences of readers, and in the works that have taken up from the original text. *Jane Eyre*'s disturbing, thrilling, violent, passionate pages have been constantly remade. *Jane Eyre* is unusual in that it runs against the much broader tide of "downward mobility."[59] Along with a clutch of other works, Brontë's novel occupies the venerated, isolated outcrop visible above the waves below which most nineteenth-century print has disappeared. The glowing light of canonical status shines on the very small selection of works poised there. The shine is of gold as well as glory. The book has a rising stock as a material object, in particular, in its "original," first edition form. The "good paper, clear type and seemly outside" in which Smith, Elder published the first copies of *Jane Eyre* now carry a value far beyond the words on the page. That value is not in reading but in owning one of a highly select group of titles that fall into an asset class as "investment collectables." In Christie's New York auction rooms a first edition of *Jane Eyre* was sold in December 2012 for $68,500.[60] At the same time, thousands of new copies in various highly affordable editions, and even cheaper secondhand copies, are readily available for sale. Not all *Jane Eyres* are equal.

Across the great variety of print cultures and readerships within which *Jane Eyre* has found a place, the book has taken aim at the legitimacy of authority, opening a pathway of resistance. Jane's voice against the men who seek to control her destiny has spoken strongly against the gendered structures of imperial power. But this has not been its only place. *Jane Eyre* has also consolidated an empire-in-print, inscribing in the global imagination a notion of Englishness, of sovereignty, and of the superior value of the bound volume (and the reading with which it is associated).

Jane Eyre continues to perform multiple work as a product and narration of empire, as inspiration of resistance to authority and in dismantling the culture of imperial "Englishness." Brontë's book sustains several lives. Jane, the small, slight, plain orphan governess, wins out over the enormous forces ranged against her, triumphing over the dominating Rochester and the virtuously authoritarian Rivers. Rochester and Rivers are men of imposing social status and forceful character, through whose presence imperial possibilities and histories are sunk deep into provincial England. Jane's story, ultimately, is one of resistance followed by reconciliation on terms she can set; a contented domestic life at Ferndean is where she "speaks" to us from. The specter of Bertha has been dispatched. Jane remains alive in the minds and hearts of readers. But Jane's life has never come to an end. Her repose at Ferndean is now disturbed by new events at Thornfield Hall (and earlier still in Antoinette Cosway's life in Dominica and Jamaica with

Rochester). At the end of Rhys's *Wide Sargasso Sea* Cosway tells us that now she knows "why I was brought here and what I have to do." She sets fire to Thornfield Hall, before jumping from its rooftop battlements—to her death, into the pages of Brontë's *Jane Eyre*, or back to her life in the Caribbean? *Jane Eyre* continues to be a consolidating and challenging feature in the imperial commons. Transcending the time and place of its setting and creation, *Jane Eyre* is as alive in a postcolonial age, as a text of contention, as it was in the first decade of its existence.

NOTES

Thanks to Fran Parkin, Susann Liebich, Martin Staniforth, Simon Hay, and to the editors and fellow contributors for their inspiration and responses to an early draft.

1. Charlotte Brontë to Smith, Elder & Co, 19 October 1847, in Brontë, *Letters of Charlotte Brontë*, 2 vols., ed. Margaret Smith (Oxford: Oxford University Press, 1995), 1:552.

2. Currer Bell, ed., *Jane Eyre: An Autobiography* (London: Smith, Elder, 1847), sold in three volumes for £1 11s. 6d.

3. In this sense it can be considered to be words in motion in the sense conveyed by Carol Gluck and Anna Lowenhaupt Tsing, eds., *Words in Motion: Toward a Global Lexicon* (Durham, NC: Duke University Press, 2009).

4. The latest film adaptation of Jane Eyre was released in early 2011: director, Cary Joji Fukunaga; screenplay, Moira Buffini; Focus Features / BBC. John Sutherland, preface to rev. ed., *Victorian Fiction: Writers, Publishers, Readers* (Basingstoke, England: Palgrave Macmillan, 2006), and *Can Jane Eyre Be Happy? More Puzzles in Classic Fiction* (New York: Oxford University Press, 1997). Antoinette Burton, "Recapturing *Jane Eyre*: Reflections on Historicizing the Colonial Encounter in Victorian Britain," *Radical History Review* 64 (Winter 1996): 58–72, and *Empire in Question: Reading, Writing and Teaching British Imperialism* (Durham, NC: Duke University Press, 2011), ch. 10, 174–183.

5. Gayatri Chakravorty Spivak, "Three Women's Texts and a Critique of Imperialism," *Critical Inquiry* 12, no. 1 (1985): 243–261.

6. "Good reading" in the terms Leah Price introduces in her *How to Do Things with Books in Victorian Britain* (Princeton, NJ: Princeton University Press, 2012).

7. Mrs. Gaskell, *The Life of Charlotte Bronte* (1857) (Harmondsworth, England: Penguin, 1975), 326.

8. See especially James A. Secord, *Victorian Sensation* (Chicago: University of Chicago Press, 2000); Leslie Howsam, "What Is the Historiography of Books? Recent Studies in Authorship, Publishing, and Reading in Modern Britain and North America," *Historical Journal* 51, no. 4 (2008): 1089–1101, and *Old Books and New Histories. An Orientation to Studies in Books and Print Culture* (Toronto: University of Toronto Press, 2006).

9. Kate Flint, *The Woman Reader 1837–1914* (Oxford: Clarendon Press, 1993); Martyn Lyons, *A History of Reading and Writing in the Western World* (Basingstoke, England: Palgrave Macmillan, 2010).

10. Alexis Weedon, *Victorian Publishing: The Economics of Book Production for a Mass Market 1836–1916* (Aldershot, England: Ashgate, 2003), 34, ch. 2 passim. See also Lyons, *History*, 137–139; Howsam, "Historiography of Books," and *Old Books and New Histories*; Simon Eliot, " 'Never Mind the Value, What about the Price?': Or, How Much Did *Marmion* Cost St. John Rivers?," *Nineteenth-Century Literature* 56, no. 2 (September 2001): 160–197.

11. Margaret Drabble, ed., *Oxford Companion to English Literature* (Oxford: Oxford University Press, 1985), 913; Brontë, *Letters*, 2:xxxix. For more on the history of Smith, Elder in India, see Priya Joshi, *In Another Country: Colonialism, Culture and the English Novel in India* (New York: Columbia University Press, 2002), 107.

12. Lyons, *History*, 147. See also George Routledge's *Railway Library* series, published from 1849.

13. Gluck and Tsing, *Words in Motion*.

14. Mary Taylor to Charlotte Brontë, June–July 1848, in Brontë, *Letters*, 2:87.

15. Charlotte Macdonald, "Intimacy of the Envelope: Fiction, Commerce and Empire in the Correspondence of Friends Mary Taylor and Charlotte Bronte, c. 1845–55," in *Moving Subjects: Gender, Mobility, and Intimacy in an Age of Global Empire*, ed. Tony Ballantyne and Antoinette Burton (Urbana: University of Illinois Press, 2009), 89–109.

16. Mary Taylor to Charlotte Brontë, June–July 1848, in Brontë, *Letters*, 2:88.

17. Jane Maria Richmond, "Springholm," Merton, Wimbledon, to Miss Margaret Taylor, Wiesbaden, 17 June 1848, Richmond-Atkinson Papers, MSY-2770, vol. 38, 72, Alexander Turnbull Library, Wellington. See Frances Porter, *Born to New Zealand: A Biography of Jane Maria Atkinson* (Wellington: Allen and Unwin / PNP, 1989).

18. Jane Maria Richmond to Margaret Taylor, January 1850, Richmond-Atkinson Papers, MSY-2770, vol. 38, 118–119, Alexander Turnbull Library.

19. Jane Maria Richmond to Margaret Taylor, 24 March 1849, Richmond-Atkinson Papers, MSY-2770, vol. 38, 100–101, Alexander Turnbull Library.

20. Jane Maria Richmond to Margaret Taylor, 28 May 1849, Richmond-Atkinson Papers, MSY-2770, vol. 38, 102–103, Alexander Turnbull Library. Richmond also read Thackeray's *Vanity Fair* and *Pendennis* and Dickens's *Dombey and Son* and *David Copperfield* as "lighter reading." She also read Mill, Ruskin, James Martineau, Carlyle, Bunyan, Machiavelli, Wordsworth, Milton, and others. Porter, *Born to New Zealand*, 20.

21. George Smith, *A Memoir* (London, 1902), Reading Experience Database (RED), entry 4370.

22. W. M. Thackeray to W. S. Williams, 23 October 1847, in Letters of Thackeray, RED, entry 4371.

23. Quoted in Kathleen Tillotson, *Novels of the Eighteen-Forties* (Oxford: Oxford University Press, 1961), 20, citing Clark's review in *Fraser's*, December 1849, 692.

24. Ruth Livesey, "Communicating with Jane Eyre: Stagecoach, Mail, and the Tory Nation," *Victorian Studies* 53, no. 4 (December 2011): 615–638.

25. Jed Esty, *Unseasonable Youth: Modernism, Colonialism, and the Fiction of Development* (Oxford: Oxford University Press, 2012), 50–51. See also Sue Thomas, *Imperialism, Reform, and the Making of Englishness in "Jane Eyre"* (Basingstoke, England: Palgrave Macmillan, 2008).

26. Gaskell, *Life of Charlotte Brontë*. An entry point for the large literature on the Brontë legend is Lucasta Miller, *The Brontë Myth* (New York: Knopf, 2004).

27. Margarete Rubik and Elke Mettinger-Schartman, eds., *A Breath of Fresh Eyre: Intertextual and Intermedial Reworkings of "Jane Eyre"* (Amsterdam: Rodopi, 2007), 25.

28. See Aaron Kamugisha, chapter 9, this volume. Also Shula Marks, ed., *Not Either an Experimental Doll* (London: Women's Press, 1987), 47n50, citing an interview with James in *Third World Book Review*, 1984.

29. Marks, *Experimental Doll*, 72.

30. Marks, *Experimental Doll*, 18. See also Shula Marks, "Changing History, Changing Histories: Separations and Connections in the Lives of South African Women," *Journal of African Cultural Studies* 13, no. 1 (2000): 94–106.

31. Marks, "Changing History."

32. Marks, *Experimental Doll*, 21.

33. Marks, *Experimental Doll*, 186.

34. Tsitsi Dangarembga, *Nervous Conditions* (London: Women's Press, 1988).

35. *Christian Remembrancer*, April 1848, xv, quoted in *The Brontës: The Critical Heritage*, ed. Miriam Allott (London: Routledge and Kegan Paul, 1974), 90.

36. E. J. Hobsbawm, *The Age of Revolution: Europe 1789–1848* (London: Weidenfeld and Nicholson, [1962] 1997).

37. *Jane Eyre* (Harmondsworth, England: Penguin Books, 1953), ch. 23, 405. Hereafter all references to *Jane Eyre* text from this source.

38. Jean Rhys, *Wide Sargasso Sea* (London: Deutsch, 1966).

39. Jean Rhys (?1890–1979), b. Dominica; C. L. R. James (1901–89), b. Trinidad.

40. Spivak, "Three Women's Texts," 250.

41. Rhys, *Wide Sargasso Sea*, 63.

42. Rhys, *Wide Sargasso Sea*, 63.

43. Gauri Viswanathan, *Masks of Conquest: Literary Study and British Rule in India* (New Delhi: Oxford University Press, 1998), 20.

44. Rhys, *Wide Sargasso Sea*, 64.

45. Rhys, *Wide Sargasso Sea*, 133.

46. Virginia Woolf, *A Room of One's Own*, edited and annotated by Mark Hussey and Susan Gubar (New York: Harcourt, 2005), 79.

47. *Jane Eyre*, ch. 34, 390–391.

48. *Jane Eyre*, 395.

49. *Jane Eyre*, 396.

50. *Jane Eyre*, 412.

51. *Jane Eyre*, ch. 35, 406.

52. *Jane Eyre*, 395.

53. Price, *How to Do Things with Books*.

54. *Jane Eyre*, ch. 38, 447.

55. *Jane Eyre*, 378. She sees her name in "Indian ink," 377.

56. Charlotte Brontë to Smith, Elder & Co, 19 October 1847, in Brontë, *Letters*, 1:552.

57. Simon Hay, "*Nervous Conditions*, Lukács, and the Postcolonial Bildungsroman," *Genre* 46, no. 3 (Fall 2013): 317–344.

58. Joseph R. Slaughter, "The Bildungsroman and International Human Rights Law," PMLA (2006): 1407b. Joseph R. Slaughter, *Human Rights, Inc.: The World Novel, Narrative Form, and International Law* (New York: Fordham University Press, 2007).

59. Derek Peterson's phrase.

60. Christie's auction, New York, 7 December 2012, Sale 2607, Lot 145, *Jane Eyre* first edition listed at $30,000–$50,000 (realized sale price of $68,500), www.christies .com, accessed 16 April 2014; see also en.wikicollecting.org/jane-eyre-first-edition-by -charlotte-bronte, accessed 16 April 2014.

Three

MACAULAY'S
HISTORY OF ENGLAND

A Book That Shaped Nation and Empire

———

CATHERINE HALL

In December 1848, in the wake of the European revolutions of that year, the first two volumes of Thomas Babington Macaulay's *The History of England from the Accession of James II* were published to rapturous applause and unprecedented sales. The sales of the next three volumes surpassed all expectations. By the turn of the century, it is estimated, probably a million copies of Macaulay's works were circulating the globe. The Great Historian, as he came to be known, was already a significant public figure in Britain, celebrated for his parliamentary oratory; his literary and historical essays on great English writers, statesmen, and empire builders; and his ballads, the *Lays of Ancient Rome*. But it was the history of England that he planned that he trusted to secure his lasting reputation, and in 1839 he set about the task of writing it. The tension for him between a life as a statesman and one as a literary man was never resolved, but the influence of Homer, he came to believe, was much longer lasting than that of Napoleon. Men's lives and imaginations were more shaped by the words they read or heard than by the deeds of conquerors. He was a man with a profound sense of the power of the book; indeed he believed that books had saved his life in the wake of traumatic events in his emotional life.[1] It was safer, he believed, to live with the dead than the living. He set his sights on his capacity to inspire readers over centuries to come, and for twenty years he devoted himself to his project. He hoped that he had written a master narrative and was convinced (correctly as it transpired) that his *History* would outlast those of his rivals. He was not disappointed: the *History* brought him immense celebrity, gave him imperial and global recognition, and made him a rich man. It has been reprinted multiple times, translated into innumerable languages, and remains in print. It is an iconic account of the nation.

He made the decision to work on the history while in India, serving as the lay member of the Governor General's Council, a very powerful position and one he used to promote the anglicization of India. The history he intended to write was a history of England, but it would stand as a universal history, for England was in his mind *the* modern nation, a nation that had progressed, was civilized, and could act as a beacon providing the model other nations could follow. Writing from India, he was able to reflect on "home" from the outside, to gain a new perspective, a much clearer recognition of the difference as he understood it between India and England, and the process whereby England had become what it was. England deserved its own history—one that would stand beside those of Greece and Rome, for "our liberty is . . . essentially English," something different.[2] England's story, as he told it, was of a transformation from barbarism to civilization. At the beginning of the twelfth century England's condition had been "more miserable than the state in which the most degraded nations of the East now are." But "in the course of seven centuries the wretched and degraded race have become the greatest and most highly civilised people that ever the world saw, have spread their dominion over every quarter of the globe, have scattered the seeds of mighty empires and republics," have exercised maritime power, have developed the science of healing, have excelled in mechanical arts, manufacture, and literature, and have become "the acknowledged leaders of the human race" on questions of political improvement. The history of England was "the history of this great change in the moral, intellectual, and physical state of the inhabitants of our own island."[3] This was a story to be proud of, a story of progress.

The opening of the first volume made clear that this was to be an epic. The historian placed himself in the center of the frame, his authoritative voice telling his readers the history of "our country." At the center of his story was the Glorious Revolution of 1688, the revolution that terminated the long struggle between the monarchy and their parliaments, and secured "the rights of the people" and the title of the reigning dynasty. "Under that settlement, the authority of law and the security of property were found to be compatible with a liberty of discussion and of individual action never before known." It was from this "auspicious union of order and freedom" that unparalleled prosperity sprang, and "our country, from a state of ignominious vassalage, rapidly rose to the place of umpire among European powers." Her "opulence and her martial glory" grew alongside the wonders of the Bank of England, a "gigantic commerce" and maritime power. Scotland was united to England, the American colonies "became far mightier and wealthier" than the Spanish, an empire as grand as that of Alexander was established in Asia. But the duty of the historian was to record disasters and "great national crimes" as well as triumphs. Expansion brought abuses, "evils from which poor and rude societies are free." In North America "imprudence and obstinacy . . . broke the ties to the parent state." Ireland was "cursed by the domination of race over race and of religion over religion." It "remained indeed a member of the empire, but a withered and distorted member, adding no strength to the body politic, and reproachfully pointed at by all who feared or envied the greatness of England." Yet, he maintained, "unless I greatly deceive myself, the general effect of this chequered narrative will be to excite thankfulness in all religious minds, and hope in the breasts, of all patriots. For the history of our country during the last hundred and sixty years is eminently the history of physical, of moral, and of intellectual improvement." He aimed to tell of battles and sieges, of parliaments and kings, but also "the history of the people," of art and religion, of manners and customs. He would place before the English of the nineteenth century a true picture of the life of their ancestors and make them proud of those ancestors—for those who had no pride in the past would leave no lasting legacies themselves.[4] Constitutional government for the people, the rule of law, individual freedom, security of property, prosperity and imperial power, these were the key elements of Macaulay's triumphalist account. He initially intended that his chronological scope should reach to 1832, his own times. In fact the five volumes ended in 1701, offering an account of the late seventeenth century, *the* formative time, in his understanding, for the making of the modern nation. And although the work was entitled *History of England*, it was in fact the history of Britain and Ireland—all subsumed in Macaulay's mind into one hegemonic category, England.

How was the *History* received, not just in Britain but across the empire? This essay can only give some small indications, for it was a book with truly global reach.[5] On publication the enthusiasm for the *History* in Britain matched the excitement over Scott's *Waverley* decades previously, and the books sold on the scale of Dickens. It was consumed by readers of every class, both men and women, and Macaulay received innumerable letters of thanks from all levels of society. "My dear Macaulay" wrote Lord Jeffrey, erstwhile editor of the *Edinburgh Review*, a man who had fostered him as a young author, "the mother that bore you, had she been yet alive, could scarcely have felt prouder or happier than I do at this outburst of your graver fame."[6] Maria Edgeworth, by this time an elderly literary lady, named it "immortal" and was especially thrilled that she was mentioned and Scott was not. Mr. Brontë read it in the Haworth vicarage and greatly enjoyed it. Harriet Martineau was much less complimentary, regarding it as a romantic fantasy. A number of intellectuals criticized its complacency and homespun philosophy. Farmers turned to it in the long winter evenings; public schoolboys bewailed the difficulties in getting hold of the volumes. An officer committed to prison for a fortnight for knocking down a policeman had his French novels taken away from him but was allowed to keep his Bible and Macaulay's *History*: a clear indication as to how it was viewed by the authorities.

The *History* was perfect for reading aloud, with its strong narrative, its simple language that made use of the vernacular, its great melodramatic setpieces, its vivid word pictures, its romance of the powerful combined with its many doses of Victorian common sense. It educated and entertained (making few critical demands) while civilizing its readers, offering them identities as proud subjects of the greatest nation on earth. Macaulay read much of it to his sister Hannah and her family as he completed chapters and was ready to try them out. Much to his annoyance, his brother-in-law, Charles Trevelyan, often fell asleep, but Hannah and her daughter were always full of praise, convincing him that his history, as he hoped, would displace the novels of fashionable young ladies on their drawing-room tables. Jane Maria Richmond's brother borrowed it from the library, as Charlotte Macdonald records (chapter 2, this volume), and it was read aloud in her family circle. She described it as "quite a Young Ladies' history in ease and cleanness; it leaves nothing for the poor female intellect to do; all the ideas are made smooth and easy of comprehension."[7] In later years Millicent Fawcett, a leading feminist, remembered her older sister, Elizabeth Garrett, gathering her siblings around her on a Sunday evening and telling them stories from Macaulay. Virginia Woolf recorded in May 1897 that she had just finished the fifth and last volume of "my beloved Macaulay."[8] Woolf might have felt less enthusiastic about him if she had known how hostile he was to "bluestockings"—a breed he regarded as hateful. Women, in Macaulay's view, were suited to being the educated companions of men, but their ambitions should reach no higher. He reproduced entirely conventional Victorian views of gender relations in the *History*, seeing family as the bedrock of social order, men as actors in the world, and woman's place as being in the home.

Those wanting to educate or improve their employees or congregations seized on it. A gentleman in Lancashire invited his poorer neighbors to come to his house every evening after their work was finished, and he read the *History* aloud to them from beginning to end. Macaulay himself particularly prized a letter that he received from a Unitarian minister offering thanks from a group of working people who had been attending the schoolhouse regularly on Wednesday evenings to hear the *History* and who appreciated the fact that workingmen could understand it. His longtime servant William Williams requested a copy of the *History* when he was pensioned off; this was the book he could enjoy by his fireside at his retirement home, Macaulay Villa. Access was not confined to those able to buy the books, for circulating libraries bought multiple copies. Cheap editions were not produced immediately—indeed, the publisher, William Longman, did not want his profits to be reduced in this way. As the *British Journal* noted in 1852:

> The number of readers in this country is rapidly extending ... we hope the day is not far distant when the original works of our highest minds—the fictions of Bulwer and the histories of Macaulay—will be published in shilling volumes and penny parts, and the poorest reader in the kingdom have thus an opportunity of sharing in a luxury now reserved only for the rich, or the comparatively rich. It is when a book is *new* that it is most keenly relished, and as the mind of the nation is continually moving onwards, one class of the community should not be left, in intellectual taste, a generation behind another.[9]

Soon enough there were selections and popular editions on the market in response to this demand.

The *History* was also a great success both on the Continent and in the United States. An English-language edition was published in a paperback series in Germany, and by 1856 there were six translations into German in progress. Editions appeared in all the major European languages and were enthusiastically consumed across the Continent. Messrs. Harper of New York were astonished by the success; the *History* had taken the country by storm. The absence of copyright protection meant that twenty thousand copies of the unauthorized edition were sold alongside forty thousand of the authorized edition, all in the first year. This demonstrated for Macaulay that his critics who claimed he was too preoccupied with "mere local and temporary feelings" had been proven wrong. "I wrote with a remote past and a remote future constantly in my mind," he recorded in his journal.[10] His *History* could have universal application—for who did not want to live in a prosperous and self-governing nation?

Macaulay's success lay in his creation of a myth of the birth, infancy, adolescence, and maturity of a great nation. While continental Europe was suffering the trauma of revolution, England had remained secure. The nineteenth century was a time of social, economic, and political transformation. In his view the historian's work in such unsettling times was to represent the nation as coherent and stable, a safe place to be. What made England so special, he argued, was its capacity to reform in time—to avoid the bloody revolutions that had disturbed the continent. The revolution that was the "least violent," that of 1688, had been the most beneficial. A union had been made between Crown and Parliament that meant that "this was our last revolution." There was no need among "wise and patriotic Englishmen" for resistance to established government, for "the means of effecting every improvement which the constitution requires may be found within the constitution itself." "All around us," he continued, "the world is convulsed by the agonies of great nations." Governments have been overthrown, capital cities of western Europe "have streamed with blood," "the antipathy of class to class, the antipathy of race to race have broken loose from the control of divine and human laws." Industry had been paralyzed, trade had been suspended, fear and anxiety had stalked millions, dangerous doctrines that "would make the fairest provinces of France and Germany as savage as Congo or Patagonia" had been abroad, "Europe has been threatened with subjugation by barbarians." Meanwhile, "in our fair island the regular course of government has never been for a day interrupted. The few bad men who longed for license and plunder have not had the courage to confront for one moment the strength of a loyal nation, rallied in firm array around a parental throne. . . . It is because we had a preserving revolution in the seventeenth century that we have not had a destroying revolution in the nineteenth century."[11] Despotic kings had been defeated, Parliament had come to represent "the people," order had been established, fanatics had been expelled, moderation had triumphed, property was secure, men could rest peacefully in their homes, which were their castles.

Macaulay's political intervention was intended to erase dissent and minimize class, gender, and ethnic conflict. He was born in 1800; his childhood was shadowed by the French Revolution and the Napoleonic wars. Growing up in a conservative evangelical household, he learned to fear revolution and despise what was construed as "mob politics." In 1831–1832, when revolution seemed a serious possibility, his speeches in the House of Commons arguing for parliamentary reform and the political incorporation of middle-class men were widely interpreted as having made a significant impact. In 1848 he was a member of the Whig cabinet at a time when once again there were real fears of violent disruption both in Britain and in Ireland. Poverty and unemployment were rife, Chartist claims for universal male suffrage were winning widespread support, and the example of Paris was inspiring. There was panic in London in April 1848, when the Chartist petition was due to be presented to Parliament after a monster meeting at Kennington Common and the city was barricaded with the army at the ready. In the event 150,000 met peaceably, the Chartist leaders declared their peaceful intentions and asked the crowd to disperse, heavy rain contributing to the collapse of Chartist hopes. The danger of revolution seemed to be over. A year later Macaulay recorded in his journal: "remembered this day last year. The great turning point—the triumph of order over anarchy."[12] His *History* was his most potent contribution to the political settlement inaugurated in 1832. A new sense of the nation had to be crafted, one appropriate to a modern urban world, one that could deal with a greatly expanded electorate. He was fully committed to the Whig project of governing *for* the people, winning consent to the rule of the propertied. As trustees of the nation, the governing class would deliver peace and prosperity. "The people" now had to be redefined as responsible men of property, citizens of the nation. Women, workers, Catholics, Jews, the Scots and the Irish, all those partially or totally excluded from the full benefits of citizenship, must know that they belonged to the nation, could claim an identification with it, could be English. Subjects of empire could learn that over time they, too, could enjoy these liberties.

This mythic story of the birth and triumph of the nation became the common sense, as Macaulay's critics recognized only too well. His account provided the benchmark against which others had to argue. It was a reference point within popular culture—a text people knew about even if they had not read it. In the much-quoted chapter 3, Macaulay aimed to demonstrate how life had improved immeasurably for all classes over the period between 1685 and the 1840s, how the nation had enjoyed "a change to which the history of the old world furnishes no parallel." And it was the "lower orders" who had benefited most, not just in material terms, the better wages and standard of living, but also from the "mollifying influence of civilisation on national character." In future times, he concluded, people might look back on the Victorian age as the time when "England was truly merry England, when all classes were bound together by brotherly sympathy, when the rich did not grind the faces of the poor, and when the poor did not envy the splendour of the rich."[13]

Such assertions were hard for Chartists to take as they struggled with the bleak realities of unemployment, underemployment, poverty, and want. Yet their challenges were confined to his claims about the working classes, not to his broader narrative or to his writerly skills: he was regularly referred to as "the brilliant historian." For Ernest Jones, a radical Chartist, "he was unequalled . . . as an historian of the past," as he put it in a lecture in 1850 at the Mechanics Institute in Chancery Lane. Yet only months before, in an address to a meeting at Leicester titled "Bread and Freedom," he had taken issue with Macaulay's assumptions as to the ways conditions were improving for the laboring poor, pointing to the increases in rent and the decreases in wages at the same time that this population was increasing and food production was declining. "The labourer had been progressing," Jones concluded, but it was "to starvation."[14] Similarly, Lloyd Jones, also on the radical wing of the Chartist movement, attacked Macaulay for his misstatements concerning the conditions of the working classes in his recently published *History* and regretted that "in a time of such boasted civilisation as the present, the working men of England were so degraded, so oppressed."[15] Yet in 1867 Lloyd Jones, together with J. M. Ludlow, published his widely read book *Progress of the Working Classes*, with its account of the improvements in conditions. The narrative of progress of which Macaulay was an arch protagonist took a deep hold. Karl Marx was one of those who was not vulnerable to it: he denounced Macaulay as that "Scotch sycophant and fine talker," "a systematic falsifier of history," defrauding the populace "in the interests of the Whigs and the bourgeoisie." "What eyes, and especially what ears he must have" to see only progress where there was daily retrogression.[16] But all this went to demonstrate how Macaulay provided a paradigm against which critics had to rail and which few had the capacity to unseat. The book provoked some, delighted others, but it reigned undisputed as *the* history of England.

In a period "after the achievement of mass literacy but before radio and television working-class culture was saturated by the spirit of mutual education" and Macaulay's writing had great appeal.[17] His works often featured on lists of books read by autodidacts, from Welsh miners to print workers and early Labour MPs. Some cited the new forms of self-expression it gave them, others the wider conception of history as an all-embracing world process. The drama and the accessibility of Macaulay's writing were much appreciated, and the criticisms of professional historians, which focused on the absence of adequate archival research and referencing and the work's populist appeal, cut little ice. Kathleen Woodward, a young factory worker, read the *History* twice through at her machine. "I derived great pleasure from these histories," she recorded, "which, as I grew up, I heard slighted, maligned. The colour and movement of Macaulay, the onward swing from Parliament to Parliament and from King to King daily transported me; nor was my pleasure spoiled by any awareness of his prejudices or inaccuracies."[18] For the "national commons" the *History* could be a resource, something that educated, but enjoyably.

Macaulay's father was born in the Highlands, but like so many of his generation migrated south. The son regarded himself as an Englishman and told a story in his *History* of how the Scots and English had become one people, mirroring his own experience of assimilation. Aspects of his account were vigorously disputed by some critics, but once again it was particular details that were challenged rather than the narrative of progress. John Paget particularly objected to Macaulay's dramatic version of the Massacre of Glencoe and found his "vituperative ... spiteful ... and grotesque" picture of the barbarism of the Highlands deeply offensive, only explicable in the context of an attack on his ancestors. "No quarrel is so bitter as a family quarrel," he wrote, "when a man takes to abusing his father or his mother he does it with infinitely greater gusto than a mere stranger."[19] But his was a lone voice, and Edinburgh voters twice elected Macaulay as their MP despite strong disapproval from some Presbyterians of his tolerance toward Catholics.

The account Macaulay gave of Ireland raised many more problems. It was impossible for him to secure "the sister kingdom" firmly into his narrative of an integrated nation. Since the Act of Union it had been neither fully metropolitan nor colonial, ruled differently from England on account of its unruly Catholic population yet part of the United Kingdom, with elected representatives at Westminster. Throughout Macaulay's political life Ireland represented a major problem for the British government. He was a firm supporter of Catholic emancipation, for Catholics had to be brought into the nation. Yet emancipation had solved nothing, and the 1830s and 1840s witnessed severe unrest, demands for repeal of the Union, and the horrors of the Famine, culminating in the abortive uprising of Young Ireland in 1848. Macaulay was firmly of the opinion that the only future for Ireland lay in a closer union with England; the tragedy of the Irish was that they had not become English. His hostility toward Catholics and Catholicism, despite his commitment to their political emancipation, was all too evident in the *History*. The book met with a sharp critical response from the *Irish Quarterly Review*, which judged it "a political romance . . . false in its facts, uncandid in its criticisms, illogical in its reasoning, and unjust in its conclusion."[20] At the same time his racialized depictions of the "aboriginal" Irish belied his universalist principles. He had grown up both with evangelical notions of a universal human family hierarchized according to level of development and with assumptions about imperial responsibility for those unable to govern themselves. These remained guiding principles, albeit in a secular form. He believed that the human family was descended from common stock, but racial hierarchies were in the order of things. Cultural differences could in theory be overcome, but delineating those differences opened up the scale of the heights to be climbed for those rescued from or still locked in barbarism. The liberal reforming vision of both nation and empire espoused by Macaulay rested on a contradiction: a formal and legalistic universalism was underpinned by an acceptance of inequality, whether of race, ethnicity, class, or gender, as the necessary foundation for any stable society. His narrative of Irish barbarism in need of civilization by the English could not pass unchallenged and was a particular provocation for Young Ireland, a romantic nationalist movement.

Charles Gavan Duffy, a passionate advocate of Young Ireland, left his native country in 1856 for Australia, disillusioned of any hopes for a better future, and spent his last years in France, writing a history both of himself and of Ireland, taking issue with English historians. Carlyle and Macaulay loomed large for him. Irish nationalism, like all anticolonial nationalisms, was forged in relation to British imperial power. As David Lloyd argues, "the power of nationalism lies in its countering of an imperial model of identity, for which the colonised people represent a primitive stage in a universal history of civilisation whose apex is the colonising power, with another, formally similar model that seeks to forge an oppositional identity from within."[21] Duffy's imperial antagonists set the terms that he had to counter. Recovering a national history was a key project for Young Ireland; centuries of oppression had to be recast into a narrative of national survival with origins, heroes, and continuities. Duffy greatly admired Macaulay's literary skills and sought his approval for his ballads, an approval that was withheld. The narrative Duffy attempted to construct was of a nation with a long-established history, its national spirit forged by Christianity in the fifth century, beset by foreign invaders, and subjugated by colonizers whose self-interests were always paramount. Across the British Empire, he maintained, "the dependent state only existed for the benefit of the paramount state."[22] The vaunted "British liberties," so dear to Macaulay, had a different meaning for the Irish. England had suspended "the laws of public morality" in the case of Ireland. "To trouble a foreign invader in England was meritorious" for Macaulay: when it came to the Irish, however, their resistance to foreign domination was seen as the "turbulence and discontent native to the Celtic race." Duffy hoped to puncture Macaulay, the "liberal rhetorician" who in both his political practice and his history writing was quite prepared to appeal to brute force when it came to the Irish. Nations had the right to determine their own futures, Duffy insisted: "but the mass of the English people have never been able to recognise any equity which countervails their interests, or alarms their pride. And this blind doltish obstinacy, Mr. Macaulay clothed in the vesture of rhetoric and eloquence."[23] Duffy's history, however, failed to unseat Macaulay's hegemony.

Despite the fact that the colonies of white settlement had no place in the *History*, for they were unknown territories in the seventeenth century, Macaulay was widely read in Australia and New Zealand, offering an identity for white colonists that was enthusiastically endorsed. As Alexis Weedon demonstrates, the export of books to the empire rose steadily from the early nineteenth century as communications speeded up and white settlements expanded, particularly in the Antipodes, Canada, and Southern Africa.[24] Macaulay's writing had a powerful appeal for this "imperial commons." The New Zealand press in the nineteenth century abounded with advertisements for the *History*, acclaiming it as "first class." It figured as a school prize, in presidential addresses, even in discussions over land tenure and the importance of freehold. In Australia it took a deep hold. By the end of the 1840s the settlers were keen to expunge the association with convictism, after their struggles over transportation and despotic military rule. They "took as their ideal a British derived ideal of liberty and a belief in universal human progress."[25] Aboriginal people were never imagined as part of this settlement, and Macaulay's total silence on the claims of "natives" suited them well. Macaulay drew on Whig thinking on empire, which had been shaped by the traumas associated with the American Revolution. A negotiated settlement should have been possible, for the colonists were Englishmen. Utilizing the language of family, "young colonies," as they were constructed, had to mature; then there were only two possibilities— full incorporation or separation. When it came to colonies of white settlement, the model of empire with which Macaulay worked was clear. During his years in politics, Australia, New Zealand, and Canada all claimed forms of responsible government and this, to his mind, was entirely appropriate. They could not be incorporated. They were far from the metropole, and their significant populations were Anglo-Saxon, Englishmen, valuing their liberties. As in the case of the United States, over time separation had to occur. This was a conclusion that chimed well with the hopes of settlers in Australia.

The *History* was widely available in New South Wales and beyond very soon after publication, with multiple advertisements in the press. As early as 1850 "A working man" wrote to the *Launceston Examiner* complaining that there were no copies available in the Mechanics Institute and that this must be remedied since it would "raise the public taste . . . enlighten . . . and inform."[26] By the later 1850s grateful pupils were presenting their teachers with copies of the *History*, and it was becoming a standard school prize. By the 1870s a traveler in Australia reported that "the three books he found on every squatter's shelf . . . were Shakespeare, the Bible and Macaulay's *Essays*."[27] Political leaders and newspaper editors identified enthusiastically with a Whig vision of history. "If we wished to look for a 'Model' it is to the Constitution of England we should look modified so as to suit the wants and requirements of the present age" proclaimed the *People's Advocate*. England "enjoyed a larger store of personal liberty and rational freedom than is perhaps enjoyed by any other country in the world, not excepting even America."[28] Regarding themselves as freed from aristocratic privilege and the other backward features of England, the colonists of New South Wales could achieve a more egalitarian body politic.

The most prominent leader in New South Wales in the 1850s was Henry Parkes, a Birmingham Chartist who had left England hoping for a better future in 1839. Parkes was the son of a Warwickshire tenant farmer who had lost his livelihood in the economic crisis of 1825. Henry, aged ten, migrated with his family to Birmingham, a major industrial center for the metal industries. The youngest of six siblings, he had to contribute to the family's survival, first working in a brick pit and then apprenticed to an ivory turner, one of the skills associated with the town's so-called toy trade in buttons and jewelry. Life was hard for the family, and Henry's fond childhood memories were concentrated on his mother, who succored him with stories of that quintessential white imperial man Robinson Crusoe. The years 1831–1832 were tempestuous in Birmingham, with its Political Union, uniting middle-class and working-class men and setting the pace with its demands for parliamentary reform. Henry Parkes was an excited spectator of the turbulent political events; he "was a man of 1832," wrote his biographer, Allan Martin, formed in the cauldron of reform.[29] He began to write poetry and prose, joined the Mechanics Institute, and later recollected that the great orators whom he had heard in Birmingham had been his teachers. He was gripped by the words of Daniel O'Connell, known as "The Liberator," who had led the struggle for Catholic emancipation, a struggle that was successfully concluded in 1829, providing a model for the Birmingham Political Union. Parkes attended the meeting of a quarter of a million people held in Birmingham in an effort to pressure the House of Lords to accept the Reform Bill. Many of these reformers were also engaged in the struggle against slavery, believing that slavery and freedom could not be reconciled in a land of liberty.

The Reform Act that was passed in 1832, however, was a deep disappointment to Parkes and his friends: only the propertied had been enfranchised, and working-class men whose property lay in their labor were excluded. In 1837 the Birmingham Political Union was reestablished, soon to become the Chartist movement and committed to universal male suffrage. Parkes was an enthusiastic supporter, but Birmingham was suffering from a trade recession and together with his wife, Clarinda, he moved to London, looking for work. Life was no easier there, and in 1839 they emigrated to New South Wales, hoping that the colony would provide a better future for "unhappy Englishmen."[30] As his daughter Annie later wrote, Australia, "to their untutored minds, must indeed have appeared a veritable land of convicts and blackfellows, but still 'the land of promise' where they might prosper as they could not at home."[31] Henry initially got work on a farm, then as a customs officer, before being able to set up in business as an ivory and bone turner. The legacy of 1832 and of Birmingham radicalism stayed with him and shaped the distinctive politics he espoused from the late 1840s. He opposed convictism and cheap foreign labor and at the same time was deeply critical of the pastoral elite. Employers wanted cheap labor from abroad; they were accustomed "to having the convicts toil for nothing" and did not want to pay for "a free man. Hence they would fain have the poor coolie from India, bound to them for a number of years—a slave in everything but in name."[32] Parkes wanted a free and prosperous society for the colony's working men as well as the middle classes. "Blackfellows" were erased from the picture: the Australian myth was one of a pristine land to be taken.

In 1850, when Australia was granted limited self-government, Parkes was a moving figure in the foundation of *Empire*, a new weekly, which committed itself in its first issue to "COLONIAL RADICALISM—OUR OWN CREED." "Every man," the paper announced, "should stand erect, as a freeman should," knowing "that the glorious sun over his head, and the fruitful soil beneath his feet, were made for him."[33] Parkes edited *Empire* for seven years and during that time entered politics as a colonial nationalist. Australia would build on the traditions of the Old Country but would be more democratic. His powerful sense of history and of the traditions of the freeborn Englishman informed his politics: he denounced the proposal made by a conservative politician, Charles Wentworth, that a hereditary upper house should be established on the model of the British, citing Macaulay's denunciation of an earlier Wentworth, a renegade parliamentarian who had taken the side of the king, an indication of how "the Great Historian" provided a widely recognized point of reference.[34]

The *History* was on sale, in a variety of editions, in the bookshop of William Piddington, the largest radical bookseller in Sydney and a keen supporter of Parkes.[35] Parkes followed Macaulay in seeing 1688 as the establishment of rule by "popular prescription" and in constructing the English as an imperial race, a race with the capacity to settle in new parts of the globe and carry their civilization with them, to remain just as English as the English. "He was as much an Englishman as any man present," he told his audience in Birmingham when he returned there in 1861. "The people in Australia were as thoroughly English as the people of the mother-country; they had forfeited nothing by going a distance of 14,000 miles. Shakespeare and Milton belonged as much to them as to the people of England; they possessed by right of inheritance an equal share in the grand traditions, the old military renown, the splendour of scientific recovery, and the wealth of literature, which had made England the great civilising power of the world."[36] His heroes were Milton, Oliver Cromwell, Hampden, all subjects of Macaulay's *Essays*: this was the Protestant lineage. And it was this inheritance that Macaulay was convinced it was the work of empire to transmit: the time for military conquest was over, he told himself and his readers, ignoring the continued military campaigns across the empire; now was the time to anglicize the globe. As he famously put it, the greatest gift Britain could bestow was "the empire of our arts and morals, our literature and our laws."[37] Making the empire English was Macaulay's dream; this was to be a benevolent empire, an empire of freedom. Yet Parkes's variety of radicalism and his espousal of universal suffrage would have received short shrift from "the great historian." Macaulay's writing could be articulated to dreams he would not share. Indeed, it became a resource for others, an aspect of the "imperial commons."

Macaulay was the son of a prominent abolitionist and was opposed to slavery, which he believed stood as the antithesis of English liberty. England's early modern empire consisted of Ireland and the colonies of the Caribbean and North America. Yet in the *History* only Ireland was deemed worthy of inclusion. Macaulay ignored the acquisition of the Atlantic empire and its central importance to trade and war. The empire was assumed, a backdrop to the nation, a necessary part of England's expanding naval and commercial power. Its peoples—the savage Indians of the New World, the enslaved Africans of the Caribbean—marked the outer peripheries, the absent presences of the *History*. Their central place in the story of the transformation from barbarism to civilization remained untold. In Macaulay's mind there was nothing significant to be said about the Caribbean, those colonies were not yet History, they had not entered the modern world. Slavery had been abolished in 1833, and by the mid-1840s the "great experiment," as it was constructed, as to whether Africans *would* work as free labor was not going well in the eyes of many Britons. (It was in this context that Brontë wrote *Jane Eyre*, published the year before the *History*.) The Caribbean islands no longer dominated sugar production and were increasingly irrelevant to global economics and politics. There was no story of progress there. Africa and the Caribbean were banished to the uttermost margins of his volumes. Their peoples and politics were irrelevant to his history, as was the huge flow of wealth from Caribbean slavery and Atlantic trade. Despite the development of the Royal Africa Company under Charles II and James II, there was no discussion of the slave trade or plantation slavery, though they were central to England's wealth and power. But slavery was a system Macaulay preferred to forget. It was abolition and imperial benevolence that should be memorialized, not the country's investment in the plantations. Slavery was a denial of human freedom and as such should be opposed, but freed slaves were not "like us." His opposition to slavery never extended to any sympathy for Africans or indigenous peoples, and he had no time for canting abolitionists or humanitarians. There was no contradiction for him between opposing slavery and having a commitment to empire.

In the period of colonial liberalism in New South Wales, Britishness—for Englishness was not a sufficiently inclusive category, given Scots, Irish, and Welsh emigration—was not defined in exclusively racial terms. By the 1870s, however, Parkes and others had moved to a more racially based notion of nation. His earlier opposition to cheap labor on the grounds of exploitation had shifted to an opposition on the basis of race, as he argued for the exclusion of the Chinese. Now the key influences were the conservatives Carlyle and Froude, rather than the Whiggish Macaulay. "The crimson thread of kinship," as Parkes famously put it, "runs through us all. We know that we represent a race . . . for the purposes of settling new colonies, which never had its equal on the face of the earth."[38] His populist nationalism was increasingly associated with the notion of a white man's country: "Britishness, once evoking a set of liberties . . . came to be overlaid by faith in the singular race patriotism of its bearers . . . to become modern was to become white."[39] The association of whiteness with citizenship and power was an inference that could be drawn from Macaulay but was never explicitly made. Offices should be open regardless of race or creed, he maintained. Theoretically he held open the possibility of "brown Englishmen": in practice, liberalism operated multiple exclusions. Indians, for example, were never quite ready in Macaulay's judgment to assume positions of authority within the Indian Civil Service. It was this paradoxical character of liberalism that meant it could be articulated to both anticolonial and feminist claims, and that such claims could be endlessly deferred.

Macaulay's history was of the making of the multiethnic white nation named England, an example of the route to modernity, laying out a path that others could follow. Colonial rule was imagined as the only route to modernity for "others." Representative government was for Britain and colonies of white settlement; India should be ruled despotically in order to deliver liberties. Macaulay's assumption was that England's route was *the* route: it was, in theory, universally applicable. It was this universalism that C. L. R. James was to undermine in *The Black Jacobins*, his majestic account of the connections between the Haitian and the French revolutions and the centrality of black agency to Atlantic history.[40] Macaulay's paradigm of the rise and triumph of the white West was broken, yet the power of that paradigm has remained and resurfaced only too effectively among conservative historians in recent times.[41] The work of deconstruction is never done.

NOTES

Thanks to Zoe Laidlaw and Keith McClelland.

1. For a longer account of Macaulay, his family, and his work, see Catherine Hall, *Macaulay and Son: Architects of Imperial Britain* (New Haven, CT: Yale University Press, 2012).

2. Thomas Babington Macaulay, "History," in *The Works of Lord Macaulay*, ed. Lady Trevelyan, 8 vols. (London: Longmans, Green and Co, 1866), 5:122–161.

3. Thomas Babington Macaulay, "Sir James Mackintosh," in *Literary and Historical Essays Contributed to the Edinburgh Review*, 2 vols. (London: Oxford University Press, 1913), 2:293–294.

4. Thomas Babington Macaulay, *The History of England from the Accession of James II* (1848), 3 vols. (London: Dent, 1906), 1:9–10.

5. On the reception of the *History* see Theodore Koditschek, *Liberalism, Imperialism and the Historical Imagination: Nineteenth-Century Visions of a Greater Britain* (Cambridge: Cambridge University Press, 2010), 143–148. Leslie Howsam is currently engaged in a project investigating the reception of Macaulay across the British Empire, with a particular focus on Canada, New Zealand, and British India, that will significantly increase our understanding of the ways Macaulay traveled and was translated. There is a particularly complex story to be investigated in India, where Macaulay's legacy is still highly contested. His enthusiasm for the use of the English language as the medium of instruction in government-funded schools for the elite as a way of anglicizing India has been strongly criticized by anticolonial and nationalist writers.

6. George Otto Trevelyan, *The Life and Letters of Lord Macaulay* (London: Longmans, Green and Co, 1881), 507.

7. Cited in Charlotte Macdonald, chapter 2, this volume.

8. Virginia Woolf, *A Passionate Apprentice: The Early Journals 1897–1909*, ed. Mitchell A. Leaska (London: Pimlico, 2004), 87.

9. *British Journal*, 7 February 1852.

10. Thomas Babington Macaulay, entry of 25 October 1849, in *The Journals of Thomas Babington Macaulay*, ed. William Thomas, 5 vols. (London: Pickering and Chatto, 2008), 2:160.

11. Macaulay, *History*, 2:210–215.

12. Macaulay, entry of 10 April 1849, in *Journals*, 2:67.

13. Macaulay, *History*, 1:218, 328–329.

14. *Northern Star and National Trades' Journal*, 14 December 1850 and 7 September 1850.

15. *Northern Star and National Trades' Journal*, 23 February 1850.

16. Karl Marx, *Capital*, trans. Ben Fowkes, 3 vols. (Harmondsworth, England: Penguin, 1976), 1:385n88, 876n1.

17. Jonathan Rose, *The Intellectual Life of the British Working Classes* (New Haven, CT: Yale University Press, 2001), 83.

18. Cited in Rose, *Intellectual Life*, 130.

19. John Paget, *The New "Examen" or an Inquiry into the Evidence Relating to Certain Passages in Lord Macaulay's History* (Edinburgh: William Blackwood and Sons, 1861), 130.

20. Cited in Koditschek, *Liberalism*, 147.

21. David Lloyd, *Nationalism and Minor Literature: James Clarence Mangan and the Emergence of Irish Cultural Nationalism* (Berkeley: University of California Press, 1987), x.

22. Charles Gavan Duffy, *Young Ireland: A Fragment of Irish History 1840–1850* (London: T. Fisher Unwin, 1880), 122.

23. Duffy, *Young Ireland*, 87, 653.

24. See Macdonald, chapter 2, this volume, for the figures derived from Alexis Weedon, *Victorian Publishing: The Economics of Book Production for a Mass Market 1836–1916* (Aldershot, England: Ashgate, 2003).

25. Neville Meany, "'In History's Page': Identity and Myth," in *Australia's Empire*, ed. Dereck M. Schreuder and Stuart Ward (Oxford: Oxford University Press, 2008), 364.

26. *Launceston Examiner*, 12 October 1850.

27. John Morley, *Nineteenth-Century Essays*, selected and with an introduction by Peter Stansky (Chicago: Chicago University Press, 1970), 74.

28. *People's Advocate*, 21 April 1849, 13 November 1852, cited in Meany, "History's Page," 364.

29. A. W. Martin, *Henry Parkes: A Biography* (Melbourne: Melbourne University Press, 1980). For two short discussions of Parkes, see Catherine Hall, *Writing Histories of Difference: New Histories of Nation and Empire*, pamphlet from Allan Martin Lecture (Canberra: Australian National University, 2005), and Bill Schwarz, *The White Man's World*, vol. 1, *Memories of Empire* (Oxford: Oxford University Press, 2011), 130–148.

30. Henry Parkes, *An Emigrant's Home Letters* (London: Simpkin, Marshall, Hamilton, Kent and Co, 1897), 27.

31. Parkes, *Home Letters*, 10.

32. Parkes, *Home Letters*, 123.

33. Parkes, *Home Letters*, 76.

34. Meany, "History's Page," 364.

35. Thanks to Paul Pickering for this information. *People's Advocate*, 12 August 1854.

36. Henry Parkes, *Australian Views of England: Eleven Letters Written in the Years 1861 and 1862* (London: Macmillan, 1869), 2.

37. Thomas Babington Macaulay, *Speeches on Politics and Literature by Lord Macaulay* (London: J. M. Dent and Sons, 1909), 125.

38. Martin, *Henry Parkes*, 391.

39. Schwarz, *White Man's World*, 143.

40. See Aaron Kamugisha, chapter 9, this volume.

41. For a powerful counternarrative see Pankaj Mishra, *From the Ruins of Empire: The Revolt against the West and the Remaking of Asia* (London: Allen Lane, 2012).

Four

"THE DAY WILL COME"

Charles H. Pearson's *National Life
and Character: A Forecast*

MARILYN LAKE

The Eye of the Tiger

When Charles Pearson's *National Life and Character: A Forecast* was first
published in London and New York, in 1893, its vision of a postcolonial
order in which Africans and Asians would take their place as social and political equals in the world caused a sensation on both sides of the Atlantic
and across the color line. To colonized peoples, such as the African nationalist Setseele Molema, it encouraged hopes for black freedom.[1] To anxious
Europeans it foretold the prospect of humiliation, as pride of race gave way
to loss of place.[2] In the new world imagined by Pearson, "white men" would
wake to find themselves "elbowed and hustled, and perhaps even thrust
aside by peoples whom we have looked down upon as servile and thought
of as bound always to minister to our needs. The solitary consolation will
be that the changes have been inevitable."[3]

Not many agreed that such a dramatic transformation of the global order,
as envisaged by Pearson, was inevitable nor indeed likely. Self-styled "white
men's countries"—in South Africa, North America, and Australasia—
resolved to keep such forces at bay by enacting racial segregation on a local

and global scale and implementing ever harsher immigration restriction measures—including in British countries against British subjects—to maintain their countries as the inheritance of white men. But these initiatives sparked in turn fresh political mobilizations among Africans and Asians and international demands for racial equality, such as that presented by Japan at Versailles in 1919, demands that ironically helped bring about the very changes Pearson warned about.

The international impact of Pearson's book was vividly described, fifteen years after it was published, in the London journal *Fortnightly Review* in an article called "Asia Contra Mundum." The article's anonymous author, "Viator" (thought to be Valentine Chirol of the *Times*), noted that "half a generation had passed since the thought of the world had been startled by the late Charles Pearson's theories upon the inevitable decay and fall of white civilization."[4] It is a resonant description. Pearson's book had anticipated by twenty-five years Oswald Spengler's better-known *Decline of the West*, which appeared ten years after the retrospective assessment by "Viator" of Pearson's "theories upon the decay and fall of white civilization." *National Life and Character* was well known in Germany—one of its enthusiastic readers was Kaiser Wilhelm, who allegedly coined the phrase "yellow peril." When President Woodrow Wilson's right-hand man, Colonel House, traveled to Germany during World War I, in an effort to negotiate a peace deal, based on their common Anglo-Saxon origins, he found the kaiser "ranted on about the demographic strength of Asia."[5]

It seemed to "Viator," writing fifteen years after the publication of *National Life and Character*, that the book had been "an act" as much as "a treatise": "It shook the self-confidence of the white races and deprived them of the absolute sense of assured superiority which had hitherto helped them to dominate. To Asiatic students, the mental pioneers of the eastern renaissance, it revealed what some of them had suspected—that the impassive forehead of the white man was part of a brazen mask, the mind within being full of doubt and trouble prone to self-dissolving reflection. The effect was like the first moment when the trainer's glance flinches before the eye of the tiger." As white self-confidence was shaken, Asians' self-consciousness was quickened by *National Life and Character*.[6]

Sadly for Pearson, historian, journalist, and colonial politician, whose quest for academic recognition had met only frustration, fame came too late. He died from a chest infection just a year after his book was published and thus did not live to see the long-term impact of his work or that it went into several editions, with a Japanese version appearing in 1909 and a final English edition published in 1913. Pearson's forecast alarmed apprehensive whites and encouraged, as "Viator" suggested, the growth of nationalist and Pan-Asian movements to combat the global offense of the ascendant politics of whiteness.[7] It gave rise, as Akira Iriye has noted, to talk in government and naval circles of a coming war between the East and the West, provoking anxieties that framed the organization of the Universal Races Congress in 1911, called to discuss "the general relations subsisting between the peoples of the West and those of the East, between so-called white and so-called coloured peoples."[8]

The Perils of Progress

Pearson was an academically trained historian, who early in his career had challenged, at some personal cost, the Anglo-Saxon triumphalism of the leading Teutonic historian, E. A. Freeman. It is worth quoting Pearson's objection to Freeman's historical approach, because it provides an early indication of his refusal of racial determinism in history and belief in the inevitability of transformative change:

> He is an enthusiast for Saxon institutions, and dates the History of England from Hengist and Horsa; while I follow Sir Francis Palgrave in tracing it back to Roman occupation. . . . Nothing is more tempting than to group all events under a symmetrical theory, and to refer every institution and fact to a Saxon or a Roman original. But the life of a great society does not arrange itself in this manner, and even if the Saxons, when they came to England, made a clean sweep of the cities and its inhabitants, as Mr Freeman seems to suppose, they must, from the very circumstances of a new settlement, have made some changes to the "old Teutonic constitution."[9]

The author of a history of England during the "early and middle ages," Pearson had lectured at King's College, London, and the University of Cambridge, and following his migration to the Australian colonies—but before taking up a career as a radical liberal politician—he had also taught at the University of Melbourne. His forecast of the "inevitable decay and fall of white civilization," as Viator described it, had two strands—the decline of the West and the rise of Asia—that rested on two distinct historical arguments.

On the one hand Pearson claimed that political developments in liberal democratic societies were leading to the state assuming responsibility for more and more aspects of life, such as education, family relations, industry, housing, and transport, culminating in fully fledged systems of "state socialism," whose tendencies were evident, in his view, in the colony of Victoria, where "the State builds railways, founds and maintains schools, tries to regulate the wages and hours of labour, protects native industry, settles the population on the land and is beginning to organise systems of state insurance."[10] Australia was rapidly creating a "State Socialism," he wrote in *National Life and Character*, "which succeeds because it is all embracing."[11]

These developments, Pearson suggested, somewhat perversely, although valuable reforms in themselves, would ultimately lead to a loss of energy, initiative, and vigor among European populations and a diminution in personal and national character. Life would become more gray, less interesting. Furthermore, as patriarchal family structures weakened, women would seek to limit their families, and the subsequent decline in population would usher in a "stationary state." As a feminist and liberal, a former principal of a secondary college for girls, and minister for public instruction in the government of Victoria, Pearson was an author of some of the social reforms that had made these changes possible, as his critics were quick to point out. His whole book, the *Saturday Review* charged, was a labored and, to a great extent, successful attempt to prove that

> the substitution of the State for the Church, the decay of the family, the equalisation of rights and privileges, the dominance of industrial organisations . . . will destroy character, weaken the interest of life, kill genius, favour only the lower races and individuals . . . ; yet he is imperturbably sure that it was quite the right thing to enlarge the suffrage, to allow a legal status, and practically a free hand to Trade Unions, to impair the authority of husbands and fathers, to abolish class distinctions, to vulgarise education. His paradox is quite different from the old one; he abhors the end, but delights in the means.[12]

The second strand of Pearson's argument was that recent progress among "the black and yellow races" showed that their capacity, industry, and population growth would lead them to take an equal place in the world. White men were not destined to rule forever. China would become a great power. India would become independent. Africans would follow Haiti in forming black republics. He was impressed by the progress made by Haiti after reviewing—and reading against the grain—Spencer St. John's book *Hayti, or The Black Republic*, published in 1884. St. John, a former English representative in Haiti, was predictably negative in his assessment of Haiti's prospects, but Pearson used the evidence St. John offered to present a more optimistic view, "though the author assuredly did not intend to convey it." The fact that "a community of slaves and coloured freedmen should have been able to preserve a centralised government and national unity," "kept itself free," and produced exports to the value of 2 million pounds a year, had defied the expectations of those who considered blacks to be incapable of self-government. In a review of Pearson's essay "The Black Republic," the *Spectator* praised it as "a perfect marvel in its absence of prejudice or forgetfulness of truth." His conclusions were "far more favourable to the Haytians than English opinion usually is."[13]

It was in Asia, however, especially in China and Chinese settlements in southeast Asia, the Pacific, the Americas, and Australasia that Pearson saw the changing world order take shape: "With civilisation equally diffused the most populous country must ultimately be the most powerful; and the preponderance of China over any rival—even over the United States of America—is likely to be overwhelming."[14] In just a short period of time, Singapore, to Australia's north, had transformed from a small British trading post into a thriving Chinese settlement. Indeed so remarkable was Chinese migration across southeast Asia and the Pacific that Pearson's erstwhile colleague in history at Oxford, Goldwin Smith, who had himself migrated to the United States and then Canada, wrote of his doubt as to whether the Anglo-Saxon race would continue to rule settler lands. In the case of Australia, it seemed increasingly likely, he ventured, that the vast "reservoir of industrial population of China" would ultimately "inherit" the southern continent, where China already had "a strong foothold."[15] "Chinese colonisation of the Straits settlements," wrote Pearson, "shows what the race is capable of."[16] The future would see China take "its inevitable position as one of the great Powers of the world."

Significantly, Pearson had witnessed the international respect accorded the Chinese Empire as a great power at first hand, when as acting chief secretary in the government of Victoria he had joined numerous dignitaries in welcoming the Ch'ing imperial commissioners General Wong Yung Ho and Mr. C. Tsing to Melbourne in 1887 when they arrived on their tour of inspection.[17] They came on a mission to inquire into the treatment of their subjects abroad, their investigation having been suggested by the Chinese foreign minister, Marquis Tseng, who had made a widely publicized pronouncement on Chinese foreign policy published in the *Times* and *Asiatic Quarterly Review*, demanding respect and recognition for the Chinese people "in accordance with the place which China holds as a great Asiatic power." On receipt of a series of reports from around the world, Marquis Tseng had concluded it was time to protest against the "outrageous treatment to which Chinese subjects residing in some foreign countries have been subjected."[18] The Australian poll tax, introduced in Victoria in 1881, symbolized this unjust and discriminatory treatment. The British Foreign Office advised the Colonial Office, which advised the Australian governors of the planned tour of investigation and asked that the imperial commissioners be afforded "every courtesy."[19]

In *National Life and Character*, Pearson warned in ringing tones of the emergence of a new postcolonial world order in words that would be quoted around the world: "The day will come and perhaps is not far distant, when the European observer will look round to see the globe girdled with a continuous zone of the black and yellow races, no longer too weak for aggression or under tutelage, but independent, or practically so, in government, monopolising the trade of their regions, and circumscribing the industry of the Europeans ... represented by fleets in the European seas, invited to international conferences and welcomed as allies in the quarrels of the civilized world."[20] It was a prophecy, as we shall see, that drew heavily—in its cadence, sentiments, and language—on the writings of Chinese themselves, thousands of whom had migrated to Melbourne, and who wrote protest booklets, petitions, and remonstrances that demanded an end to racial discrimination, invoked international law, warned of the global consequences of ill treatment, and called for recognition of their "common human rights."[21] The writings of Chinese colonists in Melbourne had a profound effect on Pearson, but the first seeds of *National Life and Character* were sown when he traveled across the United States in the 1860s. An early version of chapter 1 of his book, "The Unchangeable Limits of Higher Races," first appeared as an article in *Contemporary Review* in 1868.[22]

Radical Reformer

Pearson was born and educated in England. One of the "lights of liberalism" at Oxford in the 1850s, he earned a reputation for his "extreme Liberal opinions" (in the words of Lord Robert Cecil) and as an eloquent and skilled debater.[23] In the early 1860s he decided to emigrate to the colonies and try his hand at farming in South Australia, but he was defeated by prolonged drought. Back in England he lectured in support of the higher education of women and wrote an essay in praise of the Australian experiment in democracy for *Essays on Reform*. He then accepted an appointment as lecturer in modern history at the University of Cambridge, where he joined his colleagues Henry and Millicent Garrett Fawcett in forming a republican club, its guiding principle "a hostility to the hereditary principle as exemplified in monarchical and aristocratic institutions and to all social and political privileges depending on difference of sex."[24]

In 1868, Pearson traveled, as did many of his friends at that time, to the United States, in part to express support for the cause of the North in the civil war. While traveling across the American continent Pearson had an epiphany: the frontier was closing, and vacant land was fast disappearing. Anticipating Frederick Jackson Turner's frontier thesis by some twenty-five years, he pondered the implications of the closing frontier for Americans and Englishmen who would soon find themselves "cramped for land." The "temperate zone" was being steadily occupied by successive waves of migrants, from Britain, Europe, and China. Would it be possible for societies to live in a stationary state? He wrote down his thoughts in an essay published in *Contemporary Review* called "The Land Question in the United States," which became the basis for the first chapter of *National Life and Character*.[25]

As a historian, journalist, and world traveler, Pearson had been thinking about changing world forces for some years. He thought about the implications of the greatly increased movement of peoples and transfer of cultures in a framework we might now call world history. He had been amassing evidence for his magnum opus over decades, drawing on his travels and wide reading. In San Francisco he noted the thriving Chinatown and wrote about it in a series of articles for the U.S. journal the *Nation*. When he arrived in Melbourne, finally to settle, in 1872, he also found a thriving Chinatown, one of the oldest in the world, in the heart of the city on Bourke Street. Tens of thousands of Chinese had migrated to the colony of Victoria from the early 1850s, mainly to try their luck on the goldfields, but also to pursue associated opportunities in trade, commerce, banking, manufacture, and agriculture. Melbourne was a bustling commercial city that supported impressive public institutions, including a public library, museum, art gallery, and university, on whose council Pearson would serve.

Pearson had long worked as a journalist for English, American, and Australian papers, but he was keen to participate directly in politics and entered the parliament of Victoria on his second attempt, in 1878, as a member of the Legislative Assembly for the gold-mining district of Castlemaine. His reform efforts focused on a number of measures directed at extending democratic equality and opportunity. He proposed a progressive land tax; the breaking up of big estates to give small settlers access to land; opening the public library, museum, and art gallery on Sundays; the introduction of technical training; and the extension of free public education at all levels. As a member of the council of the University of Melbourne, he lobbied for the admission of women to university degrees and more generally supported campaigns for women's suffrage.

Recognizing China

In the year that Pearson entered the Victoria parliament, the southeastern colonies were engulfed by a seamen's strike, called in response to moves by the Australasian Steam Navigation Company to follow the Hong Kong Eastern Australian Mail Steamship Company in employing Asian labor on its Pacific run to Fiji and New Caledonia, at half the cost. Lively public meetings debated the issue in Melbourne and Sydney. A visiting British journalist, John Wisker, wrote about the strike's national significance for the *Fortnightly Review*: "It was a strike against the yellow man. Thus it acquired a sacred character; it became an Australian movement, securing universal sympathy, and what was more to the purpose substantial support."[26] But the campaign against the employment of Chinese did not go uncontested. Three leading Chinese community leaders wrote a defense of their countrymen's rights to migration and employment in a widely circulated booklet, *The Chinese Question in Australia*, published in Melbourne in 1879.

The booklet's authors were Lowe Kong Meng, Cheok Hong Cheong, and Louis Ah Mouy, educated men of standing: Lowe Kong Meng a wealthy merchant, Cheok Hong Cheong a Christian evangelist, and Louis Ah Mouy a trader and banker.[27] In their booklet they explained why their fellow countrymen had migrated to the Australian colonies and argued their right to do so under international law. Their countrymen suffered extensively from the consequences of famine, poverty, and civil war. China's population already exceeded 400 million, and people had heard there was a large country in close proximity that was sparsely populated but rich in resources. The authors explained that the international treaties enacted between the British and Chinese Empires guaranteed the right of travel and quoted the "illustrious Vattel"—Emmerich de Vattel—to highlight the obligations of reciprocity under the law of nations.[28] They cited a number of universal authorities: Confucius, Thomas Jefferson, the Bible, Mencius.

They also challenged the idea that the Chinese were inherently cheap labor. "Human nature [was] human nature all the world over," and "the Chinaman [was] just as fond of money, and just as eager to earn as much as he can, as the most grasping of his competitors."[29] Once settled in new communities, Chinese colonists would quickly adapt to the European mode of living: "Living among people who have invented thousands of artificial wants, and thousands of means of gratifying them, the expenditure of the Asiatic will soon rise to the European level, because his habits and his mode of living will approximate to those of his neighbours." The authors objected to arguments that Chinese were ill-educated and uncivilized. They were stigmatized as "ignorant pagans" by people who were themselves ignorant, who knew nothing about Eastern civilization and had never been to China.[30] "Are we an inferior race?" they asked. "No one can say so who knows anything of our history, our language, our literature, our government, or our public and private life. China had reached a very high stage of civilization when Britain was peopled by naked savages. The art of printing, the use of gunpowder, and the mariner's compass were known to us centuries before they were re-invented by Europeans. . . . In the next place, ours is a well-educated people. Indeed, it is but seldom that you could discover a Chinaman incapable of reading, writing and ciphering."[31]

Despite their protestations, or because of them, the Victoria government moved in 1881 to introduce new immigration restrictions, including a poll tax on Chinese, and to disenfranchise those who enjoyed the vote under the local provision for manhood suffrage. Charles Pearson, MP, was a leading supporter of the legislation: "He had read the Bill with satisfaction, and he considered it reflected great credit upon the Government." His speech to the Victorian parliament also suggested that he had read *The Chinese Question in Australia* with some care. He began with reference to the population figure quoted therein, a figure that would become a touchstone in future debate. "The population of China was nearly 400,000,000," he said, adding that "the mere natural increase of that population in a single year would be sufficient to swamp the whole white population of the colony"[32] (a sentence that would be reproduced in the first chapter of *National Life and Character*).

Another aspect of his argument that echoed *The Chinese Question in Australia* was his reference to the fact that the Chinese were well informed about Australia. "Australia was now perfectly well known to the Chinese," he told the Victorian parliament; "communication between the two countries was thoroughly established; and in the event of famine or war arising in China, Chinamen might come here at any time in hordes."[33] Whereas Lowe Kong Meng and his coauthors had asserted that Chinese migrants had just as much a right to occupy unsettled parts of Australia as did the British ("Did man create it or did God?") Pearson's thinking on the land question and the limited amount remaining in the "temperate zone" led him to argue that countries such as Australia must remain the heritage of the white man. They were, to use the phase that became common parlance, "white men's countries."

The Place of China as a Great Asiatic Power

Six years after the passage of the new immigration restriction legislation that also introduced the poll tax, the Chinese imperial commissioners arrived in Australia to investigate reports of discriminatory treatment of their overseas subjects. They had left China in September 1886 and visited Manila, Singapore, Malaya, Penang, Rangoon, Sumatra, Java, Port Darwin, and Sydney. After leaving Melbourne they would travel to Brisbane, Cooktown, Singapore, Siam, and Cochin China. U Tsing would then take up the position of consul in San Francisco. Newspaper reports about the commissioners' travels emphasized their international standing and level of education. The "readiness, fluency and correctness with which General Wong Yung Ho expressed himself in the English language" took most by surprise.[34]

For their overland trip from Sydney to Melbourne, the commissioners were provided with a state carriage and met by an official welcome party at Spencer Street railway station, composed of British officials, including the governor's aide-de-camp, Captain Traill, local Chinese leaders, including Lowe Kong Meng (who was an old schoolmate of General Wong Yung Ho from the English school in Penang), and a guard of honor consisting of a dozen Chinese dressed in the costume of their country. During their stay of around three weeks in Melbourne, the commissioners were provided with lavish accommodation in a suite of rooms in the Oriental Hotel, which became a kind of "Eastern Court," sufficient to house their large retinue of servants, attendants, and officials, who received a daily stream of visitors paying their respects.[35]

They were invited to lunch at Government House by His Excellency the Governor Sir Henry Loch, who had lived some years in China, and Lady Loch. During the following week they were shown around the public library, the art gallery and museum, Parliament House, the law courts, and the university. The president of the Chamber of Manufactures took them on a tour of the principal shops, factories, and warehouses in and around Melbourne, and they were taken to the wine cellars at Chateau Tahbilk. In the evening of 1 June, the commissioners worshiped at the Chinese temple at South Melbourne and made offerings, watched by a large number of local Chinese. They were visited at their quarters by the political leaders of all parties, including representatives of Trades Hall. On 7 June, they attended the opening of Parliament. Their stay culminated in a banquet hosted by Chief Justice George Higinbotham, in the presence of the governor, who proposed a toast to "The Good Ally of Our Beloved Queen, the Emperor of China." Also present at this gathering was Acting Chief Secretary Charles Pearson.

For their part, the commissioners reiterated on all possible occasions their objection to the poll tax, "the obnoxious tax" that discriminated against Chinese immigrants. "We should not mind the poll tax if it were imposed on other nationalities," explained Wong Yung Ho, "but when it is against Chinese alone it seems hard and unjust."[36] In an interview with a local journalist he elaborated: "We should never think of objecting to any laws that were general in their application. Our objection is to laws which deprive us of liberties and privileges enjoyed by other people."[37] From the point of view of the Chinese Empire, Wong Yung Ho told the Melbourne journalist in 1887, "there is absolute free trade on our part; our men and women can go at will; you can come at will; we do not tax you for coming, nor prevent them from going." The conservative, imperial-minded free trade newspaper the *Argus* was persuaded of the international logic of the Chinese position, which in its view trumped the local nationalist argument about "the superior rights of superior races."[38] The Chinese demand— "Treat us as others, that is all we ask"—was a justifiable one in the view of the *Argus*, and it was entirely proper that Australians should "give to others the liberties and privileges we demand from them."[39] Liberties, privileges, and rights should be enjoyed in common.

As a result of the Chinese commissioners' visit to the Australian colonies and their representations to the British imperial government, the poll tax was dropped, but the determination of colonial political leaders to exclude Chinese migrants through more stringent immigration restrictions strengthened. At a conference in Sydney in 1888 they agreed to enact uniform legislation to achieve this end. When the resulting legislation was introduced into the Victoria parliament, Pearson was again one of its strongest supporters. By 1888 he had formulated the issue of immigration restriction as one of national sovereignty, the right of a self-governing, "free and independent state" to self-preservation. When his old friend the liberal William Shiels spoke in defense of "the best traditions of freedom, which we inherited from the mother country," Pearson responded: "I look upon it as important not so much to the personal liberty of aliens as to the national existence of the whole people of Victoria. That is what is really at stake."[40] As Adam McKeown has pointed out, the justification by settler countries of immigration restriction in terms of national sovereign rights—and conversely the definition of sovereignty as a matter of border control—set an example for the modern globalized world.[41]

Victoria's new immigration restriction legislation departed from tradition in ignoring the special status accorded to British subjects across the empire. As Victoria's premier, Duncan Gillies, explained: "The existing law provides that Chinese who are naturalized British subjects shall be exempt from its operation, and in consequence of that, the Chinese of Hong Kong have been able to come here; but those people, although naturalized British subjects, are still Chinese, and therefore are as objectionable as if they were to come from the centre of China."[42] Chinese community leaders in Australia were outraged by these new developments and protested against them in a series of letters, petitions, and remonstrances that were given further publicity when published in newspapers and discussed in Parliament. They continued to insist on recognition of the Chinese as a civilized people and China's coming greatness as a modern power.

At the 1888 conference in Sydney, in an address titled "Address to the Representatives of the Australian Governments, in Conference Assembled," Cheok Hong Cheong, on behalf of Louis Ah Mouy, Shi Green, Sun Suey Shing, and James Moy Ling, warned of the possible consequences of continuing Australian insult. Did not Australians realize the foolishness of giving offense to a nation that was surely destined for greatness? "Our own land has no equal on earth for fertility and resources which by and by will cause her to weight heavy in the scale of nations." Evil treatment would bear bitter fruit, and wounds would fester. "A time may come," they warned, in language that would echo five years later in *National Life and Character*, "nay, probably will come sooner than is supposed, when the presence and power of China as a great nation will be felt in these seas, and it lies with you to say, as wise men or otherwise, if this be for good or evil."[43]

Cheok Hong Cheong's warning subsequently became the subject of lively debate in the Victoria parliament. "Here was an extraordinary sentence," said David Gaunson, lawyer and member for Emerald Hill, "a sentence of absolute downright meaning—a sentence of unmistakable and pregnant importance."[44] "As soon as the Chinese were induced to avail themselves of the practical appliances of western civilization," he suggested, in an idea that Pearson would make his own, "Chinese merchants would take their maritime commerce into their own hands, and dictate prices in London as they were already doing at Hangshow and Shanghai. As a matter of fact, in the Philippines, and in the other islands of the great Australian archipelago, Chinese merchants were practically running British merchants clean out of existence." Moreover, Gaunson continued, "China now possessed a more powerful fleet than Great Britain could command in Australasian waters; and . . . if the Russians and the Chinese were to coalesce, the position of Australasia would be disastrous in the extreme."[45] Pearson, then minister for public instruction, took note. Both Cheok Hong Cheong's warning—"a time may come"—and Gaunson's arguments in the Victorian parliament about the international implications of Chinese commercial power were incorporated into his famous passage of prophecy. *National Life and Character* can be seen, then, as an imperial coproduction, in Antoinette Burton's terms: an outcome of the encounter between subjects of the British and Chinese Empires in Australia.[46]

"Strikingly Original": The Reception of National Life and Character

Pearson's book impressed its British readers as "strikingly original." It was, said reviewers, "remarkable," "novel," "disturbing," "extremely disquieting." Its forecast took most quite by surprise, as he alerted his readers to the "rise of Asia" more than one hundred years before that phrase became a cliché of our own times. One of his most thoughtful reviewers, writing in 1893 in the London *Athenaeum*, noted the significance of Pearson's geographical perspective to his forecast, the distinctiveness of his "Australian point of view": "The forecast will take many by surprise, because the view it presents is not only not fashionable, but is fundamentally different from that which we have been accustomed since 'progress' became a catchword among us. . . . In another respect, too, he quits the beaten track of anticipation. His view is not purely or mainly European, nor does he regard the inferior races as hopelessly beaten in the struggle with Western civilisation." "The reader," the *Athenaeum* noted, "can indeed discern that Mr Pearson's point of view is not London or Paris, but Melbourne." "He regards the march of affairs from the Australian point of view, and next to Australia what he seems to see most clearly is the growth of Chinese power and of the native populations of Africa. In this forecast, in fact, Europe loses altogether the precedence it has always enjoyed. It appears here as not only the smallest, but as the least important continent."[47] Pearson's view was not only unfashionable, as the reviewer suggested, but fundamentally at odds with the British triumphalism popularized in the last decades of the nineteenth century by the several editions of Charles Dilke's *Greater Britain* and J. R. Seeley's *Expansion of England*.[48] Indeed one Australian Britisher, W. H. Fitchett, writing in the *Review of Reviews*, angrily accused Pearson of being a traitor to his race for refusing to admit the "superiority" of the Anglo-Saxon and for expecting his own people "to vanish before a procession of coffee-coloured, yellow tinted or black-skinned races."[49]

Pearson's prognostications were also at variance with the racial determinism of Benjamin Kidd's *Social Evolution*, published just one year after *National Life and Character*. The two books were often reviewed together, with their contrasting arguments noted. Whereas Pearson pointed to the equal prospects of the "black and yellow races," Kidd argued that they must remain subordinate for all time. As Llewellyn Davies, writing in a review in the *Guardian* titled "Are All Men Equal?" pointed out:

> Both these authors have something prophetic to say about relations of the Western and more civilised races to the less civilised; and their forecasts are in curious contrast to each other. Mr Pearson sees the Chinese, the races of the Indian peninsula, the Negroes, all increasing round the European races, and threatening to squeeze them into anaemic languor: Mr Kidd sees the Teutonic races, because they surpass other races in reverence and a sense of duty, tending to rule the whole earth. And instead of having fanciful notions as to the equality

or equal rights of inferior races, he sets himself to argue us out of any such notions.[50]

Across the Atlantic, Theodore Roosevelt also expressed doubts about Pearson's claims as to the capacity of blacks, Chinese, and Indians, and like other readers he was unsettled by Pearson's forecast. Roosevelt reviewed *National Life and Character* at length in *Sewanee Review* and wrote to tell Pearson of the "great effect" of the book on "all our men here in Washington." "They were greatly interested in what you said. In fact, I don't suppose that any book recently, unless it is Mahan's 'Influence of Sea Power' has excited anything like as much interest." It encouraged Roosevelt in his imperial turn of the mid-1890s.[51]

In the United States the publication of *The Influence of Sea Power* and *National Life and Character* at much the same time shaped the reception and reading of both texts. Together they increased discussion of a coming war between the East and West for worldwide supremacy. In 1893, the same year Pearson's book was published, Mahan wrote an essay titled "Hawaii and Our Future Sea Power" in which he called for an American takeover of the Pacific Islands because of their strategic value as a coaling station: "Shut out from the Sandwich Islands as a coal base, an enemy is thrown back for supplies of fuel to distances of thirty-five hundred miles."[52] The Pacific Ocean began to be seen as the site of the coming war between the East and the West. By the end of the nineteenth century, the Hawaiian monarchy had been overthrown and the islands annexed by the United States. The war against Spain saw the Philippines pass into American control.

Pearson's forecast of Chinese power was popularized in a number of alarmist plays and novels that were published from the 1890s, most notably M. P. Shiel's novel *The Yellow Danger*, which appeared in 1898.[53] Some contemporary critics described this novel as a fictionalization of Pearson's book, and Shiel's Asian villain, Dr. Yen How, has been seen as a possible basis for Sax Rohmer's much better known Dr. Fu Manchu. As Sascha Auerbach has noted, these novels spoke to the perceived threat of a resurgent China, and it is not surprising that *National Life and Character* was also republished in London in 1913 in response to the new sense of crisis about the Chinese in Britain itself.[54]

In Australia, Pearson's book had a direct influence on political leaders and policy formation at the highest level. In 1901, when the new Australian prime minister, Edmund Barton, rose to speak in the first federal Parliament in support of the Immigration Restriction Bill, aimed at excluding all "Asiatics" from the new Commonwealth, he cited "Professor Pearson," "one of the most intellectual statesman who ever lived in this country," as the "strong authority" whose writings gave legitimacy to the legislation. Pearson had been dead for seven years when Barton held his book high in Parliament and read two passages from it. In the first, he interpolated his own comment to emphasize the difference in circumstances between Australia and Britain:

> The fear of Chinese immigration which the Australian democracy cherishes, and which Englishmen at home find it hard to understand—(naturally because they have never had the troubles we have had)—is, in fact, the instinct of self-preservation quickened by experience. We know that coloured and white labour cannot exist side by side; we are well aware that China can swamp us with a single year's surplus of population; and we know that if national existence is sacrificed to the working of a few mines and sugar plantations, it is not the Englishman in Australia alone, but the whole civilized world that will be the losers.[55]

Barton then read Pearson's famous passage of prophecy, its cadence and content echoing Cheok Hong Cheong's warning of 1888 and the subsequent discussion in the Victorian Parliament:

> The day will come, and perhaps is not far distant, when the European observer will look round to see the globe girdled with a continuous zone of the black and yellow races, no longer too weak for aggression or under tutelage, but independent or practically so in government, monopolizing the trade of their own regions, and circumscribing the industry of the Europeans . . . represented by fleets in the European seas, invited to international conferences, and welcomed as allies in the quarrels of the civilized world. . . . It is idle to say that if all this should come to pass our pride of place will not be humiliated.[56]

Pearson the historian saw these historic changes as inevitable. Prime Minister Barton the politician asked, rather: "Is that not something to guard against?" This was the aim of the government's White Australia policy: to guard against being "elbowed and hustled, and perhaps even thrust aside by peoples whom we have looked down upon as servile"; to guard against the prospect of racial humiliation. The policy's central plank of immigration restriction would be emulated in the following decades in other British Dominions—White Canada and White New Zealand—as well as in the republic of the United States, where Lothrop Stoddard, author of *The Rising Tide of Colour*, who referred to Pearson's book as "epoch-making," was a key lobbyist for the Johnson-Reed Immigration Act of 1924.[57]

The East May Now Repel the West

In 1905, the Japanese victory over Russia at Tsushima seemed to dramatically confirm Pearson's prediction of the rise of Asia, though his focus, in 1893, had been on the power of China, not Japan. He had not lived to see the Japanese military defeat of China in 1895, or predicted the startling rise of Japan as a modern military power, but even so, the meaning of Japan's shocking defeat of a European power was understood in the discursive framework provided by Pearson's prophecy, read by so many as the prediction of a coming race war between East and West and a struggle between white and nonwhite peoples for global dominance. Across the world there was tremendous excitement with the Japanese victory, which was proclaimed by colonized and colored peoples including African, Chinese, and Indian political leaders as a triumph of "the down-trodden Eastern peoples."[58]

European statesmen and theorists also hailed the significance of Japan's victory. Goldwin Smith, by then settled in Canada, wrote to Lord Rosebery: "How far will Japan go? The East may now repel the West. No more spheres of influence for predatory Powers. What is the ultimate outlook for Australia or even for the British Empire in India?"[59] At Oxford, Alfred Zimmern, lecturer in classics and future internationalist, told his class he was setting aside Greek history that morning, explaining: "I feel I must speak to you about the most important historical event which has happened or is likely to happen in our lifetime, the victory of a non-white people over a white people."[60] And even Gandhi applauded the fact that the Japanese had forced Russia to "bite the dust on the battlefield": "The peoples of the East will never, never again submit to insult from the insolent whites."[61] At the end of 1905 his magazine *Indian Opinion* published an extract from Pearson's prophecy under the heading "A Word for Londoners."[62] It had been supplied, perversely, by L. E. Neame, who later published *The Asiatic Danger in the Colonies* (with Pearson's prophecy as his preface) to urge the imperial government to "support the Colonies in the ideal of a White Man's Country."[63]

This was the historical context, created by the repercussions of Japan's defeat of Russia, in which "Viator" wrote his long, reflective article "Asia Contra Mundum" in *Fortnightly Review*. Recent events had "re-opened the colour conflict along the whole line of European and Asiatic relations" and called to mind the strange predictions of Charles Pearson, "that disquieting thinker." Fifteen years after *National Life and Character* appeared, it appeared to "Viator" to be a "more extraordinary book than when it was written. We must admit there was more truth in it than the great majority believed. We must admit that there was more truth in it than almost anyone believed."[64] It had also become clear that *National Life and Character* was in some ways a self-fulfilling prophecy, creating the very future it warned about, with "Anglo-Saxon democracies throughout the world, whether expressed by yellow elections in [Britain], by race-riots upon the Pacific slope, or by restrictive Immigration Laws in the Commonwealth and the Transvaal, galvanizing the political unity of India and the fighting unity of Asia."

The imperial government, concluded "Viator" in 1908, would surely be forced to choose between its white self-governing democracies, who couldn't be forced to "commit social suicide in the name of justice to Asia," and "the utter alienation of all the races in our Eastern dependency."[65] Britain was being forced to betray its promise of equality and freedom for all British subjects as increasingly the divide between white colonies and others deepened. To ameliorate this betrayal, "Viator" suggested that the creation of a "brown man's country" in British East Africa might provide a solution to the Indian desire to emigrate and "strengthen our moral and strategical hold on India itself." If white men persisted, however, in trying to exclude nonwhites from four of the five continents, then Pearson's vision might well come to pass:

> Let the sense of the common grievance rise steadily and dominate; let it be asserted that there shall be white men's countries in every other Continent, but that brown men and yellow men, no matter how much they increase or how far they progress, shall never have any countries but their own; let the conception of *Asia contra mundum* gradually arouse all its races for a colossal crusade; let Japan be invoked by China as a leader and by India as a liberator and let the black races feel that the white man is like to be swept back at last; and then indeed the strangest dreams of the eclipse and extinction of Western civilisation might come true.[66]

Conclusion

In this chapter I have pointed to evidence of the widespread impact of Charles Pearson's unsettling predictions of a postcolonial world order in which the "black and yellow races" would take their place as the equals of "white men," predictions that became in some ways a self-fulfilling prophecy, as "white men's countries"—from southern Africa to northern America and to Australasia—proceeded to enact global policies of racial segregation while colonized and colored peoples mobilized in turn to demand racial equality, national independence, and an end to white men's rule. Though arguing against racial determinism, *National Life and Character* nevertheless made the binary divide between whites and nonwhites, Europeans and "Asiatics," East and West central to understanding changing world forces.

Pearson was not an advocate of racial science or social Darwinism but a student of political history, who saw the future power of Asia in world affairs as an inevitable development. And although he used the terms "lower and higher races" to explicate his argument, he was careful to explain that this did not signify a belief in innate racial inferiority and superiority. When Benjamin Kidd, a believer in Teutonic superiority, finished writing *Social Evolution* just after *National Life and Character* appeared, he read Pearson's book and its early reviews before his own was printed and was moved to add a long footnote, criticizing Pearson for "the serious mistake" of "estimating the future by watching the course of events outside the temperate regions" rather than attending to "the progress amongst the Western peoples." In other words, Pearson had made the mistake of treating the "black and yellow races" as historical agents capable of shaping their own future and taking an equal place in the world.[67]

The racial determinism of books such as Kidd's *Social Evolution* would serve as a powerful weapon for those who wanted to prove Pearson's predictions wrong and that his views of the capacity of the "black and yellow races" were misplaced. Racial determinists helped ensure that the future equality and independence of blacks and Asians, foretold by Pearson as "inevitable," would be resisted for many decades to come. Ironically, however, Pearson's prophecy also helped make race thinking central to discussions of imperial and international relations and gave currency to predictions of a coming war between white and nonwhite, the East and the West. *National Life and Character*'s legacy was to constitute "whiteness" not as a source of superiority but as a condition of anxiety fueled by apprehension of imminent loss.

NOTES

1. Seetsele Molema, *The Bantu: Past and Present* (Edinburgh: W. Green and Son, 1920), 346.

2. L. E. Neame, *The Asiatic Danger in the Colonies* (London: Routledge, 1907). Neame quoted Pearson in his preface.

3. Charles H. Pearson, *National Life and Character: A Forecast* (London: Macmillan, 1893), 85.

4. Viator, "Asia Contra Mundum," *Fortnightly Review*, 1 February 1908, 185.

5. Godfrey Hodgson, *Woodrow Wilson's Right Hand: The Life of Colonel Edward M. House* (New Haven, CT: Yale University Press, 2006), 112; David Walker, *Anxious Nation: Australia and the Rise of Asia 1850–1939* (St. Lucia: University of Queensland Press, 1999), 3.

6. Walker, *Anxious Nation*, 3.

7. Viator, "Asia Contra Mundum," 186.

8. Akira Iriye, *Pacific Estrangement: Japanese and American Expansion, 1897–1911* (Cambridge, MA: Harvard University Press, 1972), 29; Marilyn Lake and Henry Reynolds, *Drawing the Global Colour Line: White Men's Countries and the International Challenge of Racial Equality* (Cambridge: Cambridge University Press, 2008), 251.

9. Quoted in John Tregenza, *Professor of Democracy: The Life of Charles Henry Pearson 1830–1894: Oxford Don and Australian Radical* (Melbourne: Melbourne University Press, 1968), 49.

10. Pearson, *National Life and Character*.

11. Pearson, *National Life and Character*, 17–18.

12. *Saturday Review*, 25 February 1893. Clippings, Charles Henry Pearson Papers, ms 7518-9, box 432, State Library of Victoria, Melbourne.

13. Charles Pearson, "The Black Republic," in *Reviews and Critical Essays*, ed. H. A. Strong (London: Methuen, 1896); review, *Spectator*, 25 April 1896, Clippings, Charles Henry Pearson Papers, ms 7518-9, box 432, State Library of Victoria, Melbourne.

14. Pearson, *National Life and Character*, 30.

15. Goldwin Smith, *The Political Destiny of Canada* (London: Chapman and Hall, 1878), 41–42.

16. Pearson, *National Life and Character*, 29.

17. Ching-Hwang Yen, *Coolies and Mandarins: China's Protection of Overseas Chinese during the Late Ch'ing Period (1851–1911)* (Singapore: Singapore University Press, 1985).

18. John Fitzgerald, *Big White Lie: Chinese Australians in White Australia* (Sydney: UNSW Press, 2007), 112.

19. Colonial Office to Foreign Office, 25 May 1886, Enclosure no. 2, *Chinese Immigration*, part 1, Government Correspondence, Victorian Parliamentary Papers (Melbourne: Government of Victoria, 1888), 4.

20. Pearson, *National Life and Character*, 84–85.

21. Cheok Hong Cheong et al., *Chinese Remonstrance to the Parliament and People of Victoria, together with Correspondence with Government of the Same, and Address to Sydney Conference* (Melbourne: Wm. Marshall and Co., 1888), 6.

22. C. H. Pearson, "The Land Question in the United States," *Contemporary Review*, September–December 1868, 347–354.

23. Christopher Harvie, *Lights of Liberalism: University Liberals and the Challenge of Democracy 1860–86* (London: Allen Lane, 1976).

24. Tregenza, *Professor of Democracy*, 54.

25. Pearson, "Land Question," 347–354.

26. John Wisker, "The Coloured Man in Australia," *Fortnightly Review*, 1 July 1879, 82.

27. Yong Ching Fatt, "Cheong Cheok Hong," *Australian Dictionary of Biography 1851–1900*, vol. 3 (Melbourne: Melbourne University Press, 1969), 385–386; Yong Ching Fatt, "Lowe Kong Meng," in *Australian Dictionary of Biography 1851–1900*, vol. 3 (Melbourne: Melbourne University Press, 1969), 106–107; Yong Ching Fatt, "Ah Mouy, Louis," in *Australian Dictionary of Biography 1851–1900*, vol. 5 (Melbourne: Melbourne University Press, 1974), 19; Marilyn Lake, "Lowe Kong Meng Appeals to International Law: Transnational Lives Caught between Empire and Nation," in *Transnational Lives*, ed. Desley Deacon, Penny Russell, and Angela Woollacott (London: Palgrave, 2009), 223–237.

28. Lowe Kong Meng, Cheok Hong Cheong, and Louis Ah Mouy, *The Chinese Question in Australia 1878–1879* (Melbourne: FF Bailliere, 1879), 28.

29. Kong Meng et al., *Chinese Question*, 20.

30. Kong Meng et al., *Chinese Question*, 12.

31. Kong Meng et al., *Chinese Question*, 9–10.

32. Victorian Legislative Assembly, *Victorian Parliamentary Debates*, 4 October 1881, 220.

33. Victorian Legislative Assembly, *Victorian Parliamentary Debates*, 4 October 1881, 220.

34. *Argus*, 27 May 1887.

35. *Argus*, 28 May 1887.

36. *Argus*, 28 May 1887.

37. *Argus*, 28 May 1887.

38. *Argus*, 30 May 1887.

39. *Argus*, 30 May 1887.

40. Legislative Assembly, *Victorian Parliamentary Debates*, 12 September 1888, 1058.

41. Adam McKeown, *Melancholy Order, Asian Migration and the Globalization of Borders* (New York: Columbia University Press, 2008), 7.

42. Legislative Assembly, *Victorian Parliamentary Debates*, 6 December 1888, 2357.

43. Cheok Hong Cheong, "Address to Australasian Conference: To the Representatives of Australian Governments, in Conference Assembled," in Cheok Hong Cheong

et al., *Chinese Remonstrance to the Parliament and People of Victoria, together with Correspondence with Government of the Same, and Address to Sydney Conference* (Melbourne: Wm. Marshall and Co., 1888), 15.

44. Legislative Assembly, *Victorian Parliamentary Debates*, 18 October 1888, 1617.

45. Legislative Assembly, *Victorian Parliamentary Debates*, 18 October 1888, 1618.

46. Antoinette Burton, "Getting Outside the Global: Re-positioning British Imperialism in World History," in *Race, Nation and Empire: Making Histories, 1750 to the Present*, ed. Catherine Hall and Keith McClelland (Manchester: Manchester University Press, 2010).

47. *Athenaeum*, 4 March 1893.

48. Duncan Bell, *The Idea of Greater Britain: Empire and the Future of World Order, 1860–1900* (Princeton, NJ: Princeton University Press, 2007).

49. *Review of Reviews*, 15 August 1900, 150.

50. J. Llewelyn Davies, "Are All Men Equal?," *Guardian*, 13 June 1894.

51. Lake and Reynolds, *Global Colour Line*, 96–97.

52. Quoted in Thomas J. Osborne, *Annexation Hawaii: Fighting American Imperialism* (Waimanalo: Island Style Press, 1998), 40.

53. Walker, *Anxious Nation*, 107; 176–177.

54. Sascha Auerbach, *Race, Law, and the Chinese Puzzle in Imperial Britain* (London: Palgrave, 2009), 73–75.

55. Australia House of Representatives, *Commonwealth Parliamentary Debates*, 7 August 1901, 3503.

56. Australia House of Representatives, *Commonwealth Parliamentary Debates*, 7 August 1901, 3503.

57. Lothrop Stoddard, *The Rising Tide of Color: Against White World Supremacy* (New York: Scribner's, 1923), 281.

58. Lake and Reynolds, *Global Colour Line*, 167.

59. Lake and Reynolds, *Global Colour Line*, 166.

60. Lake and Reynolds, *Global Colour Line*, 166.

61. Lake and Reynolds, *Global Colour Line*, 168.

62. N.E.N., "A Word for Londoners," *Indian Opinion*, 30 December 1905, 874.

63. Neame, *Asiatic Danger*, 105.

64. Viator, "Asia Contra Mundum," 185–186.

65. Viator, "Asia Contra Mundum," 198.

66. Viator, "Asia Contra Mundum," 200.

67. Lake and Reynolds, *Global Colour Line*, 88.

Five

VICTIMS OF "BRITISH JUSTICE"?

A Century of Wrong as Anti-imperial
Tract, Core Narrative of the Afrikaner "Nation," and
Victim-Based Solidarity-Building Discourse

———

ANDRÉ DU TOIT

A Title in Its Context

Globally the most influential thing about *A Century of Wrong*, published
in October 1899 as a quasi-official justification for the South African Republic's (SAR) declaration of war, may well have been its title. All too obviously, the publication itself served as a polemical tract in the lopsided
conflict between imperial Britain and the puny Boer republics. But the title
spoke to larger issues of global concern that had also been at the heart of the
Hague Peace Conference a few months earlier.

From 18 May to 29 July 1899, 108 delegates from twenty-six countries,
including all the European great powers and the United States as well as
China and Turkey, met in the capacious setting of the Dutch Summer
Palace in the Hague. As a "peace" conference it was, for the most part, an
anomaly: it served as little more than a public forum for unvarnished assertions of great power interests and imperial ambitions. Implicitly, though,
the conference also responded to dimly perceived threats to the enduring
sway of this imperial order. The assembled delegates and assorted members
of international high society found that they could not ignore the outpouring

of public enthusiasm for the noble purposes of a peace conference occasioned by Tsar Nicholas II's call for a curb on the ever more ominous international arms race. As Barbara Tuchman relates in *The Proud Tower*, the skeptical and cynical delegates "became interested in spite of themselves."

The outcomes, in the form of the first Hague Conventions, remained meager and of little avail. Within three months, the military might of the British Empire was unleashed on the Boer republics of the Transvaal and the Free State. In this confrontation with socially backward agrarian communities, the British Empire claimed to represent progress and modern civilization. Chamberlain and Milner and their high command confidently expected an easy war; once the imperial army was in place, the war would be concluded in six months, perhaps even by Christmas. For his part the SAR state attorney, Jan Christiaan Smuts, believed that the British Empire was a ramshackle structure. The empire held sway over great countries largely inhabited by antagonistic peoples and, in Smuts's view, its dominium rested more on prestige and moral intimidation than on true military strength. Nothing came of Smuts's expectations that the war might instigate uprisings in India and other parts of the empire, but in South Africa itself it did prove an unexpectedly protracted conflict. When Generals Roberts and Kitchener resorted to "scorched earth" policies to counter Boer guerrilla warfare, with concentration camps to confine women and children, resulting in massive civilian casualties, Britain stood accused, both in England itself and before the "civilized" world, of employing "methods of barbarism."

In the end the republics were defeated, but at considerable cost to the necessary prestige of the British Empire. Ironically, the need for something like the Hague Conventions, which had so readily been disregarded, now began to appear in a different light; the 1899 conference was followed by other conferences and conventions; and in retrospect the initial Hague Conventions proved to be the beginnings of modern international human rights law. In a final reversal, the international anti-apartheid movement, ironically mirroring the erstwhile pro-Boer movements, mobilized this international human rights discourse against the successor regime of the erstwhile Boer republics.

In this ambivalent context, the title of *A Century of Wrong* proved both apt and prescient. Actually "A Century of Wrong" was not the most obvious translation of the Dutch original, *Een Eeuw van Onrecht*. A literal translation would have been "A Century of Injustice" (used in the U.S., German, and French translations). As a title, "A Century of Wrong" announced a more comprehensive moral indictment of imperial rule. This spoke to the popular expectations of "peace" as a humanitarian counterforce to the prevailing "realist" discourse in international politics. At the level of its title, then, *A Century of Wrong* was part of a global process through which the South African war became a humanitarian and human rights issue in Europe and beyond—while the imperial claims of "British justice" were severely dented. The domestic South African appeal of the publication's contents, though, was another matter; these contributed to an emerging Afrikaner nationalist movement in ways that prefigured the subsequent confrontation of local apartheid policies with universalistic human rights norms.

A Tract and Its Travels

A Century of Wrong was a stridently anti-imperial tract: it provided a partisan survey of the origins and causes of the war with a view to harnessing both domestic and international support for the republican cause. Put together in short order and under great pressure on the very eve of the war, the publication was a patchwork of partisan exhortation, selective résumés of colonial and republican history, appeals to international conventions, excerpts from diplomatic correspondence, refutations of alleged Uitlander grievances couched in impassioned anti-capitalist and anti-jingoist rhetoric. For a time, the identity of the "author" of this tract was a matter of some controversy, with General Smuts as the prime suspect. The first printing, produced by the government printer in the typical style and format of official publications on 9 October 1899, only days before the SAR's declaration of war, had been anonymous. For distribution purposes it was identified as "issued by" F. W. Reitz, the secretary of state and former president of the Orange Free State.[1] However, Reitz and his family disclaimed his connection and suggested that Smuts and J. de V. Roos had been responsible. Subsequently Smuts and Roos's collaborative "authorship" has been confirmed by historians and archivists.[2]

But this may not be the right question. Significantly, neither Smuts nor Roos ever publicly asserted their authorship. Smuts, the architect of postwar "conciliation," may well not have wanted to associate himself with a cause that had in the interim been taken up ever more exclusively by his nationalist opponents. It is less clear why Roos also kept quiet about his co-responsibility for what was after all a celebrated, if controversial, work. Perhaps appropriately for such a collaborative patchwork, *A Century of*

Wrong was a deliberately "anonymous" publication rather than the creation of particular "authors."

As such tracts go, this one had an immediate and pervasive impact, globally even more than locally. This was more a function of its uses in and for the available networks of distribution provided by the various pro-Boer movements abroad than due to any careful designs on certain intended audiences. The text itself was emphatically addressed to "Brother Africanders!" and concluded with a rousing appeal invoking the slogan "Africa for the Africander." Unlike "Boers" or "Burghers," this might have been calculated to include Cape Afrikaners in a pan-Afrikaner ethnic appeal. But from the initial distribution of *A Century of Wrong* it does not appear that Cape Afrikaners had been a priority. Of the first batch to be printed, twelve were dispatched to the SAR's representative in Brussels, ten to London, and six to the United States, with an English translation to follow in days. No mention is made of similar distribution efforts in the Cape. Already by early 1900 a second printing had appeared (with different editions published in London and the United States).[3] These provided a key staple for the pro-Boer movements and international anti-imperialist campaigns mounted in Europe and the United States, not least in England itself.

However, there is little indication that *A Century of Wrong* was informed by a strategic notion of particular international audiences in its polemical targets. There was no attempt, for example, to highlight geopolitical issues that might be of particular interest to Germany, at the time Britain's main rival. In this regard the Dutch case is even more surprising. The Netherlands was, of course, no great power, but ever since the 1881 revolt against the British annexation of the Transvaal there had been a substantial Dutch interest in their rediscovered ethnic kin (*stamverwanten*).[4] A lively body of popular Dutch writings on the "Afrikaner Boers" typically played up a heroic vision of Boer resistance against British "tyranny," viewed as a continuation of an eminently Dutch republican tradition. It would not have been difficult for a SAR propaganda offensive to tie into this. However, as we will see, any such Dutch-oriented perspective was notably absent from the historical narrative articulated in *A Century of Wrong*. Much the same applies to the various (actual and potential) pro-Boer constituencies in England, including some surprising alliances of, for example, liberal and feminist networks. Had these been in mind, it would have been strategic to avoid overt defenses of slavery and racial superiority, but these continued to feature prominently in *A Century of Wrong*. In short, the possible concerns of these pro-Boer movements (not to mention those in France, Russia, and further afield) cannot be said to have informed the publication's working conception of its intended audience in any serious way. What we do find in the text, instead, is a rather abstract and vague notion of "the tribunal of an impartial history."

What enabled this polemical tract to travel as far and wide as it did was access to the emerging networks of the various pro-Boer movements. In effect, these provided a tailor-made means for the tract's dissemination. Conversely, it eminently served the immediate propagandistic and solidarity-building needs of these diverse pro-Boer movements. This was most conspicuously the case in the Netherlands, where by the advent of the South African War an effective network of cultural and commercial ties with the SAR had developed. The Dutch–South African Society (NZAV), founded in 1881, complemented by the General Dutch Union (ANV) and the Christian National Boer Committee, functioned in tandem with the propaganda efforts of the diplomatic representative of the SAR, Dr. Willem Leyds, a Dutchman who had held various high offices in the Transvaal administration. When the threats of imminent war began escalating in 1899, the NZAV organized a petition with some 140,000 signatories calling on the British people to prevent an unjust war; on Christmas Day 1899 Charles Boissevain, editor of the leading daily newspaper *Algemeen Handelsblad*, published a front-page open letter to the Duke of Devonshire, and on 1 February 1900 Abraham Kuyper, who was shortly to become prime minister, published a celebrated disquisition, "La Crise Sud-Africaine," in the journal *Revue des Deux Mondes*, which was promptly translated into English (running to no less than sixteen editions), Dutch, German, and Swedish. In this context the ANV readily supported publication of *Een Eeuw van Onrecht*, which quickly became one of the most famous pro-Boer publications in the Netherlands.

In Britain the various pro-Boer committees provided a similar network geared to the ready dissemination of material bearing on the South African War. Politically based in the radical wing of the opposition Liberal Party, the British pro-Boers also included a range of independent nonconformists, humanitarians, feminists, pacifists, anti-imperialists, and rationalists. In some ways this was a somewhat unlikely alliance. Liberals and radicals had been among the most vocal and persistent critics of Boer racial oppression, or "slavery." But the Jameson Raid and other increasing evidence of Chamberlain and Milner's imperialist agenda made them into active opponents of the war. The key pro-Boer committees were only founded in 1899 as the threats of war rapidly gathered pace. Most conspicuous was the Stop-the-War Committee launched on Christmas Eve 1899 by W. T. Stead, indefatigable pioneer of the new mass journalism. Stead not only utilized his weekly *Review of Reviews* but also brought out a separate weekly magazine, *War against War in South Africa*. Within the year Stop-the-War had distributed millions of leaflets, posters, broadsheets, cartoons, and pamphlets. The various pro-Boer committees all sponsored private and public meetings while publishing and distributing an array of pamphlets and leaflets. Though the British pro-Boer movement proved politically rather ineffectual, it did provide a ready-made means for disseminating *A Century of Wrong*. The *Review of Reviews* published an English version with a preface by Stead himself (as well as a translation of Kuyper's "La Crise Sud-Africaine"). Some two thousand copies of *A Century of Wrong* were produced at a cost of about £80.

Similar manifestations of pro-Boer interest and sentiment also proliferated in a range of other countries worldwide. In a sense the pro-Boer movement became nothing less than a global phenomenon. It is understandable that the anti-imperial Boer cause in the South African War evoked passionate interest from nationalists in Ireland and extended to the Flemish and to Germany. But it is surprising to what extent this was also the case in Scandinavia, Russia, Hungary, Italy, and the United States. In short order *A Century of Wrong* was translated and published not only in Dutch and English but also in German, French, Swedish, and Russian.[5]

So what was the international reception and legacy of *A Century of Wrong*? This presents us with a telling paradox. For despite its celebrity and wide distribution there are few traces of any definite impact or lasting significance, at least in this international context. Even in the more detailed accounts of the international propaganda war associated with the South African War we find virtually no specific references to *A Century of Wrong*. Actually this is not unusual for a polemical tract of this kind. Such tracts are not meant to be closely studied but to be passed on for immediate propaganda purposes. Evidently, the various pro-Boer movements found *A Century of Wrong* eminently serviceable. But by definition such polemical uses were also transient, leaving few traces beyond the context of the war itself. The only lasting legacy was the title, which did not vanish without a trace, like so much else pertaining to this erstwhile propaganda war of global dimensions. For other and subsequent movements of imperial resistance, the title retained a kind of analogous relevance as a challenge to the waning moral claims of the British Empire. In the domestic South African context, though, *A Century of Wrong* did make a distinct and lasting contribution to the configuration of a resurgent Afrikaner nationalist movement in the longer term aftermath of the war.

Narrating the (Afrikaner) Nation

Whereas the polemics of *A Century of Wrong* were directed against the target of unjust imperial rule, the actual subject matter in the text also told a different kind of story. Implicitly and explicitly it took up the seminal concerns of an earlier tract *Wie zijn Wij?* (Who Are We?), the quasi-official SAR manifesto of the 1881 rebellion against the British annexation of the Transvaal. This had not been an introduction meant for some distant audience unfamiliar with the local population. Instead it represented the beginnings of an exercise in self-fashioning and solidarity-building, constructing the Afrikaner "nation" (fragmented as this still was in terms of Transvaal Boers, republican burghers, Cape Afrikaners) by telling a particular version of its history.

Expressions of an "Afrikaner" historical consciousness emerged by the late 1870s in the dual context of the first Afrikaans language movement initiated by the Cape Genootskap vir Regte Afrikaners (GRA) and of popular resistance to the British annexation of the Transvaal in 1877. In this regard S. J. du Toit's Afrikaans-language *Geskiedenis van Ons Land in die Taal van Ons Volk* (History of Our Country in the Language of Our People) (1877) represented a landmark. Over the following decade and more, though, such pan-Afrikaans historical consciousness effectively subsided, and the early accounts of Transvaal and Free State history (including the 1881 SAR manifesto) were mostly written by Hollanders. Only from 1896, following the Jameson Raid, did a marked pan-Afrikaans historical consciousness revive. This was also the context of *A Century of Wrong* in the even more charged circumstances at the advent of the South African War.

Though taking up the cause of the SAR, Smuts and Roos were both Cape Afrikaners, not Transvaal "Boers"; significantly, they were members of a new generation of university-educated and professionally qualified Afrikaners. Smuts had studied law at Cambridge and had entered Cape political life in 1895 as an ally of Cecil Rhodes before, disillusioned by the Jameson Raid, he relocated to the Transvaal. It was Roos who had a particular interest in Afrikaner history. Though not a trained historian, Roos took a passionate and sustained interest in archival and historical matters. During his first stay in the Transvaal, from 1890, he systematically interviewed survivors and descendants from the Trekker period in a proto–oral history project, reported extensively on the Paardekraal commemorations, and published a lecture titled "Dingaan's Day: A History Written in Blood." He tracked down key primary sources from the time of the Great Trek, such as the diary of Louis Trichardt, and ensured their preservation in the State Archive. Having returned to the Cape, he worked as research assistant for both of the main (and rival) archival historians, George MacCall Theal and Reverend H. C. V. Leibbrandt. If anyone was suited to produce an informed insider overview of Afrikaner history in short order, then that was "Jimmy" Roos. In the event, this also proved to be a seminal narrative of the Afrikaner "nation."

The genealogy of the core narrative of the Afrikaner "nation" may be traced by comparing the historical section of *A Century of Wrong* with S. J. du Toit's 1877 GRA *History* and the 1881 SAR manifesto. The GRA *History's* stated aim had been to provide an inclusive history of "our (Afrikaans) people," but it did not yet quite know how to go about this. Much of the book consisted of meandering descriptions featuring notable historical figures or telling episodes, with curious anecdotes and sententious reflections thrown in for good measure. It did not yet tell a coherent story linking the different times and settings involved as part of a collective experience. Not only did different parts deal with the Dutch period and that of British rule, but the parallel trajectories of the Dutch settlers and the French refugees were recounted in separate sections as well. Similarly, the later narrative of the "emigrant Boers" was itself dispersed into the various regional histories of Natal, the Free State, and Transvaal. While historical figures such as Van Riebeeck, Adam Tas, and Governor Tulbagh, or events like Slagtersnek and the Great Trek, were singled out for special notice, they also tended to get swamped in an indiscriminate account that gave equal prominence to anecdotes concerning minor figures and obscure happenings. Nor were key themes, such as the significance of Van Riebeeck's prayer at the founding of the settlement, sufficiently sustained or developed to frame the narrative.

By comparison the 1881 SAR manifesto clearly highlighted "freedom" and "independence" as the objectives of the Transvaal resistance against British annexation, positing these as the underlying driving forces of a long historical struggle. The current Transvaal rebellion was framed retrospectively as part of a common and enduring quest for republican liberties and self-rule. This enabled the 1881 manifesto to represent disparate historical events from Slagtersnek to the 1877 annexation of the Transvaal—all of which had also featured in the GRA *History*—as integral parts of a shared historical narrative, indeed of the longer history of Dutch and Protestant emancipatory struggle for religious freedom, civil liberties, and independence. Compared to the sometimes unfocused and aimlessly wandering narratives of the GRA *History*, this was a clear and purposefully structured epic of sustained national struggle in a quite different voice. Indeed, the 1881 SAR manifesto was written by Dr. E. J. P. Jorissen, a liberal Hollander, who had effectively appropriated the local Boer histories within the framework of contemporary Dutch cultural and political nationalism.

Coming to *A Century of Wrong*, the differences, even more than the similarities, are instructive. In line with the 1881 manifesto it agreed on republican independence as general objective. But there were some telling differences in its telling of the core narrative. The familiar series of key episodes—from Slagtersnek through the Great Trek to the founding of the republics, with the story now extended to the more recent Jameson Raid as well—was set out in a clear and tight narrative structure. But, unlike the 1881 version, this was not located in the context of Dutch cultural and political history. Significantly, the story was only taken up from the beginnings of British occupation, effectively leaving out the period of Dutch colonial rule. And so its core narrative did not start in 1652 with Van Riebeeck (who was not even mentioned) but with Slagtersnek in 1815.

What this implied was that the story of the Afrikaner/"Boer" political struggle essentially related to the British imperial context rather than to Dutch cultural-political history. Unlike the 1881 SAR manifesto, *A Century of Wrong* did not invoke any independent (i.e., Dutch) source of legitimacy and authority; it posed an internal challenge to British rule in terms of its own basic values and professed commitments: "History will show convincingly that the pleas of humanity, civilisation, and equal rights, upon which the British Government bases its actions, are nothing else but the recrudescence of that spirit of annexation and plunder which has at all times characterised its dealings with our people."[6] Paradoxically, the very challenge to British imperial power invoked the rights and liberties supposed to have been extended to (British) subjects but consistently denied to them in practice.

This narrow focus on those episodes and developments that demonstrated the Afrikaner/"Boer" experience of British (in)justice resulted in the telling omissions of some major historical developments not recognized as key events in the story of the Afrikaner "nation." Thus, the history of colonial Afrikaners in the Cape after the Great Trek was wholly ignored. Neither the continuing wars on the Cape Colony's eastern frontier in the 1840s and 1850s, nor the Anti-Convict Agitation on the eve of the granting of a Constitution and representative government to the Cape Colony, both of which featured extensively in the GRA *History*, were even mentioned. Only passing mention was made of the Highveld conflicts with the Ndebele, such as the battle of Vegkop, or the Basutho wars (except to protest the unwarranted and partisan interventions by the British); but the 1848 battle of Boomplaats, with the British forces of Sir Harry Smith featured prominently (including an impassioned account of the execution of Thomas Dreyer as nothing less than a murder, "to the shame of English reputation"[7]). The core narrative of *A Century of Wrong* concluded that with the Jameson Raid "we see to what a depth the old great traditions of British Constitutionalism had sunk" while unintentionally serving to bring about the awakening of "the national heart of Africanderdom."[8]

This core narrative would function as a template for the articulation and further development of postwar Afrikaner nationalism. In F. A. van Jaarsveld's judgment, *A Century of Wrong* remained the foundation of Afrikaner-nationalist historical consciousness until the founding of the Republic in 1961. Of course this template was also revised, not least because it had to accommodate the course and outcome of the South African war itself. But in an important sense it had already prepared the way for the postwar understanding and interpretation of such key features as the suffering and mass deaths of Afrikaner women and children in the concentration camps.

An Atrocity Narrative: The Legend and Shadow of Slagtersnek

The core narrative of Afrikaner history in *A Century of Wrong* was not merely a neutral framing. It articulated a distinctive perspective, one rooted in a discourse of political grievances, indeed of national victimization by British imperial power. At the time this was not the only narrative framing available, as may be illustrated with reference to some contemporary responses by Boer leaders to the imminent threats of war. Thus in August 1899 General Piet Joubert, as commander-in-chief of the SAR, published an open letter (in English) to Queen Victoria (instantly translated and published in the Netherlands). In it he compared the Voortrekkers with the people of Israel, "chosen by God to establish their republics in the middle of the African 'wilderness' to bring 'civilisation' here."[9] At about the same time the SAR secretary of state, F. W. Reitz, wrote a letter to his counterpart in the Orange Free State, replete with biblical metaphors and analogies and prophesying that God would be on the side of the Boers and help them withstand the imperial forces on the battlefield.[10] What is striking, when one compares A Century of Wrong to these contemporary responses, is the absence of similar biblical language and allusions and of any "chosen people" notion. Distinctive to A Century of Wrong was its resolutely secular approach and implicitly "modern" perspective. Unlike other Boer spokesmen and leaders, or President Paul Kruger himself, Smuts and Roos did not set out to counter the threats of British imperial power and of international mining capital with an archaic or Old Testament worldview; their charge was that the British Empire in its dealings with the Afrikaners/Boers was betraying its own professed standards of "justice," "rights," and "civilisation."

However, in representing the republics in this way as "victims of British justice," they also tapped into a popular discourse of national victimization. In particular, A Century of Wrong drew on the communal memories that had grown up around the legend of Slagtersnek and the "invented traditions" of the "Dingaan's Day" and Paardekraal public commemorations. It was this distinctive discourse of secular victim-based solidarity-building that would prove to be of special significance for the development of an Afrikaner civil mythology during the opening decades of the twentieth century.

A Century of Wrong thus represented the history of the Afrikaners/Boers not as a national epic but as part of a popular grievance discourse. As such, its litany of historical grievances was laced with elements of an atrocity narrative, above all the legend of Slagtersnek. The story of Slagtersnek had already had a strange career (which would continue long after A Century of Wrong).[11] The Bezuidenhout rebellion of 1815 had indeed been an episode of some historical significance. In the context of the closing frontier, with the new British administration attempting to establish a measure of law and order, and even some elements of the rule of law, the stakes were not insignificant. The court handed down an unprecedented number of death sentences to the main culprits; despite pleas for clemency, the governor confirmed that the capital punishment of six rebels should proceed. The outcome was traumatic for all concerned. At the public execution the ropes of all but one of the condemned broke; to the assembled onlookers this appeared as a divine intervention of some kind, but despite their desperate pleas for a reprieve, the execution was harshly enforced as a lesson in the meaning of "British justice."

Even so, popular memories of Slagtersnek soon faded: significantly, Slagtersnek was not mentioned among the grievances given as "reasons" for the Great Trek a generation later, nor did associates and descendants of the Slagtersnek rebels seem to figure much among the Trekkers. The story of Slagtersnek first surfaced in print in the five lectures on the "Emigration of the Dutch Farmers," given by Justice Henry Cloete in Pietermaritzburg in the 1850s.[12] Cloete was a member of one of the most prominent (and anglicized) Cape Dutch families. As a young man attached to the first Circuit Court on the frontier, he had personally witnessed some of the events associated with the Bezuidenhout rebellion and later acted as the British emissary in enforcing the 1842 British annexation of Natal despite Trekker protests. His first lecture prominently included a dramatic account of the botched execution. In this first lecture, Cloete also recounted that in 1843–1844 influential Trekkers in Natal insistently assured him: "We can never forget Slachters Nek." However, this revival of the story of Slagtersnek may have had as much or more to do with Cloete's own memories of these dramatic events than with the living memories of the Bezuidenhouts or other Trekkers. What is clear, though, is that Cloete's "Lecture" was the primary source on which both Theal (1874) and S. J. du Toit in the 1877 GRA *History* relied for their accounts of Slagtersnek, which in turn became the main sources for the late nineteenth-century proliferation of the legend of Slagtersnek: "Practically every history book in Afrikaans of the time featured the Slagtersnek episode prominently. . . . The unfortunate men of Slagtersnek had been transformed into 'martyrs' for Afrikaans freedom and victims of 'British cruelty.' "[13]

An extraordinary public cult then developed around the legend of Slagtersnek in the immediate aftermath of the Jameson Raid (1896). Nor was this only a matter of popular feelings. The SAR commissioned J. W. G. Van Oordt to produce an official history, while the Cape parliament commissioned its archivist, Reverend H. C. V. Leibbrandt, to publish all archival documents relating to Slagtersnek. Commandant Henning Pretorius, commander of the SAR State Artillery, even went to the Eastern Cape on a quest to recover the beam of the actual gallows used at Slagtersnek (but unfortunately died before he could complete his mission). Meanwhile in

Johannesburg a lynching party had been mobilized to string up the captured Jameson raiders on this beam of the Slagtersnek gallows. When Lionel Phillips and three other leaders of the Jameson Raid were convicted and sentenced to death by a SAR court, this was popularly interpreted as nothing less than a historic retribution for Slagtersnek. However, in the face of outraged public opinion, President Kruger commuted the death sentences, claiming that he did not want to repeat that atrocity of "British justice," so putting the English nation to shame.[14] Somehow Slagtersnek had become a potent symbol of the meaning of "British justice" for these crisis times, one that could be turned against the empire itself.

But just what was it about the legend of Slagtersnek that so aroused Afrikaner popular feelings on the eve of the South African War? At this time the crux of the Slagtersnek legend was not yet the earlier Bezuidenhout rebellion, as it would become in early twentieth-century Afrikaner-nationalist versions of the Slagtersnek narrative, but the botched execution. Significantly, in his account of Slagtersnek in *De Afrikaner-Boer en de Jameson-Inval* (*The Afrikaner Boer and the Jameson Raid*, 1896), Nico Hofmeyr rejected the proposal to erect a monument for the Slagtersnek rebels and distanced himself from this "abominable history" that had become such a "rock of offence" to Afrikaners, commenting that it did not reflect well on either Boer or Brit.[15] It was not the rebellion as such, and even less its cause, that lived in Afrikaner memories but the terrible fate of the five convicted. At a human level the traumatic story—of the gallows ropes breaking and the men then being strung up again one after the other with the only piece of sound rope available, despite the most desperate pleas for clemency—obviously raised basic issues of "justice" and "mercy." The main thrust of the story of Slagtersnek, though, was not that the conviction of the rebels had been a miscarriage of justice. But for the breaking of the gallows rope, "justice" would have been done to the rebels and accepted as such all round. The outrage was that when the gallows rope did break—in some fateful intervention—the death sentences were still enforced, despite the most desperate pleas for mercy. *That* could not be "justice," or if it was, then "justice" itself was an outrage against humanity. If such a brutal execution was an instance of "British justice," then the horror of the event revealed it to be nothing but the exercise of brute and merciless power.[16]

And so *A Century of Wrong* referred to Slagtersnek as an atrocity committed in the name of the law: "The horrible occurrence of the 9th of March 1816, when six of the Boers were half hung up in the most inhuman way in the compulsory presence of their wives and children. Their death was truly horrible . . . and the eyes of posterity still glance back shudderingly through the long vista of years at that tragedy of horror." As the opening episode in the narrative of a "century of wrong," the function of this atrocity story of Slagtersnek was that it revealed "British justice" as a hypocritical mask for brutal repression: "This was, however, but the beginning. Under the cloak of religion British administration continued to display its hate against our people and nationality, and to conceal its self-seeking aim under cover of the most exalted principles."[17]

As an atrocity story, the botched Slagtersnek execution may be compared with a similar but less renowned episode in the national narrative set out in *A Century of Wrong*: that of the battle of Boomplaats and the fate of Thomas Dreyer. Unlike the Bezuidenhouts, Dreyer has disappeared as a historical figure from post-nineteenth-century histories. The significance of the otherwise obscure Dreyer becomes clearer when we refer to the account of Boomplaats provided in the 1877 GRA *History*. According to this account, Dreyer had not been a combatant at all but was a local simpleton who—on foot, unarmed, and barely clothed—had unwittingly wandered onto the terrain of battle. Sir Harry Smith insisted that he had to be arraigned before a British military tribunal, which, as retribution for their own losses in the battle, sentenced him to death. If true, this would have been a war crime, "a murder and deed of shame." The story of the judicial killing of Thomas Dreyer, like that of Slagtersnek, was calculated to reveal the brutality of "British justice" at the most basic human level.

Even so, there was an underlying ambivalence in the approach to "British justice" expressed in this discourse of national victimization. As much as *A Century of Wrong* excoriated "British justice" as hypocritical and nothing but a mask for the brutal realities of asserting its imperial might, it still continued to invoke that same ideal of "justice": "The traditions of the greatest people on earth are tarnished. . . . But the sky which stretches its banners over South Africa remains blue. The justice to which Piet Retief appeals when our fathers said farewell to the Cape Colony, and to which Joachim Prinsloo called aloud in the Volksraad of Natal . . . the justice to which the burghers of the Transvaal entrusted their case at Paarde Kraal in 1880, remains immutable."[18] Despite appearances, *A Century of Wrong* did not set out to reject the imperial values of "justice" and "civilisation" in the name of some alternative "republican" ideal; its basic demand was that the imperial ideal of "justice" should be applied equally and fairly also in relation to the republics. In effect, this was an internal critique of the applications of "British justice" that located itself within the world of the British Empire. In principle, it followed that if "British justice" would only be properly applied in the case of the republics and the Afrikaners/Boers, then there would be no reason why the latter could not come to a political accommodation with the imperial powers. In this sense there was no inconsistency in Smuts and Roos, as the "authors" of *A Century of Wrong*, taking up leading political and administrative positions in the Transvaal and then Union government's alliance with the new British Liberal government only a few years after the South African War.

Aftermath: From the Afrikaner-Nationalist Appropriation of a Victim-Based Solidarity-Building Discourse to Its Ironic Reversal

In retrospect it might appear that *A Century of Wrong*, published *prior* to the South African War, prepared the way for the nationalist understanding of the most traumatic episode of Afrikaner loss and suffering, that of the "scorched earth" policy and especially of the mass deaths of women and children in the British concentration camps during the latter part of the South African War. As many as twenty-eight thousand died in the camps, more than six times as many as the forty-five hundred who had been killed in combat and amounting to some 10 percent of the Afrikaner population at the time. *A Century of Wrong* provided a ready-made template within which this human and national disaster could be interpreted in postwar Afrikaner-nationalist literature and historiography. In F. A. van Jaarsveld's words: "After the war the concentration camps assumed the importance in the historical image that Slagtersnek and the sufferings of the Voortrekkers in Natal had in that context before the war."[19]

However, this did not come about as smoothly as van Jaarsveld's statement might suggest. An occasional historical account, such as J. A. Smith's *Brit en Boer van Slagtersnek tot Jopie Fourie* (Brit and Boer from Slagtersnek to Jopie Fourie, 1917), did incorporate the war and the concentration camps into the Slagtersnek narrative, but this was a marginal publication. Nor was it a case of the living memories of the traumas of war being spontaneously expressed in line with this narrative template. In the immediate aftermath of the war there was indeed a proliferation of personal memoirs, war diaries, and other participant publications, including a significant number by surviving women recounting their sufferings in the British concentration camps. But few, if any, of these personal testimonies made connections with the core narrative of the Afrikaner "nation," or with the atrocity story of Slagtersnek. It was at a different and more symbolic level, that is, in the writings of Afrikaans poets and cultural entrepreneurs, that the personal suffering and political pain of the mass concentration camp deaths were appropriated into the narrative template of national victimization. The legacy of *A Century of Wrong* can be traced through the work of the theologian Totius (son of S. J. du Toit) and other seminal Afrikaans poets, in the campaign led by former President Steyn to commemorate the victims of the concentration camps with the Vrouemonument in Bloemfontein, in the popular nationalist writings of Langenhoven and in the cultural project of a populist historian like Gustav Preller.[20] Meanwhile, few serious historical studies of the war itself were produced in the first two or three decades of the twentieth century. It was through nationalist rhetoric and public commemoration, culminating in the Centennial of the Great Trek in 1938, that the memory of the concentration camps was made part of the core narrative. In his seminal study *The Rise of Afrikanerdom*, the sociologist Dunbar Moodie described this process of ethnic mobilization as the elaboration of an Afrikaner "civil religion." Significantly, Moodie's account relied heavily on *A Century of Wrong* for the narrative and central themes (including the legend of Slagtersnek) of its ideal-typical description of the Afrikaner "sacred history." In this victim-based discourse, the sufferings of Afrikaner women were socialized as that of the "nation": "The sufferings of these righteous, innocent victims . . . the patience and enduring faith of the women in the concentration camps carried a further message for every Afrikaner."[21]

The counterpart of this Afrikaner-nationalist appropriation of the human and historical traumas of the concentration camps was a particularistic narrowing of its significance in ethnic and racial terms. From a humanitarian and human rights perspective, the atrocities and war crimes suffered by the civilian victims of the British "scorched earth" policies and use of mass concentration camps were justifiably denounced, both at the time and later, as "methods of barbarism." But Afrikaner women and children were by no means the only such victims. Not only did the camp deaths include a not insignificant number of 1,676 men, but the mass concentration camps set up for black people (in total sixty-six camps confining more than one hundred thousand inmates) resulted in an estimated twenty thousand deaths of black women and children.[22] Though this discourse was victim-based, its solidarity-building did not extend to all civilian victims, and the mass black deaths in the concentration camps were not recognized as part of the story of the "nation," and indeed virtually disappeared from general historical consciousness in twentieth-century South Africa.

The exclusive ethnic focus on Afrikaner women and children as victims of the concentration camps may also be compared with the humanitarian project of Emily Hobhouse. It was primarily Hobhouse's intervention that brought the civilian deaths and atrocious conditions in the camps to public attention in Britain. Though she had some connections to British pro-Boer circles, Hobhouse's motives were broadly humanitarian, not political or nationalist. At the time her campaign also did not extend to the similar fate of black women and children in the concentration camps, reflecting her limited sources and contacts in the prevailing wartime conditions. However, the subsequent Afrikaner-nationalist commemoration of the human and political traumas of the concentration camps came to be quite deliberately defined in exclusive ethnic and racial terms. In time these duly contributed to the human disasters of apartheid forced resettlement practices. Arguably, the humanitarian concerns of a Cosmas Desmond for the millions of "discarded peoples" who became the victims of apartheid "homelands" and resettlement policies by the later twentieth century can be regarded in line with Hobhouse's legacy.[23]

The inversion whereby "South Africa" once again became a global humanitarian and human rights concern, with the descendants of the Boers no longer cast as the victims of imperial injustice but now as perpetrators of apartheid injustice, was reflected in the ironic afterlife of A Century of Wrong as a title for the construction of counter-narratives of South African history from a Black or Africanist perspective. Significantly, this occurred in politically charged commemorative contexts. Thus Three Centuries of Wrong by Melanchton (the pseudonym of Patrick Duncan, who would later become a member of the Pan-Africanist Congress) appeared in 1952, at the time of the tercentenary celebrations of the Van Riebeeck festival. Other publications, such as Three Hundred Years, by Mnguni (Hosea Jaffe), also set out to construct an Africanist counter-narrative, even if not explicitly using the same title. Also in 1952 Dr. S. M. Molema, historian and treasurer of the African National Congress, published two articles in Bantu World titled "A Historical Parallel and Warning."[24] These inversions involved more than the appeal of a catchy title. Just as A Century of Wrong had developed an internal critique of "British justice," these counter-narratives set out to turn the tables on the erstwhile "Boer" victims of imperial might by publicly shaming them with reference to shared notions of "justice" and "civilisation." In due course Sharpeville and other political atrocities of apartheid rule would come to serve as established way stations in the alternative victim-based solidarity-building discourse of anti-apartheid resistance, though the international anti-apartheid movement would prove more substantial and sustained than the pro-Boer movements had ever been. By this time, too, not only the Boer republics but also the British Empire itself had made way for a new international order subscribing to a notion of "justice" for which *A Century of Wrong* had, even if only indirectly, in some sense prepared the way.

NOTES

1. *A Century of Wrong*, issued by F. W. Reitz (London: Review of Reviews, 1899); 2nd ed. of 1900 with preface by W. T. Stead, 1 January 1900 (this is the version cited here).

2. Anna de Villiers, " 'n Historiese Geheim Opgeklaar: Wie die Skrywer van 'Een Eeuw van Onrecht' is," *Die Huisgenoot*, 6 July 1934; W. J. de Kock, "Een Eeuw van Onrecht," *Die Brandwag*, 30 August 1957.

3. Anon., *Een Eeuw van Onrecht* (Dordrecht: Morks & Geuze, 1899); 2nd ed. 1900; anon., *A Century of Injustice* (Baltimore, 1899).

4. See G. J. Schutte, *Nederland en de Afrikaners: Adhesie en Aversie* (Franeker, the Netherlands: T. Wever, 1986), 38–44; Chris A. J. van Koppen, *De Geuzen van de Negentiende Eeuw: Abraham Kuyper en Zuid-Afrika* (Maarssen, the Netherlands: Inmerc, 1992); Vincent Kuitenbrouwer, *A War of Words: Dutch Pro-Boer Propaganda and the South African War (1899–1902)* (Amsterdam: UvA-DARE, 2010).

5. *Ein Jahrhundert voller Unrecht: Ein Rückblick auf die Süd-afrikanische Politik Englands* (Berlin: Walther, 1900); *Un Siecle d'injustice* (Paris: Dupont, 1900); *Stoletiie nespravedlivosti. Sbornik materialov po anglo-burskoi voine v Yuzhnoi Afrike* (St. Petersburg, 1900), vol. 3.

6. *A Century of Wrong*, 3.

7. *A Century of Wrong*, 17.

8. *A Century of Wrong*, 49.

9. Kuitenbrouwer, *War of Words*, 182.

10. Kuitenbrouwer, *War of Words*.

11. M. C. E. van Schoor, "Die Galgeskaduwee van Slagtersnek," *Die Taalgenoot*, March–April 1957; L. M. Thompson, "The Strange Career of Slagtersnek," in *The Political Mythology of Apartheid* (New Haven, CT: Yale University Press, 1985), 105–143.

12. Henry Cloete, *Five Lectures on the Emigration of the Dutch Farmers from the Colony of the Cape of Good Hope and Their Settlement in the District of Natal* (1856).

13. F. A. van Jaarsveld, "The Afrikaner's Image of His Past," in *The Afrikaner's Interpretation of South African History* (Cape Town: Simondium, 1964), 56. Ironically,

Theal's own later *History of the Boers in South Africa* (London: Swan Sonneschein, 1887), 70, made a point of playing down the significance of Slagtersnek.

14. J. F. van Oordt, *Paul Kruger en de Opkomst van de Zuid-Afrikaansche Republiek* (Amsterdam: HAUM, 1898), 754–756; C. N. J. du Plessis, *Uit de geschiedenis van de Zuid-Afrikaansche Republiek en van de Afrikaanders* (Amsterdam: De Bussy, 1898), 185–187.

15. N. Hofmeyr, *De Afrikaner-Boer en de Jameson-inval* (1896), 21.

16. The popular meaning of "Slagtersnek" was reinforced by the name itself, which literally meant "Butchers' Neck" and has no doubt been taken by many to refer to the historical location of the botched execution. In fact, though, this was a double mistake. The name of the actual Slagtersnek referred to its having been the location where butchers' agents from Cape Town came to buy sheep and cattle from the colonists, but that was not the scene of the execution of the Bezuidenhout rebels, which took place at Van Aardtspos, twelve miles south of Slagtersnek. The "story of Van Aardtspos" would not have carried the same force.

17. *A Century of Wrong*, 6.

18. *A Century of Wrong*, 96–97.

19. Van Jaarsveld, "Afrikaner's Image," 56.

20. Irving Hexham, "Afrikaner Nationalism 1902–1924," in *The South African War: The Anglo-Boer War 1899–1902*, ed. Peter Warwick (London: Longman, 1980), 386–403.

21. T. Dunbar Moodie, *The Rise of Afrikanerdom: Power, Apartheid and the Afrikaner Civil Religion* (Berkeley: University of California Press, 1975), 17–18.

22. Stowell V. Kessler, "The Black and Coloured Concentration Camps," in *Scorched Earth*, ed. Fransjohan Pretorius (Cape Town: Human & Rousseau, 2001), 132–154.

23. Cosmas Desmond, *The Discarded People: An Account of African Resettlement in South Africa* (Johannesburg: Christian Institute, 1969).

24. See also P. S. Joshi, *The Tyranny of Colour: A Study of the Indian Problem in South Africa* (Durban: E. P. & Commercial Printing Co., 1942), 8–11.

Six

THE TEXT IN THE WORLD, THE WORLD THROUGH THE TEXT

Robert Baden-Powell's *Scouting for Boys*

ELLEKE BOEHMER

When in the years following its first publication Robert Baden-Powell's primer *Scouting for Boys* (1908) generated the soon-to-be global Scout movement, intended in part to secure the empire, it also disseminated principles of brotherhood and fellowship around the world.[1] These principles, which the empire-backing Father of Scouting had derived from like-minded imperialists such as Cecil John Rhodes and Rudyard Kipling, he alchemized through the medium of his charismatic text. The core ideas that animated the handbook therefore not only were borrowed from elsewhere, hence in a sense already networked, but also, more interesting, were, like the book, planetary and leveling, both in the outreach they implied and in the democratizing influence they in fact had. Moreover, while Scouting's sources and appeal were on one level gendered male, its generic forms—the value placed on survival and endurance, the importance of team building—bore a distinct feminine imprint, and this ensured a significant outreach to girls and young women.

Scouting for Boys was published only a decade before the conflagration of empires that was World War I. The vision of global friendship the handbook expressed went on to ramify along divers surprising routes, stimulating anti-imperial and internationalist responses across the British Empire and beyond. So Rabindranath Tagore in his 1917 indictment of Western imperialism, the essay "Nationalism," looked forward, not unlike Baden-Powell, to the bonds of amity that he believed alone might save the nations of the world from waging war on one another.

In Téa Obreht's 2011 Orange Prize–winning novel *The Tiger's Wife*, set in the aftermath of the Bosnian war of the early 1990s, Rudyard Kipling's *The Jungle Book* figures as an important talisman.[2] The narrator's grandfather, who has always taken her to see the tigers at the Belgrade zoo, across his life carries a yellowed copy of *The Jungle Book* in his breast pocket. It is to the granddaughter irrefutable proof that he has died, rather than gone missing, when his copy of the book disappears, though his other personal effects are rescued. In the course of the novel we learn that Kipling's text bears a profound significance for him because it harks back to an important period in his childhood, when he joined forces with a dumb pariah girl in his village, the so-called tiger's wife, in befriending an escaped tiger. In an unlettered community with no knowledge of tigers, the grandfather's copy of *The Jungle Book*, with its illustrations of Shere Khan, allowed him to identify the tiger when it first arrived in the area. Thereafter, he forms common cause with the girl as she is able to "read" the illustrations and recognize, as he does, that the tiger is not a devil, as the community thinks, and therefore that the tiger's friends, like the girl, should not be considered pariahs either. The recessive if insistent presence of the female in the tale is noteworthy, and will crop up again in interesting ways in this only-on-one-level masculine history of the worldwide reception and influence of *Scouting for Boys*.

As a colonial-era collection of tales for British children, *The Jungle Book* (1894) has no meaning for Obreht's grandfather. Its effect on him, sharpened by his youthful acquaintance with the girl, is to teach respect for the wild and compassion for the underdog. Subsequently, as he grows up, the book turns into a constant, indestructible presence in his life, almost a superhandbook, or a spiritual companion. After any crisis he brings it out as a touchstone of what's important and what endures; even in extremity he refuses to give it up.[3] *The Jungle Book* lies in more ways than one close to his hand and his heart.

The concept of the book that operates in transformative if unpredictable ways both as a physical presence and as a set of ideas, which is dramatized in Obreht's novel, resonates throughout my account of Robert Baden-Powell's influential *Scouting for Boys*. (The template book in this case was

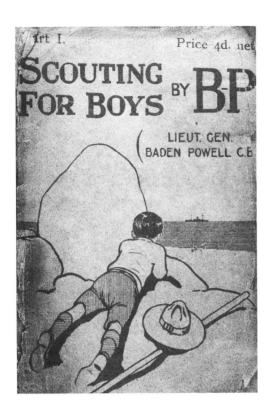

also, not insignificantly, a book by the empire laureate, Rudyard Kipling.) In spite of its overt imperialist message and the jingoist context out of which it emerged, Baden-Powell's primer had far-reaching leveling effects, moving colonial relations along less hierarchical axes. Moreover, as an affordable handbook, carried in Scouts' pockets or backpacks and literally passed from hand to hand between them (as captured in the wear and tear of the Parts edition cover shown in figure 6.1), these youth-to-youth leveling effects were physically expressed—in how the book was shared, jointly used, collectively pored over, bandied about, passed around and on. This concept of the book as an effective object and hence as object agent connects with Carol Gluck's notion that words—and books—do work in the world, "organizing, mobilizing, inspiring, excluding."[4] A book, as both Obreht and Gluck acknowledge, can come to stand for a single popular and reproducible idea—in respect to Baden-Powell's handbook, friendship regardless of cultural, racial, or social divides. Taking Obreht's grandfather's experience as an illustrative lesson, this essay will consider how a principle, here of scouting as same-sex, not exclusively fraternal, bonding, encapsulated for

Baden-Powell in the figure of Kipling's eponymous character Kim, "friend of all the world," could be serialized and creatively expanded within a cultural text, notably Baden-Powell's Scouting primer. It will also consider how this serialization and expansion produced changed social structures and cultural perceptions—for women as well as for men, for Indians and Africans as well as for Europeans and people of European descent.

A Brotherly Book

Scouting for Boys (1908), the handbook that generated a worldwide youth movement, persuasively disseminated an ideal of brotherly fellowship around the British Empire—something that till then had been concentrated largely in elite political circles in Britain and among some white men in the colonies. Through the democratizing medium of cheap, accessible print, first, and through its explicit citation of national and international circuits and their mobilizing ideas, second, as will be seen, the handbook quickly mobilized local, regional, national, and global readerships. The text, almost in spite of itself, or its author's ideological make-up, cast the hierarchical vision of imperial bonding between strong men, which the chief scout had derived from imperialist thinkers like Rudyard Kipling and Cecil John Rhodes (who in turn had it from Charles Dilke and J. R. Seeley), onto a horizontal axis. Its direct mode of address to boys (though not always explicitly excluding girls) invited the wide world of Baden-Powell's experience and adventure reading into the text, and in consequence the text, galvanized, rapidly began to move out into that wider world.[5] In effect, the book generated a worldwide network by animating and promoting the idea of networks and networking.

By 1909, one year on from first publication, Scouting had been adopted in New Zealand, in Australia's New South Wales and Victoria, and by British boys in India, and by 1910 it had successfully taken off in the United States, the year that the Girl Guide movement was also formed, widening the Scouting network still further. Headed up first by Baden-Powell's sister Agnes, and then by his wife, Olave, the Girl Guide movement was inaugurated in response to popular appeal from the sisters and friends of the first Boy Scouts, who did not necessarily feel themselves shut out of the broad and seemingly inclusive landscape that the handbook's democratic terms of address appeared to sketch. The female version of the Scout handbook, *Girl Guiding* (1918), though it paid lip service to the importance for girls of fulfilling domestic duties, also addressed the interests of these new recruits, encouraging them to show self-reliance and to be prepared to defend the empire alongside its frontiersmen.[6] Emerging in more or less the same period as the movement for women's suffrage (from 1903), not coincidentally, the appeal of Scouting ideas to girls and young women was such that in 1913 Annie Besant, the social reformer and early feminist, started up Scouting among native Indians in India. Besant found no contradiction in seeing Scouting as a realization of her ideal commonwealth of nations, to the extent that she took the Scouting oath of loyalty before Baden-Powell in Madras on the occasion of his first visit to the subcontinent.[7] However, already some years before this time, in 1917, at the height of World War I, when Besant herself was president of the Indian National Congress, the 1913 Nobel laureate Rabindranath Tagore had outlined in his influential essay on nationalism an internationalist approach not markedly different from the crossregional and transnational interchange that Baden-Powell saw expressed in Scouting.

Baden-Powell began to write *Scouting for Boys* in about 1904 in the heady aftermath of his endeavors at the Second Anglo-Boer War siege of Mafeking (1899–1900), and in quest of a new leadership role with which he might capitalize on this success. By this stage he had talked to both Rudyard Kipling and Cecil John Rhodes about the importance for the empire of Anglo-Saxon brotherhood and of fostering a sense of duty and honor in its citizens. Along with many other military and civilian leaders at the time, including Lord Frederick Roberts and William Smith, the founder of the militaristic and Christian Boys' Brigade (1883), Baden-Powell was convinced of the need in Britain for military preparedness training, British troops in South Africa having been found to be severely lacking as physical specimens.[8] Himself a product of the British public school Charterhouse and of the British army, the future chief scout was firmly of the opinion that the virtues of physical and moral discipline and character-building offered by the school playing field should be made available further down the social hierarchy, in order that Britain's grip on its empire might be maintained. In a characteristically ad hoc, haphazard way, he addressed these conjoined personal and national anxieties by cobbling together on bits of notepaper and the backs of menus and invitation cards a "self-instructor" for boys, filled with stories and illustrations. His intention was for this crafted and collage-like handbook to demonstrate in an informal, down-home style how Britain's young men might achieve moral improvement through tracking and scouting exercises, while at the same time safeguarding the nation and securing the empire. (Baden-Powell's paratactic, "add-on" mode of composition bears some similarity with the way other authors examined in these pages, most obviously M. K. Gandhi, but also Wakefield, first assembled or cobbled together their works literally out of bits and pieces—letters, separately published newspaper articles, interviews, and other pieces of journalism.)

Scouting for Boys was eventually published in 1908, first in six fortnightly parts, then as a book. Although it emerged in a time of growing imperial disaffection not entirely propitious for the making of child imperialists, as was reflected for example in J. A. Hobson's excoriating critique Imperialism (1902) and in the 1906 Liberal landslide, the handbook with its digressive anecdotal style was a wildfire popular success.[9] By the time the sixth and final issue was published in April 1908, jam-packed with fun but instructive games and practical tips, boys as well as girls across Britain were writing to Baden-Powell about how to start Scouting—though he in fact had no formal program or structures yet in place to cater to their enthusiasm. This haphazardness is clearly on show at the level of the book's inadvertent yet strongly felt appeal to early twentieth-century modern girls, the self-aware daughters of the 1890s New Woman, who, despite the book's title and the overriding accent on fostering masculinity, did not feel themselves excluded from the book's recommendations on fitness, well-being, and survival in the wild.[10] To the contrary, many of the ideal Scout's salient features were traits to which these modern girls also aspired: independence, self-reliance, pragmatism, social service.[11]

Several interrelated explanations can be offered for the immediate popularity of this on one level derivative and partly plagiarized mishmash text. Few of its more successful popular elements had been planned with any kind of foresight by Baden-Powell or his advisors, so it was the felicitous, pick-and-mix combination of these aspects perhaps, more than anything else, that accounted for the rocketing dissemination of Scouting ideas. A key internal feature was the book's direct, no-nonsense address to its young readers, coupled with its collage-like structure, broken up into bite-sized chunks of information such as suited a young person's attention span, as Baden-Powell himself opined.[12] The book, he believed, appealed not only to the power but also the structure of its target reader's imagination; its physical look invited involvement, it welcomed wear and tear. Its model was the Boy's Own journal, which used short articles interspersed with bold section headings, wide margins, and illustrations. Transposed to *Scouting for Boys*, this eye-catching layout (nicely supplemented by Baden-Powell's charming line drawings) invited young readers in, encouraging them to explore Scouting rules, tips, and ruses on their own or with friends, to fill the gaps in the text with activity.

On advice from Pearson, Baden-Powell's handbook had been shaped throughout, both in its internal, seemingly homespun makeup and in its external "easy to use" aspect, by the mass-circulation print technology that produced it, probably as much as by the pell-mell process of its creation, as will be seen in more detail. Therefore, it actively responded to and played back into the popular print culture out of which it had emerged.[13] Affordable and widely available, in both serial and book form, the text worked hard at every level as a self-help primer, showing through the medium of accessible concrete explanation how its readers might act on its advice, with a minimum of outlay, no matter what their social status or geographical position. As long as they could read (and after the 1870 Education Act many more could now do so, including young women), most boys (and some girls) could become Scouts (or Guides) simply by acting on Baden-Powell's no-fuss guidelines and low-tech exercises, transmitted in the shape of a hospitable "fireside" story, or what I will term a charismatic form.

Complementing its physical aspects, another key feature of the primer was the shaping force of its ideas. Scouting was based, in essence, on an interconnected cluster of durable core values—self-regulation, social responsibility, conservation, a sense of personal integrity—which were to be put into practice through a range of attractive, universally realizable group activities. At the same time, as noted, both the handbook and Baden-Powell's new movement tapped into still widely dominant imperialist and racial thinking: the belief in white male superiority, the rightness of British civilization, and the importance of that civilization's implantation across the world.[14] Read against the background of the colonialist and frontier settings from which the text effectively emerged (Baden-Powell having seen action on various contested colonial borderlines—Afghanistan, Asanteland, Mashonaland, Mafeking), *Scouting for Boys* can be viewed as in this sense a textual "speaking tube." It transmitted such "pro-consular" thinking, in the words of historian Bill Schwarz, first to the British masses in danger of regression, and then to Britain's settler children around the world. The handbook's prominent ideological values and assumptions in effect cooperated with Pearson's print mechanisms to persuade its young audiences that anyone with the proper conviction, combined with common sense, energy, and an imagination, could go out and become a Scout. Indeed, so current and popular were Scouting's central concepts (also including self-help and child-centered learning, as well as the importance of physical fitness and cleanliness) that Baden-Powell could as author get away without much acknowledgment of his sources. What chiefly concerned him was the pertinence of his social message and the importance of communicating it in the most vivid way possible, not shoring it up with a scholarly apparatus. As this suggests, in *Scouting for Boys*, from the get-go, the concepts of the book as accessible printed text, and as a vehicle for the mobilizing of influential ideas, were dynamically conjoined.

One of the more durable and potent of Scouting's core ideas was its vision of world fraternity and friendship across national borders, something that the handbook advocated from its opening pages. Indeed, it must count as the book's—as much as the author's—lasting achievement to have gradually converted this at first hierarchical if already influential vision into a democratizing force. Ideals of a linked Greater Britain beyond the seas that animated both metropolitan and settler cultures in the final decades of the nineteenth century had first developed in the midcentury period as a means of consolidating the white empire.[15] The planet-spanning, "railway-girt" entity presciently conjured in Charles Dilke's travelogue *Greater Britain* of 1868 was also propagated in the writing of imperial historians both Tory and Liberal, including J. A. Froude and J. R. Seeley.[16] For these opinion makers, empire essentially involved the propagation of English ethnicity, conceived as a brotherhood, around the world. In mobilizing that brotherhood, *Scouting for Boys* therefore joined forces with works like Dilke's or Seeley's *The Expansion of England* (1883), building on the ideological foundations that these earlier books had laid down. Inculcating the "racial" values of self-discipline and service, Baden-Powell's book on one level effectively set out to expand and reinforce white Greater Britain beyond the seas. Yet even as it galvanized these at once brotherly and ethnic links, *Scouting for Boys* also propagated to audiences other than the English abroad (and also, arguably, lower middle and working classes at home) the powerful idea of a brotherly network, and in particular the way a network might inculcate a sense of identity.

Toward the century's end, from the mid-1890s up to 1906, in the years that Baden-Powell was composing his primer, the ambitious colonial secretary Joseph Chamberlain gave the idea of Greater Britain, or worldwide Englishness, a predominantly economic interpretation when he campaigned for the empire to become a *zollverein* or free trade area, an economic consolidation of the idealized network of English-speaking peoples. Chamberlain's initiatives failed, but the idea of an "English" fraternity across the seas bracketed together under one imperial government continued to underpin ideologies of Englishness and to animate the popular media as well as social and cultural policy throughout the Dominions.[17] It was now widely believed that it was in the domain of culture, where it had first emerged, rather than in the economic or political sphere, that the Greater Britain idea might best thrive, drawing the Anglo-Saxon nations closer together in mutually beneficial ways. Very much in this spirit, *Scouting for Boys* opens with a direct appeal to "Scouts of the [British] nation" and to their interconnectedness through shared values and loyalties. At the same time, the Scouting activities that are recommended clearly aim to introduce such ideals of transnational amity into the everyday lives of all young people, at first within the empire, but then, at least implicitly, far beyond. ("Greater Britain" did not necessarily exclude the United States. Moreover, Zulus and Native Americans, too, at least in Baden-Powell's estimation, as will be seen, had Scouting potential.)

Despite his carelessness about sources, Baden-Powell references Rudyard Kipling, Robert Louis Stevenson, and Arthur Conan Doyle at the end of the very first section of the first part of *Scouting for Boys*, suggesting that to him, imaginings of world brotherhood and imperial federation bore the unmistakable imprimatur of storytellers and parable makers rather than of politicians.[18] There is little doubt that it was his citation of these popular and well-known cultural narratives that massively facilitated the dissemination and democratization of Scouting as concept and as movement. In relation to Kipling, at the time the most prominent of these literary influences, Baden-Powell clearly intuited something of the extent to which the poet was plugged into, and himself was seen to electrify, the central ideals that animated the empire at its height. Therefore, by including "Kim's story" at the very head of his handbook, Baden-Powell not only cannily added the authority of this "master work of imperialism" to the Scout's work of special observation and collaboration in groups.[19] He also enlisted the figure of Kipling's already widely beloved boy hero Kim to serve as itself a channel for the transmission of fraternal ideas. The eponymous novel had been published three years before Baden-Powell began writing, in 1901.

The focus on Kipling as a key source for Scouting's charismatic handbook should not, however, obscure the force of other more recessive yet still powerful cultural narratives operating within the text—narratives that, moreover, manifest something of empire's material histories of dispossession and appropriation as these were expressed on the ground, across different geographies, and then distilled into Baden-Powell's handbook. For example, *Scouting for Boys* is full of Native American knowledge about how to survive in the wild using tracking and scouting skills, which Baden-Powell derived in the first instance from the work of Ernest Thompson Seton and James Fenimore Cooper, among others, but which white settlers in the Americas had long since taken over, if not forcibly extracted, from native cultures in order to survive in that unfamiliar environment. The "Scout's Play" titled "Pocahontas" in part 1, in which "the Princess" intercedes for John Smith with her father, encapsulates (while simultaneously sanitizing) this history of appropriation. The uneasy makeshift compromise that the playlet represents is also curiously exposed, however, in the concluding scene, when the defeated native scouts bizarrely break into a Zulu praise song.[20] Elsewhere in *Scouting for Boys*, Zulu culture as Baden-Powell understood it provides models for Scouts' exercises, "war dances," and terms of address. Even the wood badge, an important feature of a Scout leader's uniform, was reputedly copied from the *iziqu*, or wooden beads, of the Zulu king Dinizulu's ceremonial necklace, or one like it, a copy of which Baden-Powell is said to have removed from the body of a dead Zulu woman after being involved in an 1888 skirmish against a Zulu village in Natal.[21] The buried minihistory offers a telling instance of how a repressed female tradition could be transformed by appropriation and then incorporated into official Scouting practice.

On the subject of recessive narratives in *Scouting for Boys*, its dominant concern with the fit male body, as well as brotherly friendship between boys and men, raised questions across the course of the twentieth century as to whether one of its encoded discourses was not homosocial—and therefore whether Scouting as a practice carried the potential to foster homophilic or male-loving links. Under the possible double entendre of its title, commentators in this vein have noted, among other topics, the muted homosexual associations of some Scouting exercises, the explicit exclusion of girls from camping activities, and the seemingly ambiguous sexuality of the founder of Scouting himself.[22] In respect of such questions, it must at once be acknowledged that Scouting's brotherly dynamics very obviously took on the imprint of the male-male bonding that the relative freedoms of late Victorian and Edwardian imperial service made available—freedoms that were, however, disallowed at home.[23] Baden-Powell's biography suggests that he generally preferred male company, a preoccupation that is reflected in the bodily aesthetic of his text. Yet it is also clear that the text's male-male imagery is not necessarily hostile to the participation of women or of men less comfortable with homoerotic play. Ultimately, the predominant preoccupation of *Scouting for Boys* is with manliness, over and above the ambiguities of sexuality—and manliness is something that can be fostered both by way of the lone survival exercises it recommends and through bonding in the bush or on the school playing field. In effect, Baden-Powell "transmutes the problem of sexuality into the process of formulating a robust if defensive manliness."[24]

Scouting for Boys *in Mass Circulation*

Though its initial address to its target audience of British boys was based on hierarchical lines, aimed at "scouts of the empire" and national hero figures, the print channels through which *Scouting for Boys* disseminated that message were, from the beginning, democratizing: the handbook did not discriminate as to who *felt* they might be scouts. It was this leveling impact on its audience, which underwrote the handbook's paratactic and charismatic makeup, and was reinforced by its message of friendship, that communicated powerfully across national, racial, and class boundaries. The Fourth Scout Law was, indicatively, the Kim-esque, and seemingly gender-neutral, asseveration "A Scout is a Friend to All."[25]

Scouting for Boys was published in six fortnightly parts, from 15 January 1908, by Horace Cox, a printer owned by the newspaper magnate C. Arthur Pearson, proprietor of such popular papers as the *Daily Express*, *Pearson's Weekly*, and *Tit-bits*. Having personally encouraged Baden-Powell to channel his scouting and tracking experiences into a training program for urban boys, Pearson was happy to grant him this access to a guaranteed nationwide audience. He also had no objection to the book's ramshackle, thrown-together aspect; on the contrary, he seemed to appreciate that it was in this form that it would most strongly appeal to its youthful readers. On 1 May 1908 Pearson published the clothbound complete edition, and for the rest of the year the fortnightly parts and the book version reappeared as if in tandem, the parts reprinting four times, the book five. The cheap edition of the book, priced at 1 shilling, that Pearson then produced sold at a rate of about five thousand copies a month in the United Kingdom alone. In 1948, fifty years and two world wars later, about fifty thousand copies of the book were still being sold annually in Britain alone. Figures for the rest of the world are significantly greater.

To this day, *Scouting for Boys* continues to rank as one of the best-selling Anglophone works of the twentieth century and has been translated into most of the world's major languages. Until after World War II, around 1950, its publishing figures were exceeded only by those of the Bible. As this suggests, Scouting has, since its inauguration, involved nearly 350 million people across the globe and exists in virtually all the world's countries. Across the twentieth century, enduring the rise and fall of nations and empires, there has been no secular movement with a greater global reach. Moreover, while Scouting's success in Britain's former white colonies was, relatively speaking, something of a matter of course, it is significant that the movement also enjoyed prestige and success in areas far outside Greater Britain. In British colonial Africa, for example, though the colonial authorities were keen to foster Scouting in order to inculcate loyalty to the empire, African boys and girls embraced the movement on their own initiative, "because they considered it entertaining, progressive and useful": "African Scouts had little difficulty separating their commitment to the movement with their distaste for the discriminatory realities of colonialism."[26] Not only Scouting the idea but also the charismatic Scouting handbook was instrumental in achieving this success.

Considering the speed with which Baden-Powell generated the primer, it perhaps stood to reason that he cannibalized his own as well as others' work in putting it together.[27] As the fragmentary aspect of the manuscript suggests, he seems to have jotted down notes whenever an idea struck him, and possibly, being ambidextrous, using now one hand, now the other. These haphazard notes, sketches, and useful quotations Baden-Powell's assistant, Mr. Cavan, then sorted into sections and typed up, feeding the typescript back to Baden-Powell for proofing and some expansion, in an ongoing process. On 28 February 1908, for example, four weeks after the publication of part 1, Baden-Powell sent off the proofs of part 5 of "S for B" for printing. At the same time, even while finishing the text, he was involved in a program of promotional lectures that Pearson had organized for the run-up to the 15 January launch date.

Throughout the writing, Pearson also supplied advice on this as it were interactive and "hands-on" process of composition. The text's division into six parts, ten chapters, and twenty-eight yarns harmonized with the entertainment formulae of *Pearson's Weekly* and, importantly, was seen as not talking down to its young readers. Baden-Powell's own account of this approach was several times repeated in so many words across the six parts of *Scouting for Boys*: "The best way of imparting theoretical instruction [is] to give it out in short instalments with ample illustrative examples when sitting round the camp fire or otherwise resting, and with demonstrations" (303). In August 2007 Baden-Powell tested out his methods in an experimental camp at Brownsea Island in Poole Harbour, concerned to make sure that his "'scouts' training" would work in practice, with "boys of all classes," the Brownsea group having been specially selected from both Eton College and Boys Brigade youth. The mix was intended to embody the need to bring different social levels and classes together in a common national purpose. As he wrote in his report on Brownsea, included in part 6: "One wants to bring all classes more in touch with each other, to break down the existing barriers, which are only artificial after all, and to teach them to give and take in the common cause instead of being at snarls of class against class, which is snobbery all round and a danger to the state" (302). He might have added "and to the empire." The message of breaking down barriers would be taken by the book's generations of readers to refer also to the snarls of nation against nation, and race against race, in far-reaching ways that Baden-Powell himself could not have anticipated and certainly had not planned for, but that both nationalist and internationalist thinkers in places distant from Baden-Powell's Edwardian Britain were to find congenial in mounting their own cases for a future beyond empire (and ultimately beyond nationalism). Tim Parsons indicatively observes that even fervently anticolonial Mau Mau fighters in Kenya "appreciated Scouting for its prestige and discipline," as did Irish nationalists in the 1910s and 1920s.[28] As for other books with a strong local and community appeal that are covered in this volume, the text was in this sense more farsighted and radical than its author, though its leveling, bridge-building effects were significantly enhanced by Pearson's canny publicity and marketing strategies.

So it was—in this micromanaged yet hodgepodge form—that B-P's idea of global interconnection fostered through scouting in teams was launched upon the humming communications networks of the wider British world. Yet Baden-Powell's close involvement with the text—as with the emerging movement the text now triggered—did not end there. Until 1922, the year the tenth edition was published, he modified and adapted *Scouting for Boys* between every edition, not to correct it so much as to broaden and globalize its social and cultural references, in order that England and Britain no longer be placed so firmly at the turning axis of the Scouting world. The handbook's more egregious imperialistic effusions, too, were bit by bit removed. Though the text in its first incarnation was watermarked with imperialist and eugenicist assumptions, as noted, it became increasingly more directed toward practical Scouting exercises, games, and badges. By 1910, two years after the book's first publication, Baden-Powell recognized, Scouting was effectively going global. Its economies of feeling and allegiance were being transnationalized, and its terminologies had to reflect the fact. This is a key point for any analysis of *Scouting for Boys* (and of Scouting) as a world form: the book's fluidity as a text meant that its mode of address and system of transnational allusion kept being widened, not least by Baden-Powell himself. It also meant, concomitantly, that Scouting's appeal to other movements committed to social widening, such as the women's suffrage movement, kept being strengthened. As Baden-Powell wrote in a highly symptomatic March 1925 letter in which he commented on the Scouts' increasingly difficult relationship with the emergent militaristic youth movement in Germany:

> The Boy Scout and the Girl Guide movement, which has now spread itself to Germany as well as to all other civilized countries, is bringing a considerable number—about two million active members of the oncoming generation into closer touch and personal acquaintance in comradeship which has its aim the single ideal of good citizenship and friendliness. Its open air attractions appeal alike to boys and girls of all nations. It is not unreasonable to hope that with the growth of this movement and the promotion of its ideals a notable change may be brought about a few years' time in the relationship between the peoples of the different nationalities, in the direction of peace and goodwill in place of jealousies and hostility.[29]

Imperial Networking: Tracking Kipling's Kim in Scouting for Boys

What shape did Scouting's ideal of friendship and brotherhood take that so correlated with conceptions of a globalized empire, and played out with such effectiveness within that empire's interconnected communications networks? The ideal was molded through and through, like a piece of Brighton rock, by the vision of England-beyond-the-seas of Rudyard Kipling, the bard of empire, as is evoked in several of his turn-of-the-century poems, most notably perhaps "A Song of the English" (1893). An intuitive popularizer, B-P was unembarrassed about siphoning some of the Anglo-Boer War glamour attached to Kipling's name into his yet-to-be-constituted movement, joining that glamour to his own already burnished reputation following the siege of Mafeking. In political terms, too, he was keen to nail his colors to the mast of imperial solidarity with which Kipling's rhetoric at this time was associated. Toward the rousing end of part 5, for example, Baden-Powell wrote in terms that Kipling would warmly have endorsed: "We must all be bricks in the wall of that great edifice—the British Empire—and . . . stick shoulder to shoulder as Britons if we want to keep our position among the nations" (292). Knowing well that the citation of the poet and storyteller on how to be an effective imperial operator would help to win him Scouts, B-P set out proactively to bring those audiences around by encapsulating Kipling's watchwords on honor, duty, and loyalty in some of the Scout Laws.

The notion of cross-empire interconnection that Baden-Powell cherished, therefore, not only was borrowed from a highly networked writer and hence always already "networked" but also was planetary in the outreach it signified—an impact further reinforced by the planetary reputation of Kipling. If the British Empire at its height around 1897, Queen Victoria's Diamond Jubilee year, is viewed as a vast circulation of commodities, money, and technology, Baden-Powell's book can be seen in part as having risen out of that circulation and then, in its turn, as having inspired other networks to emerge and to ramify.[30] It is this amplification of imperial interconnection between classes and nations, along a predominantly horizontal axis, that lies at the heart of the empire-transforming effects of *Scouting for Boys*. With its call to brotherhood, reinforced by its accessible makeup, the primer acted as both a powerful catalyst *and* a conduit for feelings of cross-empire solidarity, carrying British nationalist yet also transnationalist sentiments onto a global stage.[31]

But the influence of Kipling on *Scouting for Boys* was not only ideological and overtly imperialist; it was also strategic and imaginative. This is clearly demonstrated in the story of "Kim," a reductive précis of Kipling's novel presented by Baden-Powell as an iconic Scouting tale immediately following the short account, with which the handbook opens, of how he himself led a corps of boys in the defense of Mafeking. As this incorporation shows, a charismatic text like *Scouting for Boys* operates through drawing into its orbit universal stories, including popular tales and catchy anecdotes. In the handbook, with Kim's distinguishing characteristics of individualism, "strong-mindedness," and resourcefulness instrumentalized into prototypical Scouting traits, the literary boy hero of the Indian empire is decisively raised up as both a historical precursor to the Scout, and a model to be emulated.[32] The complexity of his native Indian and Irish identity and his ambivalent and divided allegiances—for example, to Colonel Creighton on the one hand and the Tibetan lama on the other—are completely erased from Baden-Powell's picture. Kim, the précis concludes, shows "what valuable work a boy scout could do for his country if he were sufficiently trained and sufficiently intelligent" (18).

The same work of observation—of being aware of one's surroundings and able to read terrain in order to move safely through it—is also explored in Kipling's Boer War stories, based on his "on-the-ground" experiences as a war reporter. Most noteworthy perhaps is "The Way That He Took," written around the same time as *Kim*, in which military preparedness and national security are again matters of concern.[33] However, *Kim*, the tale of a charismatic, pathfinding youth with remarkable powers of observation, is for the specific purposes of Scouts' training the more powerful and salutary tale. It provided an excellent way, for Baden-Powell, not only of bringing some of his high-minded scouting principles down to earth but also of simplifying his vision of the Greater British world to a manageable human scale. At a different but equally important interpretative level, Kim's story is also a persuasive demonstration of the principle that imperial power is expressed and wielded through the operation of systems of knowledge, as Edward Said influentially expressed it in *Orientalism*.[34] The self-made amateur spy B-P must have been in some sense aware that *Kim* dramatizes first how an empire is run on the basis of knowledge gathering, and then how that control over knowledge is wielded through a control over networks. Kim himself, the "Government Intelligence agent" in training, is an amateur ethnographer, preternaturally able to negotiate his way around the Indian rail network, as well as to read "secret signs" and decode their significance. Added to these qualities, he is also a gifted social and ethnic chameleon, speaking different vernacular languages flawlessly, passing as a native, and welcoming identification from all quarters, not excluding most Indians.

Along with the underlying keynote of vigilance, this is perhaps the most important thread from Kipling that B-P picks up in "Kim's Story," and then weaves right through *Scouting for Boys*, to the plea for imperial solidarity at the end of part 5 and the pageants of colonial brotherhood recommended in part 6: the crucial significance of networks for both imperial control and cross-empire interaction. Although Scouting's imperialist frame of reference was replaced by 1919, in the aftermath of World War I, to some extent, by B-P's new sense of the importance of world peace, his accent on networks as such remained strong. A decade or so after its inauguration, he was well aware, the Scout movement had caught on across cultural and national boundaries, precisely through the operation of different international bonds and ties. Keen that Scouting prosper wherever possible, he further recognized that such crosscultural interconnection conferred benefits in excess of the good of empire as such, and should therefore be encouraged, in an ecumenical way. In this respect the farsighted Fourth Scout Law as it appeared in the first edition is worth repeating in full: "A Scout is a Friend to All, and a Brother to Every Other Scout, no matter to what Social Class the Other belongs." Interestingly, at the point in the text where this law is first laid down, Kim's example is again cited, in a slightly different guise from before: "'Kim,' the boy scout, was called by the Indians 'Little friend of all the world,'" Baden-Powell writes, "and this is the name that every scout should earn for himself" (45). As this implies, the figure of the boy adventurer worked as something of a valve within the Scouting text, drawing in from the novel Kipling's own advocacy for imperial networks and then, in its turn, advocating for and promoting networks not only imperial but also transnational and intercultural.

In "Scout's Work," a short section sandwiched between the Mafeking and Kim stories in the opening pages of *Scouting for Boys* (1908), the Chief Scout attempts to define "scouts of the nation" avant la lettre, whom he finds embedded in what is essentially an Anglo-Saxon genealogical network, the "History of the Empire . . . made by British adventurers and explorers," extending from Canada through West Africa to the South Pacific (13–14). In part 6 he again seeks examples of "peace scouts" in "frontiersmen of our Empire in every corner of the world," ticking off in schoolbook fashion "MEN" in the different regions of the Anglophone globe: "the ranchmen, cowboys and trappers of the West; the drovers and bushmen of Australia," and so on (300), though once again not entirely excluding girls (Mary Kingsley, Grace Darling). Insofar as Scouting exemplars were thus found in all parts of Greater Britain, Scouting as life-lesson can be seen as repeating right across the empire, hence as binding more tightly together the ties of white imperial interconnection. As also for Kipling, "Faith" in the empire was to be maintained not only via its world-embracing communications networks and blood ties but also through the "words of [English] men," not excepting the precepts of *Scouting for Boys*, that "flicker and flutter and beat" across the "deserts of the deep."[35]

In *Imagined Communities* and the later *Spectres of Comparison*, his well-known analyses of modern nationalism, Benedict Anderson discusses the ways nationalist ideas are serialized or copied from one nationalist context to another.[36] Serialization occurs where networks of capitalist reproduction in general, and print cultures in particular, order the recurrence of certain commodities and meanings across spaces and regions far apart from one another. *Scouting for Boys* the handbook, itself serialized, mass-produced and mass-marketed, worked as a particularly effective vehicle of such serialization, that is, as a powerful charismatic text. It did so because it grafted Kim's story of individualist self-assertion onto a culture of teamwork, and animated and reanimated it via the stories, exercises, games, performances, and pageantry that *Scouting for Boys* recommended. It was in this form, of the Kim-like Scout figure, and of his female counterpart, the short-haired modern Girl Guide, each a synecdoche of an interconnected if still imperial world, that the Scouting ideal traveled across continents, resonating along the ganglia-like networks of the empire through which it had itself first been constituted. From this, it is not too great a stretch to claim that where once the Scout movement had been based on the crossborder workings of imperial and then international networks, some two or three decades later it was those same networks that were in part sustained via the worldwide serialization of Scouting ideas.

Tagore's Inter-"Nationalism"

As the generative intertextual links between *Kim* and *Scouting for Boys* indicate, within only a few years of its first publication the primer was instrumental in disseminating worldwide a strong and for the time radical sense of the importance of social and cultural interaction between peoples and nations. Both the book's message of fellowship and the boundary-crossing mechanisms of mass reproduction and circulation through which that message traveled recognized that such transimperial and transnational connection took place over and above—and even beyond—empire. By the end of World War I, certainly by the time of the last edition he revised himself, in 1922, the still-imperialist yet world-oriented Baden-Powell himself acknowledged as much, struggling as ever to keep pace with the widely ramifying youth movement his primer had inaugurated.

Suggestive evidence for the global circulation of Scouting-type principles of international brotherhood—and perhaps also sisterhood—comes from the collaborations that developed between anti-imperial and nationalist groupings in different parts of the empire around the time of World War I— developments that in effect unfolded in parallel with Scouting's worldwide dissemination.[37] Indian and Irish nationalists in cities across Europe and North America, for example, maintained close contact with one another in forging their campaigns for self-determination. Women's movements and campaigns for the vote in various different countries, spurred by the common purpose of female self-representation, often shared techniques and strategies (such as symbolic protest and the hunger strike). With specific reference to Scouting history, African Scouts in Britain's various colonies across the continent mutually encouraged one another to take up Scouting despite official resistance from some quarters. Irish nationalists in the buildup to the formation of the Irish Free State embraced Scouting and are said to have used their reconnaissance skills against the British military.[38]

An even more marked instance of message sharing, however, can be found in Tagore's 1917 essay "Nationalism," which he presented as a series of three lectures in Japan within a decade of *Scouting for Boys*, by which time the Scout movement had reached Indian shores. Although Tagore would not have found Scouting in its form of organized youth movement congenial, his meditation on the youthful Asian nations and their response to modernization in his tripartite essay is characterized by its warm endorsement of nation-to-nation friendship, something with which B-P would have found it hard to disagree. Throughout, the Bengali author is concerned to indict Europe's "cannibalistic" (or imperialist) political civilization, which, "overrunning the whole world like some prolific weed, is based upon exclusiveness."[39] To avoid the West's "wholesale feeding of nation upon nation," Japan and India, he urges, should strive to express their true selves via bonds of amity and inclusiveness. The close tie of friendship, he insists, "is the only natural tie that can exist between nations" in order to combat nationalist selfishness. Two options confront the age, therefore: that of "interminable competition" between peoples, as under Western imperialism, or that of constructive cooperation (69).

Like Tagore's *Nationalism*, like the women's campaign for the vote, Baden-Powell's *Scouting for Boys* had already some years before promoted a mentality that favored modes of transnational and intercultural attachment other than the reductively hierarchical and imperial, attachment that went well beyond Britain's borders. Just as Tagore signed up to an ideal of global community undivided by nationalist feelings, so B-P saw Scouts as belonging to a worldwide interconnected community that was not split up by national borders. It is in this sense that the League of Nations, founded in 1919, can be seen as, to a degree, a grownup version of Scouting, propagating as it did, and as did Tagore, principles of lateral connection between the nations.

FROM THE TIME of its first publication in serial form, Baden-Powell's Scouting handbook incrementally transformed the British Empire by shaping the way individuals related to each other in groups, especially groups bridging social and cultural differences. In addition to the immense popular appeal of scouting activities, the powerful worldwide attractiveness and hence influence of *Scouting for Boys* lay in how it took imperial preconceptions of vertical social organization and translated them, inadvertently in part, onto a horizontal plane of international exchange. Within only a few years of the handbook's publication, Scouting was the channel through which young people not only in the empire, or the Commonwealth that succeeded it, but far further afield, could reach out to each other and forge international connections, though without compromising their nationalist feelings.

Scouting for Boys is that highly anomalous "world form" that was born out of a nation and an empire in crisis, and that came to stimulate international solidarities and anti-imperial sentiments. Indeed, it stimulated those solidarities and sentiments in part through its anomalies as a world form: it was born out of one kind of global vision (exclusive, vertical) and ended up generating another (more inclusive, more horizontal). Shaped by the fluid and even chaotic conditions of its production, it became itself highly mobile and adapted to travel. Through the handbook's worldwide circulation, the democratizing aspects of Baden-Powell's message became detached from the imperial hierarchies he believed in, convincing even those whom Scouting would otherwise not have attracted of the boons and benefits of worldwide fellowship.

NOTES

1. Robert Baden-Powell, *Scouting for Boys*, ed. Elleke Boehmer (Oxford: Oxford University Press, 2004).
2. Téa Obreht, *The Tiger's Wife* (London: Random House, 2011).
3. Obreht, *Tiger's Wife*, 157, 168, 215.

4. Carol Gluck and Anna Lowenhaupt Tsing, eds., *Words in Motion: Toward a Global Lexicon* (Durham, NC: Duke University Press, 2009).

5. Eric Bulson, "Little Magazine, World Form," in *The Oxford Handbook to Global Modernisms*, ed. Mark Wollaeger (Oxford: Oxford University Press, 2012), 283.

6. Robert Baden-Powell and Agnes Baden-Powell, *Girl Guiding* (London: C. Arthur Pearson, 1918); Bill Schwarz, *The White Man's World: Memories of Empire*, vol. 1 (Oxford: Oxford University Press, 2011), 117.

7. Elleke Boehmer, "Global Nets, Textual Webs; Or What Isn't New about Empire?," *Postcolonial Studies* 7, no. 1 (2004): 11–26.

8. Martin Crotty, *Making the Australian Male: Middle-Class Masculinity 1870–1920* (Melbourne: University of Melbourne Press, 2001), 196–202; Tim Jeal, *Baden-Powell, Founder of the Boy Scouts* (London: Pimlico, 1991), 367–369.

9. Elleke Boehmer, "Note on the Text," in Baden-Powell, *Scouting for Boys*, xl–xliv.

10. Compare Baden-Powell, *Scouting for Boys*, 301 and 305.

11. Alys Eve Weinbaum et al., eds., *The Modern Girl around the World: Consumption, Modernity, and Globalization* (Durham, NC: Duke University Press, 2008).

12. Baden-Powell, *Scouting for Boys*, 306–308.

13. Bulson, "Little Magazine," 268; Leah Price, *How to Do Things with Books in Victorian Britain* (Princeton, NJ: Princeton University Press, 2012).

14. Schwarz, *White Man's World*.

15. Duncan Bell, *The Idea of Greater Britain: Empire and the Future of World Order* (Princeton, NJ: Princeton University Press, 2007); Robert Young, *The Idea of English Ethnicity* (Oxford: Blackwell, 2008), 196–230.

16. Charles Dilke, *Greater Britain: A Record of Travel in English-Speaking Colonies during 1866 and 1867*, 2 vols. (London: Macmillan, 1868), 1:2, 400.

17. See Charlotte Macdonald, *Strong, Beautiful and Modern: National Fitness in Britain, New Zealand, Australia and Canada, 1935–1960* (Wellington: Bridget Williams Books, 2011); Young, *English Ethnicity*.

18. Baden-Powell, *Scouting for Boys*, 19, 228.

19. Baden-Powell, *Scouting for Boys*, 14–19; Edward Said, introduction to *Kim*, by Rudyard Kipling (Harmondsworth, England: Penguin Classics, 1987), 45.

20. Baden-Powell, *Scouting for Boys*, 51–62.

21. Jeff Guy, "Imperial Appropriations: The Dynamic History of the *iziqu*," *Natal Museum Journal of Humanities* 11 (December 1999): 23–42.

22. Elleke Boehmer, introduction to Baden-Powell, *Scouting for Boys*, xi–xxxix; Elleke Boehmer, "At Once A-sexual and Anal: Baden Powell and the Boy Scouts," in *Children and Sexuality: From the Greeks to the Great War*, ed. George Rousseau (Basingstoke, England: Palgrave Macmillan, 2007), 299–311.

23. Joe Bristow, *Empire Boys: Adventures in a Man's World* (London: HarperCollins, 1991); Graham Dawson, *Soldier Heroes: British Empire, Adventure, and the Imagining of Masculinities* (London: Routledge, 1994); Christopher Lane, *The Ruling Passion: British Colonial Allegory and the Paradox of Homosexual Desire* (Durham, NC: Duke University Press, 1995).

24. Boehmer, "At Once," 306–307.

25. Baden-Powell, *Scouting for Boys*, 44–45.

26. Tim Parsons, *Race, Resistance and the Boy Scout Movement in British Colonial Africa* (Athens: Ohio University Press, 2004), 4–6.

27. Boehmer, "Note on the Text," xl–xliv.

28. Parsons, *Race*, 4–5.

29. Robert Baden-Powell, letter, 2 March 1925, cited in Daniel Scott-Davies, Archive and Heritage Manager, "Report on Relations between the Scout Association and Germany in the Inter-war Years, 2012," personal communication, 4–5 October 2012.

30. Rudyard Kipling, *War Stories and Poems*, ed. Andrew Rutherford (Oxford: Oxford University Press, 1990), i.

31. Elleke Boehmer, "The Worlding of the Jingo Poem," *Yearbook of English Studies* 41, no. 2 (2011): 41–57; Laurence Kitzan, *Victorian Writers and the Image of Empire: The Rose-Coloured Vision* (Westport, CT: Greenwood Press, 2001), 43.

32. Hugh Brogan, *Mowgli's Sons: Kipling and Baden-Powell's Scouts* (London: Cape, 1987), records B-P's extensive borrowing from the animal culture of the *Jungle Books* for the 1910s elaboration of his Scouting method in the Cubs, designed for younger boys who, too, had been clamoring to scout. No doubt aware that his influence on Scouting and Scouting's creator had been laid down some time before, Kipling was happy to authorize the borrowing.

33. Kipling, *War Stories*, 127–144; Kipling, *Kim*.

34. Edward Said, *Orientalism* (London: Routledge and Kegan Paul, 1978).

35. Rudyard Kipling, *The Definitive Edition of Rudyard Kipling's Verse* (London: Macmillan, 1989), 170–176.

36. Benedict Anderson, *Imagined Communities: Reflections on the Origin and Spread of Nationalism* (London: Verso, 1991), and *The Spectre of Comparisons: Nationalism, Southeast Asia and the World* (London: Verso, 1998).

37. Elleke Boehmer, *Empire, the National and the Postcolonial: Resistance in Interaction* (Oxford: Oxford University Press, 2002).

38. Padraig Pearce, one of the leaders of the 1916 Easter Rising, is said to have formed a Scout troop at the school where he taught. Daniel Scott-Davies, personal email communication, 4–5 October 2012.

39. Rabindranath Tagore, *Nationalism*, Great Ideas Series 95 (Harmondsworth, England: Penguin, 2010), 7–10.

Seven

HIND SWARAJ

Translating Sovereignty

TRIDIP SUHRUD

Written in 1909, Gandhi's manifesto *Hind Swaraj* has proved itself to be a text for the twenty-first rather than the twentieth century. Across the course of the last century, the book was misunderstood, ignored, or consciously rejected. Jawaharlal Nehru famously dismissed it as "completely unreal," while Gandhi's mentor G. K. Gokhale thought it "so crude and hastily conceived that he prophesied that Gandhiji would himself destroy the book after spending a year in India."[1] These views have been echoed by others, and apart from an enthusiastic reception in the United States, *Hind Swaraj* remained marginal and unread, even as Gandhi himself came to be internationally feted.

Nonetheless, over the last decade a powerful resurgence of interest in the text has occurred, sparked in part by its centenary in 2009 but equally by a group of scholars interested in understanding Gandhi's thinking on sovereignty outside the realm of abstract rights and the nation-state. In a recent book Faisal Devji notes that Gandhi's ideas far exceeded any notion of freedom in a national framework but were rather a much larger experiment with India as its instantiation. "India's mission, therefore, was not simply to liberate herself from imperialism, but set the precedent that would free the world as a whole from violence."[2]

This view was rooted in Gandhi's conviction that human society persists through the force of love and nonviolence, which enables the world to survive despite wars and violent events. Yet, as Gandhi noted, "history does not and cannot take note of this fact." As Devji notes, "only violence . . . was historical, because it was sporadic and therefore transformative in the limited way that allowed historians to define it as either a cause or an effect."[3]

Hind Swaraj offers a thoroughgoing critique of this configuration of violence, event, cause and effect, beginnings and endings. In a worldwide anti-imperial century, obsessed with just such endings and beginnings, it is hardly surprising that Gandhi's logic has remained recessive. As we move into an era invested in unpicking the nation-as-method as well as understanding the persistence of imperial structures in the world, Gandhi's text has started to come into its own.

Hence this essay explores *Hind Swaraj* as a text that has changed our ideas of empire retrospectively, by fundamentally challenging the nexus of history and causality itself. Gandhi spoke of *Hind Swaraj* as his seed text: as the seed comes to life, the seed itself is extinguished. Life within the seed may lie still and silent for a long time. Gandhi's ideas in *Hind Swaraj* have long lain dormant. This essay explores the radical proclivities and implications of the text by paying attention to its bilingual character and the nature of the ideas that this character enabled Gandhi to generate.

HIND SWARAJ WAS WRITTEN between 13 and 22 November 1909 aboard the steamer *Kildonan Castle* as Gandhi returned from England to South Africa. Ten days of almost continuous writing on the ship's stationery was marked by a restless intensity that Gandhi had never known before. He wrote when he could no longer "restrain" himself. The handwritten manuscript consists of eighty-eight questions posed by a "Reader" and eighty-eight responses by an "Editor" in twenty chapters spread over 271 pages, with an introduction in five pages. When the right hand tired, Gandhi wrote thirty-eight pages with his left hand. Those pages strangely bear a hand more firm and clear. No question was left unanswered. The manuscript bears 228 marks of erasures and corrections. Of these, twenty-one pertain to the questions by the Reader and bring a sharper focus to the large questions *Hind Swaraj* seeks to formulate: the meaning of human life and its possibility in modern civilization.

The journey aboard a ship is also a metaphor that can help us understand the fluidity of the text. It's a text in motion. The very form of dialogue suggests motion, conversation, poser and counterposer, where both the question and its response could explore doubt, hesitation, and uncertainty. Gandhi's choice of the form of dialogue was careful and deliberate. At once, he drew on the long tradition of exploring philosophical questions through the dialogic form and simultaneously sought to make the ideas more accessible to his readers. The essay form in Gujarati was not more than six decades old and was an acquired literary style.

This text was printed with meticulous exactness (in two installments, 11 and 18 December 1909) in *Indian Opinion*, the journal Gandhi nurtured as the voice of the struggle for Indian-Asiatic rights in South Africa and of Satyagraha as a mode of thought and of resistance. Gandhi's own sense of his relationship with the text is complex and elusive. Three days after drawing the final line on the text, Gandhi wrote to his spiritual companion Hermann Kallenbach about his experiences aboard the *Kildonan Castle*. Almost as an afterthought, in the postscript he wrote: "I have . . . written an original book in Gujarati."[4] This is perhaps the only instance of Gandhi making a claim of this kind in which he sets forth an idea of authorship based on originality.

In the foreword to the text Gandhi wrote: "These views are mine, and yet not mine. They are mine because I hope to act according to them. They are part of my being. But, yet, they are not mine, because I lay no claim to originality. They have been formed after reading several books. That which I dimly felt received support from these books. The views I venture to place before the readers are, needless to say, held by many Indians not touched by what is known as civilisation, but I ask the reader to believe me when I tell him that they are also held by thousands of Europeans."[5] What does this "mine" and yet "not mine" indicate? As I have explained elsewhere, Gandhi

seeks to clarify a relationship to the text that is at a distinct remove from the modern conception of text and authorship as something new and original. In the pre-modern Indic universe such a clarification would have been unnecessary. It is a relationship premised on the belief that the utmost given to a writer-composer is to be able to say in and for one's time and context, that which has been known and recognised to be true. Authorship and text therein are a journey and a quest to discover the authentic and true. They are not meant to intrinsically embody and signify the invention or creation of something "new" and "original."[6]

Gandhi suggests that the claim of the text being his rests not so much on the authorship as on conduct. He said that the views were his because "I hope to act according to them." He reiterated this claim in the last line of *Hind Swaraj*. "I have endeavoured to explain it [Swaraj], and my conscience testifies that my life henceforth is dedicated to its attainment."[7] The questions of authorship and originality for Gandhi are located within the domain of conduct, in one's ability to dedicate oneself to truth as perceived.

We need to comprehend the choice of language and the form of the text that Gandhi chose. As he sat down to write it, he must have been aware that his attempt was without precedent and entailed an endeavor to measure the meaning and worth of the modern impulse from a ground of cognition that lay beyond its ambit. Already in 1909 a large part of the world had been substantially recast according to the requirements of modern transformation set in motion in Europe. The few voices in Europe of caution and warning against the modern were confined to the lonely margins. In the world beyond Europe, critiques of the modern were confined to the details of Europe manipulating the stupendous gifts of modern civilization for its narrow selfish purpose. Aware of these debates, Gandhi chose to write *Hind Swaraj* in the form of a dialogue and in Gujarati. At first glance, every possible consideration seems to militate against this choice. In Gujarati, or indeed in any other modern Indian language, there was at that time nothing that could be read or seen as a rejection of modern civilization. In fact the modern capacity to transform and reorder the wherewithal of life was universally accepted as promising and good. The critique of colonization was cast in terms of impassioned denunciations of colonial exploitation and racial arrogance. The text had little bearing on the aspirations of the struggle in South Africa; in fact there are only two references to South Africa in the text. Gandhi's prime referents were India and Europe, modern civilization and meaning of life. In writing *Hind Swaraj* in Gujarati—a language on the remote margins of the modern—Gandhi affirmed two cardinal concepts on which the fact and possibility of human equality is predicated: (1) inherence in language of a capacity to make sense and take measure of things utterly unfamiliar and unknown, and (2) Gujarati as an opportunity to access folk and vernacular discourses. The sheer simplicity of the original text is striking in the extreme. In the words of Gandhi, it seems "crude."[8] A reader is sometimes utterly overtaken by the raw rustle of the prose. Vinoba Bhave, one of Gandhi's closest associates and a man whose feel for the languages and literary traditions of India was incomparable, commented on the "crudeness" of the language of *Hind Swaraj*:

> I have said crude because the words ... which he [uses] later are not the words to be found in it. Just as the language of the *Upanishads* sounds crude to the ears, the language of *Hind Swaraj* also seems crude. When we look at Shankara's *Bhasya*, the neatness of its language, its mode of explanation, the capacity to explain everything through argument, the language of the *Upanishads* in comparison to that appears crude. But the life and vigour that dwells in the crude language of *Upanishads* is not to be found in other languages of argument and science.[9]

Gandhi continued to believe that the cognitive universe of *Hind Swaraj* could be best captured in a language that had its roots in the Indic civilization and modes of thought. It is not a coincidence that *Hind Swaraj* was the only work Gandhi wrote that he chose to translate.

IT IS IN THE way Gandhi made this translation that this work bears the marks of a bilingual text. Bilingualism is not just the ability to think and express oneself in two languages. Rather, it indicates simultaneity and suggests a process whereby an idea is conceived and thought in one language and expressed in another—that is, whereby it becomes possible to express a concept, a notion, that is alien to one linguistic/semantic universe through another tongue. I propose that *Hind Swaraj* is a bilingual text in this sense.

It is most instructive to examine this idea through the notion that forms the core of *Hind Swaraj*, the idea of Sudhar, rendered in English as Civilization. Sudhar in Gujarati has a lineage. Before Gandhi, the term was used largely to indicate the idea and process of social and religious reform. In this sense, Sudhar encompassed the idea that Su-dhar was the good path, the righteous path (Su indicating the quality of goodness); hence Sudharo is equated with "good conduct." But until *Hind Swaraj*, Sudharo had been used in the sense of reform (and largely continues with this meaning). Gandhi, by contrast, defines Sudharo as that which makes possible self-knowledge and self-rule. It is "that mode of conduct that points out to man the path of duty," where "performance of duty and observance of morality" become "convertible terms," which allow us to "attain mastery over our mind and passion," and "so doing, we know ourselves."[10]

Gandhi had a choice of two other and more prevalent usages to indicate civilization. These are *sabhyata* and *sanskriti*. In fact, when Gandhi writes in the English rendering that the Gujarati equivalent for civilization means "good conduct," he is referring to *sabhyata* rather than *sudharo*. The Gujarati lexicon *BhagvadGoMandal*, in fact, says that *sanskriti* means civilization. Gandhi may not have preferred a notion of civilization that is intrinsically tied to Sanskrit and all the modes of thought and practices that were articulated through that language. But this still does not explain the choice of the term "Sudhar."

Gandhi was clearly invoking Sudhar in two senses, which have been latent in Gujarati. First, Su-dhar is not simply a good path but one that holds, bears; from the Sanskrit root *dhri, dharayati*. It holds and bears human society; it is *sudhar*; and only such Sudhar could make manifest to humanity the path of duty and open the possibility of self-knowledge. Sudhar is civilization in this sense. Second, Sudhar, unlike *sabhyata* or *sanskriti*, has a sense of movement. Sudhar, according to *BhagvadGoMandal*, suggests a movement toward virtue. It entails a choice in favor of the good and active, shunning all that is undesirable. It was this active, choice-enabling, virtue-enhancing possibility of Sudhar that Gandhi desired from civilization. Moreover, Sudhar in the more prevalent usage could also suggest reform, progress, contemporariness, change, and the influence of the modern West, all these senses being present in the English rendering.

There are instances in the Gujarati text where Gandhi has qualified the term "Sudharo." The term "modern civilization" that is used in the English translation by Suresh Sharma and myself occurs in three distinct ways in the Gujarati text; as Sudharo, as *aaj-kal no Sudharo*, and as *adhunik Sudharo*. The term *aaj-kal* in Gujarati literally means "today and tomorrow." It is used to indicate the contemporary and therefore transient nature of things; the term "modern" lacks this pronounced sense of transience. Interestingly, the term *adhunik*, which occurs only twice in the Gujarati text, also has a sense of transience, of lack of permanence, in Gujarati. By describing civilization as *adhunik Sudharo* Gandhi wished to emphasize not so much its modernity but the transient nature of that reality which passes under the name "civilization." Therefore Gandhi declared that "this civilisation is such that one has only to be patient and it will be self-destroyed." In the Gujarati text he emphasized the self-destructive nature of modern civilization by stating "te Sudharo nashkarak ane nashvant che" (this civilization is destructive and certain to be destroyed).[11] This added emphasis is absent in the English text. In today's Gujarati, both Sudharo as Civilization and *adhunik* as "ephemeral" have become recessive; we speak of *adhunik* in the sense of *navin* and hence modern.

In the Gujarati text, the term "Kudhar/Kudharo" (the wrong path) creates a play between Sudhar and Kudhar. This term, which occurs nine times in the Gujarati text, has been rendered as "civilisation only in name," "civilisation as a disease," and "reverse of civilisation." In fact, six out of nine times Gandhi did not render the term "Kudhar" in the English text. This is true of many idiomatic Gujarati phrases. Gandhi either does not render them in English or chooses to provide a literal translation. He does not resort to equivalent idiomatic usages in English. For example, the Gujarati idiom "Miya ne Mahadev ne Na Bane" (Miya and Mahadev will always quarrel) is used to frame the argument about Hindu–Muslim relations and the *had ver* (inborn enmity) between the two communities. This idiom is used twice in the Gujarati text. Gandhi chose not to render it in English at all. In one instance he rendered it as "our very proverbs prove it," and in the second instance as "the proverbs you have quoted." While in case of "Jenu man changa che tene gher bethe ganga che," Gandhi provided this literal English translation: "Those whose hearts were aglow with righteousness have the Ganges in their own home."[12]

Gandhi does something similar with the English phrases that occur in the Gujarati text. For instance, in the cases of the terms "extremists" and "moderates" he chose to explicate these terms in nonpolitical idioms: *dhima* (slow), *utavala* (impatient), *bikan* (timid), and *himatvala* (bold). Curiously, this explanation found its way into the English text as well. Where cultural practices that could approximate the English phrase were available, Gandhi used both terms in Gujarati. He explained "segregation" through the notion of ritual and in some cases temporary impurity, *sutak*. He invoked the outlaws of Saurahstra to explain guerrilla warfare: *baharvatiya* (literally, those who walk away). In case of the term "boycott," he invoked much deeper cultural fears by describing it in terms of untouchability. The term *abhadchet* suggested that British cloth and machine-made things had not only to be shunned but were defiling. In what would be one of the most creative transpositions, Gandhi coined the phrase *daya bal* (force of pity or love) in Gujarati to capture the Christian sense of the active and transformative power of love, compassion, and pity.

This kind of intertextuality between Gujarati and the English text is most evident in the case of four cognate terms: *daru-golo, hathiyar bal, top bal,* and *mara mari.* An entire range of fluid and interchangeable meanings is attributed to these four terms in Gandhi's English text. He renders *daru-golo* as "brute-force," "arms and ammunitions," "gunpowder," and "use of force." The term "brute-force," a force that is beastly, he employs to denote all those forces that oppose what Gandhi calls, in his English translation, "soul-force." Apart from *daru-golo,* the term "brute-force" is used for *hathiyar bal* (force of arms), *top bal* (force of canons), *sharir bal* (body-force), and *mara mari* (violence). Both the act of violence and the instrumentality of violence he sought to convey through these terms.

Thus, in many of its central concerns, *Hind Swaraj* is a bilingual text; it was conceived simultaneously in two linguistic frames and rendered in two languages. It needs to be read in both languages as two original texts and not one as original and the other as a derivative translation.

HIND SWARAJ IS philosophically located at a fleeting, tantalizing moment in human history, in many ways aptly symbolized by the author's journey aboard the *Kildonan Castle.* It is located at a moment where it is still possible to conceive of life outside the realm of the modern universe. In this moment, two modes of life and thought are present simultaneously. The first we may call amodern. Amodern is not antimodern. It is not nonmodern in the sense that "nonmodern" signifies absence of modernity. Amodern refers to something that lies outside the modern realm and has to be conceptualized without a necessary and inevitable referent to the modern. The other mode of life and thought that is present is modern civilization. *Hind Swaraj* should be read as a text that was written at a moment in history where both the amodern and modern universes existed simultaneously as large facts—however fleeting that moment might have been.

Gandhi's deep unease with modern civilization stems from his argument that the purpose of a civilization is to make possible for those who live under it to know themselves. It is this capacity for self-understanding that defines civilization for Gandhi. "Civilisation is that mode of conduct that points out to man the path of duty. Performance of duty and observance of morality are convertible terms. To observe morality is to attain mastery over our mind and our passions. So doing, we know ourselves."[13] A civilization that makes possible knowledge of oneself is Sudhar, and one that precludes that possibility is Kudhar, or "reverse of civilization."

For Gandhi, the essential character of modern civilization—Kudharo—is not represented by either the empire, the speed of railways, the contractual nature of society brought about by Western law, or the vivisection of modern Western medicine. Kudharo is also not represented by the use of violence as a legitimate means of expressing political dissent and obtaining political goals. The essential character of modern civilization is represented by denial of a fundamental possibility: the possibility of knowing oneself. Describing modern civilization, Gandhi says: "Its true test lies in the fact that people living in it make bodily welfare the object of life."[14] This is an inadequate rendering of the original Gujarati, which could be rendered as "its true identity is in the fact that people seek to find in engagement with the material world and bodily comfort, meaning and human worth." When the principal *purushartha* (four principal human endeavors) becomes a search for meaning and fulfillment in the material world and bodily comfort, it shifts the ground of judgment about human worth from the human person to the body and the material world. It is for this reason that Gandhi characterized modern civilization as "irreligion," a "Satanic Civilisation," and the "Black Age." By shifting the locus of human endeavor outside the human person—to objects of bodily welfare—modern civilization also precludes the possibility of Swaraj (self-rule and rule over the self). "It is Swaraj when we learn to rule ourselves."[15] This capacity to rule oneself is different from Home Rule or political freedom.[16] Swaraj is predicated on Sudharo, a civilization that makes self-understanding its central concern.

Gandhi argued that Swaraj could not be obtained so long as Indians and the British remained in the vise-like grip of modern civilization. *Hind Swaraj* claims that this civilization is self-destructive and is certain to be obliterated. Anything that leads one away from oneself cannot be permanent for Gandhi. Despite decrying modern civilization and its emblems, *Hind Swaraj* is not a text of hatred. In fact, it is moved by deep love and empathy for those caught in the fire of modern civilization. *Hind Swaraj* is a theory of salvation, not only for India but also for Britain. Gandhi is at pains to point out that India's struggle cannot be against the British but against the civilization they represent. He reminds the British that they are religious people, that their basic constitution as a people and a society is not flawed. Gandhi's plea is that Britain be Christian in the true sense, and if they become moral and acknowledge that their pursuit is both irreligious and destructive, then the English can stay in India becoming moral people, not votaries of modern civilization and the empire that this civilization creates. *Hind Swaraj* is a rare document of contemporary thought that does not seek annihilation of the oppressor but in fact seeks their salvation. The duty of India for Gandhi is unique; it must not only realize Swaraj for itself but also free the British from the fires of modern civilization.

Hind Swaraj is a meditation on the question of means and ends. Violence for Gandhi is indelibly linked to modern civilization. Violence has to be shunned not only because Ahimsa (nonviolence, love, noninjury, nonkilling) represents a superior morality but also because violence creates a distance between the self and the pursuit of Truth. "The more he took to violence, the more he receded from Truth."[17] Violence for Gandhi makes the possibility of knowing oneself even fainter. He therefore decries the argument that ends justify the means. He says: " 'As is the God, so is the votary' is a maxim worth considering."[18] He likens means to a seed and ends to a tree, "and there is just the same inviolable connection between the means and the end as there is between the seed and the tree."[19] Not only is the relationship between means and ends inviolable, Gandhi argues for purity of both the means and the ends. One cannot worship God by the means of Satan. This emphasis on the purity of means and ends and their inviolable relationship between them is a unique contribution of *Hind Swaraj*.

THE MEANS ARE MEDIATED through the human agency; in the final analysis, the pure means are those that are wielded by a pure person. It was this relationship between objects of senses and the attachment for them that attracted Gandhi to the Bhagavad Gita. He read the Gita first in Sir Edwin Arnold's verse translation—*The Song Celestial*—with theosophist friends in England. The poem struck him as one of "priceless worth." Verses 62 and 63 of the second discourse made a deep impression:

> If one
> Ponders on objects of the sense, there springs
> Attraction; from attraction grows desire,
> Desire flames to fierce passion, passion breeds
> Recklessness; then the memory—all betrayed—Lets noble purpose
>   go, and saps the mind,
> Till purpose, mind, and man are all undone.[20]

More than thirty years later at the time of writing his autobiography, these verses still rang in his ears. These verses claim that those—both individuals and, Gandhi would argue, civilizations—that make bodily welfare their object and measure human worth in and through them are certain to be ruined. The verses describe a state that is opposed to that of *brahmacharya*. When Gandhi read these stanzas in 1888–1889, he was still far from taking a vow of *brahmacharya*, even in the limited sense of chastity and celibacy, a central quest of his life. But what awakened in young Gandhi was a religious quest and longing that was to govern his entire life henceforth. The Gita became his lifelong companion. He translated the Gita as *Anasakti Yoga* in Gujarati. His engagement with the Gita, though deep, was in no way singularly unique. India's national movement displayed a marked preference for the Gita.

The path of the Gita for Gandhi was neither that of contemplation nor of devotion but that of *anasakta* (desire-less, unattached) action. This idea is embodied in the Gita in the image of the *sthitpragnya* (one whose intellect is secure); who acts without attachment either to the action or fruits thereof. Gandhi adopted two modes of self-practice to attain the state where one acts yet does not act. These two modes were *yajna* (sacrifice; a traditional Hindu concept) and Satyagraha; both deeply personal and simultaneously political.

The Gita declared that "together with the sacrifice did the Lord of beings create."[21] Gandhi saw this idea of sacrifice—of the self and not a symbolic, ritualistic sacrifice—as the basis of all religions. The ideal, of course, was Jesus; Gandhi said that the word *yajna* had to be understood in the way Jesus lived and died. "Jesus put on a crown of thorns to win salvation for his people, allowed his hands and feet to be nailed and suffered agonies before he gave up the ghost. This has been the law of *yajna* from immemorial times, without *yajna* the earth cannot exist even for a moment."[22] But how is one to perform such sacrifice in daily life? Gandhi's response was twofold: for one he turned to the Bible, and the other was uniquely his own. "Earn thy bread by the sweat of thy brow," says the Bible. Gandhi made this central to the life at the ashram and borrowed the term "bread labour" to describe it. The other form of *yajna* was peculiar to his times: it referred to the spinning that was an obligatory ashram observance, each member being required to spin 140 threads daily, each thread measuring four feet. This spinning was called *sutra-yajna* (sacrificial spinning). As his conviction regarding spinning as the true *yajna* deepened, his ashram, hitherto called Satyagraha Ashram, was renamed Udyog Mandir (literally, temple of industry). Explaining the term *udyog*, Gandhi said: "Udyog has to be read in the light of the *Bhagvad Gita*."[23]

If the *Gita* and the state of the *sthitpragnya* informed and guided Gandhi's spiritual quest to attain self-realization, Satyagraha was his chosen means to attain Swaraj.

HIND SWARAJ ONLY SUGGESTS and alludes to the idea of a *satyagrahi* and the practice of Satyagraha. Gandhi wrote an account of the struggle of the Indian people in South Africa, *Dakshin Africa Na Satyagraha No Itihas* (Satyagraha in South Africa). He wanted this account to be read alongside his autobiography, almost as a companion volume: "I need hardly mention that those who are following the weekly chapters of *My Experiments with Truth* cannot afford to miss these chapters on Satyagraha, if they would follow in all details the working out of the search after Truth."[24] Gandhi clearly saw his spiritual quest and political striving as enjoined and stemming from the same root. Satyagraha has its roots in a pledge, taken in the name of God and with God as witness. Satyagraha as a philosophy and a practice is recognition of the humanity of others. Without this recognition no dialogue about the nature of truth can take place. Gandhi insisted that Truth could not be one's own relative, constricted idea of truth.

Gandhi increasingly came to believe that a person who wielded such a pure means had to be pure. In *Hind Swaraj* and *Satyagraha in South Africa*, this aspect is recessive, though he does mention the need for voluntary poverty, *brahmacharya*, and fearlessness. The reason for this recessive presence lies in the fact that during his South African years his understanding of the ashram and ashram observances had not fully matured. He had established two "ashram-like" communities in South Africa, but one was a "settlement" (Phoenix Settlement) while the other was a "farm" (Tolstoy Farm). Ruskin's *Unto This Last* provided the initial impulse for Phoenix. Though it had a religious basis, "the visible object was purity of body and mind as well as economic equality."[25] Celibacy was not regarded as essential, in fact, coworkers were expected to live as family men and have children. Gandhi began to look on Phoenix as a deliberate religious institution after 1906, when he took the vow of *brahmacharya* and celibacy that became an imperative for a life devoted to service. In 1911, the establishment of Tolstoy Farm was recognition that Satyagraha required a community where the families of *satyagrahis* could live and lead a religious life.

Gandhi as a *satyagrahi* is understood only when we understand him as an ashramite. Gandhi wrote two works, *Satyagraha Ashram No Itihas* (Ashram Observances in Action) and *Mangal Prabhat* (From Yeravda Mandir), to explain the philosophy and practice of ashram life. On his return to India Gandhi established an ashram at Kochrab in Ahmedabad on 25 May 1915. It shifted to the banks of the Sabarmati River in Ahmedabad in 1917 and was called Satyagraha Ashram, as it owed its very existence to the "pursuit and attempted practice of Truth."[26] Gandhi described the ashram as a community of men of religion. The emphasis was both on community and religious life. The word "religion" indicated a nondenominational idea of dharma. What gave the inhabitants an idea of being part of a religious community were a set of eleven vows (*ekadash vrata*).[27] Three of these were Gandhi's response to his times and context (removal of untouchability, equality of all religions, and Swadeshi), while the inclusion of bread labor was an innovation in the Indian context, where notions of social and ritual purity and impurity are determined also by the materials that one deals with. The other seven were part of many Indic traditions. Gandhi's originality lay in the fact that he made them central to the political realm. Ashram observances were essential for those who wished to wield the pure means of Satyagraha.

Thus, Gandhi's *Hind Swaraj*, his *Satyagraha in South Africa*, and his autobiography make sense only when read along with the ashram observances. In the last lines of *Hind Swaraj*, Gandhi made an assertion and a dedication: "In my opinion, we have used the term 'Swaraj' without understanding its real significance. I have endeavoured to explain it as I understand it, and my conscience testifies that my life henceforth is dedicated to its attainment."[28] The true meaning and significance of a life dedicated to the attainment of Swaraj can be understood only when one understands Gandhi as an ashramite.

FINALLY, ONE MUST FACE the question of lack of comprehension and unease that *Hind Swaraj* has aroused, both in Gandhi's times and in ours. The possible answers might lie in the fluidity of the text. The meaning of the term "Hind Swaraj" kept evolving with Gandhi. It was no longer a text; it became sets of practices: Satyagraha, voluntary poverty, ashram life, constructive work in villages, his lifelong striving to understand and eradicate untouchability and to secure Hindu–Muslim unity. When Gandhi spoke of *Hind Swaraj* as his seed text, he was referring to all these manifestations of its ideals. Text and life became inseparable. Another explanation for the lack of comprehension and unease is that *Hind Swaraj* came to be seen as an antimodern manifesto. Nehru's response was characteristic of it. All those who wanted a modern nation-state found the Gandhi of *Hind Swaraj* dispensable. Equally significant was a response from those who were oppressed by tradition—women, Dalits, religious and other minorities. They took Gandhi's critique of modernity as an advocacy for obscurantism, oppressive tradition. His argument that modern civilization precludes the possibility of self-recognition was both alien and unacceptable to them. They also found Gandhi's insistence on self-recognition as the sole ground from which Swaraj and Civilization emanates contrary to modern political practices and discourse. This is so because in Gandhi's estimation it is the spiritual and the moral that are primary over the realm of the political, while contemporary politics sees itself as the final arbitrator of all questions, even questions of first principles.

But it is because of these multiple, divisive readings that *Hind Swaraj* invites us to engage with it again and again. It urges us to keep its ideas in motion.

NOTES

1. Jawaharlal Nehru, *A Bunch of Old Letters* (London: Asia Publishing House, 1958), 505; M. K. Gandhi, "A Message to 'The Aryan Path,' " n1, in *Collected Works of Mahatma Gandhi*, 100 vols. (New Delhi: Government of India, 1956–1994) (CWMG), 81:319–321.

2. Faisal Devji, *The Impossible Indian: Gandhi and the Temptation of Violence* (Cambridge, MA: Harvard University Press, 2012), 3.

3. Devji, *Impossible*; Gandhi quote from 89, 5.

4. M. K. Gandhi to Hermann Kallenbach, 25 November 1909, CWMG, 96:36–38.

5. M. K. Gandhi, *M. K. Gandhi's Hind Swaraj: A Critical Edition*, annotated, translated, and edited by Suresh Sharma and Tridip Suhrud (Delhi: Orient Blackswan, 2010), 9–10. All subsequent references to the text of *Hind Swaraj* are from this bilingual edition.

6. Suresh Sharma and Tridip Suhrud, editors' introduction to *M. K. Gandhi's Hind Swaraj*, xiii.

7. Gandhi, *M. K. Gandhi's Hind Swaraj*, 98.

8. Speech at Gandhi Seva Sangh Meeting, Brindaban, CWMG, 69:197.

9. Vinoba Bhave, *Vinoba Sahitya*, vol. 20 (Wardha, India, 2001), quoted in Gandhi, *M. K. Gandhi's Hind Swaraj*, 365. Suresh Sharma's translation from original Hindi.

10. Gandhi, *M. K. Gandhi's Hind Swaraj*, 56.

11. Gandhi, *M. K. Gandhi's Hind Swaraj*, 32.

12. Gandhi, *M. K. Gandhi's Hind Swaraj*, 42.

13. Gandhi, *M. K. Gandhi's Hind Swaraj*, 56.

14. Gandhi, *M. K. Gandhi's Hind Swaraj*, 30.

15. Gandhi, *M. K. Gandhi's Hind Swaraj*, 59–60.

16. The term "Swaraj" occurs fifty-six times in the Gujarati text. The English rendering alternates between "Home Rule" and "Swaraj," the choice being guided by the context of usage and the distance or proximity that Gandhi wished to suggest with his own vision. Out of fifty-six occurrences of the term "Swaraj" in Gujarati, it has been rendered as "Home Rule" in twenty-eight instances.

17. M. K. Gandhi, *From Yeravda Mandir* (1932), translated from the original Gujarati by Valji Govindji Desai (Ahmedabad: Navajivan, 2005), 5.

18. Gandhi, *M. K. Gandhi's Hind Swaraj*, 81.

19. Gandhi, *M. K. Gandhi's Hind Swaraj*, 81.

20. Sir Edwin Arnold's translation. Gandhi's own rendering reads: "In a man brooding on objects of the senses, attachment to them spring up; attachment begat craving and craving begets wrath. Wrath breeds stupefaction, stupefaction leads to loss of memory, loss of memory ruins reason, and the ruin of reason spells utter destruction." Discourse II: 62, 63. Mahadev Desai, *The Gospel of Selfless Action or The Gita According to Gandhi* (1946) (Ahmedabad: Navajivan, 2004), 163.

21. Gita III, 10.

22. CWMG, 20:404.

23. CWMG, 43:203.

24. M. K. Gandhi, *Satyagraha in South Africa* (1950), translated from the original Gujarati by Valji Govindji Desai (Ahmedabad: Navajivan, 2003), vii.

25. CWMG, 50:189.

26. Gandhi, *From Yeravda Mandir*, 3.

27. They are Satya (truth), Ahimsa (nonviolence or love), Brahmacharya (chastity), Asvad (control of the palate), Asteya (nonstealing), Aparigraha (nonpossession or poverty), Abhaya (fearlessness), Ashprushyata Nivaran (removal of untouchability), Sharer Shrama (bread labor), Sarva Dharma Samabhav (tolerance or equality of religions), Swadeshi.

28. Gandhi, *M. K. Gandhi's Hind Swaraj*, 98.

Eight

TOTARAM SANADHYA'S
FIJI MEIN MERE EKKIS VARSH

A History of Empire and Nation in a Minor Key

MRINALINI SINHA

Fiji Mein Mere Ekkis Varsh (My Twenty-One Years in Fiji), a slim Hindi-language book by Totaram Sanadhya (1876–1948), is not a major publication. Published in November 1914 by an obscure Hindi-language press in Firozabad in Agra district, in the United Provinces of Agra and Oudh (U.P.), the book did for a time enjoy some success.[1] By 1916, for example, it was already in its third edition, and it had also been published in four Gujarati translations, two Bengali, one Marathi, and one Urdu.[2] The vibrant Indian-language press as well as some of the Indian-owned English-language newspapers in India reported favorably on the book. Sanadhya's "shudra pustak" (humble book), as he put it, even managed to garner a brief mention in the corridors of power at the India Office and the Colonial Office in London. Yet the fact that until 1991 the book was not published in an English-language translation—an acid test for any claim to empire-wide significance—is a reminder of its parochial reputation.[3] The "minor" status of the book, however, is in itself deserving of attention: it illuminates an important, albeit inassimilable, moment—an interregnum between the Age of Empires and the Age of Nations—in the political history of the twentieth century.[4]

The book appeared approximately midway into a political campaign in India to end the notorious system that deployed Indian indentured labor overseas. The British government, ever since the abolition of Atlantic slavery, had been drawn into coordinating an elaborate system of recruitment and transportation of labor from India to colonial plantations overseas, replacing emancipated Africans with indentured Indians, in order to safeguard a continued supply of cheap labor. The system, from its inception, was beleaguered by criticisms and was subject throughout its existence to various reforms to check some of its grossest abuses. On the eve of World War I, however, the working of the entire system had come under serious attack in a concerted campaign in India for the abolition of indentured emigration. Sanadhya's firsthand account of the indentured system in *Fiji Mein Mere Ekkis Varsh* was a salvo in the anti-indenture movement or what has been called the "second abolition," following the abolition of Atlantic slavery.

The abolition of indenture, with the stopping of recruitment in 1917 and the commutation of the last indenture contracts in Fiji in 1920, was a significant break in the typical pattern of reforms in the British Empire: it was spurred by *Indian* political agitation and was the product of a shift in *Indian*, and not British, public opinion. The fate of the system, indeed, was decided in "dependent India, and not in metropolitan Britain."[5] The British government and the British public, despite the belated and weak-kneed interventions of the once redoubtable Anti-Slavery and Aborigines Protections Society in London, were slow to join in the abolitionist fervor; hence this time the British Empire was robbed of the moral redemption it had once claimed on the basis of Britain's leading role in the abolition of Atlantic slavery.

Anti-indenture sentiment in India was initially a by-product of M. K. Gandhi's various campaigns in South Africa, most notably by the 1913 strike of indentured workers in Natal, but it soon became the subject of a political mobilization of its own. Just as South Africa had dominated discussions in India about the general condition of Indians overseas, Fiji—the last of the British colonies to still remain substantially dependent on the export of Indian labor—featured prominently in the debate about indenture in particular. This shift, moreover, was not just geographical: it entailed also the widening, and deepening, of what had hitherto constituted Indian public opinion.

The abolition movement may have started out as a "sentimental" affair, and for colonial officials this always remained the essence of the movement, which they saw as reflecting nothing more than the desire of Indian politicians to redeem national "honor" from the stigma of racial inferiority. But the movement evolved quickly, albeit unevenly, into a much broader popular movement centered squarely on the plight of exploited workers themselves. Beneath the radar of high-profile political speeches, conferences, and resolutions against indenture was a simmering popular movement that was capturing small towns and villages across northern India, especially in the western districts of Bihar and in the U.P., which by the early twentieth century had become the primary catchment area for overseas recruits under indenture. Sanadhya's "minor" publication stands as a testimony to this important, but unevenly digested, dimension of the movement.

Fiji Mein Mere Ekkis Varsh was not the first book in India to publicize widely the condition of indentured workers overseas, nor was it the book whose presumably incontrovertible revelations laid to rest the possibility of the system's continuation. These honors belong, arguably, to the English-language texts penned by three lieutenants of Gandhi: *The Indians of South Africa: Helots within the Empire and How They Are Treated* (1909), by Henry S. L. Polak, and *Report on Indentured Labour in Fiji* (1916), by Reverend Charles F. Andrews and W. W. Pearson.[6] The importance of *Fiji Mein Mere Ekkis Varsh* lies elsewhere: in bringing into focus the expansive contours of the first—predating the more famous Gandhian campaigns by a few years—village-based mass movement in India on an all-India issue. And at stake in its minor status, then, is precisely the meaning of this inaugural moment of mass politics.

Sanadhya's combined personal and collective record of the life of indentured and time-expired (ex-indentured) workers from India in Fiji—what we might today call a testimonio—written in simple and idiomatic Hindi is especially suited to reveal the historic role of this abolition movement. The immediacy and urgency of the many personal stories in *Fiji Mein Mere Ekkis Varsh* notwithstanding, the book did more than simply add firsthand testimony of indenture to the public debate. Even before Sanadhya's book, individual stories of indentured workers had already entered into the public discussion of indenture. Polak's 1909 book, even though its primary aim was to publicize Gandhi's South African campaign, had alerted the Indian public to the injustice of the system with heartrending individual stories of indentured workers. By 1912, when the Indian politician G. K. Gokhale moved the first resolution for the abolition of indenture in the Legislative Council in India, the speeches in support of the resolution testified that the Indian political class had become sufficiently educated on the particular problems arising out of the indentured system. This was a far cry from just a few years before, when vague sentimental expressions about indenture were still the norm. The anti-indenture cause, even before Sanadhya's publication, had begun to move out of the shadow of Gandhi's South African campaigns, and the general problem of racial discrimination faced by Indians in the Dominions or the colonies of "white" settlement, to focus squarely on the issues arising out of the operation of the indentured system itself.

Many of the general contours of the anti-indenture arguments in Sanadhya's book, moreover, would have been familiar in the proabolition circles in India: the seduction (*bahakana*) of ill-informed villagers by the unscrupulous practices of the unlicensed recruiters or *arkatis*; the breakdown of the social customs and prejudices, including the religious practices, of the recruits in the emigration depots and on the long ocean voyages to the colonies; the exploitation as well as the atrocities and injustices experienced by the workers (*kasht*) on the plantations; the inadequate facilities for medical care and education of Indians in the colonies; and the alarmingly high murder and suicide rates among the indentured population, especially in Fiji. Even the theme for which the book became most noted— the sexual abuse of women, which according to Sanadhya was inherent in the working of the system itself—was anticipated in the few sensational reports from Fiji (for at least one of which Sanadhya was responsible) that were published in proabolition Hindi-language papers, for example the *Bharat Mitra* of Calcutta. This theme, which brought country-wide public meetings of women to join the national debate on indenture, became the special burden of that other indefatigable anti-indenture activist: Charles Freer Andrews.[7] Its fullest articulation, albeit with more of a patriarchal bias (arising out of his overwhelming concern with sexual immorality), was found in Andrews's writings, which followed and expanded on Sanadhya's lead. More, perhaps, than adding any new content to the anti-indenture argument, therefore, *Fiji Mein Mere Ekkis Varsh* is notable simply for what it was: a printed book about the indenture experience told from the perspective of one who had served his time under indenture. In the canon of Indian abolitionist literature, indeed, *Fiji Mein Mere Ekkis Varsh* stands out: it was the first and only book about indenture authored by a person who had himself served under indenture to be published during the lifetime of the system itself.

Even though analogies to the abolition of Atlantic slavery abounded in the anti-indenture movement, including the formation of several Anti-Indenture Emigration Leagues and Indentured Coolie Protection Societies, the genre of the "slave narrative" does not seem to have translated in contemporary discussions of *Fiji Mein Mere Ekkis Varsh*. The idea for Sanadhya's book was born almost by serendipity. It had its origins in Firozabad at the Hindi Pustakalaya (library), one of a growing number of public libraries in small towns and villages across India, established by the Bharati Bhavan, an institution associated with the nineteenth-century Hindu reformist-nationalist organization the Arya Samaj. On 15 June 1914, the Bhavan manager at the library, Lala Chiranji Lal Jain, introduced Sanadhya, freshly returned from Fiji to his village, Hirangaui, near Firozabad, to an as-yet-unkown government schoolteacher and aspiring journalist, Benarsidas Chaturvedi.[8] Having read Sanadhya's writings in some of the leading Hindi newspapers of the time, such as the *Bharat Mitra* of Calcutta and the *Sri Venkateshwara Samachar* of Bombay, Chaturvedi recommended that Sanadhya publish his experiences in a printed book. When Sanadhya, uncertain of his literary skills, demurred, Chaturvedi volunteered to be his amanuensis for what became *Fiji Mein Mere Ekkis Varsh*. This was the start of a close collaboration between the two on the concerns of Indians overseas, first with Andrews at Shantiniketan in Bengal and then with Gandhi at his ashram in Sabarmati, Gujarat.

Although Sanadhya apparently spoke, according to an acquaintance who spent time with him at that ashram, in a "theth dehati Hindi" or very rustic Hindi, his authorship of a book written in a more standard modern Hindi seems to have gone largely unremarked in the Indian press.[9] The first three editions of *Fiji Mein Mere Ekkis Varsh*, which were published during Sanadhya's lifetime, carried only his name as the author. In the fourth edition of the book, published in 1973, Chaturvedi was listed as the publisher of the book and as the author of a new introduction and preface that told the story of their collaboration. He insisted that Sanadhya had had "ninyanve feesdi shey" (99 percent share) in the writing of the book and that his own contribution consisted chiefly in arranging sections of the book and in "dressing up the language."[10] His reason for remaining anonymous, he explained, was because at the time he had a job as a teacher at a government school that might have been jeopardized through his association with the book.

Nonetheless, as if responding to the public's curiosity about Sanadhya, the second edition of the book of 1915 did include an interesting note about the author from the publisher, identified in the text simply as "a member of Bharati Bhavan," though one Madhuri Prasad of the Bharati Bhavan was listed as the official publisher of the book.[11] The note assured readers that Sanadhya was neither, as some seemed to believe, nothing but a "coolie," nor some great man. He was, the publisher insisted, just an "aam admi" (common man), who could read and write in Hindi; was a student of the Fijian language; and had a little broken English. In a nod to his collaboration with Chaturvedi, perhaps, the note added that Sanadhya needed to rely on the help of others for Hindi–English translations. The publisher's note went on to acknowledge this "common man" as a "great patriot" and detailed his work for the anti-indenture cause both in Fiji and, since his return, in India. Only the Special Branch of the Police of the Government of the U.P. in 1915 seemed to give much attention to the existence of Sanadhya's possible collaborator.[12] The Police report, on the basis of the opinion of the government translator, found the book's writing to have some pretensions to literary merit and its vocabulary interspersed with a few Sanskrit words, indicating, it suggested, a level of education that Sanadhya could not be expected to possess. The existence of a collaborator, and the possible identity of such a person, had the U.P. government stumped, but these questions were apparently of less concern to the audience for Sanadhya's book.

The extant editions of the book bear a few traces of the Sanadhya-Chaturvedi collaboration. Consider the following example. The book occasionally uses the term *girmit*, a neologism made popular by indentured workers from Bihar and the U.P. to refer to the English word "agreement," referring to the contract to which workers supposedly gave their informed consent before embarking for work in the colonies. Likewise, the term *girmitiya* (or "people of the girmit")—what one scholar has identified as an early example of a critical self-appellation adopted by a subordinated and stigmatized people—appears a few times in Sanadhya's text.[13] The Indian audience of *Fiji Mein Mere Ekkis Varsh* might have been expected to respond to the neologisms *girmit* and *girmitiya*—especially popular in Fiji—in much the same manner, perhaps, as did Gandhi when he first encountered the terms in Natal: as merely a "*corrupt* form of the English word 'agreement.'"[14] More often, therefore, the text uses the more standard terms *shartname* (contract) and *shartbandhe mazdoor* (bonded/bound workers). By the same token, Fiji Hindi, a lingua franca for the Indians on the islands that was made up largely of Awadhi and Bhojpuri, representing the regions in northern India whence the majority of the Indians came, and interspersed with borrowings from several South Indian languages as well as from English and Fijian, does not otherwise seem to have left a mark on the text.[15] Sanadhya's influence on the language of the text was most evident, perhaps, in the book's eschewal of the hated term "coolie" as a supposedly neutral descriptor for indentured workers.

Sanadhya's book pointed to the interjection of new concerns and, even more, of new voices in the national debate about indenture: that is, a growing recognition of the *aam admi*, or the "common person," as it were, as both the subjects and the objects of the movement. The entire genre of working-class autobiographies and memoirs that scholars are discovering from the 1920s and 1930s in India, in a sense, might be considered the heirs of *Fiji Mein Mere Ekkis Varsh*. When the Gandhian socialist leader Jayaprakash Narayan visited the Firozabad Bharati Bhavan in 1963, he wrote in the visitor's book that he was grateful to the institution for publishing Sanadhya's book, which had a major impact on him as a young student in Bihar.[16] Indeed, the Firozabad Bharati Bhavan had the honor of providing the abolition movement in India with a text that was, perhaps, the closest thing to the "slave narratives" made famous during the movement for the abolition of Atlantic slavery.

The novelty of Sanadhya's book—a printed book by an ex–indentured worker—was a product of the "democratization of print" in late colonial India. Sanadhya, an impoverished Brahmin by caste, although listed in his emigration pass as of the Thakur (a Kshatriya) caste (a deceit resorted to commonly because recruiters were expressly discouraged from recruiting Brahmins, who were considered allegedly unfit for the rigors of agricultural work on the plantations), was no stranger to the world of print. Before leaving for Fiji as an indentured laborer at the age of seventeen, he had received a limited education in Hindi at the Hiraungi Patshala (village school), which would not have been unusual, especially after Charles Wood's Education Dispatch of 1854, which had redirected the attention of the Government of India toward primary and secondary education in the "vernacular" languages.[17] For the most part, however, Sanadhya was self-taught in Fiji. While still under indenture, for example, he had worked out a mutually profitable arrangement with a European shopkeeper on the plantation for exporting books from India that were in demand among the Indians of Fiji.

These were mainly religious and other popular romances that were mass produced, at least since the last quarter of the nineteenth century, for an expanding market by large Indian-owned Hindi presses such as the Nawal Kishore Press in Lucknow and the Sri Venkateshwar Press in Bombay.[18] These books, though available only in limited numbers of copies on the various plantations in the islands, were rented out to readers—one book, according to Sanadhya, rented for 2 rupees with an initial deposit of 10 rupees—and were typically part of a collective or shared reading experience: books were read aloud at public gatherings on both ordinary and special occasions. Sanadhya's self-study in Fiji helped in his transformation into a "pundit" (learned man), a sobriquet associated with him ever afterward. Yet in Fiji Sanadhya would have had no precedent for considering the printed book a suitable vehicle for narrating the lives of ordinary indentured laborers or as a medium that could be used by a person with his limited literary skills.

Indian newspapers, which covered "any printed, including cyclostyled, periodical work containing public news, or comment on public news," and which were available in Fiji, were a different matter.[19] The readers and listeners—for newspapers too were read aloud to people who could not read—of Indian newspapers in Fiji kept abreast of the raging public debates over indenture. Gandhi's campaigns in South Africa, duly covered in the Indian press, especially caught the imagination of Indians in Fiji. Indians from different parts of the islands raised funds for the South African struggle, collecting a total of 40 pounds (600 rupees) to send to Gandhi. Sanadhya's own first appearance in print under his own name was probably in Gandhi's paper in South Africa, the *Indian Opinion* (1904). The paper published a letter from Sanadhya on behalf of the recently formed (1911) British Indian Association of Fiji requesting Gandhi to send an Indian barrister to Fiji who would fight for justice for the indentured workers. Sanadhya's call in the *Indian Opinion* was answered by Manilal Maganlal Doctor, a Gujarati barrister like Gandhi, who on Gandhi's advice had set up his practice in Mauritius in 1907 to provide legal aid to the Indians on the plantations.[20] Manilal (who changed his name to Doctor Manilal sometime after his arrival in Fiji in 1912) had followed Gandhi's lead, starting a trilingual newspaper in English, Hindi, and French, published from Port Louis in Mauritius, called the *Hindusthani* (1909), which he used to publicize his own anti-indenture activism. In Fiji, Manilal started in 1913 what was perhaps Fiji's first Hindi paper, a cyclostyled sheet that became a precursor for the

English-language *Indian Settler*, which he launched in 1917.[21] Such precedents would likely have influenced Sanadhya, who in his own apotheosis as anti-indenture activist and publicist was quick to make use of newspapers to publicize stories of, by, and for indentured workers.

The Calcutta-based *Bharat Mitra* offered an early example. The paper, with a circulation of four thousand and a distribution that extended beyond Calcutta, was one of the more popular Indian papers in Fiji because of, as Sanadhya recalled, its consistent coverage of the situation of Indians in Fiji. The paper had close connections to the Marwari Association of Calcutta, which had been active since 1912 in the anti-indenture cause, rescuing and providing assistance to recruits lured into the emigration depots in Calcutta before embarkation for the plantations overseas.[22] Between October and November 1913, the paper began publishing a series of sworn statements from emigrants returned from several places, including Fiji, Trinidad, and British Guiana, that provided personal testimonies of men and women tricked into indentured service. The *Bharat Mitra* had also published accounts by Ram Narain Sharma, an Indian barrister from Georgetown, British Guiana, about the legal difficulties of indentured workers there.[23] The paper was thus an obvious choice for Sanadhya and Ram Manoharanand Saraswati, an Arya Samaj activist who had recently arrived in Fiji, for publicizing the situation of Indians in Fiji. These two, as subsequent investigations by the Fiji government suggested, were probably responsible for the famous letter, purportedly written by Kunti, identified as a low-caste Chamar woman originally from Gorakhpur district in the U.P., that was published in the 8 May 1913 issue of the *Bharat Mitra*.[24] The letter helped publicize in India the story of the attempted sexual assault on Kunti by a white overseer on a plantation in Nadewa, Fiji.

When Sanadhya left Fiji in 1914, with the avowed aim of taking his struggle to the small towns and villages in India, he was exposed to the connections that existed between Hindi newspapers and the Hindi book industry. The spread of vernacular education combined with the Hindi-language movement—a movement for the promotion of the Devnagiri or Nagri script as the common script for the majority of the Indian languages and consequently of Hindi written in the Nagiri script as the *rashtra bhasha* (national language)—had produced a vibrant Hindi print culture in India.[25] Ambikaprasad Vajpeyi, the coeditor of the *Bharat Mitra*, a paper that was unusual among Indian-language newspapers in paying its editors a steady salary and employing its own stable of reporters, gave Sanadhya access to the Hindi press, including some of the leading papers other than his own, to publicize his stories.[26] By contrast, the world of the Firozabad Bharati Bhavan in the U.P. was more circumscribed and provincial. However, it had access to the numerous small printing presses in the province that had become the heartland of the Hindi movement. These presses, whose proliferation owed much to the introduction of cheap lithographic technology, depended for their survival on diversification, including the printing of newspapers, forms, leaflets, posters, and cheap printed books in Hindi and Urdu, as well as contracting out for occasional job work.[27] The Hindi print-world in the U.P. was thus primed to provide the abolition movement with a cheap printed book about the conditions of indenture in Fiji.

Sanadhya's book was created when he on Chaturvedi's invitation spent fifteen days in Chaturvedi's house telling him his stories from Fiji while Chaturvedi wrote them all down and produced a handwritten manuscript that was longer than the published text of *Fiji Mein Mere Ekkis Varsh*. The book was published by the Firozabad Bharati Bhavan as the second work in its Bharati Granth Mala Series (Bharati Book Series). It was printed at Kunvar Hanuvant Singh Raghuvansa's Rajput Anglo-Oriental Press, a printing press in nearby Agra, an urban center with a long history of printing presses. This press, which was associated with the Kshatriya Upkarni Maha Sabha (Society for the Welfare of Kshatriyas), counted among its members several large landowners (*zamindars*), as well as maharajas, from all across India. It published books in English, Hindi, and Urdu, as well as two Hindi newspapers: the bimonthly *Rajput* (circulation eighteen hundred) and the monthly *Swadesh Bandhwa* (five hundred).[28]

Even though often there was not a distinction between the publisher and the printer, in the case of *Fiji Mein Mere Ekkis Varsh* this distinction, presumably because the Firozabad Bharati Bhavan did not have a press of its own, was especially useful. Chaturvedi, anticipating a government search for the manuscript at the premises of the Bharati Bhavan, instructed one of the workers at the Bhavan to take the original manuscript to Hanuvant Singh at the press for safekeeping, probably in the belief that the press, with its connections to a class of socially prominent Indians, would be protected from official harassment.[29] By the terms of the new Press Act of 1910, enacted in the wake of the upsurge of anticolonial revolutionary activism provoked by the government's unpopular decision to partition Bengal in 1905, the local governments were empowered to proscribe objectionable printed material without having to go through the courts. The U.P. government, however, found nothing that was either seditious or obscene in *Fiji Mein Mere Ekkis Varsh* and did not proscribe the book, a point that was widely used in the Indian-language press to argue that even the government could not come up with anything to controvert Sanadhya's revelations.[30]

The Firozabad Bharati Bhavan had one thousand copies of the book printed in 1914, a fairly impressive print run for a noneducational and nonreligious title, and priced it at 6 annas each.[31] All the copies of the book were presumably sold within the year: even the U.P. government by the end of the year was unable to procure a second copy of the book. There is, to the best of my knowledge, no extant copy of this first edition of the book in any of the major libraries around the world. In October 1915, the Bharati Bhavan published a second edition of Sanadhya's book, at the price of 1 rupee, and, relieved from the fear of official harassment, had it printed this time at an even more obscure press, the Onkar Press in Allahabad. The second edition, with a print run of two thousand copies, appeared under a slightly revised title, *Fiji Dweep Mein Mere Ekkis Varsh* (My Twenty-One Years in the Fiji Islands), which was the title used in all subsequent editions of the book, since they all came to rely on this edition.[32] The second edition presumably differed from the first only in the slight change in the title and in the additions of a note from the publisher and a brief preface by Sanadhya.

Sanadhya's preface foregrounds the cooperation in the Indian-language media on abolition that catapulted a Hindi-language book to all-India attention. Sanadhya lists by name several Indian-language newspapers across the country that helped in more ways than just publicizing the book. The staff of several newspapers, as in the case of Shri Sitakant, the chief editor of the Marathi-language paper *Lokmitra* (Khanapur, Belgaum), volunteered to translate Sanadhya's book into other Indian languages; even more, they also helped the book financially. Sanadhya thanks them for enabling him to distribute four hundred free copies of his book at the annual meetings of the Indian National Congress in Madras and of the Hindi Sahitya Sammelan (Hindi Literature Conference) at Lucknow and, more important, at the Maha Kumbh Mela (fair) in Haridwar in 1915. This particular fair, held every twelve years, and which that year was also attended by Gandhi, himself newly returned from South Africa, inevitably drew the attention of the government, not just because of the enormous crowds that gathered at the fairs but also because the fairs, ever since the early advent of print in India, had been popular for the distribution of printed propaganda.[33] Because of its presence at the Kumbh Mela, *Fiji Mein Mere Ekkis Varsh*, unlike the case of its earlier, more routine examination conducted by the U.P. government, which was entrusted with the task of examining all the books published in the province under the Press and Registration of Books Act XXV of 1867, now drew the attention of the Criminal Investigation Department (CID) of the Government of India in Delhi.[34] The CID inquiry into the book, however, managed to slip through the cracks in the exchanges between the two governments, an indication, perhaps, that *Fiji Mein Mere Ekkis Varsh* did not quite rise to a level to engage the full attention of the authorities.

Fiji Mein Mere Ekkis Varsh largely fell below the radar of concerted official scrutiny, and after its initial honeymoon it received only intermittent mention even in those English-language papers most noted for their consistent attention to the anti-indenture cause. However, as testimony to a movement whose existence did not depend only on the English-reading public, the book continued to have a vibrant presence in the Indian-language press, especially in the U.P. A third edition—the last edition before the final legal vestiges of indenture were abolished in 1920—was published in 1916 by the Pratap Pustakalay (Pratap Book Publishing Company) of Kanpur, which published the popular Hindi weekly the *Pratap* (1913).[35] The founder-editor and principal writer of *Pratap*, Ganesh Shankar Vidyarthi, and the "keeper of the press," Shivnarain Misra, were widely respected both by the public (as evidenced by the fact that the circulation of *Pratap* jumped from the inaugural five hundred in 1913 to six thousand by 1916) and, more grudgingly, by the government monitors.[36]

With the new Pratap edition, Sanadhya's book entered the circles of the more explicitly antigovernment politics associated with the Home Rule Leagues and the revolutionaries spawned by the antipartition movement of 1905. While copyright laws, introduced in India in 1847, operated more in the breach, with piracy and unlicensed reprints of popular books not uncommon, Sanadhya was probably himself involved in the Pratap Pustakalaya edition of his book. Vidyarthi and his paper were early converts to the abolition cause, publishing articles and letters against the system, including a controversial article by Sanadhya in its 16 August 1915 issue.[37] The article, in a reprise of the story of Kunti published in the *Bharat Mitra*, was this time about a Muslim woman, Bachi, the wife of a man named Mohammed Beg in Fiji, who had sent Sanadhya a written declaration accusing Mr. Stafford, of the Vunisei plantation in Rewa, of raping her. The publisher's note in the third edition, moreover, acknowledged the earlier editions by the Firozabad Bharati Bhavan and explained that the decision had been made to produce a new edition because, beyond lip service, the government had done nothing as yet to actually abolish the conditions of which the book had written. The Pratap edition, with a print run of two thousand and the backing of a completely committed publisher, was meant to keep up the pressure of public opinion for abolition.

This edition was the twenty-first book to be published in the Pratap Granth Mala (Pratap Book Series), a series of works that the company's editors considered most important.[38] Some of the other books in Hindi published in the series reflected the eclectic political bent of the series: they included Gandhi's account of his jail experiences in South Africa, a history of the Indian National Congress, an account of the movement for Swarajya (self-rule) in India, a book on Irish Home Rule and another on the question of the national ("mother-tongue") language in Ireland, a book on secret political societies in Russia, a collection of German spy stories, and a world history of battles. The "Granth Mala" was apparently a relatively recent innovation of the Pratap Press, which relied on a membership system whereby members paid an entry fee of 2 rupees and became entitled to receive new titles in the series, as well as any of the earlier titles, at a discounted rate. While members could choose any book they wished to buy from the previous titles, they were not given this option with the new titles in the series, which were shipped to them after a week's notification. This arrangement probably provided some stability for a press that was constantly financially strapped and survived through the sheer determination of Vidyarthi and of a loyal following of readers and of fellow newspaper editors.

The Pratap Press, after Sanadhya's book, went on to publish several compilations of material in Hindi against indenture, and Vidyarthi subsequently became an important champion of the cause of peasants and workers. He opened the columns of his paper to writings on and from striking mill workers in Kanpur; was a critic of the forced labor system in the Kumaun region of the U.P.; and was an early supporter of the cultivators on the indigo plantations in Champaran, Bihar. His engagement with Sanadhya's book, indeed, came at the start of a self-conscious effort on his part, and on that of his press, to reflect and represent a more expansive understanding of what hitherto had constituted the Indian public: a *sadharan samaj* (ordinary public).[39] *Fiji Mein Mere Ekkis Varsh* as the product of, and catalyst for, this expanded world of print in India thus appeared sufficiently ordinary to warrant little commentary on the novelty of its intervention.

The desire to reach an expanded public meant that Sanadhya's book necessarily spilled over the boundaries of a discrete printed text. The book was part of an assemblage that included both written and spoken words, as well as direct action aimed at paralyzing the indenture system. It included, in addition to a legal strategy aimed at rescuing potential recruits from the emigration depots with help from junior Indian officials in the courts and in the police, a campaign of direct propaganda among the people.[40] Sanadhya, as the Agra representative of the Anti-Indenture League of Calcutta, an organization affiliated with the Marwari Association of Calcutta, was part of a network of ambulating village activists in north India who gave public talks and distributed leaflets against indenture in market centers in small towns and villages, as well as on railway carriages that carried potential recruits to the emigration depots in Calcutta.[41] Sanadhya's debut as a public speaker in India was in the more august circumstances of the annual session of the Indian National Congress in Madras in December 1914, which he attended as a delegate of the Indians in Fiji, who had paid his expenses to get there. Extending the five minutes initially allotted him to speak from the Congress platform to a full half hour, Sanadhya tried to interest a public that was distracted by other political priorities and largely content with the rumors of official sympathy for abolition. Henceforth Sanadhya concentrated his energies, and used his personal finances, to prevent recruitment for indenture at its source.[42] He spent twelve days at the Maha Kumbh Mela, where apart from distributing his book, he gave talks and distributed leaflets warning people about the actual conditions of indenture. The Abhyudaya Press of Allahabad, which published the popular Hindi weekly *Abhyudaya*, published Sanadhya's speeches in 1915 in the form of a tract appropriately titled *Kuli-Pratha* (The Coolie [Indentured] System).[43]

The work of Sanadhya, and other itinerant activists, through talks and leaflets, was making a sufficient impact for the colonial officer in charge of recruitment in Benares, A. Marsden, to lodge a formal complaint to the Colonial Office about the difficulties created for his recruiters in filling their quota for colonial recruitment.[44] A translation of a sample leaflet in Hindi found in Muzaffarpur in Bihar, under the name of a Puroshottam Das, and with twenty thousand copies printed at the Narayan Press of Muzzafarpur, reads as follows:

ESCAPE FROM DECEIVERS
Escape from the Depot People
Beware! Beware! Beware!
It is not service. It is woe.

Do not fall into their snare.

They will ruin you

You will weep your life along

Instead of rupees, rubbish will fall (on you).

They are taking you across the sea! To Mauritius, to Demerara,

  to Fiji, to Jamaica, to Trinidad, to Honduras.

They are not islands; they are hell

The leaflet concluded by requesting "anyone who wishes, [to] ask for this notice free of charge." Another leaflet, after the common references to indenture as *gulami* or slavery and to the colonies as jails, ended by inviting people who wished to learn more about the evils of indenture to read Sanadhya's book on Fiji.[45] The similarities in the texts of leaflets found in several places across the recruiting districts suggest some degree of coordination, perhaps by the Anti-Indenture League of Calcutta with its branches in Agra, Allahabad, and several other towns across northern India.

The leaflets—with the names, duly noted by law, of their publishers and of the presses where they were printed, which included small printing presses in places such as Muzaffarpur in Bihar and Allahabad in the U.P., as well as the better-known Arya Samaj presses in Delhi—seemed almost to taunt the government to take action. But the Government of India, which was largely sympathetic to the anti-indenture movement, was content to leave Marsden and the Colonial Office to initiate any legal proceedings. The danger for Marsden in prosecuting the anti-indenture activists was that it would make recruitment more difficult at a time when recruits were already becoming difficult to find. The activities of only some of the village-level activists merited the government's attention; for example, the Arya Samajist Satya Dev, who had returned from the United States and who operated in the districts of Patna, Darbhanga, and Muzaffarpur in Bihar and was suspected by the U.P. government, because of his U.S. education, as the possible collaborator on Sanadhya's book. The Government of Bihar and Orissa warned the district magistrates and the superintendents of police in the province against this "dangerous agitator," inasmuch as his proselytizing against indenture sometimes spilled over into direct criticism of the government. He walked through villages giving public talks that, according to one police report, drew attention to the "sorry condition of black races all over the world."[46]

Fiji Mein Mere Ekkis Varsh also inspired several creative literary endeavors. Sanadhya, who is credited with having organized Fiji's first Ramlila (a popular performance of the life of Lord Ram drawn from the Hindu epic the *Ramayana*), recognized the potential of the Ramlila for popularizing his book in India. He volunteered to put up a public performance, based on his book, at the annual Ramlila in Agra in 1915.[47] Even though Sanadhya was not ready in time, the idea for converting the book into a play apparently took hold. Lakshman Singh, the husband of the Hindi littérateur Subhadra Kumari Chauhan and an accomplished Hindi writer in his own right, wrote a play, *Kuli-Pratha arthat Biswi Shatabdi Gulami* (The Indentured System: A Twentieth-Century Slavery), based loosely on Kunti's story from *Fiji Mein Mere Ekkis Varsh*.[48] The Pratap Press published the play in 1916. The play, with its overtly antigovernment stand, was proscribed by the U.P government, which also forfeited, and raised the amount of, the deposit demanded from the press. The Pratap Relief Fund, subscribed to by readers and by other Indian newspapers, managed to rescue the press financially. The play itself went on to acquire further notoriety when a group of young revolutionaries from Mainpuri in the U.P. decided, in an act of defiance, to sell publications proscribed by the U.P. government at the 1917 annual session of the Indian National Congress in Delhi.[49] The U.P. government responded swiftly by seizing all the publications and issued a warrant for the arrest of these young men, at least some of whom managed to escape into hiding. In the trial that followed, which came to be known as the Mainpuri Conspiracy Case of 1918, the play was produced as evidence in the charges against the defendants in absentia.

The outpouring of creative writing around *Fiji Mein Mere Ekkis Varsh*, and around the cause of abolition more generally, took its cue from the earlier South African campaigns of Gandhi that had generated several plays and poems in India about Gandhi's unusual weapon, satyagraha.[50] Likewise, the abolition movement, and Sanadhya's book in particular, inspired several popular poems in the Indian-language press, most notably one by Maithili Sharan Gupta, the *rashtra kavi* (national poet), whose poem *Kisan* (Peasant), published in 1916, is supposed to have drawn its inspiration from Sanadhya's book.[51] The popular literary responses generated by the abolition movement also harked back to earlier oral genres: that is, to the numerous rural folk songs and stories against the hardships of indenture that circulated in the villages of eastern India and on the plantations wherever indentured workers worked overseas.[52]

Ultimately, however, as befitting a relatively minor publication, the traces of *Fiji Mein Mere Ekkis Varsh*'s influence are, at best, oblique.[53] The famous

Andrews-Pearson report on Fiji—the most important of the anti-indenture texts that finally rendered any public defense of the indenture system politically unviable—owed both its genesis and its form in some sense to Sanadhya's prior text. Andrews was already convinced after his visit to Gandhi in South Africa in 1914 of the need for an independent, nonofficial inquiry into indenture. Sanadhya's book, which demanded just such an inquiry in the wake of his disillusionment with the official commission of inquiry that had visited Fiji in 1913, provided the excuse. On the publication of Sanadhya's book, Andrews immediately wrote to the Bharati Bhavan for a copy, enclosing 6 annas for the book and 1 anna for postage.[54] His poem "The Indentured Coolie," in which he claimed that he saw Christ in the figure of the indentured worker and which he wrote at about the time he was reading Sanadhya's book, was very likely a reference to Sanadhya.[55] As Andrews prepared to participate in the independent, nonofficial inquiry that was now cosponsored by the Anti-Indenture Emigration League of Calcutta and the Imperial Indian Citizenship Association of Bombay, he had an English translation of Sanadhya's book made for his personal use to take with him to the inquiry in Fiji.[56] On 14 February 1916, if the report of the Special Branch of the U.P. Police is to be believed, Andrews met Sanadhya in Delhi on his return.[57] In Fiji, in no small part because he had been introduced to the network of anti-indenture activists in India, including Sanadhya, Andrews was able to convince the planters, whose support was necessary for abolition, of the nature of the movement in India.[58] The movement, he informed them, went far beyond the usual political class active in anticolonial agitation and constituted a genuinely popular mobilization that reflected a widespread and implacable revulsion against the system.

Even when the public agitation in India against indenture had entered into the public lore of colonial officials, however, Sanadhya and his book were soon enough forgotten. Take the following example.[59] In 1924 Sanadhya wrote to the Fiji government in response to an exposé by Chaturvedi in the Hindi paper *Aj* (Benares) on the continuing problems confronting Indians in Fiji. The Indian expert of the Fiji government, J. S. Neill, was able to identify both Chaturvedi and *Aj* as abettors of political agitation in India, but, only ten years after the publication of *Fiji Mein Mere Ekkis Varsh*, he had never heard of Sanadhya.

Likewise, the book's expanded understanding of the public only indirectly marked the advent of the new era of mass politics in India associated with the emergence of Gandhi as an all-India leader. The anti-indenture movement was the vehicle that allowed Gandhi to make the transition from South African leader to leader of the nationalist movement in India.[60] Abolition was the only political cause Gandhi embraced on his arrival in India during the period when he had promised to take a hiatus from politics so as to acquaint himself with the conditions in India. Gandhi's involvement, closely associated with the cause in the minds of the public, was the link that connected the political leadership in India more closely to the popular village-level abolition movement.

By early 1917, when the government had still not taken any concrete steps toward abolition, Gandhi at a public meeting gave the government an ultimatum. If indenture was not abolished by 31 May 1917, he threatened to launch his first all-India satyagraha. Drawing on a ready army of anti-indenture activists, he proposed directly interfering with the "coolie ships" to prevent them from leaving the ports of India. The Government of India, by hastily stopping indenture through the special Defense of India Regulations, on the pretext of safeguarding wartime recruitment, managed to postpone its first confrontation with Gandhian satyagraha. But in bypassing abolition through the legislative initiatives of Indian politicians, the government also tacitly gave the victory for abolition to a realm of extra-constitutional, mass-based politics.[61] This popular politics, which predated Gandhi, was of course that with which he would henceforth be identified. Sanadhya's book, albeit only indirectly, was at the threshold of these momentous developments that would eventually shake the entire British Empire to its foundations.

Sanadhya's book—always just below, and in angular relationship to, the major current, whether in the canon of abolitionist literature or in the genealogy of mass-based politics—reveals the most about this inaugural moment of mass politics. To give the abolition of indenture recognition via new legislation, the Government of India eventually, in cooperation with Indian politicians, produced the controversial Indian Emigration Act of 1922. This act prohibited not only indentured labor but all emigration for unskilled labor overseas, with the exception of a few places.[62] In the name of protecting workers from abuses in the colonies, the act curtailed the mobility of labor. Through asserting control over emigration, in a reversal of the Dominion colonies' control over immigration, Indian politicians began to delineate the proper boundaries of national concern in limited territorial terms. Indians overseas were now slowly excluded from this new territorial-national imagination as a separate, and secondary, class of their own as "overseas Indians." *Fiji Mein Mere Ekkis Varsh* is a casualty of precisely this shrinking of political horizons in the aftermath of abolition.

Sanadhya's book—because of, and not despite, the fact that it is minor—demonstrates the ideological nature of what has been considered "major" about Indian abolition. The book was part of a political assemblage that includes other writings of the time, some published and others unpublished, as well as Sanadhya's continued work on behalf of returned emigrants from the colonies, who often found themselves unwelcome on their return. His book represents, as such, an alternative vision of a postemancipation polity. The cause of ex–indentured workers, as he recognized in a foreword to a compilation of Hindi materials on Indians overseas, depended on maintaining porous boundaries between India and the colonies that were not unlike the subcontinent's connections to Southeast Asia in the ancient past.[63] The book belongs to a moment—and a movement—whose critiques of empire and demands for redistributive justice in the name of a *sarva-sadharan janta* (ordinary public) did not lead necessarily, and certainly not automatically, to the territorial form of the nation-state. Sanadhya's humble book—a detritus of the abolition movement—is a stubborn reminder of what is occluded from the incorporation of abolition in a supposedly continuous and progressive unfolding of the transition from empire to nation.

NOTES

1. Totaram Sanadhya, *Fiji Mein Mere Ekkis Varsh* (Agra: Rajput Anglo-Oriental Press, 1914). The official registration gives the publication date "December 20, 1915"; Statement of Particulars Regarding Books and Periodicals Published in the U.P., Registered under Act XXV of 1867, [Statement of Books], during the Quarter Ending, March 1915, U.P. State Archives, Lucknow (U.P. Archives).

2. Totaram Sanadhya, *Fiji Dweep Mein Mere Ekkis Varsh* (Prakashak: Pt. Benarsidas Chaturvedi; Shivlal Agarval & Co, Agra, 1973) (*FDMMEV*).

3. John Dunham Kelley and Uttara Kumari Singh, *My Twenty-One Years in Fiji; And The Story of the Haunted Line*, ed. and trans. T. Sanadhya (Suva: Fiji Museum, 1991).

4. Here I use "minor" in the sense of Sudesh Misra, who draws on Deleuze, to refer not to something that is forgotten or neglected, but to something that is not—and cannot be—integrated into the major narrative. In other words, a minor history functions something like the footnote or the endnote in a text: its presence cannot be entirely ignored but, nevertheless, it does not quite make it into the main text. See Sudesh Misra, "Girmit as Minor History," *Australian Humanities Review* 52 (May

2012), available at www.australianhumanitiesreview.org/archive/Issue-May-2012
/mishra_s.html, accessed 15 July 2012.

5. Hugh Tinker, *A New System of Slavery* (1974) (London: Hansib, 1993), 288. The
most detailed account of abolition is in Karen A. Ray, "The Abolition of Indentured
Emigration and the Politics of Indian Nationalism, 1894–1917" (Ph.D. diss., McGill
University, 1980).

6. H. S. L. Polak, *The Indians of South Africa* (Madras: G. A. Natesan, 1909); C. F.
Andrews and W. W. Pearson, *Report on Indentured Labour in Fiji* (Calcutta: Star Printing, 1916).

7. Benarsidas Chaturvedi and Marjorie Sykes, *Charles Freer Andrews: A Narrative*
(London: Allen and Unwin, 1949).

8. R. Ratnes, *Patrikarita Ke Yug Nibharta: Benarsidas Chaturvedi* (Delhi: Prabhat
Prakashan, 2010).

9. Balavantsinha, *Under the Shelter of Bapu*, trans. Shri Gopalrau Kulkarni (1956)
(Ahmedabad: Navajivan Publishing House, 1962), 15–16.

10. Chaturvedi in FDMMEV, 2 October 1972, 18–24.

11. "Prakashak ka Nivedan," in T. Sanadhya, *Fiji Dweep Mein Mere Ekkis Varsh*
(Allahabad: Onkar Press, 1915).

12. Commerce and Industry, Emigration, May 1916, 10–16, pt. B, National Archives
of India, New Delhi (NAI).

13. Sudesh Mishra, "Time and Girmit," *Social Text* 82, no. 23 (Spring 2005): 15–36.

14. Mishra, "Time and Girmit," 15.

15. Rodney Moag, "The Linguistic Adaptations of the Fiji Indians," in *Rama's Banishment*, ed. Vijay Mishra (Auckland: Heineman, 1973), 112–138.

16. Chaturvedi in FDMMEV, 18–24.

17. B. Chaturvedi, "Totaram Sanadhya," in *Sansmaran* (Kashi: Bharitya Gnanpith,
1958), 180–189; and Jaganath Lahiri, *Janam Shatabdi Ke Punya Avsar Par, Sri Totaram
Sanadhya Samarika (1876–1976)* (Ferozabadh: Ferozabad Sandesh Press, n.d.).

18. Ulrike Stark, *An Empire of Books: The Naval Kishore Press and the Diffusion of the
Printed Word in Colonial India* (New Delhi: Permanent Black, 2007).

19. Madan Gopal, *Freedom Movement and the Press: The Role of Hindi Newspapers*
(New Delhi: Criterion, 1990), 13.

20. Tinker, *New System*, 306–309.

21. Pavan Kumar Jain, *Videsom Mein Hindi Patrikarta* (New Delhi: Radha, 1993), 121.

22. B. Chaturvedi, "Bikhri Hui Baten," in *Balmukund Gupta Smarak Grantha*, ed.
Jhabamal Sharma and B. Chaturvedi (Calcutta: Gupta Smaraka Grantha Prakashan
Samiti, 1950).

23. Revenue, Emigration, File no. 3E-6, Proceedings, nos. 5–7, Nov. 1915, West Bengal State Archives, Kolkata (WBA); Commerce and Industry, Emigration, Dec. 1915,
nos. 43–54, pt. A, NAI.

24. Commerce and Industry, Emigration, Nov. 1914, nos. 17–20, pt. B, NAI.

25. Alok Rai, *Hindi Nationalism* (Delhi: Orient Blackswan, 2001).

26. B. S. Kesavan, *History of Printing and Publishing in India*, vol. 3 (Delhi: National
Book Trust of India, 1997), 286–288.

27. Stark, *Empire of Books.*

28. *Memorandum on Indian-Owned Newspapers in the United Provinces during the Year 1914* (Allahabad: Government Press, U.P., 1915), U.P. Archives.

29. Chaturvedi in FDMMEV, 18–24.

30. *Hindi Kesari* (Benares), 18 November 1915, in Selection from Indian Owned Newspapers in U.P., 1915, U.P. Archives. However, the Marathi translation of the book, Sitakant, *Fiji Kantatal Manji 21 Varsh*, was banned; see Graham Shaw and Mary Lloyd, eds., *Publications Proscribed by the Government of India: A Catalog of the Collections in the India Office Library and Records and the Department of Oriental Manuscripts and Printed Books, British Library Reference Division* (London: British Library, 1985).

31. Statement of Books, during the Quarter Ending March 1915, U.P. Archives.

32. Statement of Books, during the Quarter Ending December 1915, U.P. Archives.

33. Kama Maclean, *Pilgrimage and Power: The Kumbh Mela in Allahabad, 1765–1954* (New York: Oxford University Press, 2008).

34. Commerce and Industry, Emigration, May 1916, nos. 10–16, pt. B, NAI.

35. M. L. Bhargava, *Ganesh Shankar Vidyarthi* (New Delhi: Government of India, Publications Division, 1988).

36. Statement of Books, During 1917, U.P. Archives.

37. Commerce and Industry, Emigration, May 1916, nos. 10–16, pt. B, NAI.

38. Prakashak, Shiv Narain Misra, "Kuch Shabd," 1 December 1916, in T. Sanadhya, *Fiji Dweep Mein Mere Ekkis Varsh* (Kanpur: Pratap Pustakalya, 1916).

39. Francesca Orsini, "What Did They Mean by 'Public'? Language, Literature and the Politics of Nationalism," *Economic and Political Weekly* 34, no. 7 (February 1999): 409–416.

40. Commerce and Industry, Emigration, May 1916, nos. 10–16, pt. B, NAI.

41. Commerce and Industry, Emigration, May 1916, nos. 10–16, pt. B, NAI.

42. Sanadhya, "Prastavna," in "Ek Bharitiya Hriday," in *Fiji Mein Bharatiya Prati-bandh: Kuli-Pratha* (Kanpur: Pratap Press, 1919), 1–54.

43. Statement of Books, during the Quarter Ending March 1915, U.P. Archives.

44. Commerce and Industry, Emigration, Dec. 1915, nos. 43–54, pt. A, NAI.

45. Depot Walon Ka Phanda, Commerce and Industry, Emigration, May 1916, nos. 10–16, pt. B; and Commerce and Industry, Emigration, Dec. 1915, nos. 43–54, pt. A, NAI.

46. *Sri Swami Satya Dev Parivrajaka* (Patiala: Bhasha Vibhag, 1988); and Rita Chaturvedi and S. R. Bakshi, *Bihar through the Ages*, vol. 3 (New Delhi: Sarup and Sons, 2007), 355–356.

47. Commerce and Industry, Emigration, May 1916, nos. 10–16, pt. B, NAI.

48. "Indentured Immigration: Summary of the Hindi Book Prohibited in the United Provinces under the Press Act," L/P/J/6/1479, Asian and African Collections, British Library (BL); and Satyendra Kumar Taneja, *Sitama Ki Intiha Kya Hai: Ata zabtasuda Hindi Nataka* (New Delhi: Rashtriya Naya Vidyalaya, 2010).

49. Mainpuri Conspiracy Case, file 3, U.P. Archives.

50. Surendra Bhana and Neelima Shukla Bhatt, *A Fire That Blazed in the Ocean* (New Delhi: Promila, 2011); and on indenture, *Navajivan* (Allahabad), July 1915; *Pratap*, 9 Nov. 1915, in Selection of Native Newspapers, U.P., 1915, U.P. Archives.

51. Chaturvedi in *FDMMEV*, 18–24.

52. Ved Praksh Vatuk, "Protest Songs of East Indians in British Guiana," *Journal of American Folklore* 77, no. 305 (July–Sept. 1964): 220–235; and Mousumi Majumdar, ed., *Kahe Gaile Bides? Where Did You Go? On Bhojpuri Migration since the 1870s and Contemporary Culture in Uttar Pradesh, Bihar, Suriname and the Netherlands* (Amsterdam: KIT Press, 2010).

53. Misra, "Girmit as Minor History."

54. Andrews to Sir, n.d., Benarsidas Chaturvedi Papers, 1/B-387, NAI.

55. Chaturvedi and Sykes, *Charles Freer Andrews*, 112–113.

56. Chaturvedi in *FDMMEV*, 18–24.

57. Commerce and Industry, Emigration, May 1916, nos. 10–16, pt. B, NAI.

58. Commerce and Industry, Emigration, May 1916, no. 6, pt. A, NAI.

59. John Dunham Kelley, "Addenda," in Kelley and Singh, *Twenty-One Years.*

60. Ray, "Abolition."

61. Ray, "Abolition."

62. *Legislative, Assembly & Council*, July 1922, nos. 1–19, pt. A, NAI. I owe this insight about the Act of 1922 to Radhika Singha, "A 'Proper Passport' for the Colony: Border Crossing in British India, 1882–1920," available at the website of Yale University, www.yale.edu/agrarianstudies/colloqpapers/16singha.pdf, accessed 21 April 2014.

63. Sanadhya, "Prastavna," 1–54. Sanadhya's extended account about Fiji was published by Brij V. Lal and Yogendra Yadav, *Bhut Len Ki Katha: Totaram Ka Fiji* (New Delhi: Saraswati Press, 1994), and Totaram Sanadhya, *Bhut Len Ki Katha: Girmit Ki Anubhav*, edited by Brij V. Lal, Ashutosh Kumar, and Yogendra Yadav (New Delhi: Rajkamal Press, 2012).

Nine

C. L. R. JAMES'S
THE BLACK JACOBINS AND
THE MAKING OF THE
MODERN ATLANTIC WORLD

. AARON KAMUGISHA

Published in 1938 on the brink of World War II, C. L. R. James's book *The Black Jacobins: Toussaint L'Ouverture and the San Domingo Revolution* is the finest single accomplishment of the figure many consider to be the outstanding Anglophone Caribbean intellectual of the twentieth century.[1] *The Black Jacobins* is not merely the most enduring and influential history of the Haitian Revolution in the English language, and rightly in its epic sweep called by some the Caribbean's *War and Peace*, but in its tracing of the relationship between metropole and colony it anticipated much of late twentieth-century work in Atlantic and postcolonial studies. It introduced the question of the momentous importance of the Haitian Revolution to audiences throughout the world, and directly influenced later texts that would inaugurate the argument that the development of the West was inseparable from the exploitation of enslaved labor from Africa, principally *Capitalism and Slavery*, by Eric Williams. *The Black Jacobins* is also arguably the single most important work of history by a twentieth-century Caribbean historian, in that because of it, generations of Caribbean people have realized that through the Haitian Revolution they announced themselves as a people to the world, and that every historical-cultural movement and political conundrum in the wider region since—neocolonialism, black consciousness, the debt burden—first revealed itself there. *The Black Jacobins* has thus played a decisive role in the education of three generations of radical activists and intellectuals about the meaning of slavery and freedom in the Western Hemisphere.

These are daring claims, to be sure. Part of the challenge of tracing the influence of this classic text of the black radical tradition lies in distinguishing the impact of its author from that of the reception of the text. James was one of the quintessential figures of the twentieth-century black world, an insightful Pan-Africanist and Marxist theoretician of great subtlety and charisma, and in his six decades of radical activity attracted an immense range of revolutionary comrades, fellow travelers, and admirers. While the precise influence of this text on persons whose lives were changed by their encounter with James might be difficult to discern, an audience with James inevitably meant an encounter with the ideas given coherence in *The Black Jacobins*. In this chapter, I will seek to consider the impact of *The Black Jacobins* in a meditation that will take me from Haitian revolutionary studies to interrogations of the modern in postcolonial studies, from Caribbean historiography to the meaning of Haiti in the Western imagination. The intellectual legacy of *The Black Jacobins* is particularly intriguing, as it appeared first as a play under the title *Toussaint Louverture* (1936) and as a chapter in a broader history, James's *A History of Negro Revolt* (1938). *The Black Jacobins* looks back to slavery and the mechanics of empire in anticipation of a future decolonization—indeed James indentified the book as being less about the Caribbean than about Africa and its coming freedom struggle. In his 1936 history of the Communist International, *World Revolution 1917–1936*, James commented: "We may well see, especially after the universal ruin and destruction of the coming war, a revolutionary movement which . . . will sweep the imperialist bourgeoisie out of power, not only in every country in Europe, but in India, China, Egypt and South Africa."[2] Written and researched between London and Paris, *The Black Jacobins* was conceptualized in the heart of the British Empire, whose abolition James was determined to usher in, and at the crossroads of the anti-imperialist networks and friendships that stimulated the most single productive period in James's life.[3] The half century that he lived post its publication allowed him the time to write a riveting appendix and important revisions to a second edition, deliver a series of lectures on *The Black Jacobins* in 1971, and contribute a new introduction and autobiographical sketches that add to the book's enduring weight and value.

Beyond Vindicationism

A presentation of *The Black Jacobins* as James's finest work may suggest that it is the culmination of his life's work—a strange argument to make about a figure who lived for five decades after its publication and produced an enormous amount of influential scholarship in that time. It is better seen as the culmination of a specific trajectory in his intellectual life that began before his departure from Trinidad for England in 1932. James was born in 1901 in colonial Trinidad, and staked a claim as a public intellectual through his participation in the launch of the literary magazines *Trinidad* and the *Beacon* in the late 1920s and early 1930s, and as a fiction writer of distinction. His first published essay, "The Intelligence of the Negro," was a response to a racist diatribe by a Dr. Sydney Harland titled "Racial Admixture," and takes a fairly classical vindicationist line of response to that article.[4] By "vindicationism" I refer to a form of African diaspora historicism that Wilson Moses defines as constituting a "project of defending black people from the charge that they have made little or no contribution to the history of human progress. Sometimes vindicationism may imply the even more basic struggle to secure recognition of the fact that black people are human at all."[5] Early twentieth-century racism meant that vindicationism was a discourse that a black intelligentsia could hardly refuse, a mode of emplotment in historical writing shared by many both before and after James. A comment by James in his 1971 lecture "How I Wrote *The Black Jacobins*" about his life in the Caribbean before he left for England in 1932 is instructive here. In it James describes his knowledge of himself as a person of African descent living in the Caribbean at that time:

> I don't know too much about black people, but nevertheless I don't believe all that they tell me. They tell me more or less that black people are lowly people, that we came to the Caribbean as slaves, and that it was a benefit to us to have come rather than to have stayed in backward Africa. I didn't so much believe it, but I didn't disbelieve it. I didn't think that it was what they were saying, but one thing, we moved about among white and black people, and Englishmen

came and went. We met them on a level. There was nobody who came there who made me feel inferior—by inferior I mean intellectually subordinate.[6]

This observation by James well illustrates his status as a middle-class intellectual within Trinidad at that time. His remark that he "didn't so much believe it, but I didn't disbelieve it" shows well the ways he could, and did, maneuver within a society that was predicated on racism but offered spaces where the educated middle classes could develop a confidence and belief in themselves far beyond what colonialism offered. Despite its popularity as a form of historical discourse and popular history from the nineteenth century through the twentieth century, especially among a self-taught black intelligentsia, the vast majority of James's work always lay outside the often reactive nature of vindicationist arguments and their historical-civilizationist-redemptive limits. His essay "The Intelligence of the Negro" remains important for a reason beyond his shredding criticism of Harland. In this 1931 essay, written a year before he left for England, James advances the story of Toussaint L'Ouverture as a counter to Harland's ideas about the paucity of black achievement and displays more than a passing knowledge of, and interest in, the revolution in St. Domingue. The key question for James at this stage, however, is not the revolution but the singular greatness of its main leader, which gives the lie to theories of black inferiority.

James arrived in England in 1932, and over the next six years became a revolutionary and scholar of global sympathies, with a prodigious intellectual output.[7] In the same year that *The Black Jacobins* was published, it appeared as a chapter in James's history of black resistance to colonialism in the modern world, *A History of Negro Revolt*. This chapter does not differ substantially from the longer history, except that its content is naturally much abridged, though James does give a remarkably lucid explanation of the reasons for the British interest in abolishing the slave trade. His play *Toussaint Louverture*, with Paul Robeson as its lead, which opened in London two years before the publication of *The Black Jacobins*, constitutes a fascinating attempt by James to combine his historical and aesthetic interests in one production. In his introduction to the long-lost 1936 edition of *Toussaint Louverture* Christian Høgsbjerg makes the claim that it is "the indispensable companion work to *The Black Jacobins* . . . a literary supplement to the magisterial history."[8] This view is echoed by Fionnghuala Sweeney, who argues convincingly that *Toussaint Louverture* should not be seen as merely practice for *The Black Jacobins*, as this perspective ignores the intricate questions surrounding staging a revolutionary play in 1930s London, and the play's location within a black transatlantic aesthetic of its time.[9] The play's emphasis on heavy, somewhat stilted dialogue in its script makes it dense and not evocatively dramatic—more than slightly strange when one considers the sheer literary and rhetorical power of the historical text. However—despite the play's too heavy focus on the revolutionary leaders—the problem of government, the schemes, pondering, uncertainty, and politics of intrigue, and the choices facing the leaders of the revolution are cast into stark relief in the dramatic form. Also, vodun, mentioned but not given a very prominent role in the historical text, is an unmistakable, constantly hovering presence in the play, giving life to James's comment in *The Black Jacobins* that vodun "was the medium of the conspiracy."[10] Furthermore, *Toussaint Louverture* marked "the first time that black professionals had ever performed on the British stage in a play written by a black playwright"—marking it as a signal contribution to the history of black diaspora theater.[11] Despite its limited run of just two nights, the play received over twenty reviews in British publications, with an additional request from a Broadway producer to stage the production in New York.[12] Paul Robeson's celebrity certainly contributed to its success; he reveled in the part, as it was "the only play in which Robeson appeared that was written by a writer of African heritage."[13]

The Black Jacobins appeared in 1938, shortly before James left London for a lecture tour to the United States. It constitutes the story of the Haitian Revolution, but like all great works of the historical imagination, forges pathways beyond a chronology of events. From the preface's consideration of the problem of writing revolutionary history to the tumultuous final chapter, *The Black Jacobins* produces a series of stunning reversals to then settled understandings within Western thought. Its opening chapter on the lives of enslaved persons is an elaborate rendition of the dehumanization and violence of slavery, but simultaneously contains a powerful *rehumanization* of enslaved persons, and a consideration of the categories and forms that resistance took against slavery. The discussion of the San Domingo slave society and economy is an examination of the role of white supremacy in securing privilege and access to resources in the colonies, shattering racist stereotypes of black inferiority and unfitness for positions of power and authority. In one of the single most important arguments of the text, James declares that "the slave-trade and slavery were the economic basis of the French Revolution," highlighting not just the exploitation of the colonies by the metropolis but that the colonies actually create Europe, rather than the commonly held reverse.[14] In an allied argument, James would tie British abolition of the slave trade not to the received wisdom of humanitarianism but to the desire by the British prime minister William Pitt and his secretary of war, Henry Dundas, to ruin the colony of San Domingo, a major competitor against British sugar on the world market. The text's attention to the minutiae of battles, negotiations, and compromises highlights the imperial intrigue of the time, in which France, Spain, and England attempted to wrest control of the colony. The stakes and sheer deadliness of the politics on display is a more forceful indictment of imperialism than any polemic could ever be. While James's focus on Toussaint L'Ouverture has been criticized in later scholarship, which has justifiably said that it obscures the role of the masses in the creation and perpetuation of the revolution, James uses Toussaint to reflect productively on the problem of revolutionary leadership and organization. More than an application of Marxist categories to a third-world revolution, The Black Jacobins exists as a text through which James can forge pathways to the means by which race and class produce coloniality, and must be understood in any assessment of it: "The race question is subsidiary to the class question in politics, and to think of imperialism in terms of race is disastrous. But to neglect the racial factor as merely incidental is an error only less grave than to make it fundamental."[15]

The power of The Black Jacobins is that in rejecting the vindicationist tale, with its curious web of indignation at the denial of an African worldview and bourgeois love of civilization, it presents a story of the black presence in the modern world with the potential to dismantle the entire artifice of Eurocentric world history. Listen to James in the preface to the first edition: "The transformation of slaves, trembling in hundreds before a single white man, into a people able to organise themselves and defeat the most powerful European nations of their day, is one of the great epics of revolutionary struggle and achievement."[16] In a 1980 foreword to the Allison and Busby edition of The Black Jacobins, James states his personal motivations for writing it as how tired he was of the constant tales of black oppression from throughout the Western Hemisphere and African continent, and his personal conviction that he should write a book in which people of African descent were "taking action on a grand scale, and shaping other people to their own needs."[17] He ends the brief foreword with an anecdote about meeting South African students in Ghana in 1957 who were reading *The Black Jacobins*, which they found directly relevant to their contemporary concerns. James's jubilation here may be because, as he often noted, "the book was written not with the Caribbean but with Africa in mind."[18] The last three pages of *The Black Jacobins* show this intention and interest of James, who in the mid-1930s was a founding member of the International African Service Bureau in London. "The imperialists envisage an eternity of African exploitation: the African is backward, ignorant. . . . They dream dreams."[19] And as a closing line to the text: "The African faces a long and difficult road and he will need guidance. But he will tread it fast because he will walk upright."[20]

The Black Jacobins received generally positive reviews in the British press, except for a notorious attack in the *New Statesman*.[21] A U.S. edition was published the same year and was reviewed extensively by African American journals, while a French translation appeared in 1949 but was banned by the French government; *The Black Jacobins* only became easily available in French in 1983.[22] A review published in James's native Trinidad by his revolutionary comrade George Padmore was arguably the most prescient and discerning. Padmore wrote that *The Black Jacobins* should serve as "an inspiration to Africans and other colonial peoples still struggling for their freedom from the yoke of white imperialism."[23] James left England for the United States in 1938, originally on a speaking tour, but later residing there for fifteen years. In that time, he met Kwame Nkrumah and famously facilitated his introduction to George Padmore when Nkrumah traveled to London. Padmore, a childhood friend of James in Trinidad and a towering figure of the Pan-African left in the United Kingdom following his split with the Soviet Union in 1935, mentored Nkrumah and many other African activists and students in London, and more than any other figure in the Anglophone world laid the groundwork for the post–World War II liberation struggles on the African continent. James was somewhat removed from these concrete struggles but would later claim that "Nkrumah and other revolutionaries read and absorbed the book"—and certainly its tale of a heroic black struggle against overwhelming colonial forces resonated strongly with Pan-Africanists in the immediate post–World War II era.[24]

The transformation of the world after the war has meant that the routes of influence of *The Black Jacobins* have been complex. In what follows, I trace a number of circuits of influence of this text and attempt to show why it was one of the quintessential texts for understanding the dismantling of the ideological structures that legitimated Britain's empire.

I have advanced the claim that *The Black Jacobins* is the most enduring and influential history of the Haitian Revolution in the English language and a pioneer of transatlantic historical studies. The fulsome praise this text has consistently received in surveys of the field of Caribbean historiography, Haitian revolutionary studies, and postcolonial studies provides a place to begin an assessment of its legacy. In the most recent major history of the revolution, Laurent Dubois says *The Black Jacobins* "remains the classic account of the revolution."[25] David Geggus in his authoritative *Haitian Revolutionary Studies* has written: "Easily the most influential general study has been C. L. R. James, *The Black Jacobins* (1938), an analytical tour de force of literary distinction and extraordinary staying power."[26] Nor are these judgments limited to historians. For the Jamaican political scientist Brian Meeks, "*The Black Jacobins* is . . . arguably the single most important historical study by any writer in the Anglophone Caribbean," while the literary scholar Frank Birbalsingh declares James's magnum opus a "superlative literary achievement" and "probably the finest piece of non-fiction writing to come out of the English-speaking Caribbean."[27] Here, the lasting impression on readers is not just James's insights or methodology but that more elusive quality of style that gives his history a sweep and verve more compelling than practically any other study in Caribbean history.

This praise does not quite alert us, though, to the nature of the lasting contributions that James has made to Caribbean historiography. Barry Higman, in his *Writing West Indian Histories*, establishes a network of dedications by Caribbean historians to their past colleagues in which C. L. R. James, Elsa Goveia, and Eric Williams occur most prominently and regularly. However, Higman's treatment of *The Black Jacobins*, despite somewhat casually mentioning its "highly influential" role in the region's historiography, is limited and avoids a thorough examination of one of the most decisive impacts of that text: its role, and its author's role, in influencing the intellectual career of Eric Williams.[28]

Eric Williams's *Capitalism and Slavery* is easily the most debated and controversial historical study by an Anglophone Caribbean intellectual. Published in 1944, it emerged from his 1938 Oxford doctoral dissertation, with which Williams became the first West Indian to attain a doctorate in history. The relationship between James and Williams is the most famously acrimonious of two leading Caribbean scholars, stretching sixty years and filled with debt and counterdebt, betrayals and disavowals. The terrain here is not merely scholarship but the question of postcolonial politics and the future of the Caribbean.

We may well start with a sketch of this sixty-year relationship. It is well established that James first met Williams when he served as his tutor at Queen's Royal College, the secondary school both attended in Port-of-Spain.[29] Both left Trinidad in 1932 for Britain, James to create a career for himself as a writer, Williams for Oxford. During James's six years in Britain, they were in constant contact, and left for the United States around the same time, just before the outbreak of World War II. James's sojourn in the United States lasted fifteen years before he departed, in the face of his inevitable deportation, in 1953. Williams left a couple years later for Trinidad, where he launched the nationalist party the People's National Movement (PNM) and within a year became the chief minister of the colony. James, invited to come down to Trinidad from London to attend the launch of the Federal Parliament in 1958, stayed to work with the PNM as the editor of the party newspaper the *Nation* and as secretary of the West Indies Federal Labour Party. By July 1960 he had resigned from the PNM, amid growing differences with Williams, and left Trinidad shortly before independence, which came in 1962, with Williams as prime minister. On his return to cover cricket test matches in 1965, Williams placed him briefly under house arrest, after which James formed the Workers and Farmers Party, which contested, and was ignominiously defeated, in the 1966 general election. James left Trinidad shortly after this campaign, not to return to Trinidad again until 1980, when he visited for a few months as the guest of the Oilfield Workers Trade Union, before returning to England for the rest of his life.

The political split between James and Williams has had the effect of substantially obscuring the overwhelming intellectual debt Williams owes to James, and nowhere is this more apparent than in Williams's autobiography, *Inward Hunger*.[30] This book is polemical, boastful, and idiosyncratic in its scripted story and thus in concert with the temper of much of Williams's published work from the 1960s onward.[31] Its three references to James are revealing in their brief and dismissive nature. In Williams's reflection on his decision to return to the West Indies, James is caricatured as one who "deserted" the region for "the absurdities of world revolution"; later he is listed with George Padmore and Arthur Lewis as an associate with whom Williams discussed the PNM's draft party program and constitution. The last mention of James is the longest: an account of James's split with the PNM, the blame for which is given squarely to James, who had a "notorious political record" and "used the Party paper to build up himself and his family."[32] Yet even the fictionalized sections of Williams's autobiography cannot quite escape moments when the influence of James becomes clear. While tracing the network of influences that convinced him to do his doctoral historical research on the West Indies, Williams cites "the political education I had acquired from my international contacts in England."[33] Williams might be in a hurry to disavow any influence by James, but intellectual histories of the period place him as a fellow traveler of George Padmore and the International Friends of Abyssinia movement in mid-1930s London.[34] Williams's earlier and most famous work, long before his 1961 split with James, *Capitalism and Slavery*, also betrays him. In his bibliographical notes to that work he gives "special mention" to *The Black Jacobins*, stating that "on pages 38–41 [of *The Black Jacobins*] the thesis advanced in this book is stated clearly and concisely and, as far as I know, for the first time in English."[35]

James's comments on Williams, and attempts to trace their relationship, have the merit of greater historical veracity, if hardly less bitterness. James's best known rejoinder to Williams came in his *Party Politics in the West Indies*, a book written in some haste to clarify his position on the split between them, and the prospects for Trinidad and Tobago on the cusp of independence. The critique of Williams advanced in the section bearing his name is a study of a political personality. Williams is presented here as the prototypical charismatic leader that Archie Singham would dissect in his book *The Hero and the Crowd*: a leader who propagandizes the masses rather than mobilizes them, facilitating a political culture where demagoguery replaces a thoughtful presentation of political alternatives.[36] In many of his comments on Williams in the 1960s and onward, James presents him as a petit-bourgeois intellectual with a limited imagination, who could be profitably studied as a prototype of the leadership that would befall the postindependence Caribbean state. At the end of his lectures on *The Black Jacobins* in 1971, James mused about the possibility of writing a psychological study of Williams in his autobiography—as "I know that *petit-maitre* very well."[37]

Polemic aside, the best place to look for an examination of the intellectual differences between the two men might be James's review of Williams's first book, *The Negro in the Caribbean*. James published this review under the pseudonym W. F. Carlton, and in it he rehearses in a quite prescient manner the break he will have with Williams two decades later. Not only does James flatly assert that "Williams is no Marxist" but also he claims that "the future demands more than Williams has. It needs a conscious theory. He is a sincere nationalist and a sincere democrat, but after so sure a grasp of historical development as he shows in this history of four centuries, he displays an extreme naiveté in his forecasts of the future."[38] Williams's text is a "little triumph"; his "immediate demands—federation, national independence, political democracy—are admirable, but he commits a grave error in thinking, as he obviously does, that these will end or even seriously improve West Indian mass poverty and decay."[39] James's return to Trinidad in 1958 thus has to be understood as somewhere between the act of a reluctant conscript to a nationalist enterprise that he knew would never accommodate his politics and an indication of his sincere interest and excitement at the possibilities that could emerge in the formation of a new Caribbean nation. In a letter to George Padmore on 17 March 1958, the day after he received his official invitation to attend the inauguration ceremonies of the West Indian Federal Parliament, James wrote: "I have been badly wanting to go home for some years now. I intend to stay for a while and I intend also to take part in the undoubted crisis which the Federation faces. My view is that nothing can save them but independence with a constitution to be decided by a constitutional assembly and not handed down either by the Colonial Office or a Federal Parliament."[40] However, in his semiautobiographical *Beyond a Boundary*, he wrote: "Once in a blue moon, i.e. once in a lifetime, a writer is handed on a plate a gift from heaven. I was handed mine in 1958."[41] The irony here is that without Williams's endorsement James, who had left Trinidad twenty-six years previously, could hardly have established his reputation again so quickly or had such a decisive influence on the nationalist movement in Trinidad, and the discussions around independence throughout the Anglophone Caribbean. It is another of the cycles of debt to each other, forgotten amid the bitterness of the 1960s.

In a 1972 interview in Texas, James gives his clearest published statement about his influence on Williams's doctoral dissertation, later to become *Capitalism and Slavery*.[42] In response to a direct question on the connection between *The Black Jacobins* and *Capitalism and Slavery*, James begins by mentioning his close association with Williams throughout the 1930s and the vast amounts of time they spent in each other's company during his breaks from studying at Oxford. He further states that Williams accompanied him on his searches for archival material in France for *The Black Jacobins* and served as his research assistant on these trips. This comment is repeated in his unpublished autobiography, but with this quite astonishing addition: "and there are certain pages in *The Black Jacobins* where most of the material and all the footnotes (I would put them in sometime) are the things that Williams gave to me. I never had occasion to look them up. That is what he's done."[43] This observation complicates understandings of this relationship, which perpetually cast James in the role of mentor and Williams as the student. James does go on to suggest that Williams asked him for advice on his doctoral project, and James wrote what amounted to a draft proposal, which Williams later took and submitted to the Oxford authorities—an assertion given weight not just by Williams's bibliographical note on James but also by his biographer, Selwyn Ryan.[44]

I have written this long clarification on the relationship between James and Williams in order to show the inextricable bond between *The Black Jacobins* and *Capitalism and Slavery*, which is crucial for any appreciation of the legacy of *The Black Jacobins*. As I have already stated, *Capitalism and Slavery* is the most debated and controversial book by a Caribbean historian—indeed, for Cedric Robinson, "Williams struck a vital nerve at the ideological core of Western historiography."[45] Despite numerous critiques of its central premises, it has been very difficult to discredit the book's thesis, to the extent that Joseph Inikori could state in his magnum opus *Africans and the Industrial Revolution in England* (2002) that "the main arguments concerning the economic basis of abolition have stood the test of time. In spite of the voluminous criticism by scholars since the 1960s, those arguments can still be shown to be basically valid, logically and empirically."[46] In addition, *Capitalism and Slavery* inspired a group of radical Caribbean social scientists who would make an important contribution to the dependency school of the 1960s, and it became a classic text of black political economy.[47] Nowhere is its contemporary influence better seen than in the recent work on Britain's debt to its Caribbean colonies, whose authors cite Williams as their most important intellectual ancestor.[48]

Recognition of the contribution of *The Black Jacobins* to historiography has thus certainly not been limited to scholars interested in the field of Caribbean history. Even within Haitian intellectual circles, with a long history of writing about the revolution ignored by the Western academy, James's work is prized. Scholars of the Haitian Revolution have paid critical attention to James's work, and I have already noted the appreciation of it that two leading figures in the field, David Geggus and Laurent Dubois, have expressed. Carolyn Fick's book *The Making of Haiti: The Saint Domingue Revolution from Below* (1990), often recognized as the most important text in the field since *The Black Jacobins,* shows an incredible debt to James in its acknowledgments. For James, according to Fick, proposed the topic to her dissertation supervisor, George Rudé, and the dissertation subsequently became *The Making of Haiti*—a quite extraordinary connection between two decisive texts within the field.[49] Fick acknowledges the innovative importance of James's book, in which the "revolutionary potential of the masses is . . . an integral part of the revolutionary process" but is troubled by its emphasis on Toussaint L'Ouverture's biography and the correspond-ing lost voice of the mass of the population.[50] On this question James would agree, as in his lecture "How I Would Rewrite *The Black Jacobins,*" he criticized his earlier work on two main grounds. First, he critiqued his earlier overreliance on the account of colonial travel writers' depictions of enslaved Africans and assessments of their intellectual prowess. Instead he suggests that he would search harder for perspectives from the enslaved per-sons on their own condition. Second, he professes a strong interest in theo-rizing the sheer extent of the leadership of the revolution, the "two thousand leaders to be taken away," which will allow him to comprehend that the locomotion of the revolution was from below.[51]

The Black Jacobins also presents a significant development in the field of Marxist-inspired history, which the intellectual historian Christian Høgsbjerg has shown anticipated the development of the "history from below" school of British historians, whose most prominent names include E. P. Thompson and Eric Hobsbawm.[52] James's radical path as a Trotskyist, and in the 1930s one of the leading critics of the Soviet Union in Britain, cer-tainly influenced the reception of this work. With some candor, Hobsbawm notes that in the formation of the historians' group in the British Com-munist Party, "since CP members then segregated themselves strictly from schismatics and heretics, the writings of living non-Party members made little impact, though C. L. R. James' *Black Jacobins* was read, in spite of the author's known Trotskyism."[53] This cool reception may have contributed to the limited appreciation by key figures like Hobsbawm of James's work, which resulted in Hobsbawm's stunning silence on the Haitian Revolution in his much-heralded *Age of Revolution* (1962), which mentions that revo-lution cursorily, and only twice.[54] In James Young's reconstruction of this period, James met E. P. Thompson at the Fifth Worker's Control confer-ence in Coventry in June 1967.[55] At this meeting, Thompson's glowing com-ments about James's contribution to radicalism and to the study of society and culture led to the beginning of a friendship between the two, despite James's own pointed critique of the New Left's "May Day Manifesto," coauthored by Thompson. Yet there was little space for James's ideas in Britain's New Left. Probably even more crucial than this was the ethnocentrism and nationalism of this generation of British Marxist historians and their inability to consider empire, an inability that would have rendered James's text and the Haitian Revolution unthinkable.[56] By the 1980s, with a subsequent waning of the Trotskyite-Communist clashes of an earlier generation, and with a growing recognition of James during the last decade of his life, more on the left in Britain would have appreciated E. P. Thompson's tribute to him on his eightieth birthday: "It is not a question of whether one agrees with everything he has said or done: but everything has had the mark of originality, of his own flexible, sensitive and deeply cultured intelligence."[57]

In a discerning comment on *The Black Jacobins*, Stuart Hall has stated that "it is the first work to centre slavery in world history."[58] While we may well harbor doubts about claims to epistemological zero hours of this nature, this comment captures well the argument James made about the inseparable historical link between metropolitan powers and colonies. *The Black Jacobins* did not merely show that one cannot have a proper appreciation of the Haitian Revolution without understanding the progress of the French Revolution, but that major events in world history—from the Napoleonic Wars to the Louisiana Purchase, Simón Bolívar's liberation of South America to the abolishment of the British slave trade—would be incomprehensible without considering the actions of colonized (and in this case, recently emancipated) persons. This challenge to complacent narratives of Eurocentric visions of global history has, of course, in the last few decades become a standard part of new histories being written in the areas of Atlantic studies and postcolonial studies. In their much-cited essay "Between Metropole and Colony: Rethinking a Research Agenda," Ann Stoler and Frederick Cooper turn immediately to Haiti's Revolution following their opening paragraphs and draw on the work of James, Fick, and Michel-Rolph Trouillot in their assessment of its importance for reconsidering the metropole–colonial relationship.[59] Peter Linebaugh and Marcus Rediker's well-known work on the revolutionary Atlantic also draws significant inspiration from James.[60] For Linebaugh, James "opened up continents and races to the historian's gaze, while rebuking the racism of both capitalist and Comintern orthodoxies."[61]

The Making of the Caribbean People

> To be welcomed into the comity of nations a new nation must bring
> something new. Otherwise it is a mere administrative convenience or
> necessity. The West Indians have brought something new.
>
> C. L. R. JAMES, *The Black Jacobins* (1963)

The Black Jacobins may have been written with the African, not Caribbean, revolution in mind, but by the time James wrote the appendix to the second edition a quarter century had passed, and James had recently completed his ill-fated sojourn in Trinidad.[62] Yet the story of this period in James's life is abridged if it is reduced to the gladiatorial contest he had with Williams. James's return to the Caribbean in 1958 as secretary to the West Indian Federal Labour Party and as editor of the PNM newspaper facilitated a reintroduction to West Indian society that resulted in a number of invitations to lecture at the University of the West Indies, Mona Campus, and more widely to Caribbean audiences. In this moment we see the genesis of another period in James's life: a shift from writer and revolutionary to mentor of a succeeding generation of Caribbean and third world activists.

In the posthumously published *Walter Rodney Speaks*, Walter Rodney cites *The Black Jacobins* and *Capitalism and Slavery* as "two of the foremost texts that informed a nationalist consciousness" during his undergraduate days at Mona.[63] This statement is somewhat curious, and poses fascinating questions about the circulation of *The Black Jacobins* in the Caribbean region. Rodney's undergraduate career at Mona lasted from 1960 to 1963, and on attaining first-class honors in his last year he traveled to the School for Oriental and African Studies to pursue his doctorate. For Rodney's comment to be accurate, it seems he must have been relying on the first edition of *The Black Jacobins*, as the second was published in the year he graduated. However, according to George Lamming, *The Black Jacobins* was hardly available until its republication in the 1960s.[64] In the essay "Caliban Orders History," published in his collection *The Pleasures of Exile* (1960), Lamming spends an entire essay retelling, with extensive quotations, the story of *The Black Jacobins*, partly to reintroduce the book to readers unfamiliar with it.[65] While Rodney, as an undergraduate student of distinction, would have encountered the first edition in the library, it is more likely that the widespread influences he describes came slightly later in the decade, with the presence of the immensely popular second edition, and in the milieu of

Caribbean Black Power and late 1960s radicalism in which he was to play such an important role.

James's lectures at the University of the West Indies were part of his attempt to articulate his vision of a Caribbean identity and its relationship to the modern. His consistent reference to the people of the Caribbean as a "new people," a people "unique in the modern world," occupying a "new nation" (the emphasis on new *nation* rather than its plural is important here, as James was making an argument about the necessity of a Caribbean federation), and whose writers were involved in producing a "new view of West Indian history" provides several important insights into his view of Caribbean culture at the moment of the independence of its Anglophone territories.[66] Coming forth from every page is the sense of excitement James felt at this time—that the Caribbean would produce something new on the world stage, not just for itself but for the benefit of world civilization. These speeches attracted younger scholars like Norman Girvan and Lloyd Best to James's work and became a crucial part of the transnational community that he would forge over the next two decades. This included a study group on Marxism he ran for West Indian students in London, whose participants included Walton Look-Lai, Orlando Patterson, Richard Small, Joan French, Raymond Watts, Stanley French, and Walter Rodney.[67] According to David Austin, Norman Girvan introduced Robert Hill to C. L. R. James in London, a significant introduction, as Robert Hill would become a founding member of the C. L. R. James Study Circle and the Caribbean Conference Committee, both based in Montreal.[68] The Caribbean Conference Committee in Montreal was arguably the "most active site of exile Anglophone Caribbean *political* activity" in the late 1960s and early 1970s, and the leading personalities within it played key roles in the intraregional radicalism of this period.[69] Here James's transition from a leading theoretical and radical figure in any group with which he was associated to the status of mentor and older revolutionary figure became complete. In the last two decades of his life, for many Pan-Africanists and Caribbean intellectuals, a visit to London would not be complete unless they visited James in his apartment in Brixton.

In James's lectures and writings on the Caribbean in this period, Haiti and its revolution continue to feature prominently. His desire to introduce *The Black Jacobins* to new audiences resulted in his collaboration in a new version of his 1936 play, this time under the same title of the history and an arguably less successful production than the first play had been.[70] In his appendix to the second edition of *The Black Jacobins*, "From Toussaint L'Ouverture to Fidel Castro," James asserts that "West Indians first became aware of themselves as a people in the Haitian Revolution."[71] Reflection on this statement leads one to consider the impact of the revolution on perceptions of the possibility of black freedom in the Atlantic world, agency against the tide of history, and the sociohistorical features that have fashioned contemporary Caribbean existence. This appendix is James's most concentrated piece of writing on the potential and limits of Caribbean freedom. Caribbean history is, for James, defined by two central features, "the sugar plantation and Negro slavery," and the entire appendix is a sustained meditation on Caribbean people's response to those forms of modern colonial power. His study of the Haitian Revolution led James to understand enslaved Africans as living a modern existence in a colonial world, and he was among the first to firmly locate plantation slavery as a modern process, in a move that was heretical to both the complacent evolutionary anthropology of the early twentieth century and to Marxism-Leninism. In *The Black Jacobins* he writes: "Working and living together in gangs of hundreds on the huge sugar-factories which covered the North Plain, they were closer to a modern proletariat than any group of workers in existence at the time, and the rising was, therefore, a thoroughly prepared and organised mass movement."[72] In his appendix he highlights other features of enslaved life in the Caribbean—the highly detailed, mechanized process of sugar production, the dependence of the colonial economy on transnational flows of basic goods, principally food and clothing.[73] These insights by James have been noted by scholars interested in making an argument about the profound modernity of the Caribbean and transatlantic black experience since slavery, and indeed its primacy in debates about the modern. In the concluding chapter of Paul Gilroy's *The Black Atlantic*, he argues that "the concentrated intensity of the slave experience is something that marked out blacks as the first truly modern people, handling in the nineteenth century dilemmas and difficulties which would only become the substance of everyday life in Europe a century later."[74] Sidney Mintz, one of the most renowned anthropologists of the Caribbean of the last half century, has constantly highlighted the Caribbean's status as the site of a "precocious modernity," anticipating by generations developments in Europe, and has suggested that C. L. R. James was the first to illustrate the centrality of the Black experience in the formation of the Atlantic world.[75] Given Haiti's seismic impact on the history of the Western Hemisphere, an influence that, in James's own words, would "make history which would alter the fate of millions of men and shift the economic currents of three continents," the Black Jacobins *created* the modern Atlantic world.

The most ambitious recent attempt to think about the legacy of *The Black Jacobins* for our time is David Scott's *Conscripts of Modernity: The Tragedy of Colonial Enlightenment*.[76] Scott wishes to write against the exhaustion of progressive political projects in the postcolonial world, and the "acute paralysis of will and sheer vacancy of imagination, the rampant corruption and vicious authoritarianism, the instrumental self-interest and showy self-congratulation" that pervades our postcolonial present.[77] Scott argues that rather than the dominant tale of overcoming colonialism that has been couched in a narrative of anticolonial romance, our times demand a different emplotment: tragedy. *The Black Jacobins* is mobilized here, as between the first and second editions Scott detects a shift in registers from anticolonial romance to tragedy, which he believes to be part of a more general change in James's work in the 1950s and 1960s. James's reflections on tragedy are best seen in his revisions to the second edition of *The Black Jacobins*, specifically the seven paragraphs he inserted at the beginning of the last chapter, and are worthy of serious consideration in this moment as, according to Scott, "tragedy has a more respectful attitude to the contingencies of the past in the present, to the uncanny ways in which its remains come back to usurp our hopes and subvert our ambitions, it demands from us more patience for paradox and more openness to chance than the narrative of anticolonial Romanticism does, confident in its striving and satisfied in its own sufficiency."[78] A sense of the tragic does not condemn us to despair, but should give us a more "critical story of our postcolonial time."[79]

A consideration of James's writing in this period clearly shows this sense of the tragic; however, to me this sense is often grafted onto a cautiously liberatory narrative that does not quite correspond to either the romantic anticolonialism Scott signals as the dominant trend of the time or his own reading of James's use of the tragic. Instead, at points we get a clear awareness that one of the potential futures of the Caribbean nation may be neocolonialism, yet the acknowledgment of this real possibility is couched within a cautious tale of hope, and excitement at the possibilities of the new West Indian nation. These possibilities are clearly there in James's defiant introduction to his critique of the Trinidadian nation at the moment of independence, *Party Politics in the West Indies*, as well as his semiautobiographical masterpiece, *Beyond a Boundary*, and several essays of this period.[80] James's writings on the United States and the Caribbean in the 1950s similarly contrast them with a Europe that is dour and mired in tragedy, compared to the optimistic individualism of the United States, and the new forms of existence that are the gift of the Caribbean to the world. While I share Scott's concern over our postcolonial present, I pause at the almost totalizing nature of the exhaustion he suggests captivates the postcolonial world—a pessimism that James, always on the lookout for the new social movement, never shared.[81]

As the major history of the Haitian Revolution in English throughout the decolonizing period, *The Black Jacobins* served a crucial role in reeducating Caribbean and Africana people about the importance of Haiti, away from imperial lies about its existence. The daring pathways opened by the text's reconsideration of the plantation, modernity, and Caribbean history have led to assessments of it as the "beginning of Caribbean social theory."[82] Singham speaks glowingly about the connection of *The Black Jacobins* to the work of later Caribbean scholars, specifically citing Eric Williams, Elsa Goveia, and Lloyd Best and suggesting that the "basic questions of pluralism" raised by M. G. Smith and Lloyd Braithwaite were given voice in its pages, but makes these scholars seem too derivative of James's work. The assessment of Lewis Gordon that James is "perhaps the most prolific of all Caribbean social theorists" may more accurately depict the tendrils of influences emanating from this enormously influential book and its author.[83]

Haiti's Song

Yet the story of Haiti cannot escape its agonies of the last two hundred years, the almost incomprehensible reversals and sufferings of its people since its independence. If the Haitian Revolution was the most important event in the Caribbean since Columbus first established permanent contact between the region and Europe, the earthquake of 12 January 2010, with over three hundred thousand lives lost, is the greatest tragedy the Caribbean has had to bear since slavery. It is here that Haiti as a site of wonder emerges in the Caribbean and Africana imagination, a place whose revolution reshaped the meaning of freedom in the Caribbean, an island with a fabulous intellectual tradition generations ahead of their Anglophone peers in debates about race and imperialism, economic nationalism and dependency.[84] However, too often, this wonder takes an unsavory turn in discourses about Haiti in the contemporary Caribbean. Rather than a reckoning of Haiti that honors its past even when discomfited by its present predicament, instead too often we see a lapse into Western tropes of inferiority, barbarism, and accursedness—a view of Haiti as a place with little to teach the Caribbean or world, a community to fortify national borders against, in need of paternalistic guidance and trusteeship.

Against this defeat, the voices of Africana thinkers have continued to resonate for over a century in their acknowledgment of the mesmerizing power of Haiti and of their debt to it and its revolution. Haiti, where for Aimé Césaire "negritude rose for the first time and stated that it believed in its humanity."[85] Haiti, the subject of Derek Walcott's first dramatic production and of plays by Edouard Glissant and Aimé Césaire.[86] As Timothy Brennan reminds us, Haiti educated a number of the most prominent literary-cultural figures of the African diaspora, including Zora Neale Hurston, who started *Their Eyes Were Watching God* there; Langston Hughes, reared on tales of the Haitian Revolution; and Alejo Carpentier.[87] Kamau Brathwaite has insisted that we "Dream Haiti"; David Rudder offers an apology for our forgetfulness.[88] The question Haiti poses the contemporary Caribbean is a despair, less over past injustice than over the coloniality of the present and our seemingly potential futures. It is unlikely that we would have progressed so far in dismantling the tissue of lies that have stifled the recognition of Haiti's unique contribution to the world without *The Black Jacobins*.

NOTES

Thanks to George Lamming, Peter Hudson, Christian Høgsbjerg, David Austin, Antoinette Burton, Isabel Hofmeyr, and the 10 Books collective for their insightful comments on this essay.

1. C. L. R. James, *The Black Jacobins: Toussaint L'Ouverture and the San Domingo Revolution*, 2nd ed. (New York: Vintage Books, 1989), ix. Hereafter, I am referring to this edition of *The Black Jacobins*, unless I specify another edition.

2. C. L. R. James, *World Revolution 1917–1936: The Rise and Fall of the Communist International* (Atlantic Highlands, NJ: Humanities Press, 1993), 36–37. This Trotskyite history of the Communist International was considered subversive enough that nine thousand kilometers away the South African state would open a file on James. See file: "CLR James: Negro," 7607, 67/328, South African Archives Depot, Native Affairs Department, Johannesburg. I am indebted to Isabel Hofmeyr for this reference.

3. On these networks, see Minkah Makalani, *In the Cause of Freedom: Radical Black Internationalism from Harlem to London, 1917–1939* (Chapel Hill: University of North

Carolina Press, 2011), and Susan D. Pennybacker, *From Scottsboro to Munich: Race and Political Culture in 1930s Britain* (Princeton, NJ: Princeton University Press, 2009).

4. C. L. R. James, "The Intelligence of the Negro," in *From Trinidad: An Anthology of Early West Indian Writing*, ed. Reinhard W. Sander (London: Hodder and Stoughton, 1978).

5. Wilson Moses, *Afrotopia: The Roots of African American Popular History* (Cambridge: Cambridge University Press, 1998), 21. The second part of this definition threatens to encompass the whole of the African diasporic intellectual tradition, but Moses suggests that the vindicationists' main concern is with black achievement in the past.

6. C. L. R. James, "Lectures on *The Black Jacobins*," *Small Axe* 8 (2000): 66.

7. The following are James's major works of this period: *The Life of Captain Cipriani: An Account of British Government in the West Indies* (1932), *Minty Alley* (1936), the play *Toussaint Louverture: The Story of the Only Successful Slave Revolt in History* (1936), *World Revolution: The Rise and Fall of the Communist International* (1937), *The Black Jacobins: Toussaint L'Ouverture and the San Domingo Revolution* (1938), *A History of Negro Revolt* (1938). *The Life of Captain Cipriani* and *Minty Alley* were written before James left for London. In addition, James was the ghostwriter for Learie Constantine's autobiography *Cricket and I*, translated into English, and Boris Souvarine's biography of Stalin; was editor of the *International African Opinion*, the journal of the International African Service Bureau; and wrote many articles on cricket for the *Manchester Guardian*.

8. Christian Høgsbjerg, introduction to *Toussaint Louverture: The Story of the Only Successful Slave Revolt in History*, by C. L. R. James (Durham, NC: Duke University Press, 2013), 2. This constitutes the first publication of the 1936 edition of the play.

9. Fionnghuala Sweeney, "The Haitian Play: C. L. R. James' *Toussaint Louverture* (1936)," *International Journal of Francophone Studies* 14, nos. 1 and 2 (2011): 146–147.

10. James, *Black Jacobins*, 86.

11. Høgsbjerg, introduction, 2.

12. These reviews are reproduced in C. L. R. James, *Toussaint Louverture: The Story of the Only Successful Slave Revolt in History* (Durham, NC: Duke University Press, 2013), 164–186.

13. Colin Chambers, *Black and Asian Theatre in Britain: A History* (London: Routledge, 2011), 98, as cited in Høgsbjerg, introduction, 2.

14. James, *Black Jacobins*, 47.

15. James, *Black Jacobins*, 283.

16. James, *Black Jacobins*, ix.

17. C. L. R. James, foreword to *The Black Jacobins: Toussaint L'Ouverture and the San Domingo Revolution* (London: Allison and Busby, 1980), v.

18. James, foreword, vi.

19. James, *Black Jacobins*, 376.

20. James, *Black Jacobins*, 377.

21. Reviews of the British edition include Arthur Ballard, "The Greatest Slave Revolt in History," *New Leader*, 9 December 1938; two by Dorothy Pizer, "How Blacks

Fought for Freedom," *International African Opinion* 1, no. 4 (October 1938): 11–12, and "A Lesson in Revolution," *Controversy*, no. 28 (January 1939): 318–320; K.A., "Review," *Keys* 6, no. 2 (October–December 1938), and the hatchet piece by Flora Grierson, "Man's Inhumanity to Man," *New Statesman*, 8 October 1938.

22. The following reviews of the American edition appeared: Harold Courlander, "Revolt in Haiti," *Saturday Review of Literature*, 7 January 1939; Rayford W. Logan, "Reviews—Caribbean History," *Opportunity: Journal of Negro Life* 17, no. 2 (1939); James W. Ivy, "Break the Image of the White God . . . ," *Crisis* 46, no. 8 (August 1939); W. G. Seabrook, "Review," *Journal of Negro History* 24, no. 1 (January 1939); anon., "The Black Jacobins of San Domingo's Revolution," *New York Times*, 11 December 1938; Ludwell Lee Montague, "Review," *Hispanic American Historical Review* 20, no. 1 (February 1940); George E. Novack, "Revolution, Black and White," *New International* 5, no. 5 (May 1939). On the French translation, see James D. Young, *The World of C. L. R. James: His Unfragmented Vision* (Glasgow: Clydeside Press, 1999), 334. A review of the French edition prompted a rejoinder by C. L. R. James. See the review by Louis Ménard in *Les Temps Modernes* 52 (February 1950); C. L. R. James's and the editors replies were carried in *Les Temps Modernes* 56 (June 1950). An Italian translation appeared in 1968. I am indebted to Christian Høgsbjerg for copies of these reviews. Finally, the first Spanish edition appeared in February 2010, courtesy of the Cuban publishing house Casa de las Americas.

23. George Padmore, "Toussaint, the Black Liberator," *People*, 12 November 1938, 10–11, continued 19 November 1938, 4.

24. C. L. R. James, *Nkrumah and the Ghana Revolution* (London: Allison and Busby, 1977), 66.

25. Laurent Dubois, *Avengers of the New World: The Story of the Haitian Revolution* (Cambridge, MA: Harvard University Press, 2004), 2.

26. David Geggus, *Haitian Revolutionary Studies* (Bloomington: Indiana University Press, 2002), 31. Geggus goes on to state that *The Black Jacobins* has been the dominant book on the Haitian Revolution in the Anglophone world for sixty years.

27. Brian Meeks, "Re-reading *The Black Jacobins*: James, the Dialectic and the Revolutionary Conjuncture," *Social and Economic Studies* 43, no. 3 (September 1994): 75–103; Frank Birbalsingh, "The Literary Achievement of C. L. R. James," *Journal of Commonwealth Literature* 19, no. 1 (1984): 108–121.

28. B. W. Higman, *Writing West Indian Histories* (London: Macmillan, 1999).

29. James was ten years Williams's senior, and returned there to teach in his twenties. Ivar Oxaal, *Black Intellectuals Come to Power: The Rise of Creole Nationalism in Trinidad and Tobago* (Cambridge, MA: Schenkman, 1968), 65; Richard Sheridan, "Eric Williams and Capitalism and Slavery: A Biographical and Historiographical Essay," in *British Capitalism and Caribbean Slavery: The Legacy of Eric Williams*, ed. Barbara L. Solow and Stanley L. Engerman (Cambridge: Cambridge University Press, 1987), 317.

30. Eric Williams, *Inward Hunger: The Education of a Prime Minister* (London: Deutsch, 1969).

31. For a summary of criticisms of Williams's work in this period, see Selwyn Ryan, *Eric Williams: The Myth and the Man* (Kingston, Jamaica: University of the West Indies Press, 2009), 46–54.

32. Williams, *Inward Hunger*, 77, 143, 267–268.

33. Williams, *Inward Hunger*, 49.

34. Susan D. Pennybacker, *From Scottsboro to Munich: Race and Political Culture in 1930s Britain* (Princeton, NJ: Princeton University Press, 2009), 81.

35. Eric Williams, *Capitalism and Slavery* (Chapel Hill: University of North Carolina Press, 1994), 268.

36. Archie Singham, *The Hero and the Crowd in a Colonial Polity* (New Haven, CT: Yale University Press, 1968).

37. James, "Lectures," 112.

38. C. L. R. James, "On *The Negro in the Caribbean* by Eric Williams," in *C. L. R. James on the "Negro Question,"* ed. Scott McLemee (Jackson: University Press of Mississippi, 1996), 118.

39. James, "On *The Negro*," 125.

40. James to George Padmore, 17 March 1958, folder 105, box 5, C. L. R. James Archive, University of the West Indies, St. Augustine, Trinidad and Tobago.

41. C. L. R. James, *Beyond a Boundary* (Durham, NC: Duke University Press, 1994).

42. C. L. R. James, interview by Ian Munro and Reinhard Sander, in *Kas-Kas: Interviews with Three Caribbean Writers in Texas* (Austin: African and Afro-American Research Institute, University of Texas at Austin, 1972), 22–41. For a shorter and more vitriolic account, see the statement by James quoted in Ryan, *Eric Williams*, 55.

43. C. L. R. James, "Eric Williams," unpublished autobiography, C. L. R. James Archive, University of the West Indies, St. Augustine, Trinidad and Tobago.

44. Ryan, *Eric Williams*, 35, 43–44.

45. Cedric Robinson, "Capitalism, Slavery and Bourgeois Historiography," *History Workshop* 23 (Spring 1987): 128. See Barbara L. Solow and Stanley L. Engerman, eds., *British Capitalism and Caribbean Slavery: The Legacy of Eric Williams* (Cambridge: Cambridge University Press, 1987), and Heather Cateau and S. H. H. Carrington, eds., *Capitalism and Slavery Fifty Years Later: Eric Eustace Williams—A Reassessment of the Man and His Work* (New York: Peter Lang, 2000).

46. Joseph Inikori, *Africans and the Industrial Revolution in England: A Study in International Trade and Economic Development* (Cambridge: Cambridge University Press, 2002), 6.

47. Hilary McD. Beckles, "'The Williams Effect': Eric Williams's *Capitalism and Slavery* and the Growth of West Indian Political Economy," in Solow and Engerman, *British Capitalism*, 303–316.

48. Hilary Beckles, *Britain's Black Debt: Reparations for Caribbean Slavery and Native Genocide* (Kingston, Jamaica: University of the West Indies Press, 2013), xiv; Nicholas Draper, *The Price of Emancipation: Slave Ownership, Compensation and British Society at the End of Slavery* (Cambridge: Cambridge University Press, 2010). See also the insightful discussion of Draper's book in *Small Axe* 37 (March 2012): Christer Petley,

"British Fortunes and Caribbean Slavery," 144–153; Susan Thorne, "Capitalism and Slavery Compensation," 154–167; Nicholas Draper, "Capitalism and Slave Ownership: A Response," 168–177.

49. Carolyn Fick, *The Making of Haiti: The Saint Domingue Revolution from Below* (Knoxville: University of Tennessee Press, 1990), xiii.

50. Fick, *Making of Haiti*, 4.

51. James, "Lectures," 106, 108.

52. Christian Høgsbjerg, "C. L. R. James: The Revolutionary as Artist," *International Socialism* 112 (2006), www.isj.org.uk/?id=253, accessed 1 July 2012.

53. Eric Hobsbawm, "The Historians' Group of the Communist Party," in *Rebels and Their Causes: Essays in Honour of A. L. Morton*, ed. Maurice Cornforth (London: Lawrence and Wishart, 1978), 23.

54. Eric Hobsbawm, *The Age of Revolution: Europe 1789–1848* (1962) (London: Weidenfeld and Nicholson, 1997). In his select bibliography, Hobsbawm writes: "C. L. R. James, *The Black Jacobins* (1938) describes the Haitian Revolution" (336). The two references to the revolution are one-liners about the Jacobins' abolishment of slavery, and another about "movements of colonial liberation inspired by the French Revolution (as in San Domingo)" (69, 89). Here, the Haitian Revolution is positioned as no more than a derivative event, while the Jacobins' abolishment "helped to create the first independent revolutionary leader of stature in Toussaint-Louverture."

55. James D. Young, *The World of C. L. R. James: His Unfragmented Vision* (Glasgow: Clydeside Press, 1999), 261–264.

56. See Paul Gilroy, *"There Ain't No Black in the Union Jack": The Cultural Politics of Race and Nation* (Chicago: University of Chicago Press, 1991), 49–50, 55; Paul Gilroy, *The Black Atlantic: Modernity and Double Consciousness* (Cambridge, MA: Harvard University Press, 1994), 14. Young, *World of C. L. R. James*, 200–201, 262–267. I borrow the idea of the Haitian Revolution as an unthinkable event from Michel Rolph-Trouillot; see *Silencing the Past: Power and the Production of History* (Boston: Beacon Press, 1997).

57. E. P. Thompson, "C. L. R. James at 80," in *C. L. R. James: His Life and Work*, ed. Paul Buhle (New York: Allison and Busby, 1986), 249.

58. Bill Schwarz, "Breaking Bread with History: C. L. R. James and *The Black Jacobins*: An Interview with Stuart Hall," *History Workshop Journal* 46 (Autumn 1998): 22.

59. Ann Laura Stoler and Frederick Cooper, "Between Metropole and Colony: Rethinking a Research Agenda," in *Tensions of Empire: Colonial Cultures in a Bourgeois World*, ed. Frederick Cooper and Ann Laura Stoler (Berkeley: University of California Press, 1997), 2.

60. See here Peter Linebaugh, "All the Atlantic Mountains Shook," *Labour / Le Travailleur* 10 (Autumn 1982): 109, 118; Peter Linebaugh, "What If C. L. R. James Had Met E. P. Thompson in 1792?," in Buhle, *C. L. R. James*, 212–219.

61. Linebaugh, "What If," 218.

62. The epigraph to this section is from C. L. R. James, "Appendix: From Toussaint L'Ouverture to Fidel Castro," in *The Black Jacobins: Toussaint L'Ouverture and the San Domingo Revolution* (1963) (New York: Vintage Books, 1989), 417.

63. Walter Rodney, *Walter Rodney Speaks: The Making of an African Intellectual* (Trenton, NJ: Africa World Press, 1990), 14. In a recent interview, Orlando Patterson notes that James was a "legendary figure" during his undergraduate days at Mona (1959–1962) but does not specifically mention *The Black Jacobins* as a reason for this towering reputation. See David Scott, "The Paradox of Freedom: An Interview with Orlando Patterson," *Small Axe* 40 (March 2013): 137.

64. David Scott, "The Sovereignty of the Imagination: An Interview with George Lamming," *Small Axe* 12 (September 2002): 135. George Lamming, resident in Trinidad in the late 1940s, has told me that he does not remember seeing a copy of *The Black Jacobins* in Trinidad—he encountered it for the first time in London. Similarly, no less a figure than Stuart Hall, resident in the United Kingdom from 1951, doubts he read it before its republication in 1963! See Schwarz, "Breaking Bread with History," 22.

65. George Lamming, "Caliban Orders History," in *The Pleasures of Exile* (Ann Arbor: University of Michigan Press, 1992), 118–150.

66. C. L. R. James, "West Indian Personality" (lecture at the University College of the West Indies, 1959/1960), *Caribbean Quarterly* 35, no. 4 (December 1989): 11–14; "The Making of the Caribbean Peoples," lecture delivered at the Second Conference on West Indian Affairs, Montreal, summer 1966; "The Birth of a Nation," in *Contemporary Caribbean: A Sociological Reader*, vol. 1, ed. Susan Craig (Maracas, Trinidad and Tobago: College Press, 1981), 3–35; "A New View of West Indian History" (lecture at the University College of the West Indies, 3 June 1965), *Caribbean Quarterly* 35, no. 4 (December 1989): 49–70; "A National Purpose for Caribbean Peoples," in *At the Rendezvous of Victory* (1964) (London: Allison and Busby, 1984).

67. David Austin, "In Search of a National Identity: C. L. R. James and the Promise of the Caribbean," in *You Don't Play with Revolution: The Montreal Lectures of C. L. R. James* (Oakland, CA: AK Press, 2009), 9.

68. Austin, "In Search."

69. Austin, "In Search," 11, italics original.

70. See Høgsbjerg, introduction, 28.

71. James, "Appendix," 391.

72. James, *Black Jacobins*, 86. This line is repeated verbatim in the chapter "San Domingo" in James's text of the same year, *A History of Negro Revolt*. See *A History of Negro Revolt* (Chicago: Frontline Books, 2004), 9.

73. James, *Black Jacobins*, 392.

74. Gilroy, *Black Atlantic*, 221. Gilroy gestures to *The Black Jacobins*, and cites at length the key passage on slave life and the modern on pp. 251–252.

75. Sidney W. Mintz, "Enduring Substances, Trying Theories: The Caribbean Region as *Oikoumene*," *Journal of the Royal Anthropological Institute* 2, no. 2 (1996): 289–311.

76. David Scott, *Conscripts of Modernity: The Tragedy of Colonial Enlightenment* (Durham, NC: Duke University Press, 2004).

77. Scott, *Conscripts of Modernity*, 2.

78. Scott, *Conscripts of Modernity*, 220.

79. Scott, *Conscripts of Modernity*, 221, 14.

80. Nowhere is Scott's reading of James more forced than in his conscription of *Beyond a Boundary* into his project, through James's attention in that text to ancient Greece. *Beyond a Boundary,* a classic text about the birth of a new Caribbean nation beyond coloniality, shows the difficulties with Scott's claim that there is a distinctive switch in James's work of this period from a revolutionary anticolonial romance to tragedy.

81. My own concerns about the Caribbean present can be seen in the special issue of the journal *Race & Class* that I edited with Alissa Trotz, "Caribbean Trajectories: 200 Years On," *Race & Class* 49, no. 2 (October 2007).

82. A. W. Singham, "C. L. R. James on the Black Jacobin Revolution in San Domingo—Notes toward a Theory of Black Polities," *Savacou* 1 (June 1970): 86.

83. Lewis Gordon, *An Introduction to Africana Philosophy* (Cambridge: Cambridge University Press, 2008), 165n14.

84. Gordon K. Lewis, *Main Currents in Caribbean Thought: The Historical Evolution of Caribbean Society in Its Ideological Aspects, 1492–1900* (Baltimore: Johns Hopkins University Press, 1983), 253–254, 257, 261.

85. Aimé Césaire, *Notebook of a Return to the Native Land,* trans. Annette Smith and Clayton Eshleman (Middletown, CT: Wesleyan University Press, 2001), 15. This was also the first time that the word "negritude" was used by its inventor, Césaire, in print.

86. Derek Walcott, *Henri Christophe: A Chronicle in Seven Scenes* (Bridgetown, Barbados: Advocate, 1950); Edouard Glissant, *Monsieur Toussaint: A Play,* trans. Michael J. Dash (Boulder, CO: Lynne Rienner, 2005); Aimé Césaire, *La Tragédie du roi Christophe* (Paris: Présence Africaine, 1970). See also Aimé Césaire, *Toussaint Louverture: La Révolution française et le problème colonial* (Paris: Présence Africaine, 1981).

87. Timothy Brennan, introduction to Alejo Carpentier, *Music in Cuba,* trans. Alan West-Durán (Minneapolis: University of Minnesota Press, 2001), 34.

88. Kamau Brathwaite, "Dream Haiti," in *The Oxford Book of Caribbean Short Stories,* ed. Stewart Brown and John Wickham (Oxford: Oxford University Press, 2001); David Rudder, *Haiti* (Warner Brothers / London Records, 1988).

Ten

ETHNOGRAPHY AND CULTURAL INNOVATION IN MAU MAU DETENTION CAMPS

Gakaara wa Wanjau's *Mīhīrīga ya Agīkūyū*

DEREK R. PETERSON

Gakaara wa Wanjau found his literary voice during the 1950s, while he was held—for eight long years—in colonial Kenya's detention camps. Superintended by British officials, the camps were places of extraordinary privation, where thousands of Gikuyu men and women who supported the Mau Mau movement were subjected to psychological coercion and physical maltreatment. For Gakaara, the experience of detention was an occasion for ethnographic work. He conducted research with other detainees and composed a series of manuscripts on Gikuyu religion, culture, and kinship. In 1956 Gakaara confessed before British officers to his involvement with Mau Mau. He was employed as a staff member as a reward for his cooperation. Under the watchful eye of the camp commandant, Gakaara wrote at least five plays for detainees to perform. He also edited the detention camp newspaper.[1] During his eight years in detention he also composed dozens of songs, carried on an extensive correspondence with his wife, negotiated through the mail over his sister's remarriage, directed litigation over land he had inherited from his father, and kept a diary.[2]

His greatest achievement was *Mīhīrīga ya Agīkūyū*, "The Clans of the Gikuyu People," published in 1960, the year he was finally released. It is a work of homespun ethnography, bursting with vivid details about the character, mentality, and accomplishments of each of the ten Gikuyu clans. Gakaara did not compose a literature of resistance. Neither did he defend Gikuyu traditions against the threat of cultural imperialism. His imaginative book was about the obligations wives bore to their husbands, about the character of Gikuyu womanhood, and about the civic institutions that upheld moral order and cemented kinship. The book was never translated into English, and it never found a readership outside Kenya. That is the point. This was a text directed to a specific audience who needed the instruction it could provide. *Mīhīrīga ya Agīkūyū* was an entry in the large library of books through which colonized people worked to define their culture, organize gender relations, and earn a respectable place in the public sphere.

The historian Caroline Elkins has recently illuminated the awful inhumanity of colonial Kenya's detention camps. Her book, published in the United Kingdom under the title *Britain's Gulag: The Brutal End of Empire in Kenya*, documents the horrific abuses British officials perpetrated against Gikuyu men and women.[3] In Elkins's account the politics of 1950s Kenya are cast in a prefabricated pattern. Gikuyu were either part of a "Mau Mau population" or they were British loyalists who moved in "lockstep with the British to ensure their common collective interests."[4] Detention camps were machines for crushing Mau Mau sentiments. In the camps "space, time and social exchange were completely organized and routinized," Elkins writes. "Freedom was eliminated, and violence, or the threat of it, was part of every waking and sleeping moment."[5] Isolated from their kin, humiliated, and subjected to coercive indoctrination, long-term detainees were made "socially dead."[6]

In this chapter I argue that detention camps not only were places of punishment but also were crucibles for cultural innovation. In Kenya and elsewhere, decolonization occasioned a contest over moral (not only political) legitimacy. Africa's patriots sought to surpass their colonial rulers, to project an image of integrity and responsibility that testified to their fitness to govern themselves. "Why am I fit to rule?" is a hard question to face, for it is an audit of personal integrity.[7] The 1950s and 1960s—the era of African independence—was therefore also an occasion for moral reform. Dozens of ethnic welfare associations were founded. As spokesmen for Luo, Haya, Ganda, or Gikuyu people, the leaders of these associations sought to reform their people's manners and earn other people's respect.[8] Mau Mau partisans shared a sensibility and a project with these architects of ethnic patriotism. In their violent guerrilla war, Gikuyu men and women struggled to uphold family life and defend their people from the debilitating threat of cultural amnesia. Gakaara and the many other Gikuyu men and women who took an oath in the late 1940s and 1950s were involved in a moral project, not a straightforward political war. After they were detained by the British, Gakaara and other entrepreneurs carried these discourses about family life and political self-mastery forward. Lumped together in cloistered cells with other men, isolated from their families, and uncertain about their wives' loyalty, detainees did ethnographic work in order to ensure their wives' fidelity, get leverage over brothers and clansmen, and uphold their own reputations. *Mĩhĩrĩga ya Agĩkũyũ* changed the British Empire by giving a colonized people resources with which to renovate their family values.

Mau Mau and Moral Order

Gakaara wa Wanjau spent most of his literary career casting about for a secure position from which to write.[9] He had served in the colonial military during World War II; on his return to Kenya he moved to the town of Nakuru, where he worked for the local government. In a newspaper editorial he complained at the poor quality of municipal housing.[10] "You would find an African employee, a driver, mechanic, clerk etc. wandering about during the night suffering for somewhere to sleep," he wrote. "It is even shameful to state how these people sleep in one small room." Gakaara himself was living in a single room together with other government employees. He had used his wartime salary to finance his marriage, but in Nakuru his straitened financial circumstances obliged him to live apart from his wife, who stayed in his parents' home. Early in 1949 Gakaara, desperate for money, was compelled to hawk cigarettes and foodstuffs.[11] It was during this dark period that he filled out an application for a correspondence course at the "British Institute of Practical Psychology." The application illuminates the way poverty had endangered Gakaara's sense of volition. "I have much propaganda to make me a big man," he wrote, "whereas I have no ways." When asked "Do you feel your life lacks purpose?" he replied "Yes, because of poverty." And when asked "Are you inclined to turn your eyes away when people look straight at you?" he replied "Big people, more educated and very rich."[12]

Gakaara was not alone in his predicament. In the late 1940s rural class formation had left many Gikuyu men without land, endangering their social lives. Wartime profits invited wealthy farmers to expand their holdings, forcing tenants and junior men off gardens they had long cultivated. Lacking enough land for subsistence, smallholders became proletarians in increasing numbers. In 1943 and again in 1947, Nyeri—the district from which Gakaara came—produced the most migrant workers per capita of all districts in Kenya colony.[13] Without sufficient land with which to support their families, impoverished men found it impossible to claim other people's attention or respect.[14] Commodity farmers used wartime profits to monopolize marriageable women, stifling young suitors' hopes. They and other wealthy men drove up brideprice. The frequency of church marriages throughout central Kenya dropped precipitously in the 1940s.[15] Formal marriage was too expensive for the poor, who saw their path to adulthood closed off.

In 1948, Gakaara joined the Rift Valley Agikuyu Union, which was one of many ethnic associations that campaigned against the corruptions of city living. The Union expelled a number of prostitutes from the township; those who refused to leave were imprisoned.[16] The Union also had its eye on men: members resolved that "men who live on women's earnings should be prosecuted."[17] It was at this time that Gakaara published his pamphlet *Wanawake wa Siku Hizi* (Women of These Days). Its aim, Gakaara explained, was to "abhor the bad reputation brought up by lazy African women who roam about shamefully in town with nothing to do but prostitution," while also encouraging "the African girls who lead good ways of life in progressing the country."[18] The book was one of a series of pamphlets about marriage and family life that Gakaara composed during the late 1940s. His first book, *Ūhoro Wa Ūgurani* (Marriage Procedures), was published in 1946; the pamphlet *Kīguni gīa Twana* (Manners of Children) was published in 1949. *Kīguni gīa Twana* listed "some usual good manners which are common to Kikuyu children" and encouraged them to "respect their superiors and parents etc."[19]

Spurred by the insecurity he felt over his own conjugal life, Gakaara wa Wanjau was creating a textual architecture to uphold a conservative social order. His literary and political work was part of a larger field of morally conservative thought. One newspaper editorialist complained that many Gikuyu girls, "beautiful, strong, very fit for mothers at home still loiter on Nairobi streets disguised as Alimas and Fatumas."[20] Another editorialist wanted Gikuyu prostitutes to remember that "the result of the havoc they are doing will be to bring into existence a new tribe of half-castes and bastards." "Their fiendish game is one of the best ways of exterminating a tribe," he averred.[21] "The evils of prostitution are a greater enemy than the Germans or the Japanese during the world wars," wrote a third editorialist.[22] With their demographic future in mind, Gikuyu editorialists debated the mechanisms by which refractory women could be brought into line. One editorialist invited readers to subscribe money toward the building of a special jail wherein prostitutes could be confined.[23] Another wanted rural chiefs to nominate three people from their localities who would go to Nairobi, seek out prostitutes who came from their home areas, and compel them to return to their homes.[24]

Gakaara wa Wanjau took a Mau Mau oath in July 1952. He and other oath-takers promised to stay away from prostitutes' lairs, support their families, deny themselves alcoholic drinks, and keep their mouths closed.[25] Gakaara was inspired by these promises, thinking them to be an inducement to moral discipline. In August he called two colleagues to his Nairobi office, where he had arranged to give them the oath.[26] He paid the fee required of all Mau Mau oath-takers on their behalf.[27] When in September Gakaara saw one of his colleagues drinking beer at a bar, he reported him to Mau Mau authorities. Mau Mau partisans practiced a stern morality. Women, too, were obliged to comport themselves with honor. Mau Mau oaths demanded that young women commit themselves to their marriages, abjure the business of prostitution, nurture their children, and break off relationships with men who were not Gikuyu.[28] The thousands of young men who in 1953 and 1954 went into central Kenya's forests as Mau Mau guerrilla fighters were protagonists in this battle against moral indiscipline.[29] The young men of the forest named their mountaintop strongholds *cīhaarīro*, "council grounds," historically the spaces where respectable elders had gathered to deliberate over matters of political importance.[30] The dispossessed men of Mau Mau were claiming the reputable status of elders, with family responsibilities. The guerrilla leader Dedan Kimathi ran a centralized welfare system for deserted wives of Mau Mau partisans, sending money home in installments of twenty shillings.[31] Guerrilla leaders often punished rapists with death. When Gucu wa Gikoyo came upon a Mau Mau fighter raping a woman during a raid, he and others hacked the man to pieces.[32] General Mwariama carried an abandoned baby for three full weeks, feeding it with food from his own mouth.[33]

The Mau Mau war was not a straightforwardly political battle between British loyalists and anticolonial nationalists. Its advocates were, like

Gakaara, marginal men whose marriages were endangered and whose access to land was increasingly foreclosed. In the Mau Mau movement they staked a claim to respectability. From a position of insecurity they created institutions and composed texts that aimed to uphold moral order, reinforce standards of sexual discipline, and bring a new generation to life.

Cultural Work in Mau Mau Detention Camps

On 20 October 1952 Gakaara wa Wanjau was arrested and accused of fomenting Mau Mau ideology. The government's evidence against him was the "Creed of Gikuyu and Muumbi," which Gakaara had published in 1952. It was a rewriting of the Apostles' Creed. When Gakaara appealed against his detention, the British officers who reviewed his file concluded that he was "probably a sincere fanatic of unstable mental balance. If set at large he might be very dangerous."[34] Gakaara was detained for eight years: first at Kajiado; then at Manda Island and Takwa camps, on the Indian Ocean coast; at Athi River camp; and finally at Hola Open Camp, in Kenya's arid east. He was one of the tens of thousands of people, most of them men, who were crowded into Kenya's 176 camps, prisons, and detention centers.[35] Kenya's prison population in 1956 was ten times greater than Great Britain's.[36] In all, more than 150,000 Gikuyu men and women spent some time in detention camps during the course of the rebellion.[37]

As detainees, Mau Mau partisans carried forward their long war against social and moral indiscipline. At Takwa camp, detainees made a point of honoring the wives of their warders. "We always tried to behave respectfully, and there wasn't a detainee who would not try to help a woman on the path," remembered Gakaara wa Wanjau. Their self-discipline earned them the respect of their jailors. Detainees regularly drank tea in their warders' homes, and "even we loved their children; they greeted us with pleasure when they saw us."[38] At Yatta camp, in eastern Kenya, detainees punished any among their compatriots who drank alcohol, took bhang, or consorted with loose women. Even "talking words of love to a girl" was punishable, and offenders were compelled to crawl, on their knees, back and forth on a concrete floor.[39] At Perkerra camp, where detainees lived in semisupervised open villages, the detainees' committee resolved that inhabitants should be "men of strong character, and able to control their desires, which often led them into ruin."[40] The committee ordered that women from the surrounding communities should be barred from entering the village at nighttime.[41]

Detainees were imposing impressively strict standards of discipline on themselves, but they could not be sure that their wives were doing the same. Outside the wire, detainees had alarmingly little influence. They were terrified that their wives, left to fend for themselves, would forfeit their fidelity. They had good reason to worry. In the mid-1950s, the ratio of women to men in central Kenya was seven to one.[42] Some abandoned wives, desperate for support, found it impossible to resist the advances of opportunistic suitors. "I know that any man cannot play around with you and convince you to offer them your body recklessly," Gakaara wrote in a nervous letter to his wife.[43] "Never agree to such a thing as offering your body to anyone who comes with the lies that he will help you. These are all lies." Worried over their wives' fidelity, detainees also worried over their male relatives' greed. Many detainees were junior members of their families, with older brothers who stood to inherit the bulk of their father's property.[44] Detainees' property was particularly imperiled after 1954, when government surveyors set out to consolidate Gikuyu landholders' scattered gardens into larger, more economic units.[45] The scheme was part of the Kenya government's larger effort to encourage the growth of a landed African peasantry. Detainees regarded the plan with trepidation. An editorialist in the detention camp newspaper warned readers that their property was in danger. "Land is being consolidated and it is only the owner of the land who may know everything concerning his land," he wrote. "If you are in a camp far from home this will be difficult."[46] Detainees had to rely on wives, brothers, or cousins to represent them before government surveyors. They worried that their greedy relatives would take advantage of the situation. In 1957 detainee Anderson Mureithi was refused parole by his village chief. His brother, Mureithi learned, did not want him to receive land from their father and so objected to his release.[47] Gakaara wa Wanjau was involved in protracted litigation against members of his own clan over land he had inherited from his father. "I have heard a lot of complaints here in detention from the detainees because they are shortchanged on land . . . even from people from the same clan," he wrote to his wife.[48] But Gakaara had also heard "many women praised because of how strongly they defended their family's land."

For men like Gakaara, detention was not only a time of physical privation. By making it impossible for them to exercise their duties as husbands, fathers, and kinsmen, the experience of detention made Gikuyu men feel that their family lives were in crisis. In reality detainees' dystopian nightmares were exaggerated. In their husbands' absence, most wives worked faithfully to hold their families together. The hundreds of women held as detainees at Kamiti camp brought their infants with them, badgering warders for supplies of fresh milk and stitching children's tattered clothes together.[49] They plied sympathetic British missionaries for news of home.[50] Shifra Wairire, Gakaara's wife, was detained at Kamiti. "Do not think that I have forgotten the home people," she wrote to Gakaara. "At every moment I am remembering the home."[51] After her release in 1957 Shifra dedicated herself to her children, building a six-room, grass-thatched house for them to live in. Gakaara was discomfited by his wife's hard work. "Sometimes I laugh on my own when I realize that I had never thought I would be asking you about such a thing as construction," he wrote. "Just imagine that the things I ask you are the ones you are supposed to be asking me. Things have really changed."[52] For Gakaara, as for other detainees, wives' novel powers were an unwelcome reminder of their own failure of responsibility.

It was out of this sense of anxiety that Gakaara composed "Which Clan Do You Belong To?"—the work later published under the title *Mīhīrīga ya Agĩkũyũ*.[53] The manuscript was written, with a pencil, in six exercise books, spirited out of Manda Island camp in the hands of a colleague, and stored at the bottom of a box by Gakaara's wife.[54] For Gakaara the detention camps were an opportunity to conduct ethnographic research. In the preface to the published work he thanks his "former detention colleagues" whose "inspiration and rich source of information about each clan enabled me to write this book."[55] Drawn together from distant corners of central Kenya, detainees compared their customs and developed a comprehensive picture of each clan's character. Gakaara's book lists ten different clans, identifying each clan's "behavior," its "manners," "statesmanship and courage," "wealth," "witchcraft," and "attraction to women."[56]

These stereotypes were a novelty. Never before had the psychology and character of Gikuyu clans been described in print. Gikuyu clans were alliances of convenience, not lineages with a shared culture and history. They had been formed by the immigrant people who settled in central Kenya and set to work clearing its forests in the eighteenth and nineteenth centuries.[57] The earliest ethnographies emphasized the culturally and linguistically disparate origins of the Gikuyu clans. One government administrator, writing in 1908, heard leaders of the Anjiru clan claim descent from the Chuka people. Aceera people claimed to have come from the Kamba, while Ethaga people said that they had sprung from the Chagga people of Kilimanjaro.[58] "Anyone enquiring into the descent of those present at a meeting of Kikuyu elders will find an extraordinary number of tribes represented," the administrator reported. No one could agree on the number of clans: in 1910 two ethnographers reported that the Gikuyu people were divided into thirteen clans; in 1911 a government officer counted nine; in 1921 another officer thought there were twelve.[59] As is fitting for a people with diverse origins, Gikuyu people embraced disparate origin myths. One story held that the original couple had been a brother and sister, virgins both, who devoted themselves to hunting. When they partook of the waters of a flowing stream, they were overcome with lust, copulated, and became the parents of all living people. The story contrasted the unproductive, shiftless work of hunting with the biologically and socially procreative labor of irrigated agriculture.[60] Another origin story similarly defined Gikuyu people by their shared commitment to agriculture: it described how God had given his Maasai son a spear with which to defend his cattle, his Okiek son a bow and arrow for hunting, and his Gikuyu son a digging stick.[61]

The creation of a singular Gikuyu cultural system—with a dominant origin story and a standard set of institutions—occurred in the space of the imperial commons, the area of textual exchange wherein imperial subjects could borrow, plagiarize, and expound on texts generated elsewhere.[62] The key text was the 1924 reading primer *Karirikania*, the set text for all Gikuyu-language learners in Kenya's Protestant schools. The first line in the primer went:

> Ngai nĩaheete Gĩkũyũ bũrũri mwega ũtaagaga irio kana maĩ kana gĩthaka. Wega no Gĩkũyũ kĩgocage Ngai hĩndĩ ciothe nĩ ũndũ anagĩtanahĩra mũno.[63]

> God has given Gikuyu a good country that lacks neither food nor water nor forested land. It is good that Gikuyu should be praising God always, for he has been very generous to them.

The Scots missionary who composed the primer meant to impress a sense of gratitude on Gikuyu people. But for early Christian converts—called *athomi*, "readers" in the Gikuyu language—these sentences were the outline for an origin story. They positioned a singular ancestor—the man Gikuyu—in a direct relationship with God and defined an Edenic landscape as Gikuyu's personal possession. No other origin story was so much expounded on or so politically useful. In 1929, the Kenya government appointed a committee of inquiry to look into Gikuyu people's complaints about the land that British settlers had expropriated from them. Gikuyu witnesses used the 1924 primer to cement their claim over disputed land. "God set us here and gave us the land," argued a delegation from Fort Hall district. "We began to cut the forest and to cultivate. We have no tradition of having migrated here from elsewhere."[64] The origin myth pruned away Gikuyu pioneers' history of migration, positioning them as autochtons, with better claim to Kenya's productive soil than British émigrés. The myth also helped to paper over the diverse, multicultural genealogies of disparate Gikuyu clans. "We are descended from one ancestor named Mugikuyu, and various clans are named after his daughters," the Fort Hall delegation told the commissioners. The notion that Gikuyu clans were descended from a single ancestor was a novelty: knowledgeable observers had not heard of it prior to the late 1920s.[65] Invented or not, the origin story helpfully shrouded Gikuyu people's disparate origins.[66] Christian readers found it particularly good to think with. Writing in the Gikuyu-language journal *Mwigwithania* in 1929, the same year the commission was collecting evidence, an editorialist personified the origin story: he referred to "our ancestor, Kikuyu," to whom God, from his seat on Mount Kenya, had given the land from Kabete to Meru.[67] Another writer noted that "there is a name for the father of a man, but what is the name of a man's mother? Know that a man's mother's name is Muumbi."[68] As the father and mother of all Gikuyu people, Gikuyu and Muumbi turned disparate clans into a homogeneous people with a common parentage. It was this origin story that was piped into the English language through Jomo Kenyatta's 1938 book *Facing Mount Kenya*. Kenyatta—who had begun his career as editor of *Mwigwithania*— told his British readers that "according to the tribal legend," the man Gikuyu had been taken to a mountaintop by God and shown a place to settle, an Eden full of fig trees called Mokorwe wa Gathanga. There he was given a beautiful wife named Muumbi. Their daughters were the founders of the Gikuyu clans.

The story of Gikuyu and Muumbi was not born, whole, from the Gikuyu past. It was assembled through the expository writing of Gikuyu intellectuals, who used a snippet from a missionary reading primer as a prompt with which to develop a new theory of their people's origins. In subsequent decades Gikuyu autoethnographers devoted themselves to developing and elaborating on the story. In his 1947 book *Kīrīra kīa Ūgīkūyū*, M. N. Kabetu asked his readers "Was Gikuyu created at Mukurue-ini wa Gathanga, or was he settled there by God from elsewhere?"[69] The answer, Kabetu admitted, was difficult to know, since there are "not many older Gikuyu people at present who can . . . narrate the story." In the absence of confirmation from oral history, Kabetu thought the best evidence could be found in the 1924 reading primer. "At the beginning when people started to live on the earth, that is the point at which Gikuyu was given this land by God his creator, just as it used to be said," Kabetu wrote.[70] In Gikuyu and in English, Kabetu's sentence echoes the phraseology of the 1924 primer. It was common knowledge, a phrase that a whole generation of Gikuyu readers came to know as a fact through their basic reading lessons. For Kabetu, the phrase established the reality of the Gikuyu ancestor's presence at the very beginning of time.

Gakaara wa Wanjau's *Mĩhĩrĩga ya Agĩkũyũ* shows that Mau Mau detainees were very much interested in these discussions over culture and origins. Gakaara had Kabetu's 1947 book at his elbow as he completed his ethnographical work in the late 1950s. In a few paragraphs he quotes word for word the whole of Kabetu's discussion regarding the location of Gikuyu's creation.[71] Like Kabetu, Gakaara and his colleagues thought it important to establish Gikuyu's presence as an autochton, indigenous to colonial Kenya's landscape. What was new about Gakaara's account was his emphasis on the personality, the psyche, of each of the Gikuyu clans. Earlier authorities had nothing to say on the subject. The consolidated account of origins birthed out of the late 1920s discourses about Gikuyu and God had pruned away the disparate histories and experiences of each of the Gikuyu clans. It would have been positively dangerous to reflect on the specificities, the distinctiveness, of each clan. When the earlier autoethnographers mentioned clans, they did so in numbered lists, identifying the name of the founding matriarch and the name of the clan she birthed. That was as much as Kenyatta felt able to say in *Facing Mount Kenya*. The Presbyterian schoolmaster Stanley Kiama Gathigira offered slightly more material in his 1933 book *Mĩikarĩre ya Agĩkũyũ* (The Ways of Staying of the Gikuyu).[72] He was willing to describe the distinctive shouts that women of each clan gave when they were surprised or astonished, but beyond these bare facts he was silent about the identities of the Gikuyu clans.

Gakaara's book is bursting with idiosyncratic, judgmental insights into the specific mentality of each clan. The book helps us see how detainees' exegetical discussions must have proceeded: each section begins with a folktale, or a proverb, and then expounds on the text to derive insights about the clan's character. Concerning the Aceera clan, for example, the book describes how a Ceera man, traveling with a friend to look at a piece of property, crossed a river on a log and then turned and removed the log before his companion could cross. The Ceera man then raced ahead and claimed the land as his own. The story gave detention-camp ethnographers the evidence with which to make judgments on Ceera men's character. Hasty and acquisitive Ceera men "are not good friends of the poor," says the book, and they are "impatient before they understand a matter."[73] The character of the Airimu clan is similarly diagnosed by reference to a folktale. The book describes how a young Irimu man once happened on a beautiful young girl while cutting firewood. He offered to assist her in her work and then pretended to have been wounded when a tree fell on him. Carried away to the girl's father's home, he impregnated her and claimed her hand in marriage. The story helped detention-camp ethnographers show that Irimu men were "poor courtiers" and were "not good at womanizing."[74] In documenting the personalities of central Kenya's several clans, Gakaara and other detention-camp ethnographers were doing something quite new in Gikuyu intellectual history. Where earlier homespun ethnographers had pruned away the multilingual histories of the Gikuyu clans, Mau Mau detainees populated the sparse architecture of clanship with human psychology, dispositions, and sentiments.

Their ethnographic work was part of a wider effort to create crosscutting institutions that could impose order on the camps' disparate inmates. The most pertinent question detainees faced was this: by what authority could they oblige other detainees to act with a unity of purpose? In August 1953 Gakaara and other members of the Mau Mau Central Committee in Manda Island resolved to go on strike in protest against the manual labor their British warders compelled them to perform.[75] Not everyone shared their convictions, and in exchange for better rations and other preferments several detainees agreed to cooperate fully with their British warders. It was, Gakaara wrote, a time of "great hatred between non-cooperators and cooperators." He injured his hand while throwing notes "accusing people who wanted to work" over the barbed-wire fence that divided his compound from his neighbors'.[76] Central Committee leaders secretly convened trials wherein the cooperators were subjected to a variety of fines—from a fat ram to a tin of honey to a bull—to be paid after their release.[77] These proleptic sanctions were never enough to impress the cooperators. When the cooperator John Mungai was called before Gakaara and his colleagues on Manda Island, he refused to be tried, saying that he would not acknowledge the court's legitimacy. It was in this context that detainees conducted their

ethnographic inquiries into clanship. Their work was urgent and important, for it helped to create a structure by means of which to hold other detainees accountable to the public will. Associations proliferated in Manda
Island camp. Detainees were organized into districts; each district had its
own chairman and secretary. There were associations of age groups—five
in number—and members' names were written in a register.[78] Clans were
likewise bureaucratized: each clan had a chairman and a membership roll,
so that every "member of the clan should know each other."[79]

Mīhīrīga ya Agĩkũyũ was animated by this organizational work. Its stereotypes about the behaviors and mentalities of each of the Gikuyu clans
reflected detainees' efforts to invest cultural institutions with authority, to
make people feel beholden to purposes larger than their own self-interest.
The book illuminates detainees' urgent search for cultural footings on which
to organize themselves. *Mīhīrīga ya Agĩkũyũ* was an aspect of a larger effort
to codify men's political and social commitments.

The book was also a guidebook to the feminine mystique. Cut off from
their families, desperate detainees were casting about for intellectual and
rhetorical leverage over their wives. The book helps us see how detainees worked to predict, and control, their wives' eccentricities. Chapter by
chapter, it chronicles the personalities of each clan's women. The exemplary woman of the Anjiru clan is said to "love her husband and always
protects his property." She is "very open handed and will take care of guests
very well," and she is "very particular about firm boundaries. Should a fight
break out at her home she quickly takes part in it."[80] Women of the Aga-
chiku clan are not said to be "very kind in giving food but will take care of
their husbands and guests." Their great strength is their industriousness:
the Gachiku woman "marks her garden boundaries well in advance by
plaiting grass and so she has few boundary quarrels."[81] Ambui women are
said to "stick to their husbands when they marry, and help their husbands
to earn more." But Ambui women are also known to be "domineering and
can dominate their husbands in case they relax."[82] Detainees needed to
know whether their wives would guard their interests. Many of them were
depending on their wives to protect their property. *Mīhīrīga ya Agĩkũyũ* illuminates the anxious conversations that detainees were conducting about
the managerial capacities of Gikuyu womanhood.

Mau Mau detention camps were full of advice about household management and other technical skills. In October 1956 the staff at Athi River detention camp launched a newspaper called *Atīrīrī*. Typed and duplicated on

a Roneo machine, some one thousand copies of *Atīrīrī* appeared in Gikuyu language each week. Gakaara wa Wanjau—who by that time had confessed to his involvement with Mau Mau—edited the newspaper under the supervision of the camp commandant. The greater part of *Atīrīrī* was populated with advice columns. There was a feature titled "Manners and Speech." There was a series of articles titled "An Advocate and His Profession." There was a long-running column about banking, interest rates, checkbooks, and other aspects of financial management. The contributors were Gikuyu men and women employed in government service. The world they conjured up was full of possibilities. Detainees were urged to interest themselves in world affairs, cultivate gentlemanly hobbies—stamp collecting was the subject of a long series of articles—and develop managerial capacities. British officers thought that *Atīrīrī* and other "rehabilitation" programs could help to "re-educate these Africans and . . . convince them that our plans are better and hold promise of a brighter future than those of the Mau Mau."[83] The newspaper was a tremendously popular undertaking: the editors had space to publish just a third of the contributions they received each week.[84]

The chief concern of *Atīrīrī*'s correspondents was conjugality. Gakaara, the editor, set the tone. Over the course of several editions he published a novel titled "She Must Quit This Home." Its subject was the difficulty of managing kin relations from afar. It featured a young man, recently married to a woman of whom his mother did not approve. While the young man labored in a faraway place, his bride, residing with his parents, was subjected to nighttime visitations from a threatening, ghostly voice. Overcome with fear, the young woman sank into an incoherent stupor. It was only when the young man returned to his home that the truth came out: the ghostly voice had been the man's mother, who had hoped to intimidate the young woman into separating from her son. Gakaara's message was clear: household management required men's constant attention. *Atīrīrī* gave its readers the skills they needed to supervise their families from afar. A series of over twenty articles titled "Family Life" featured technical advice about the organization of social occasions. Wedding parties had to be carefully planned; brides and grooms should ensure that invitations were sent out well in advance, so that the appropriate amount of refreshments could be prepared for the guests' enjoyment.[85] Each guest could be expected to consume two sandwiches, two cakes, and one scone.[86] The series "The Woman and Home Cleanliness" described the configuration of the ideal village house, with garden plots measuring one hundred by fifty yards, hedges four feet in height, kitchens in an orderly and sanitary arrangement, and walls painted white.[87] In *Atīrīrī* family life was stripped of its sentimentalities and made into an enterprise demanding technical competence.

Emboldened by the expertise they derived from *Atīrīrī*, guided also by their ethnographic insights into women's competence and character, detainees kept up a correspondence with their families. They used the postal system to project their supervisory authority into a domestic arena where they otherwise had little leverage. Early in 1956 Gakaara sent his wife a package containing several handkerchiefs, an Oxford reader, two exercise books, and a fountain pen. "Get one educated woman to teach you English," he told her. "I want you to improve your handwriting. It will be of much help to you and me in future."[88] The next year he sent his wife a copy of the government newspaper *Tazama*, calling her attention to a feature story about how to welcome visitors. "I would very much like you to read the story keenly," wrote Gakaara. "I have marked with pen all the area I think are important."[89] In the same package he sent his wife a set of teacups. "Keep them from children and maybe you should be using them only when you have visitors," he advised her. Gakaara was managing appearances from afar.

In its evaluations of women's capacities, skills, and aptitudes, *Mīhīrīga ya Agīkūyū* was an instrument that detainees could use to exert a supervisory authority over their complicated family lives. The book was a curriculum vitae, offering men information about their wives' competences and administrative skills. There was no space here for independent women. The book placed husbands—their property, their interests—at the center of family life. One of the first chapters in the book described how—in the ancient past—Gikuyu men had thrown off the despotic government of their wives. Husbands had once been subject to all manner of indignities: they were obliged to care for children while their wives governed; they were made to sit quietly while their wives danced; they were beaten, scourged, and mocked by their domineering brides. One day, the book recounts, husbands took matters into their own hands: they impregnated their wives all at once, and when the women were incapacitated by pregnancy, they physically overcame them and established a patriarchal government over Gikuyuland. The parable was a fantasy, allowing detainees to imagine a time when they, like their ancient forefathers, would assert patriarchal authority and reclaim their place as family heads.[90] *Mīhīrīga ya Agīkūyū* is a record of the reassuring stories that anxious men must have told themselves as they worried over their wives' apparently excessive powers.

Lifted from a missionary reading primer, a two-sentence fragment became the framework wherein the architects of Gikuyu moral community could define what held them together. As the sparse text passed through the hands of successive Gikuyu writers, it was populated with new characters, inhabited with sociology and culture, and codified into common knowledge. *Mĩhĩrĩga ya Agĩkũyũ* was one fruit of this ongoing work of textual self-imagination. In its stereotypes regarding the particular characteristics of Gikuyu clans, the book made clans into substantial, sociable organizations that deserved support. And in its judgments on women's capabilities, the book gave worried men resources that would enable them to involve themselves in their families' lives. The men who composed *Mĩhĩrĩga ya Agĩkũyũ* were themselves detainees. That is why they found ethnography so important. They were renovating institutions that promoted social order. Their literary and intellectual work gave them means of holding their families accountable to a patriarchal moral discipline.

Postcolonial Literature

Gakaara wa Wanjau emerged from his long incarceration in Mau Mau detention camps in 1960. He had a substantial amount of material ready for publication: there were manuscripts titled "How Kikuyu Governed Themselves Before the Whiteman Came," "Brideprice and Marriage," and "Mysteries of the Kikuyu Witchdoctor" and manuscripts on several other subjects.[91] He initially planned to publish the whole of his ethnographic work in one large volume, but financial constraints made it necessary for him to print each manuscript separately. His first publication was *Mĩhĩrĩga ya Agĩkũyũ*. It came out in January 1960, the same month the Kenya government finally lifted the State of Emergency. Lacking funds with which to finance the printing costs himself, Gakaara convinced the printer to produce advance copies, sold them, and used the profits to finance a larger print run. He hoped to place the book on the official syllabus for Kenya's intermediate schools. "Ninety percent of our present children and even some grown up young people of our tribe have no knowledge of Kikuyu clans," he told the minister of education. He meant his book to "play an important part in teaching [young people] . . . our customs and traditions."[92]

The government official who reviewed the book disputed the accuracy of Gakaara's ethnographic stereotypes. He averred that Anjiru women—who in Gakaara's book were said to "love [their] husband[s] and always protect his property"—were actually harridans. They were "known to be the most inhospitable, very harsh, and they like to possess anything they can lay their hands on," the official argued.[93] This criticism notwithstanding, *Mīhīrīga ya Agīkūyū* became a recommended text for use in central Kenya's intermediate schools. Gakaara reprinted the book four times over the course of the 1970s and 1980s. In 1998 he rewrote much of the content and published it again, with line drawings that he crafted. The new edition featured five pages of questions, meant to remind the reader of the key points in the text.[94]

Gakaara had great plans for his publishing business. His aim, he told a visiting British publisher, was to "run a big and popular bookshop, where while writing I can deal with selling of books from other countries, be an agent for books and periodicals, school materials, stationeries, sports equipment etc."[95] But his finances were always precarious, and for the whole of his career Gakaara spent much of his time negotiating over debts he owed, keeping accounts, and searching anxiously for sources of revenue. He applied for a government loan in 1960 to finance the purchase of his own printing machines, telling the director of trade and supplies that "we have great need to keep records of our happenings, old and new."[96] In 1966 Gakaara opened a print shop in his hometown, Karatina. Over the course of three decades he brought out dozens of books: there was a clutch of reading primers for students of Gikuyu, Dholuo, Kalenjin, and Kikamba; a series of moralistic novelettes; hymnbooks; ethnographic texts; and historical studies. Many of these texts had been conceived during his long incarceration in Mau Mau detention camps. Even the name of his first book series—"Atīrīrī"—was borrowed from the title of the detention camp newspaper.

In 1986, the eminent Kenyan writer Ngũgĩ wa Thiong'o famously announced that he would henceforth write entirely in the Gikuyu language. Ngũgĩ argued that vernacular languages grow directly out of the historical experience of a people: language is "inseparable from ourselves as a community of human beings with a specific form and character, a specific relationship to the world," he wrote.[97] But in fact the relationship between a particular people and a particular language has never been straightforward. The Gikuyu vernacular was a site of cultural and intellectual innovation, not a repository for a people's unique historical experience. In the early 1980s Gakaara went through the government-approved reading primer, highlighting places where words from other languages were used instead of Gikuyu terms. The adulterated language taught in the official reading primers, he argued, was a "shame to Gikuyu people." "It is difficult to rightly [teach children their culture and history] without first teaching them how to read and write correctly in their own language," he wrote.[98] In 1991 Gakaara brought out a series of three reading primers, published under the title *Mwandīkīre wa Gũgĩkũyũ Karīng'a* (Writing of Proper Gikuyu). It established a new standard of Gikuyu grammar and orthography, a standard Ngũgĩ himself now uses in the composition of his Gikuyu-language novels.

Gikuyu vernacular literature was made through the creative work of intellectuals like Gakaara wa Wanjau. Gakaara and his colleagues were not spokesmen for already-established cultural norms. They worked from a position of extreme insecurity, and this insecurity lent urgency to their ethnographic and cultural work. It is on this grounding that the library of Kenya's postcolonial literature stands.[99]

NOTES

Archival sources are referenced as follows: KNA: Kenya National Archives, Nairobi; GW: Gakaara wa Wanjau Papers, Yale University Library; EUL: Edinburgh University Library; TT: Tumutumu Church archives, Nyeri District, Kenya; AIM: Africa Inland Mission archives, Nairobi; PCEA: Presbyterian Church of East Africa archives, Nairobi; SOAS: School of Oriental and African Studies archive, London; Bristol: Imperial and Commonwealth History Museum, Bristol, England.

1. Gakaara to Community Development office, 27 July 1957, AB 11/61, KNA.

2. Gakaara wa Wanjau, *Mwandīki wa Mau Mau Ithamīrio-inī* (Nairobi: Heinemann, 1983); Gakaara wa Wanjau, *Mau Mau Author in Detention* (Nairobi: Heinemann, 1988).

3. Caroline Elkins, *Britain's Gulag: The Brutal End of Empire in Kenya* (London: Jonathan Cape, 2005).

4. Elkins, *Britain's Gulag*, 60.

5. Elkins, *Britain's Gulag*, 190.

6. Elkins, *Britain's Gulag*, 156.

7. John Lonsdale, "Writing Competitive Patriotisms in Eastern Africa," in *Recasting the Past: History Writing and Political Work in Modern Africa*, ed. Derek R. Peterson and Giacomo Macola (Athens: Ohio University Press, 2009), 251–267.

8. I have discussed this wider field of moral reformism in Derek R. Peterson, *Ethnic Patriotism and the East African Revival: A History of Dissent, c. 1935–1972* (Cambridge: Cambridge University Press, 2012).

9. I have discussed other aspects of Gakaara's work in "The Intellectual Lives of Mau Mau Detainees," *Journal of African History* 49, no. 1 (2008), 73–91, and in *Ethnic Patriotism*, ch. 10. His biography is given in Cristiana Pugliese's excellent *Author, Publisher, and Gikuyu Nationalist: The Life and Writings of Gakaara wa Wanjau* (Bayreuth: Bayreuth African Studies, 1995).

10. Gakaara to editor, *Baraza*, 3 March 1948, "Correspondence, 1948–49" file, GW.

11. Gakaara to District Commisssioner Nakuru, 2 March 1949, "Correspondence, 1948–49" file, GW.

12. Enrollment form, British Institute of Practical Psychology, n.d. [1949], "Correspondence, 1948–49" file, GW.

13. Nyeri District Annual Report, 1943, Provincial Commissioner Central Province (PC/CP) deposit 4/4/2; Nyeri District Annual Report, 1947, PC/CP/4/4/3, KNA.

14. This analysis is from John Lonsdale, "The Moral Economy of Mau Mau: Wealth, Poverty, and Civic Virtue in Kikuyu Political Thought," in *Unhappy Valley: Conflict in Kenya and Africa*, ed. Bruce Berman and John Lonsdale (London: James Currey, 1992).

15. Philp to Irvine, 24 July 1942, "Correspondence with Chogoria" file, TT.

16. *Mumenyereri* (newspaper), 6 June 1949, quoted in Kenya Information Office, "Summary of Opinions Expressed in the Kenya Press," 6 June 1949, District Commissioner Kisumu deposit 1/28/56, KNA.

17. *Mumenyereri*, 27 June 1949, quoted in Kenya Information Office, "Summary of Opinions Expressed in the Kenya Press," 1–15 June 1949, District Commissioner Kisumu deposit 1/28/56, KNA.

18. Gakaara to East Africa Command, n.d. [1948], "Correspondence, 1948–49" file, GW.

19. Gakaara to Secretary, District School Committee, n.d. [1948], "Correspondence, 1948–49" file, GW.

20. *Gikuyu Times*, 27 January 1948; quoted in Kenya Information Office, "Summary of Opinions Expressed in the Kenya Press," 15–31 January 1948, District Commissioner Kisumu deposit 1/28/56, KNA.

21. *Mucemanio*, 14 August 1948; quoted in Kenya Information Office, "Summary of Opinions Expressed in the Kenya Press," 1–15 August 1948, District Commissioner Kisumu deposit 1/28/154, KNA.

22. *Baraza*, 23 October 1948; quoted in Kenya Information Office, "Summary of Opinions Expressed in the Kenya Press," 15–30 October 1948, District Commissioner Kisumu deposit 1/28/154, KNA.

23. *Mumenyereri*, 5 July 1948; quoted in Kenya Information Office, "Summary of Opinions Expressed in the Kenya Press," 1–15 July 1948, District Commissioner Kisumu deposit 1/28/154, KNA.

24. *Gikuyu Times*, 19 August 1948; quoted in Kenya Information Office, "Summary of Opinions Expressed in the Kenya Press," 16–31 August 1948, District Commissioner Kisumu deposit 1/28/154, KNA.

25. Officer in Charge, Manyani, to Minister of Defence, 6 April 1956, AB 1/83, KNA.

26. Confession report, AWC 1209: Stephen Wangara, 23 September 1955, JZ 7/45, KNA.

27. No author, "Athi River," 8 June 1956, "Detention Correspondence" file, GW.

28. Ruth Wambuku, "Second Oath Confession Form," 7 April 1955, II/G/4, PCEA.

29. Luise White, "Matrimony and Rebellion: Masculinity in Mau Mau," in *Men and Masculinities in Modern Africa*, ed. Lisa Lindsay and Stephan Miescher (Portsmouth, NH: Heinemann, 2003), 177–191.

30. A. R. Barlow, notes on *kĩhaarĩro*, Gen. 1785/2, EUL. The definition of the word is given in T. G. Benson, *Kikuyu-English Dictionary* (Oxford: Clarendon Press, 1964), 135.

31. Confession report, AWC 1213, Karioki Muchemi, 19 November 1955, JZ 7/45, KNA.

32. Gucu wa Gikoyo, *We Fought for Freedom* (Nairobi: East African Publishing House, 1979), 149.

33. David Njagi, *The Last Mau Mau Field Marshals* (Meru: Ngwataniro Self-Help Group, 1993), 56.

34. Sidney Fazan, marginal comments on Petition no. 632, Gakaara Wanjau, 12 July 1954, JZ 7/26, KNA.

35. G. Heaton, "Report on the General Administration of Prisons and Detention Camps in Kenya" (Nairobi, 1956), "Letter from Prison" file, CBMS A/T 2/5, box 278, SOAS. David Anderson gives the daily average of Mau Mau detainees as 71,346 in December 1954, in *Histories of the Hanged: The Dirty War in Kenya and the End of Empire* (New York: Norton, 2005), 313.

36. No author, "Medicine for Mau Mau," n.d. [1956], JZ 8/1, KNA.

37. Anderson, *Histories of the Hanged*, 5.

38. Entry for February 1956, "Detention Diary Ms." file, GW.

39. J. M. Kariuki, *"Mau Mau" Detainee: The Account by a Kenya African of His Experiences in Detention Camps, 1953–1960* (Nairobi: Oxford University Press, 1963), 83.

40. Village Committee meeting, 5 October 1957, AB 18/30, KNA.

41. Senior Rehabilitation Assistant, Perkerra, to District Officer Marigat, 10 December 1957, AB 18/30, KNA.

42. Dr. Shannon, "The Changing Face of Kenya," *Kikuyu News* 210 (October 1955); Daniel Branch, *Defeating Mau Mau, Creating Kenya: Counterinsurgency, Civil War, and Decolonization* (Cambridge: Cambridge University Press, 2009), 112.

43. Gakaara to Shifra, n.d. (mid-1957), "Detention Correspondence" file, GW.

44. Community Development Officer to District Commissioner Nakuru, 15 December 1956, AB 18/10, KNA.

45. For the Swynnerton Plan, see Gavin Kitching, *Class and Economic Change in Kenya* (New Haven, CT: Yale University Press, 1980), and M. P. K. Sorenson, *Land Reform in the Kikuyu Country: A Study in Government Policy* (Nairobi: Oxford University Press, 1967).

46. Kibuchi Ndiangui, editorial letter, *Atĩrĩrĩ* 1, 51 (21 September 1957), AB 11/61, KNA.

47. Anderson Mureithi at Hola Camp to Community Development Officer, Saiyusi, 29 May 1957, AB 1/94, KNA.

48. Gakaara to Raheli Warigia, 8 July 1957, "Detention" file, GW.

49. Officer in Charge of Rehabilitation to Stanley Morrison, 8 February 1955, AB 1/112, KNA.

50. "Miss Martin" file: Martin to Greaves, 19 April 1958, CBMS A/T 2/6 box 279, SOAS.

51. Shifra to Gakaara, 18 October 1956, "Detention" file, GW.

52. Gakaara to Shifra, 4 November 1957, "Detention" file, GW.

53. Gakaara wa Wanjau, *Mīhīrīga ya Agīkūyū* (1960) (Nairobi: Gakaara Publishing Services, 1963).

54. Gakaara to Shifra, 12 July 1958, "Detention" file, GW.

55. Gakaara, *Mīhīrīga*, ii.

56. Gakaara, *Mīhīrīga*, 31–32.

57. On the multifarious origins of the Gikuyu clans, see Godfrey Muriuki, *A History of the Kikuyu, 1500–1900* (Nairobi: Oxford University Press, 1974), 37–61, 113–115.

58. K. R. Dundas, "Notes on the Origin and History of the Kikuyu and Dorobo Tribes," *Man* 8 (1908): 136–139.

59. W. Scoresby and Katherine Routledge, *With a Prehistoric People* (London: Edwin Arnold, 1910), 20; McClure, file note, January 1911, District Commissioner Nyeri deposit 1/6/1; District Commissioner Fort Hall, file note, 19 May 1921, Provincial Commissioner Central Province deposit 6/4/3, KNA.

60. Leonard Beecher, *The Kikuyu* (Nairobi: Ndia Kuu Press, 1944).

61. Scoresby and Routledge, *Prehistoric People*, 283.

62. Burton and Hofmeyr, introduction, this volume.

63. Marion Stevenson, *Karirikania* (Nyeri: Tumutumu School, 1924).

64. Kenya Land Tenure Commission, "Evidence given at Fort Hall baraza," September 1929, I/F/9, PCEA.

65. A. R. Barlow, notes on "Muumbi," Gen. 1785/2, EUL.

66. See John Lonsdale, "Contests of Time: Kikuyu Historiography, Old and New," in *A Place in the World: New Local Historiographies from Africa and South Asia*, ed. Axel Harniet Sievers (Leiden: Brill, 2002), 201–254.

67. Ng'ondu wa Kabuitu, "Preserving Kikuyu Characteristics," *Mwigwithania* 2, 2 (July–Aug. 1929), District Commissioner Machakos deposit 10B/13/1, KNA.

68. H. M. Gichuiri, "A Parable," *Mwigwithania* 1, 7 (Nov. 1928).

69. M. N. Kabetu, *Kīrīra kīa Ūgīkūyū* (1947) (Nairobi: Kenya Literature Bureau, 1991). My thanks to Joseph Kariuki Muriithi for his help with the translation of Kabetu's text.

70. Kabetu, *Kīrīra*, 2.

71. Gakaara, *Mīhīrīga*, 1–2.

72. S. K. Gathigira, *Mīikarīre ya Agīkūyū* (1933) (Nairobi: Scholars Publications, 1986).

73. Gakaara, *Mīhīrīga*, ch. 15.

74. Gakaara, *Mīhīrīga*, ch. 16.

75. Gakaara, *Mau Mau Author*, 35. See also Kariuki, *"Mau Mau" Detainee*, 116.

76. Notes on January and February 1954, "Detention Diary Correspondence" file, GW.

77. Breckenridge Papers, confession report, John Michael Mungai, 21–28 September 1956, file with no cover, Bristol.

78. Gakaara, *Mau Mau Author*, 101.

79. Breckenridge Papers, John Michael Mungai, 21–28 September 1956, file with no cover, Bristol.

80. Gakaara, *Mīhīrīga*, 30–31.

81. Gakaara, *Mīhīrīga*, 34–35.

82. Gakaara, *Mīhīrīga*, 32–33.

83. Tom Askwith, *From Mau Mau to Harambee*, ed. Joanna Lewis (Cambridge: Cambridge African Studies Centre, 1995), 101.

84. James Breckenridge, *Forty Years in Kenya* (Bridport, England: Creeds the Printers, n.d.), 237; Kame Muhoro, editorial letter, *Atīrīrī* 2, 6 (9 November 1957), AB 11/61, KNA.

85. Njeri, "The Family Life," pt. 17, *Atīrīrī* 2, 2 (12 October 1957).

86. Njeri, "The Family Life," pt. 18, *Atīrīrī* 2, 3 (19 October 1957).

87. Milika Wanjiru Jackson, "The Woman and Home Cleanliness," *Atīrīrī* 2, 7 (16 November 1957).

88. Gakaara to Shifra, 26 January 1956, "Detention Correspondence" file, GW.

89. Gakaara to Shifra, 2 July 1957, "Detention Correspondence" file, GW.

90. Kenyatta's *Facing Mount Kenya*, ch. 1, contains a similar account of an ancient matriarchal tyranny.

91. Gakaara wa Wanjau to Director of Trade and Supplies, 27 July 1960, "Correspondence, 1959–70" file, GW.

92. Gakaara wa Wanjau to Secretary to the Education Minister, 18 September 1960, "Correspondence, 1959–70" file, GW.

93. The critic was Fred Kago, author of a series of three reading primers published under the title *Wīrute Gūthoma* (Nairobi: Evans Brothers, 1953). Fred Kago, Education Officer, Keruguoya, to District Education Officer, Nyeri, 16 November 1960, "Correspondence, 1959–70" file, GW.

94. Gakaara wa Wanjau, *Mīhīrīga ya Agīkūyū* (Karatina: Gakaara Press, 1998).

95. Gakaara to Alden Clark of Franklin Publications, 14 April 1964, "Correspondence, 1959–70" file, GW.

96. Gakaara to Director of Trade and Supplies, 27 July 1960, "Correspondence, 1959–70" file, GW.

97. Ngugi wa Thiong'o, *Decolonizing the Mind: The Politics of Language in African Literature* (London, 1986).

98. Gakaara wa Wanjau, "The Gikuyu Language Committee," n.d., "Correspondence, 1960s, 1970s" file, GW.

99. This argument is developed in Peterson, *Creative Writing: Translation, Bookkeeping, and the Work of Imagination in Colonial Kenya* (Portsmouth, NH: Heinemann, 2004), ch. 9.

BIBLIOGRAPHY

Collections and Archives

Alexander Turnbull Library, Wellington, New Zealand
    Richmond-Atkinson Papers
Asian and African Collections, British Library, London
Bodleian Library, Oxford
    Charles Henry Pearson papers
C. L. R. James Archive, University of the West Indies, St. Augustine, Trinidad and
    Tobago
Edinburgh University Library
Imperial and Commonwealth History Museum, Bristol, England
    Breckenridge Papers
Kenya National Archives, Nairobi
National Archives of India, New Delhi
    Benarsidas Chaturvedi Papers
    Commerce and Industry, Emigration, November 1914, December 1915, May 1916
    Legislative, Assembly & Council, July 1922
    Depot Walon Ka Phanda, Commerce and Industry, Emigration, May 1916
SAPPHIRE (Scottish Archive of Print and Publishing History Records),
    www.sapphire.ac.uk
School of Oriental and African Studies Archive, London
Scout Association Headquarters Archive, Gilwell Park, Chingford, Essex
South African Archives Depot, Native Affairs Department, Pretoria
State Library of Victoria, Melbourne
    Charles Henry Pearson Papers
Tumutumu Church Archives, Nyeri District, Kenya
U.P. State Archives, Lucknow, India
    Mainpuri Conspiracy Case
    *Memorandum on Indian-Owned Newspapers in the United Provinces during the Year
        1914.* Allahabad: Government Press, U.P., 1915
    Selection from Indian Owned Newspapers in U.P., 1915
    Selection of Native Newspapers, U.P., 1915

Statement of Books, during 1917
Statement of Books, during the Quarter Ending December 1915
Statement of Particulars Regarding Books and Periodicals Published in the U.P.,
    Registered under Act XXV of 1867, [Statement of Books], during the Quarter
    Ending March 1915
Victorian Parliamentary Papers, State Library of Victoria, Melbourne
West Bengal State Archives, Kolkata
Yale University Library, New Haven, Connecticut
    Gakaara wa Wanjau Papers

Books and Articles

An Account of Ireland, Statistical and Political. 2 vols. London: Longman, Hurst, Rees,
    Orme and Brown, 1812.
Allott, Miriam, ed. *The Brontës: The Critical Heritage.* London: Routledge and Kegan
    Paul, 1974.
Anderson, Benedict. *Imagined Communities: Reflections on the Origin and Spread of
    Nationalism.* London: Verso, 1991.
Anderson, Benedict. *The Spectre of Comparisons: Nationalism, Southeast Asia and the
    World.* London: Verso, 1998.
Anderson, David. *Histories of the Hanged: The Dirty War in Kenya and the End of Em-
    pire.* New York: Norton, 2005.
Andrews, C. F., and W. W. Pearson. *Report on Indentured Labour in Fiji.* Calcutta: Star
    Printing, 1916.
Anon. "The Black Jacobins of San Domingo's Revolution." *New York Times,* 11 Decem-
    ber 1938.
Anon. *A Century of Injustice.* Baltimore, 1899.
Anon. *A Century of Wrong.* Issued by F. W. Reitz. London: Review of Reviews, 1899.
Anon. *A Century of Wrong.* 2nd ed. With preface by W. T. Stead. London: Review of
    Reviews, 1900.
Anon. *Een Eeuw van Onrecht.* Dordrecht: Morks & Geuze, 1899.
Anon. *Een Eeuw van Onrecht.* 2nd ed. Dordrecht: Morks & Geuze, 1900.
Apter, Emily. *Against World Literature: On the Politics of Untranslatability.* London:
    Verso, 2013.
Ashforth, Adam. *The Politics of Discourse in Twentieth-Century South Africa.* Oxford:
    Clarendon Press, 1990.
Askwith, Tom. *From Mau Mau to Harambee.* Edited by Joanna Lewis. Cambridge:
    Cambridge African Studies Centre, 1995.
Auerbach, Sascha. *Race, Law, and the Chinese Puzzle in Imperial Britain.* London:
    Palgrave, 2009.
Austin, David. "In Search of a National Identity: C. L. R. James and the Promise of the
    Caribbean." In *You Don't Play with Revolution: The Montreal Lectures of C. L. R.
    James,* 1–26. Oakland, CA: AK Press, 2009.
Azim, Firdous. *The Colonial Rise of the Novel.* London: Routledge, 1994.

Baden-Powell, Robert. *Scouting for Boys*. Edited by Elleke Boehmer. Oxford: Oxford University Press, 2004.

Baden-Powell, Robert, and Agnes Baden-Powell. *Girl Guiding*. London: C. Arthur Pearson, 1918.

Balavantsinha. *Under the Shelter of Bapu*. Translated by Shri Gopalrau Kulkarni. Ahmedabad: Navajivan, 1962. (Originally published 1956)

Ballantyne, Tony. "Reading the Newspaper in Colonial Otago." *Journal of New Zealand Studies* 12 (2011): 49–50.

Ballantyne, Tony. "The State, Politics, and Power, 1769–1893." In *The New Oxford History of New Zealand*, ed. Giselle Byrnes, 99–125. Oxford: Oxford University Press, 2009.

Ballard, Arthur. "The Greatest Slave Revolt in History." *New Leader*, 9 December 1938.

Barber, Karin, ed. *Africa's Hidden Histories: Everyday Literacy and the Making of the Self*. Bloomington: Indiana University Press, 2006.

Barber, Karin. "Audiences and the Book." *Current Writing* 13, no. 2 (2001): 9–19.

Barber, Karin. "Authorship, Copyright and Quotation in Oral and Print Spheres in Early Colonial Yorubaland." In *Staging the Immaterial: Rights, Style and Performance in Sub-Saharan Africa*, ed. Ute Röschenthaler and Mamadou Diawara. Oxford: Sean Kingston, forthcoming.

Barber, Karin. "Introduction: Hidden Innovators in Africa." In *Africa's Hidden Histories: Everyday Literacy and the Making of the Self*, ed. Karin Barber, 1–24. Bloomington: Indiana University Press, 2006.

Bayly, C. A. *Empire and Information: Intelligence Gathering and Social Communication in India, 1780–1870*. Cambridge: Cambridge University Press, 1996.

Beckles, Hilary. *Britain's Black Debt: Reparations for Caribbean Slavery and Native Genocide*. Kingston, Jamaica: UWI Press, 2013.

Beckles, Hilary McD. " 'The Williams Effect': Eric Williams's *Capitalism and Slavery* and the Growth of West Indian Political Economy." In *British Capitalism and Caribbean Slavery: The Legacy of Eric Williams*, ed. Barbara L. Solow and Stanley L. Engerman, 303–316. Cambridge: Cambridge University Press, 1987.

Beecher, Leonard. *The Kikuyu*. Nairobi: Ndia Kuu Press, 1944.

Bell, Bill. "Crusoe's Books: The Scottish Emigrant Reader in the Nineteenth Century." In *Across Boundaries: The Book in Culture and Commerce*, ed. Bill Bell, Philip Bennett, and Jonquil Bevan, 116–129. New Castle, DE: Oak Knoll Press, 2000.

Bell, Currer, ed. *Jane Eyre: An Autobiography*. London: Smith, Elder, 1847.

Bell, Duncan. *The Idea of Greater Britain: Empire and the Future of World Order*. Princeton, NJ: Princeton University Press, 2007.

Benson, T. G. *Kikuyu-English Dictionary*. Oxford: Clarendon Press, 1964.

Bently, Lionel. "The 'Extraordinary Multiplicity' of Intellectual Property Law in the British Colonies in the Nineteenth Century." *Theoretical Inquiries in Law* 12, no. 1 (2011): 161–200.

Benton, Lauren. *A Search for Sovereignty: Law and Geography in European Empires, 1400–1900*. Cambridge: Cambridge University Press, 2009.

Bhana, Surendra, and Neelima Shukla Bhatt. *A Fire That Blazed in the Ocean*. New Delhi: Promila, 2011.

Bhargava, M. L. *Ganesh Shankar Vidyarthi*. New Delhi: Government of India, Publications Division, 1988.

Birbalsingh, Frank. "The Literary Achievement of C. L. R. James." *Journal of Commonwealth Literature* 19, no. 1 (1984): 108–121.

Birnhack, Michael D. *Colonial Copyright: Intellectual Property in Mandate Palestine*. Oxford: Oxford University Press, 2012.

Bloomfield, Paul. *Edward Gibbon Wakefield: Builder of the British Commonwealth*. London: Longmans, 1961.

Boehmer, Elleke. "At Once A-sexual and Anal: Baden-Powell and the Boy Scouts." In *Children and Sexuality: From the Greeks to the Great War*, ed. George Rousseau, 299–311. Basingstoke, England: Palgrave Macmillan, 2007.

Boehmer, Elleke. *Empire, the National and the Postcolonial: Resistance in Interaction*. Oxford: Oxford University Press, 2002.

Boehmer, Elleke. "Global Nets, Textual Webs; or What Isn't New about Empire?" *Postcolonial Studies* 7, no. 1 (2004): 11–26.

Boehmer, Elleke. "The Worlding of the Jingo Poem." *Yearbook of English Studies* 41, no. 2 (2011): 41–57.

Branch, Daniel. *Defeating Mau Mau, Creating Kenya: Counterinsurgency, Civil War, and Decolonization*. Cambridge: Cambridge University Press, 2009.

Brathwaite, Kamau. "Dream Haiti." In *The Oxford Book of Caribbean Short Stories*, ed. Stewart Brown and John Wickham, 169–186. Oxford: Oxford University Press, 2001.

Breckenridge, James. *Forty Years in Kenya*. Bridport, England: Creeds the Printers, [2005].

Brennan, Timothy. Introduction to *Music in Cuba*, by Alejo Carpentier. Translated by Alan West-Durán. Minneapolis: University of Minnesota Press, 2001.

Bristow, Joe. *Empire Boys: Adventures in a Man's World*. London: HarperCollins, 1991.

Brogan, Hugh. *Mowgli's Sons: Kipling and Baden-Powell's Scouts*. London: Cape, 1987.

Brontë, Charlotte. *Jane Eyre*. Harmondsworth, England: Penguin Books, 1953.

Brontë, Charlotte. *Letters of Charlotte Brontë*. 2 vols. Edited by Margaret Smith. Oxford: Oxford University Press, 1995.

Bulson, Eric. "Little Magazine, World Form." In *The Oxford Handbook to Global Modernisms*, ed. Mark Wollaeger, 267–287. Oxford: Oxford University Press, 2012.

Burns, Patricia. *Fatal Success: A History of the New Zealand Company*. Auckland: Heinemann Reed, 1989.

Burroughs, Peter, ed. *The Colonial Reformers and Canada, 1830–1849*. Toronto: McClelland and Stewart, 1969.

Burton, Antoinette. *Empire in Question: Reading, Writing and Teaching British Imperialism*. Durham, NC: Duke University Press, 2011.

Burton, Antoinette. "Getting Outside the Global: Re-positioning British Imperialism in World History." In *Race, Nation and Empire: Making Histories, 1750 to the Present*, ed. Catherine Hall and Keith McClelland, 199–216. Manchester: Manchester University Press, 2010.

Burton, Antoinette. "Recapturing *Jane Eyre*: Reflections on Historicizing the Colonial Encounter in Victorian Britain." *Radical History Review* 64 (Winter 1996): 58–72.

Cateau, Heather, and S. H. H. Carrington, eds. *Capitalism and Slavery Fifty Years Later: Eric Eustace Williams—A Reassessment of the Man and His Work.* New York: Peter Lang, 2000.

Césaire, Aimé. *La Tragédie du roi Christophe.* Paris: Présence Africaine, 1970.

Césaire, Aimé. *Notebook of a Return to the Native Land.* Translated by Annette Smith and Clayton Eshleman. Middletown, CT: Wesleyan University Press, 2001.

Césaire, Aimé. *Toussaint Louverture: La Révolution française et le problème colonial.* Paris: Présence Africaine, 1981.

Chambers, Colin. *Black and Asian Theatre in Britain: A History.* London: Routledge, 2011.

Chand, Lal, and Sons. *State-Owned Printing Presses and Their Competition with Private Trade.* Calcutta: Lal Chand and Sons, 1923.

Chatterjee, Rimi B. *Empires of the Mind: A History of the Oxford University Press in India under the Raj.* New Delhi: Oxford University Press, 2006.

Chaturvedi, B. "Bikhri Hui Baten." In *Balmukund Gupta Smarak Grantha,* ed. Jhabamal Sharma and B. Chaturvedi. Calcutta: Gupta Smaraka Grantha Prakashan Samiti, 1950.

Chaturvedi, B. "Totaram Sanadhya." In *Sansmaran.* Kashi: Bharitya Gnanpith, 1958.

Chaturvedi, Benarsidas, and Marjorie Sykes. *Charles Freer Andrews: A Narrative.* London: Allen and Unwin, 1949.

Chaturvedi, Rita, and S. R. Bakshi. *Bihar through the Ages.* Vol. 3. New Delhi: Sarup and Sons, 2007.

Cheong, Cheok Hong, et al. *Chinese Remonstrance to the Parliament and People of Victoria, together with Correspondence with Government of the Same, and Address to Sydney Conference.* Melbourne: Wm. Marshall and Co., 1888.

Codell, Julie F. "Getting the Twain to Meet: Global Regionalism in 'East and West': A Monthly Review." *Victorian Periodicals Review* 37, no. 2 (2004): 214–232.

Codell, Julie F. "Introduction: The Nineteenth-Century News from India." *Victorian Periodicals Review* 37, no. 2 (2004): 106–123.

Cohn, Bernard S. *Colonialism and Its Forms of Knowledge: The British in India.* Princeton, NJ: Princeton University Press, 1996.

Coombe, Rosemary J. "Authorial Cartographies: Mapping Proprietary Borders in a Less-Than-Brave New World." *Stanford Law Review* 48, no. 1357 (1996): 2.

Cooper, Frederick, and Ann Laura Stoler. "Between Metropole and Colony: Rethinking a Research Agenda." In *Tensions of Empire: Colonial Cultures in a Bourgeois World,* ed. Frederick Cooper and Ann Laura Stoler, 1–56. Berkeley: University of California Press, 1997.

Courlander, Harold. "Revolt in Haiti." *Saturday Review of Literature,* 7 January 1939.

Crotty, Martin. *Making the Australian Male: Middle-Class Masculinity 1870–1920.* Melbourne: Melbourne University Press, 2001.

Dangarembga, Tsitsi. *Nervous Conditions.* London: Women's Press, 1988.

Darnton, Robert. "What Is the History of Books?" *Daedalus* 111, no. 3 (1982): 65–83.

Darwin, John. "Imperialism and the Victorians: The Dynamics of Territorial Expansion." *English Historical Review* 112, no. 447 (1997): 614–442.

Davies, J. Llewelyn. "Are All Men Equal?" *Guardian*, 13 June 1894.

Dawson, Graham. *Soldier Heroes: British Empire, Adventure, and the Imagining of Masculinities*. London: Routledge, 1994.

Deane, Bradley. *The Making of the Victorian Novelist: Anxieties of Authorship in the Mass Market*. London: Routledge, 2002.

De Kock, W. J. "Een Eeuw van Onrecht." *Die Brandwag*, 30 August 1957.

Desai, Mahadev. *The Gospel of Selfless Action or The Gita According to Gandhi*. Ahmedabad: Navajivan, 1946.

Desmond, Cosmas. *The Discarded People: An Account of African Resettlement in South Africa*. Johannesburg: Christian Institute, 1969.

De Villiers, Anna. " 'n Historiese Geheim Opgeklaar: Wie die Skrywer van 'Een Eeuw van Onrecht' is." *Die Huisgenoot*, 6 July 1934.

Devji, Faisal. *The Impossible Indian: Gandhi and the Temptation of Violence*. Cambridge, MA: Harvard University Press, 2012.

Dick, Archie. *The Hidden History of South Africa's Book and Reading Culture*. Toronto: University of Toronto Press, 2012.

Dilke, Charles. *Greater Britain: A Record of Travel in English-Speaking Colonies during 1866 and 1867*. 2 vols. London: Macmillan, 1868.

Drabble, Margaret, ed. *Oxford Companion to English Literature*. Oxford: Oxford University Press, 1985.

Draper, Nicholas. "Capitalism and Slave Ownership: A Response." *Small Axe* 37 (March 2012): 168–177.

Draper, Nicholas. *The Price of Emancipation: Slave Ownership, Compensation and British Society at the End of Slavery*. Cambridge: Cambridge University Press, 2010.

Dubois, Laurent. *Avengers of the New World: The Story of the Haitian Revolution*. Cambridge, MA: Harvard University Press, 2004.

Duffy, Charles Gavan. *Young Ireland: A Fragment of Irish History 1840–1850*. London: T. Fisher Unwin, 1880.

Dundas, K. R. "Notes on the Origin and History of the Kikuyu and Dorobo Tribes." *Man* 8 (1908): 136–139.

Du Plessis, C. N. J. *Uit de geschiedenis van de Zuid-Afrikaansche Republiek en van de Afrikaanders*. Amsterdam: De Bussy, 1898.

Edward Gibbon Wakefield and the Colonial Dream: A Reconsideration. Wellington: Friends of the Turnbull Library / GP Publications, 1997.

Ein Jahrhundert voller Unrecht: Ein Rückblick auf die Süd-afrikanische Politik Englands. Berlin: Walther, 1900.

Eliot, Simon. " 'Never Mind the Value, What about the Price?': Or, How Much Did *Marmion* Cost St. John Rivers?" *Nineteenth-Century Literature* 56, no. 2 (September 2001): 160–197.

Elkins, Caroline. *Britain's Gulag: The Brutal End of Empire in Kenya*. London: Cape, 2005.

Esty, Jed. *Unseasonable Youth: Modernism, Colonialism, and the Fiction of Development*. Oxford: Oxford University Press, 2012.

Fairburn, Miles. "Wakefield, Edward Gibbon—Biography." In *Biography Dictionary of New Zealand. Te Ara—The Encyclopedia of New Zealand.* www.teara.govt.nz/en /biographies/1w4/wakefield-edward-gibbon.

Fick, Carolyn. *The Making of Haiti: The Saint Domingue Revolution from Below.* Knoxville: University of Tennessee Press, 1990.

Finkelstein, David, and Douglas M. Peers, eds. *Negotiating India in the Nineteenth-Century Media.* London: Palgrave Macmillan, 2000.

Finnegan, Ruth. *Orality and Literacy: The Technologizing of the Word.* London: Routledge, 1982.

Fitzgerald, John. *Big White Lie: Chinese Australians in White Australia.* Sydney: UNSW Press, 2007.

Flint, Kate. *The Woman Reader 1837–1914.* Oxford: Clarendon Press, 1993.

Fraser, Robert. *Book History through Postcolonial Eyes: Rewriting the Script.* London: Routledge, 2008.

Fraser, Robert, and Mary Hammond, eds. *Books without Borders.* Vol. 1. *The Cross-National Dimension in Print Culture.* London: Palgrave Macmillan, 2008.

Frost, Mark Ravinder. " 'Wider Opportunities': Religious Revival, Nationalist Awakening and the Global Dimension in Colombo, 1870–1920." *Modern Asian Studies* 36, no. 4 (2002): 937–967.

Gakaara wa Wanjau. *Mau Mau Author in Detention.* Nairobi: Heinemann, 1988.

Gakaara wa Wanjau. *Mīhīrīga ya Agīkūyū.* Nairobi: Gakaara Publishing Services, 1963 (Originally published 1960)

Gakaara wa Wanjau. *Mīhīrīga ya Agīkūyū.* Karatina, Kenya: Gakaara Press, 1998.

Gakaara wa Wanjau. *Mwandīki wa Mau Mau Ithamīrio-inī.* Nairobi: Heinemann, 1983.

Gandhi, Mahatma. "A Message to 'The Aryan Path.' " In *Collected Works of Mahatma Gandhi,* 100 vols., 81:319–321. New Delhi: Publications Division, Government of India, 1956–1994.

Gandhi, M. K. *Collected Works of Mahatma Gandhi.* 100 vols. New Delhi: Government of India, 1956–1994.

Gandhi, M. K. *From Yeravda Mandir.* Translated from the original Gujarati by Valji Govindji Desai. Ahmedabad: Navajivan, 2005. (Originally published 1932)

Gandhi, M. K. *M. K. Gandhi's Hind Swaraj: A Critical Edition.* Annotated, translated, and edited by Suresh Sharma and Tridip Suhrud. Delhi: Orient Blackswan, 2010.

Gandhi, M. K. *Satyagraha in South Africa.* Translated from the original Gujarati by Valji Govindji Desai. Ahmedabad: Navajivan, 2003. (Originally published 1950)

Garvey, Ellen Gruber. "Scissorizing and Scrapbooks: Nineteenth-Century Reading, Remaking and Recirculating." In *New Media, 1740–1915,* ed. Lisa Gitelman and B. Geoffrey Pingree, 207–227. Cambridge, MA: MIT Press, 2003.

Gaskell, Mrs. *The Life of Charlotte Bronte.* Harmondsworth, England: Penguin, 1975. (Originally published 1857)

Gathigira, S. K. *Mīikarīre ya Agīkūyū.* Nairobi: Scholars Publications, 1986. (Originally published 1933)

Geggus, David. *Haitian Revolutionary Studies*. Bloomington: Indiana University Press, 2002.

Gichuiri, H. M. "A Parable." *Mwigwithania* 1, no. 7 (November 1928).

Gilroy, Paul. *The Black Atlantic: Modernity and Double Consciousness*. Cambridge, MA: Harvard University Press, 1994.

Gilroy, Paul. *"There Ain't No Black in the Union Jack": The Cultural Politics of Race and Nation*. Chicago: University of Chicago Press, 1991.

Glissant, Edouard. *Monsieur Toussaint: A Play*. Translated by Michael J. Dash. Boulder, CO: Lynne Rienner, 2005.

Gluck, Carol. "*Sekinin*: Responsibility." In *Words in Motion: Toward a Global Lexicon*, ed. Carol Gluck and Anna Lowenhaupt Tsing, 11–19. Durham, NC: Duke University Press, 2009.

Gluck, Carol. "Words in Motion." In *Words in Motion: Toward a Global Lexicon*, ed. Carol Gluck and Anna Lowenhaupt Tsing, 83–108. Durham, NC: Duke University Press, 2009.

Gluck, Carol, and Anna Lowenhaupt Tsing, eds. *Words in Motion: Toward a Global Lexicon*. Durham, NC: Duke University Press, 2009.

Gopal, Madan. *Freedom Movement and the Press: The Role of Hindi Newspapers*. New Delhi: Criterion, 1990.

Gordon, Lewis. *An Introduction to Africana Philosophy*. Cambridge: Cambridge University Press, 2008.

Gouger, Robert, ed. *A Letter from Sydney, the Principal Town of Australasia. Together with the Outline of a System of Colonization*. London: Joseph Cross, 1829.

Graham, Ruth. "Juvenile Travellers: Priscilla Wakefield's Excursions in Empire." *Journal of Imperial and Commonwealth History* 38 (2010): 374.

Green, Nile. *Bombay Islam: The Religious Economy of the Western Indian Ocean*. New York: Cambridge University Press, 2011.

Green, Nile. "Persian Print and the Stanhope Revolution: Industrialization, Evangelicalism, and the Birth of Printing in Early Qajar Iran." *Comparative Studies of South Asia, Africa and the Middle East* 30, no. 3 (2010): 473–490.

Grierson, Flora. "Man's Inhumanity to Man." *New Statesman*, 8 October 1938.

Gucu wa Gikoyo. *We Fought for Freedom*. Nairobi: East African Publishing House, 1979.

Guy, Jeff. "Imperial Appropriations: The Dynamic History of the *iziqu*." *Natal Museum Journal of Humanities* 11 (December 1999): 23–42.

Hall, Catherine. *Macaulay and Son: Architects of Imperial Britain*. New Haven, CT: Yale University Press, 2012.

Hall, Catherine. *Writing Histories of Difference: New Histories of Nation and Empire*. Pamphlet from Allan Martin Lecture. Canberra: Australian National University, 2005.

Harvey, David. *Companion to Marx's "Capital."* London: Verso, 2009.

Harvey, Ross. "Bringing the News to New Zealand: The Supply and Control of Overseas News in the Nineteenth Century." *Media History* 8, no. 1 (2002): 21–34.

Harvie, Christopher. *Lights of Liberalism: University Liberals and the Challenge of Democracy 1860–86*. London: Allen Lane, 1976.

Hawkins, Sean. *Writing and Colonialism in North Ghana: The Encounter between the LoDagaa and "the World on Paper," 1982–1992*. Toronto: University of Toronto Press, 2002.

Hay, Simon. "*Nervous Conditions*, Lukács, and the Postcolonial Bildungsroman." *Genre* 46, no. 3 (Fall 2013): 317–344.

Hexham, Irving. "Afrikaner Nationalism 1902–1924." In *The South African War: The Anglo-Boer War 1899–1902*, ed. Peter Warwick, 386–403. London: Longman, 1980.

Higman, B. W. *Writing West Indian Histories*. London: Macmillan, 1999.

Hobsbawm, Eric. *The Age of Revolution: Europe 1789–1848*. London: Weidenfeld and Nicholson, 1997. (Originally published 1962)

Hobsbawm, Eric. "The Historians' Group of the Communist Party." In *Rebels and Their Causes: Essays in Honour of A. L. Morton*, ed. Maurice Cornforth, 21–48. London: Lawrence and Wishart, 1978.

Hodgson, Godfrey. *Woodrow Wilson's Right Hand: The Life of Colonel Edward M. House*. New Haven, CT: Yale University Press, 2006.

Hofmeyr, Isabel. *Gandhi's Printing Press: Experiments in Slow Reading*. Cambridge, MA: Harvard University Press, 2013.

Hofmeyr, Isabel. *The Portable Bunyan: A Transnational History of "The Pilgrim's Progress."* Princeton, NJ: Princeton University Press, 2003.

Høgsbjerg, Christian. "C. L. R. James: The Revolutionary as Artist." *International Socialism* 112 (2006). Available at www.isj.org.uk/?id=253.

Høgsbjerg, Christian. Introduction to *Toussaint Louverture: The Story of the Only Successful Slave Revolt in History*, by C. L. R. James. Durham, NC: Duke University Press, 2013.

Howsam, Leslie. *Cheap Bibles: Nineteenth-Century Publishing and the British and Foreign Bible Society*. Cambridge: Cambridge University Press, 1991.

Howsam, Leslie. *Kegan Paul and Victorian Imprint: Publishers, Books and Cultural History*. Toronto: KPI and University of Toronto Press, 1998.

Howsam, Leslie. *Old Books and New Histories: An Orientation to Studies in Books and Print Culture*. Toronto: University of Toronto Press, 2006.

Howsam, Leslie. "What Is the Historiography of Books? Recent Studies in Authorship, Publishing, and Reading in Modern Britain and North America." *Historical Journal* 51, no. 4 (2008): 1089–1101.

Inikori, Joseph. *Africans and the Industrial Revolution in England: A Study in International Trade and Economic Development*. Cambridge: Cambridge University Press, 2002.

Innes, C. L. Epilogue to *A History of Black and Asian Writing in Britain*, 233–252. Cambridge: Cambridge University Press, 2008.

Iriye, Akira. *Pacific Estrangement: Japanese and American Expansion, 1897–1911*. Cambridge, MA: Harvard University Press, 1972.

Israel, Milton. *Communications and Power: Propaganda and the Press in the Indian Nationalist Struggle, 1920–1947*. Cambridge: Cambridge University Press, 1994.

Ivy, James W. "Break the Image of the White God . . ." *Crisis* 46, no. 8 (August 1939).

Jackson, Milika Wanjiru. "The Woman and Home Cleanliness." *Atīrīrī* 2, no. 7, 16 November 1957.

Jain, Pavan Kumar. *Videsom Mein Hindi Patrikarta*. New Delhi: Radha Publications, 1993.

James, C. L. R. "Appendix: From Toussaint L'Ouverture to Fidel Castro." In *The Black Jacobins: Toussaint L'Ouverture and the San Domingo Revolution*, 391–418. New York: Vintage Books, 1989. (Originally published 1963)

James, C. L. R. *Beyond a Boundary*. Durham, NC: Duke University Press, 1994.

James, C. L. R. "The Birth of a Nation." In *Contemporary Caribbean: A Sociological Reader*, vol. 1, ed. Susan Craig, 3–35. Trinidad and Tobago: College Press, 1981.

James, C. L. R. *The Black Jacobins: Toussaint L'Ouverture and the San Domingo Revolution*. 2nd ed. New York: Vintage Books, 1989.

James, C. L. R. Foreword to *The Black Jacobins: Toussaint L'Ouverture and the San Domingo Revolution*. London: Allison and Busby, 1980.

James, C. L. R. "The Intelligence of the Negro." In *From Trinidad: An Anthology of Early West Indian Writing*, ed. Reinhard W. Sander, 227–237. London: Hodder and Stoughton, 1978.

James, C. L. R. "Lectures on *The Black Jacobins*." *Small Axe* 8 (2000): 65–82.

James, C. L. R. "The Making of the Caribbean Peoples." Lecture delivered at the Second Conference on West Indian Affairs, Montreal, summer 1966.

James, C. L. R. "A National Purpose for Caribbean Peoples." In *At the Rendezvous of Victory*, 143–158. London: Allison and Busby, 1984. (Originally published 1964)

James, C. L. R. "A New View of West Indian History." *Caribbean Quarterly* 35, no. 4 (December 1989): 49–70.

James, C. L. R. *Nkrumah and the Ghana Revolution*. London: Allison and Busby, 1977.

James, C. L. R. "On *The Negro in the Caribbean* by Eric Williams." In *C. L. R. James on the "Negro Question,"* ed. Scott McLemee, 117–125. Jackson: University Press of Mississippi, 1996.

James, C. L. R. "San Domingo." In *A History of Negro Revolt*, 1–20. Chicago: Frontline Books, 2004.

James, C. L. R. *Toussaint Louverture: The Story of the Only Successful Slave Revolt in History*. Durham, NC: Duke University Press, 2013.

James, C. L. R. "West Indian Personality." *Caribbean Quarterly* 35, no. 4 (December 1989): 11–14.

James, C. L. R. *World Revolution 1917–1936: The Rise and Fall of the Communist International*. Atlantic Highlands, NJ: Humanities Press, 1993.

James, Patricia. *Population Malthus: His Life and Times*. London: Routledge and Kegan Paul, 1979.

Jeal, Tim. *Baden-Powell, Founder of the Boy Scouts*. London: Pimlico, 1991.

Jeppie, Shamil, and Souleymane Bachir Diagne, eds. *The Meanings of Timbuktu*. Pretoria: Human Sciences Research Council Press, 2008.

Johnston, Anna. *The Paper War: Morality, Print Culture, and Power in Colonial New South Wales*. Crawley: University of Western Australia Publishing, 2011.

Johnston, H. J. M. "Wakefield, Edward Gibbon." *Dictionary of Canadian Biography Online*. www.biographi.ca/en/bio/wakefield_edward_gibbon_9E.html.

Joshi, Priya. *In Another Country: Colonialism, Culture and the English Novel in India*. New York: Columbia University Press, 2002.

Joshi, P. S. *The Tyranny of Colour: A Study of the Indian Problem in South Africa*. Durban: E. P. & Commercial Printing Co., 1942.

Kabetu, M. N. *Kīrīra kīa Ūgīkūyū*. Nairobi: Kenya Literature Bureau, 1991. (Originally published 1947)

Kafka, Ben. *The Demon of Writing: Powers and Failures of Paperwork*. Cambridge, MA: Zone Books, 2012.

Kago, Fred. *Wīrute Gūthoma*. Nairobi: Evans Brothers, 1953.

Kamra, Sukeshi. *The Indian Periodical Press and the Production of Nationalist Rhetoric*. London: Palgrave Macmillan, 2011.

Kamugisha, Aaron, and Alissa Trotz, eds. "Caribbean Trajectories: 200 Years On." Special issue, *Race and Class* 49, no. 2 (October 2007).

Kariuki, Josiah M. *"Mau Mau" Detainee: The Account by a Kenya African of His Experiences in Detention Camps, 1953–1960*. Nairobi: Oxford University Press, 1963.

Kaul, Chandrika, ed. *Media and the British Empire*. Basingstoke, England: Palgrave Macmillan, 2006.

Kaul, Chandrika. *Reporting the Raj: The British Press and India, 1880–1922*. Manchester: Manchester University Press, 2003.

Kelley, John Dunham, and Uttara Kumari Singh. *My Twenty-One Years in Fiji; and The Story of the Haunted Line*. Edited and translated by T. Sanadhya. Suva: Fiji Museum, 1991.

Kennedy, Dane. "The Great Arch of Empire." In *The Victorian World*, ed. Martin Hewett, 57–72. London: Routledge, 2012.

Kenyatta, Jomo. *Facing Mount Kenya*. London: Secker and Warburg, 1938.

Kesavan, B. S. *History of Printing and Publishing in India*. Vol. 3. Delhi: National Book Trust of India, 1997.

Kessler, Stowell V. "The Black and Coloured Concentration Camps." In *Scorched Earth*, ed. Fransjohan Pretorius, 132–154. Cape Town: Human & Rousseau, 2001.

Kielbowicz, Richard B. "Newsgathering by Printers' Exchanges before the Telegraph." *Journalism History* 9, no. 2 (1982): 42–48.

Kipling, Rudyard. *The Definitive Edition of Rudyard Kipling's Verse*. London: Macmillan, 1989.

Kipling, Rudyard. *Kim*. Harmondsworth, England: Penguin Books, 1987.

Kipling, Rudyard. *War Stories and Poems*. Edited by Andrew Rutherford. Oxford: Oxford University Press, 1990.

Kitching, Gavin. *Class and Economic Change in Kenya*. New Haven, CT: Yale University Press, 1980.

Kitzan, Laurence. *Victorian Writers and the Image of Empire: The Rose-Coloured Vision*. Westport, CT: Greenwood Press, 2001.

Koditschek, Theodore. *Liberalism, Imperialism and the Historical Imagination: Nineteenth-Century Visions of a Greater Britain*. Cambridge: Cambridge University Press, 2010.

Kuitenbrouwer, Vincent. *A War of Words: Dutch Pro-Boer Propaganda and the South African War (1899–1902)*. Amsterdam: UvA-DARE, 2010.

Lahiri, Jaganath. *Janam Shatabdi Ke Punya Avsar Par, Sri Totaram Sanadhya Samarika (1876–1976)*. Ferozabadh, U.P., India: Ferozabad Sandesh Press, n.d.

Lake, Marilyn. "Chinese Warnings and White Men's Prophecies." In *Critical Perspectives on Colonialism: Writing the Empire from Below*, ed. Fiona Paisley and Kirsty Reid, 46–57. New York: Routledge, 2013.

Lake, Marilyn. "Lowe Kong Meng Appeals to International Law: Transnational Lives Caught between Empire and Nation." In *Transnational Lives*, ed. Desley Deacon, Penny Russell, and Angela Woollacott, 223–237. London: Palgrave, 2009.

Lake, Marilyn, and Henry Reynolds. *Drawing the Global Colour Line: White Men's Countries and the International Challenge of Racial Equality*. Cambridge: Cambridge University Press, 2008.

Lal, Brij V., and Yogendra Yadav. *Bhut Len Ki Katha: Totaram Ka Fiji*. New Delhi: Saraswati Press, 1994.

Lamming, George. "Caliban Orders History." In *The Pleasures of Exile*, 118–50. Ann Arbor: University of Michigan Press, 1992.

Lane, Christopher. *The Ruling Passion: British Colonial Allegory and the Paradox of Homosexual Desire*. Durham, NC: Duke University Press, 1995.

Lessig, Lawrence. *The Future of Ideas: The Fate of the Commons in a Connected World*. New York: Random House, 2001.

Lewis, Gordon K. *Main Currents in Caribbean Thought: The Historical Evolution of Caribbean Society in Its Ideological Aspects, 1492–1900*. Baltimore: Johns Hopkins University Press, 1983.

Linebaugh, Peter. "All the Atlantic Mountains Shook." *Labour / Le Travailleur* 10 (Autumn 1982): 109–118.

Linebaugh, Peter. "What If C. L. R. James Had Met E. P. Thompson in 1792?" In *C. L. R. James: His Life and Work*, ed. Paul Buhle, 212–219. New York: Allison and Busby, 1986.

Livesey, Ruth. "Communicating with Jane Eyre: Stagecoach, Mail, and the Tory Nation." *Victorian Studies* 53, no. 4 (December 2011): 615–638.

Lloyd, David. *Nationalism and Minor Literature, James Clarence Mangan and the Emergence of Irish Cultural Nationalism*. Berkeley: University of California Press, 1987.

Logan, Rayford W. "Reviews—Caribbean History." *Opportunity: Journal of Negro Life* 17, no. 2 (1939).

Lonsdale, John. "Contests of Time: Kikuyu Historiography, Old and New." In *A Place in the World: New Local Historiographies from Africa and South Asia*, ed. Axel Harniet Sievers, 201–254. Leiden: Brill, 2002.

Lonsdale, John. "The Moral Economy of Mau Mau: Wealth, Poverty, and Civic Virtue in Kikuyu Political Thought." In *Unhappy Valley: Conflict in Kenya and Africa*, ed. Bruce Berman and John Lonsdale, 315–505. London: James Currey, 1992.

Lonsdale, John. "Writing Competitive Patriotisms in Eastern Africa." In *Recasting the Past: History Writing and Political Work in Modern Africa*, ed. Derek R. Peterson and Giacomo Macola, 251–267. Athens: Ohio University Press, 2009.

Lyons, Martyn. *A History of Reading and Writing in the Western World*. Basingstoke, England: Palgrave Macmillan, 2010.

Lyons, Martyn, and John Arnold, eds. *A History of the Book in Australia 1891–1945: A National Culture in a Colonised Market*. St. Lucia: University of Queensland Press, 2001.

Lyons, Martyn, and Lucy Taksa. *Australian Readers Remember: An Oral History of Reading 1890–1930*. Melbourne: Oxford University Press, 1992.

Macaulay, Thomas Babington. "History." In *The Works of Lord Macaulay*, edited by Lady Trevelyan, 8 vols., 5:122–161. London: Longmans, Green and Co., 1866.

Macaulay, Thomas Babington. *The History of England from the Accession of James II* (1848). 3 vols. London: Dent, 1906.

Macaulay, Thomas Babington. *The Journals of Thomas Babington Macaulay*. 5 vols. Edited by William Thomas. London: Pickering and Chatto, 2008.

Macaulay, Thomas Babington. "Sir James Mackintosh." In *Literary and Historical Essays Contributed to the Edinburgh Review*, 2 vols., 2:272–334. London: Oxford University Press, 1913.

Macaulay, Thomas Babington. *Speeches on Politics and Literature by Lord Macaulay*. London: Dent, 1909.

Macdonald, Charlotte. "Intimacy of the Envelope: Fiction, Commerce and Empire in the Correspondence of Friends Mary Taylor and Charlotte Bronte, c. 1845–55." In *Moving Subjects: Gender, Mobility, and Intimacy in an Age of Global Empire*, ed. Tony Ballantyne and Antoinette Burton, 89–109. Urbana: University of Illinois Press, 2009.

Macdonald, Charlotte. *Strong, Beautiful and Modern: National Fitness in Britain, New Zealand, Australia and Canada, 1935–1960*. Vancouver: University of British Columbia Press, 2011.

Mackenzie, Donald. *An Engine, Not a Camera: How Financial Models Shape Markets*. Cambridge, MA: MIT Press, 2008.

Maclean, Kama. *Pilgrimage and Power: The Kumbh Mela in Allahabad, 1765–1954*. New York: Oxford University Press, 2008.

Majeed, Javed. "What's in a (Proper) Name? Particulars, Individuals, and Authorship in the Linguistic Survey of India and Colonial Scholarship." In *Knowledge Production, Pedagogy, and Institutions in Colonial India*, ed. Daud Ali and Indra Sengupta, 19–39. New York: Palgrave, 2011.

Majumdar, Mousumi, ed. *Kahe Gaile Bides? Where Did You Go? On Bhojpuri Migration since the 1870s and Contemporary Culture in Uttar Pradesh, Bihar, Suriname and the Netherlands*. Amsterdam: KIT Press, 2010.

Makalani, Minkah. *In the Cause of Freedom: Radical Black Internationalism from Harlem to London, 1917–1939*. Chapel Hill: University of North Carolina Press, 2011.

Malthus, T. R. *An Essay on the Principle of Population*. 3 vols. 5th ed. London: John Murray, 1817.

Mandler, Peter. "The Problem with Cultural History." *Cultural and Social History* 1 (2004): 95–117.

Marks, Shula. "Changing History, Changing Histories: Separations and Connections in the Lives of South African Women." *Journal of African Cultural Studies* 13, no. 1 (2000): 94–106.

Marks, Shula, ed. *Not Either an Experimental Doll*. London: Women's Press, 1987.

Martin, A. W. *Henry Parkes: A Biography*. Melbourne: Melbourne University Press, 1980.

Marx, Karl. *Capital: A Critique of Political Economy*. Vol. 1. Translated by Ben Fowkes. London: Penguin, 1990.

Matthews, Nicole, and Nickianne Moody, eds. *Judging a Book by Its Cover: Fans, Publishers, Designers and the Marketing of Fiction*. Aldershot, England: Ashgate, 2007.

McGill, Meredith L. *American Literature and the Culture of Reprinting, 1834–1853*. Philadelphia: University of Pennsylvania Press, 2003.

McKeown, Adam. *Melancholy Order, Asian Migration and the Globalization of Borders*. New York: Columbia University Press, 2008.

Meaney, Neville. " 'In History's Page': Identity and Myth." In *Australia's Empire*, ed. Dereck M. Schreuder and Stuart Ward, 364–387. Oxford: Oxford University Press, 2008.

Meeks, Brian. "Re-reading *The Black Jacobins*: James, the Dialectic and the Revolutionary Conjuncture." *Social and Economic Studies* 43, no. 3 (September 1994): 75–103.

Meng, Lowe Kong, Cheok Hong Cheong, and Louis Ah Mouy. *The Chinese Question in Australia 1878–1879*. Melbourne: F. F. Bailliere, 1879.

Mill, John Stuart. *Principles of Political Economy: With Some of Their Applications to Social Philosophy*. Boston: Charles C. Little and James Brown, 1848.

Miller, Lucasta. *The Bronte Myth*. New York: Knopf, 2004.

Millgate, Jane. *Walter Scott: The Making of the Novelist*. Toronto: University of Toronto Press, 1984.

Mills, Richard Charles. *The Colonization of Australia (1829–42): The Wakefield Experiment in Empire Building*. London: Sidgwick and Jackson, 1915.

Mineka, Francis E., and Dwight N. Lindley, eds. *The Later Letters of John Stuart Mill, 1849–1873*. Toronto: University of Toronto Press, 1972.

Mintz, Sidney W. "Enduring Substances, Trying Theories: The Caribbean Region as Oikoumene." *Journal of the Royal Anthropological Institute* 2, no. 2 (1996): 289–311.

Mishra, Pankaj. *From the Ruins of Empire: The Revolt against the West and the Remaking of Asia*. London: Allen Lane, 2012.

Mishra, Sudesh. "Girmit as Minor History." *Australian Humanities Review* 52 (May 2012). Available at www.australianhumanitiesreview.org/archive/Issue-May-2012/mishra_s.html. Accessed 15 July 2012.

Mishra, Sudesh. "Time and Girmit." *Social Text* 82, no. 23 (Spring 2005): 15–36.

Moag, Rodney. "The Linguistic Adaptations of the Fiji Indians." In *Rama's Banishment*, ed. Vijay Mishra, 112–138. Auckland: Heinemann, 1973.

Molema, Seetsele. *The Bantu: Past and Present*. Edinburgh: W. Green and Son, 1920.

Montague, Ludwell Lee. "Review." *Hispanic American Historical Review* 20, no. 1 (February 1940).

Moodie, T. Dunbar. *The Rise of Afrikanerdom: Power, Apartheid and the Afrikaner Civil Religion*. Berkeley: University of California Press, 1975.

Morley, John. *Nineteenth-Century Essays*. Selected and with an introduction by Peter Stansky. Chicago: Chicago University Press, 1970.

Moses, Wilson. *Afrotopia: The Roots of African American Popular History*. Cambridge: Cambridge University Press, 1998.

Moss, David J. "Wakefield, Edward (1774–1854)." *Oxford Dictionary of National Biography*. Oxford: Oxford University Press, 2004.

Munro, Ian, and Reinhard Sander. "Interview with C. L. R. James." In *Kas-Kas: Interviews with Three Caribbean Writers in Texas*, 22–41. Austin: African and Afro-American Research Institute, University of Texas at Austin, 1972.

Muriuki, Godfrey. *A History of the Kikuyu, 1500–1900*. Nairobi: Oxford University Press, 1974.

Neame, L. E. *The Asiatic Danger in the Colonies*. London: Routledge, 1907.

Nehru, Jawaharlal. *A Bunch of Old Letters*. London: Asia Publishing House, 1958.

N.E.N. "A Word for Londoners." *Indian Opinion*, 30 December 1905.

Ngugi wa Thiong'o. *Decolonizing the Mind: The Politics of Language in African Literature*. London, 1986.

Njagi, David. *The Last Mau Mau Field Marshals*. Meru, Kenya: Ngwataniro Self-Help Group, 1993.

Njeri. "The Family Life." Pt. 17. *Atīrīrī* 2, no. 2, 12 October 1957.

Njeri. "The Family Life." Pt. 18. *Atīrīrī* 2, no. 3, 19 October 1957.

Novack, George E. "Revolution, Black and White." *New International* 5, no. 5 (May 1939).

Obreht, Téa. *The Tiger's Wife*. London: Random House, 2011.

Ogborn, Mikes. *Indian Ink: Script and Print in the Making of the English East India Company*. Chicago: University of Chicago Press, 2007.

Orsini, Francesca. "What Did They Mean by 'Public'? Language, Literature and the Politics of Nationalism." *Economic and Political Weekly* 34, no. 7 (February 1999): 409–416.

Osborne, Thomas J. *Annexation Hawaii: Fighting American Imperialism*. Waimanalo: Island Style Press, 1998.

Oxaal, Ivar. *Black Intellectuals Come to Power: The Rise of Creole Nationalism in Trinidad and Tobago*. Cambridge, MA: Schenkman, 1968.

Padmore, George. "Toussaint, the Black Liberator." *People*, 12 November 1938, 10–11. Continued 19 November 1938, 4.

Paget, John. *The New "Examen" or an Inquiry into the Evidence Relating to Certain Passages in Lord Macaulay's History*. Edinburgh: William Blackwood and Sons, 1861.

Parkes, Henry. *Australian Views of England. Eleven Letters Written in the Years 1861 and 1862*. London: Macmillan, 1869.

Parkes, Henry. *An Emigrant's Home Letters*. London: Simpkin, Marshall, Hamilton, Kent and Co, 1897.

Parsons, Tim. *Race, Resistance and the Boy Scout Movement in British Colonial Africa.* Athens: Ohio University Press, 2004.

Pearson, C. H. "The Land Question in the United States." *Contemporary Review,* September–December 1868, 347–354.

Pearson, Charles. "The Black Republic." In *Reviews and Critical Essays,* ed. H. A. Strong, 305–320. London: Methuen, 1896.

Pearson, Charles H. *National Life and Character: A Forecast.* London: Macmillan, 1893.

Pennybacker, Susan D. *From Scottsboro to Munich: Race and Political Culture in 1930s Britain.* Princeton, NJ: Princeton University Press, 2009.

Peterson, Derek R. *Creative Writing: Translation, Bookkeeping, and the Work of Imagination in Colonial Kenya.* Portsmouth, NH: Heinemann, 2004.

Peterson, Derek R. *Ethnic Patriotism and the East African Revival: A History of Dissent, c. 1935–1972.* Cambridge: Cambridge University Press, 2012.

Peterson, Derek R. "The Intellectual Lives of Mau Mau Detainees." *Journal of African History* 49, no. 1 (2008): 73–91.

Peterson, Derek R., and Giacomo Macola. "Introduction: Homespun Historiography and the Academic Profession." In *Recasting the Past: History Writing and Political Work in Modern Africa,* ed. Derek R. Peterson and Giacomo Macola, 1–30. Athens: Ohio University Press, 2009.

Petley, Christer. "British Fortunes and Caribbean Slavery." *Small Axe* 37 (March 2012): 144–153.

Peukert, Alexander. "The Colonial Legacy of the International Copyright System." In *Staging the Immaterial: Rights, Style and Performance in Sub-Saharan Africa,* ed. Ute Röschenthaler and Mamadou Diawara. Oxford: Sean Kingston, forthcoming.

Philipps, Angus. "Does the Book Have a Future?" In *A Companion to the History of the Book,* ed. Simon Eliot and Jonathan Rose, 547–559. Chichester, England: Wiley-Blackwell, 2009.

Piper, Andrew. *Dreaming in Books: The Making of the Bibliographic Imagination in the Romantic Age.* Chicago: University of Chicago Press, 2009.

Pizer, Dorothy. "How Blacks Fought for Freedom." *International African Opinion* 1, no. 4 (October 1938): 11–12.

Pizer, Dorothy. "A Lesson in Revolution." *Controversy,* no. 28 (January 1939): 318–320.

Plotz, Jonathan. *Portable Property: Victorian Culture on the Move.* Princeton, NJ: Princeton University Press, 2009.

Polak, H. S. L. *The Indians of South Africa.* Madras: G. A. Natesan, 1909.

Pollock, Sheldon. *The Language of the Gods in the World of Men: Sanskrit, Culture, and Power in Premodern India.* Berkeley: University of California Press, 2006.

Porter, Frances. *Born to New Zealand. A Biography of Jane Maria Atkinson.* Wellington: Allen and Unwin / PNP, 1989.

Potter, Simon J. *News and the British World: The Emergence of an Imperial Press System.* Oxford: Oxford University Press, 2003.

Prakashak, Shiv Narain Misra. "Kuch Shabd." In T. Sanadhya, *Fiji Dweep Mein Mere Ekkis Varsh.* Kanpur: Pratap Pustakalya, 1916.

"Prakashak ka Nivedan." In T. Sanadhya, *Fiji Dweep Mein Mere Ekkis Varsh*. Allahabad: Onkar Press, 1915.

Pretty, Graeme L. "Wakefield, Edward Gibbon (1796–1862)." In *Australian Dictionary of Biography*, vol. 2. Melbourne: Melbourne University Press, 1967. Available at adb.anu.edu.au/biography/wakefield-edward-gibbon-2763.

Price, Leah. *How to Do Things with Books in Victorian Britain*. Princeton, NJ: Princeton University Press, 2012.

Puar, Jasbir. *Terrorist Assemblages: Homonationalism in Queer Times*. Durham, NC: Duke University Press, 2007.

Pugliese, Cristiana. *Author, Publisher, and Gikuyu Nationalist: The Life and Writings of Gakaara wa Wanjau*. Bayreuth: Bayreuth African Studies, 1995.

Rai, Alok. *Hindi Nationalism*. Delhi: Orient Blackswan, 2001.

Ratnes, R. *Patrikarita Ke Yug Nibharta: Benarsidas Chaturvedi*. Delhi: Prabhat Prakashan, 2010.

Raven, James. *London Booksellers and American Customers: Transatlantic Literary Community and the Charleston Library Society, 1748–1811*. Columbia: University of South Carolina Press, 2002.

Ray, Karen A. "The Abolition of Indentured Emigration and the Politics of Indian Nationalism, 1894–1917." Ph.D. diss., McGill University, 1980.

Report from the Select Committee on New Zealand; Together with the minutes of evidence taken before them, and an appendix, and index. 1840 (582).

Report from the Select Committee on the Disposal of Lands in the British Colonies; Together with the minutes of evidence, and appendix. 1836 (512).

Rhys, Jean. *Wide Sargasso Sea*. London: Deutsch, 1966.

Richards, Thomas. *The Imperial Archive: Knowledge and the Fantasy of Empire*. London: Verso, 1993.

Rigney, Ann. *The Afterlives of Walter Scott: Memory on the Move*. Oxford: Oxford University Press, 2012.

Robinson, Cedric. "Capitalism, Slavery and Bourgeois Historiography." *History Workshop* 23 (Spring 1987): 122–140.

Robinson, Francis. "Technology and Religious Change: Islam and the Impact of Print." *Modern Asian Studies* 27, no. 1 (1993): 229–251.

Rodney, Walter. *Walter Rodney Speaks: The Making of an African Intellectual*. Trenton, NJ: Africa World Press, 1990.

Rolph-Trouillot, Michel. *Silencing the Past: Power and the Production of History*. Boston: Beacon Press, 1997.

Romani, Roberto. *National Character and Public Spirit in Britain and France, 1750–1914*. Cambridge: Cambridge University Press, 2002.

Röschenthaler, Ute, and Mamadou Diawara, eds. *Staging the Immaterial: Rights, Style and Performance in Sub-Saharan Africa*. Oxford: Sean Kingston, forthcoming.

Rose, Jonathan. *The Intellectual Life of the British Working Classes*. New Haven, CT: Yale University Press, 2001.

Rubik, Margarete, and Elke Mettinger-Schartman, eds. *A Breath of Fresh Eyre: Intertextual and Intermedial Reworkings of "Jane Eyre."* Amsterdam: Rodopi, 2007.

Rudder, David. *Haiti*. Warner Brothers / London Records, 1988.

Rukavina, Alison. *The Development of the International Book Trade, 1870–1895*. Basingstoke, England: Palgrave Macmillan, 2010.

Ryan, Selwyn. *Eric Williams: The Myth and the Man*. Kingston, Jamaica: University of the West Indies Press, 2009.

Said, Edward. Introduction to *Kim*, by Rudyard Kipling. Harmondsworth, England: Penguin Classics, 1987.

Said, Edward. *Orientalism*. London: Routledge and Kegan Paul, 1978.

Sanadhya, Totaram. *Bhut Len Ki Katha: Girmit Ki Anubhav*. Edited by Brij V. Lal, Ashutosh Kumar, and Yogendra Yadav. New Delhi: Rajkamal Press, 2012.

Sanadhya, Totaram. *Fiji Dweep Mein Mere Ekkis Varsh*. Prakashak: Pt. Benarsidas Chaturvedi; Shivlal Agarval and Co, Agra, 1973.

Sanadhya, Totaram. *Fiji Mein Mere Ekkis Varsh*. Agra: Rajput Anglo-Oriental Press, 1914.

Sanadhya, Totaram. "Prastavna." In "Ek Bharitiya Hriday." In *Fiji Mein Bharatiya Pratibandh: Kuli-Pratha*, 1–54. Kanpur: Pratap Press, 1919.

Schutte, G. J. *Nederland en de Afrikaners: Adhesie en Aversie*. Franeker, the Netherlands: T. Wever, 1986.

Schwarz, Bill. "Breaking Bread with History: C. L. R. James and *The Black Jacobins*: An Interview with Stuart Hall." *History Workshop Journal* 46 (Autumn 1998): 22.

Schwarz, Bill. *The White Man's World*. Vol. 1. *Memories of Empire*. Oxford: Oxford University Press, 2011.

Scoresby, W., and Katherine Routledge. *With a Prehistoric People*. London: Edwin Arnold, 1910.

Scott, David. *Conscripts of Modernity: The Tragedy of Colonial Enlightenment*. Durham, NC: Duke University Press, 2004.

Scott, David. "The Paradox of Freedom: An Interview with Orlando Patterson." *Small Axe* 40 (March 2013): 137.

Scott, David. "The Sovereignty of the Imagination: An Interview with George Lamming." *Small Axe* 12 (September 2002): 135.

Seabrook, W. G. "Review." *Journal of Negro History* 24, no. 1 (January 1939).

Secord, James A. *Victorian Sensation: The Extraordinary Publication, Reception, and Secret Authorship of Vestiges of the Natural History of Creation*. Chicago: University of Chicago Press, 2000.

Seville, Catherine. *The Internationalisation of Copyright Law: Books, Buccaneers and the Black Flag in the Nineteenth Century*. Cambridge: Cambridge University Press, 2006.

Shannon, Dr. "The Changing Face of Kenya." *Kikuyu News* 210 (October 1955).

Sharma, Suresh, and Tridip Suhrud. Editors' introduction to *M. K. Gandhi's Hind Swaraj: A Critical Edition*, annotated, translated, and edited by Suresh Sharma and Tridip Suhrud, xi–xxiv. Delhi: Orient Blackswan, 2010.

Shaw, Graham. "Communications between Cultures: Difficulties in the Design and Distribution of Christian Literatures in Nineteenth-Century India." In *The*

Church and the Book, ed. R. N. Swanson, 339–356. Woodbridge, England: Boydell Press, 2004.

Shaw, Graham, and Mary Lloyd, eds. *Publications Proscribed by the Government of India: A Catalog of the Collections in the India Office Library and Records and the Department of Oriental Manuscripts and Printed Books, British Library Reference Division*. London: British Library, 1985.

Shep, Sydney. "Mapping the Migration of Paper: Historical Geography and New Zealand Print Culture." In *The Moving Market*, ed. Peter Isaac and Barry Mackay, 179–192. New Castle, DE: Oak Knoll Press, 2001.

Sheridan, Richard. "Eric Williams and Capitalism and Slavery: A Biographical and Historiographical Essay." In *British Capitalism and Caribbean Slavery: The Legacy of Eric Williams*, ed. Barbara L. Solow and Stanley L. Engerman, 317–345. Cambridge: Cambridge University Press, 1987.

Singha, Radhika. "A 'Proper Passport' for the Colony: Border Crossing in British India, 1882–1920." www.yale.edu/agrarianstudies/colloqpapers/16singha.pdf. Accessed 21 April 2014.

Singham, A. W. "C. L. R. James on the Black Jacobin Revolution in San Domingo— Notes toward a Theory of Black Polities." *Savacou* 1 (June 1970): 86.

Singham, Archie. *The Hero and the Crowd in a Colonial Polity*. New Haven, CT: Yale University Press, 1968.

Slaughter, Joseph R. "Enabling Fictions and Novel Subjects: The *Bildungsroman* and International Human Rights Law." PMLA (2006): 1405–1423.

Slaughter, Joseph R. *Human Rights, Inc.: The World Novel, Narrative Form, and International Law*. New York: Fordham University Press, 2007.

Smith, Adam. *An Inquiry into the Nature and Causes of the Wealth of Nations*. 4 vols. Edited by Edward Gibbon Wakefield. London: Charles Knight, 1835–1840.

Smith, George. *A Memoir*. London, 1902. Reading Experience Database, entry 4370.

Smith, Goldwin. *The Political Destiny of Canada*. London: Chapman and Hall, 1878.

Solow, Barbara L., and Stanley L. Engerman, eds. *British Capitalism and Caribbean Slavery: The Legacy of Eric Williams*. Cambridge: Cambridge University Press, 1987.

Sorenson, M. P. K. *Land Reform in the Kikuyu Country: A Study in Government Policy*. Nairobi: Oxford University Press, 1967.

Spivak, Gayatri Chakravorty. "Three Women's Texts and a Critique of Imperialism." *Critical Inquiry* 12, no. 1 (1985): 243–261.

Sri Swami Satya Dev Parivrajaka. Patiala: Bhasha Vibhag, 1988.

Stallybrass, Peter. "What Is a Book?" Lecture, Centre for the Study of the Book, Bodleian Library, University of Oxford, 13 April 2010.

Stark, Ulrike. *An Empire of Books: The Naval Kishore Press and the Diffusion of the Printed Word in Colonial India*. New Delhi: Permanent Black, 2007.

St Clair, William. *The Reading Nation in the Romantic Period*. Cambridge: Cambridge University Press, 2004.

Stevenson, Marion. *Karirikania*. Nyeri: Tumutumu School, 1924.

Stoddard, Lothrop. *The Rising Tide of Color: Against White World Supremacy*. New York: Scribner's, 1923.

Stoler, Ann Laura. *Along the Archival Grain: Epistemic Anxieties and Colonial Common Sense*. Princeton, NJ: Princeton University Press, 2010.

Stoletiie nespravedlivosti: Sbornik materialov po anglo-burskoi voine v Yuzhnoi Afrike. St. Petersburg, 1900.

Sutherland, John. *Can Jane Eyre Be Happy? More Puzzles in Classic Fiction*. New York: Oxford University Press, 1997.

Sutherland, John. Preface to rev. ed. In *Victorian Fiction: Writers, Publishers, Readers*. Basingstoke, England: Palgrave Macmillan, 2006.

Sutherland, Kathryn. Introduction to *An Inquiry into the Nature and Causes of the Wealth of Nations: A Selected Edition*, by Adam Smith. Oxford: Oxford University Press, 1993.

Sweeney, Fionnghuala. "The Haitian Play: C. L. R. James' *Toussaint Louverture* (1936)." *International Journal of Francophone Studies* 14, nos. 1 and 2 (2011): 146–147.

Tagore, Rabindranath. *Nationalism*. Great Ideas Series 95. Harmondsworth, England: Penguin, 2010.

Taneja, Satyendra Kumar. *Sitama Ki Intiha Kya Hai: Ata zabtasuda Hindi Nataka*. New Delhi: Rashtriya Naya Vidyalaya, 2010.

Temple, Philip. *A Sort of Conscience: The Wakefields*. Auckland: Auckland University Press, 2002.

Theal, George McCall. *History of the Boers in South Africa*. London: Swan Sonnenschein, 1887.

Thomas, Sue. *Imperialism, Reform, and the Making of Englishness in "Jane Eyre."* Basingstoke, England: Palgrave Macmillan, 2008.

Thompson, E. P. "C. L. R. James at 80." In *C. L. R. James: His Life and Work*, ed. Paul Buhle, 249. New York: Allison and Busby, 1986.

Thompson, L. M. "The Strange Career of Slagtersnek." In *The Political Mythology of Apartheid*. New Haven, CT: Yale University Press, 1985.

Thorne, Susan. "Capitalism and Slavery Compensation." *Small Axe* 37 (March 2012): 154–167.

Tillotson, Kathleen. *Novels of the Eighteen-Forties*. Oxford: Oxford University Press, 1961.

Tinker, Hugh. *A New System of Slavery*. London: Hansib, 1993. (Originally published 1974)

Tregenza, John. *Professor of Democracy: The Life of Charles Henry Pearson 1830–1894: Oxford Don and Australian Radical*. Melbourne: Melbourne University Press, 1968.

Trevelyan, George Otto. *The Life and Letters of Lord Macaulay*. London: Longmans, Green and Co., 1881.

Un Siecle d'injustice. Paris: Dupont, 1900.

van Jaarsveld, F. A. "The Afrikaner's Image of His Past." In *The Afrikaner's Interpretation of South African History*, 46–70. Cape Town: Simondium, 1964.

van Koppen, Chris A. J. *De Geuzen van de Negentiende Eeuw: Abraham Kuyper en Zuid-Afrika*. Maarssen, the Netherlands: Inmerc, 1992.

Vann, J. Don, and Rosemary T. van Arsdel, eds. *Periodicals of Queen Victoria's Empire: An Exploration*. Toronto: University of Toronto Press, 1966.

van Oordt, J. F. *Paul Kruger en de Opkomst van de Zuid-Afrikaansche Republiek*. Amsterdam: HAUM, 1898.

van Schoor, M. C. E. "Die Galgeskaduwee van Slagtersnek." *Die Taalgenoot*, March–April 1957.

Vatuk, Ved Praksh. "Protest Songs of East Indians in British Guiana." *Journal of American Folklore* 77, no. 305 (July–September 1964): 220–235.

Viator. "Asia Contra Mundum." *Fortnightly Review*, 1 February 1908, 185–200.

Viswanathan, Gauri. *Masks of Conquest: Literary Study and British Rule in India*. New Delhi: Oxford University Press, 1998.

[Wakefield, Edward Gibbon.] *The British Colonization of New Zealand: Being an Account of the Principles, Objects, and Plans of the New Zealand Association*. London: John W. Parker, 1837.

[Wakefield, Edward Gibbon.] *England and America: A Comparison of the Social and Political State of Both Nations*. 2 vols. London: Richard Bentley, 1833.

Wakefield, Edward Gibbon. *Facts Relating to the Punishment of Death in the Metropolis*. London: J. Ridgway, 1831.

[Wakefield, Edward Gibbon.] *The Hangman and the Judge, or, A Letter from Jack Ketch to Mr. Justice Alderson: Revised by the Ordinary of Newgate and edited by Edward Gibbon Wakefield*. London: E. Wilson, 1833.

Wakefield, Edward Gibbon. *The New British Province of South Australia*. London: C. Knight, 1834.

Wakefield, Edward Gibbon. *The New British Province of South Australia*. 2nd ed. London: C. Knight, 1835.

[Wakefield, Edward Gibbon.] *Plan of a Company to Be Established for the Purpose of Founding a Colony in Southern Australia*. London: Ridgway and Sons, 1832.

[Wakefield, Edward Gibbon.] *Swing Unmasked, or, The Causes of Rural Incendiarism*. London: Effingham Wilson, 1831.

Wakefield, Edward Gibbon, ed. *A View of the Art of Colonization: With Present Reference to the British Empire*. London: John W. Parker, 1849.

Wakefield, Priscilla. *Excursions in North America*. 3rd ed. London: Darton, Harvey and Darton, 1819.

Walcott, Derek. *Henri Christophe: A Chronicle in Seven Scenes*. Bridgetown, Barbados: Advocate, 1950.

Wald, James. "Periodicals and Periodocity." In *A Companion to the History of the Book*, ed. Simon Eliot and Jonathan Rose, 421–432. Chichester, England: Wiley-Blackwell, 2009.

Walker, David. *Anxious Nation: Australia and the Rise of Asia 1850–1939*. St. Lucia: University of Queensland Press, 1999.

Weaver, John C. *The Great Land Rush and the Making of the Modern World, 1650–1900*. Montreal: McGill-Queen's University Press, 2003.

Weedon, Alexis. *Victorian Publishing: The Economics of Book Production for a Mass Market 1836–1916*. Aldershot, England: Ashgate, 2003.

Weinbaum, Alys Eve, et al., eds. *The Modern Girl around the World: Consumption, Modernity, and Globalization*. Durham, NC: Duke University Press, 2008.

Weston, Kath. *Long Slow Burn: Sexuality and Social Science*. New York: Routledge, 1998.

White, Luise. "Matrimony and Rebellion: Masculinity in Mau Mau." In *Men and Masculinities in Modern Africa*, ed. Lisa Lindsay and Stephan Miescher, 177–191. Portsmouth, NH: Heinemann, 2003.

Williams, Eric. *Capitalism and Slavery*. Chapel Hill: University of North Carolina Press, 1994.

Williams, Eric. *Inward Hunger: The Education of a Prime Minister*. London: Deutsch, 1969.

Wirtén, Eva Hemmungs. *Terms of Use: Negotiating the Jungle of the Intellectual Commons*. Toronto: University of Toronto Press, 2008.

Wisker, John. "The Coloured Man in Australia." *Fortnightly Review*, 1 July 1879, 80–83.

Woolf, Virginia. *A Passionate Apprentice: The Early Journals 1897–1909*. Edited by Mitchell A. Leaska. London: Pimlico, 2004.

Woolf, Virginia. *A Room of One's Own*. Edited and annotated by Mark Hussey and Susan Gubar. New York: Harcourt, 2005.

Yen, Ching-Hwang. *Coolies and Mandarins: China's Protection of Overseas Chinese during the Late Ch'ing Period (1851–1911)*. Singapore: Singapore University Press, 1985.

Yong Ching Fatt. "Ah Mouy, Louis." In *Australian Dictionary of Biography 1851–1900*, vol. 5, 19. Melbourne: Melbourne University Press, 1974.

Yong Ching Fatt. "Cheong Cheok Hong." In *Australian Dictionary of Biography 1851–1900*, vol. 3, 385–386. Melbourne: Melbourne University Press, 1969.

Yong Ching Fatt. "Lowe Kong Meng." In *Australian Dictionary of Biography 1851–1900*, vol. 3, 106–107. Melbourne: Melbourne University Press, 1969.

Young, James D. *The World of C. L. R. James: His Unfragmented Vision*. Glasgow: Clydeside Press, 1999.

Young, Robert. *The Idea of English Ethnicity*. Oxford: Blackwell, 2008.

CONTRIBUTORS

TONY BALLANTYNE is a professor of history at the University of Otago in New Zealand, where he is also head of the Department of History and Art History. He is director of Otago's Centre for Research on Colonial Culture. He has published widely on the cultural history of the British Empire in the nineteenth century, especially relating to the production of colonial knowledge, print culture, and forms of cultural mobility. His recent work has particularly focused on the development of colonial culture in southern New Zealand.

ELLEKE BOEHMER is professor of world literature in English at the University of Oxford, and Professorial Governing Body Fellow at Wolfson College. She has published *Colonial and Postcolonial Literature* (1995, 2005), *Empire, the National and the Postcolonial, 1890–1920* (2002), *Stories of Women* (2005), and the biography *Nelson Mandela* (2008). She is the author of four acclaimed novels, including *Screens against the Sky* (short-listed David Higham Prize, 1990), *Bloodlines* (short-listed SANLAM Prize), and *Nile Baby* (2008), as well as the short-story collection *Sharmilla and Other Portraits* (2010). She edited the British best seller *Scouting for Boys*, by Robert Baden-Powell (2004), and the anthology *Empire Writing* (1998), and coedited *J. M. Coetzee in Writing and Theory* (2009), *Terror and the Postcolonial* (2009), *The Indian Postcolonial* (2010), and *The Postcolonial Low Countries* (2012). She is the general editor of the Oxford Studies in Postcolonial Literatures series and holds an honorary doctorate from Linnaeus University, Sweden (2009). She is finishing two new books: *Networks of Empire 1870–1915: Indian Arrivants in the Imperial Metropolis* and *The Shouting in the Dark*, a novel.

ANTOINETTE BURTON is a feminist historian of empire at the University of Illinois, Urbana-Champaign. She has written on gender and colonialism, race and postcolonial politics, and world history. Her most recent book is an edited collection of primary sources, *The First Anglo-Afghan Wars* (Duke 2014).

CATHERINE HALL is professor of modern British social and cultural history at University College London. Her work has focused on the relation between Britain and its empire. *Civilising Subjects: Metropole and Colony in the English Imagination* was published in 2002, and a collection edited with Sonya O. Rose, *At Home with the Empire: Metropolitan Culture and the Imperial World*, in 2006. *Macaulay and Son: Architects of Imperial Britain* was published in September 2012. She is the principal investigator on the ESRC / AHRC-funded project Legacies of British Slave Ownership.

ISABEL HOFMEYR is professor of African literature at the University of the Witwatersrand in Johannesburg and Visiting Distinguished Global Professor at New York University. Her prize-winning books include *"We Spend Our Years as a Tale That Is Told": Oral Historical Storytelling in a South African Chiefdom* (1993), *The Portable Bunyan: A Transnational History of "The Pilgrim's Progress"* (2004), and *Gandhi's Printing Press: Experiments in Slow Reading* (2013).

AARON KAMUGISHA is a senior lecturer in cultural studies at the University of the West Indies, Cave Hill Campus. His current work is a study of coloniality, cultural citizenship, and freedom in the contemporary Anglophone Caribbean, mediated through the social and political thought of C. L. R. James and Sylvia Wynter. He is the editor of *Caribbean Political Thought: The Colonial State to Caribbean Internationalisms*, *Caribbean Political Thought: Theories of the Post-colonial State*, and *Caribbean Cultural Thought: From Plantation to Diaspora*.

MARILYN LAKE is professor in history and Australian Research Council Professorial Fellow at the University of Melbourne, where she researches the international history of Australian democracy and convenes a public lecture and seminar series called "Australia in the World." Her most recent books include *Drawing the Global Colour Line: White Men's Countries and the International Challenge of Racial Equality*, coauthored with Henry Reynolds, which won the Ernest Scott Prize for the best book in Australian, New Zealand, and colonization history and the Prime Minister's Prize for Non-fiction in 2009. She is currently writing a history of Australian–American Pacific crossings and progressive politics called "Our Common Ideals." Professor Lake is a fellow of the Australian Academies of Humanities and Social Sciences and president of the Australian Historical Association.

CHARLOTTE MACDONALD is professor of history at Victoria University of Wellington / Te Whare Wananga o te Upoko o Te Ika a Maui, New Zealand. Her nineteenth-century interests encompass writing and unsettlement in British colonial societies; publications include *"My Hand Will Write What My Heart Dictates,"* with Frances Porter (1996), and "Between Religion and Empire: Sarah Selwyn's Aotearoa / New Zealand, Eton and Lichfield, England, c. 1840s–1900," *Journal of the Canadian Historical Association* 19 (2008): 2 (Canadian Historical Association best article prize, 2009). Her twentieth-century interests trace the legacy of empire in cultures of body, sport, and fitness in the 1930s and 1940s: *Strong, Beautiful and Modern: National Fitness in Britain, New Zealand, Australia and Canada* (2011).

DEREK R. PETERSON teaches African history at the University of Michigan. He is the editor of several books and the author of *Creative Writing: Translation, Bookkeeping, and the Work of Imagination in Colonial Kenya* (2004) and *Ethnic Patriotism and the East African Revival: A History of Dissent* (2012) (Herskovits Prize of the African Studies Association; Martin Klein Prize of the American Historical Association). He is currently writing a history of Idi Amin's Uganda.

MRINALINI SINHA is Alice Freeman Palmer Professor in the Department of History and professor in the Department of English Language and Literature (by courtesy) at the University of Michigan, Ann Arbor. She has written on various aspects of the political history of colonial India, with a focus on anticolonialism, gender, and transnational approaches. She has recently become interested in the different forms of political imaginings, beyond the nation-state, that animated anticolonial thought in India at least until the interwar period.

TRIDIP SUHRUD has written commentaries on *Hind Swaraj* in three languages and coedited and translated a critical bilingual edition of it. He works at Sabarmati Ashram at Ahmedabad.

ANDRÉ DU TOIT is Emeritus Professor of Political Studies at the University of Cape Town. His research interests include the intellectual history of South African political thought and traditions, transitional justice, the narrative interpretation of political violence in South Africa, and academic freedom. Among other works he is the author of *Afrikaner Political Thought: Analysis and Documents, 1780–1850* (with Hermann Giliomee) (1983); "No Chosen People: The Myth of the Calvinist Origins of Afrikaner Nationalism and Racial Ideology," *American Historical Review* (1983); "Legitimate Anachronism as a Problem for Intellectual History and for Philosophy," *South African Journal of Philosophy* (1991); and "Founding and Crushing: Narrative Understandings of Political Violence in Pre-modern and Colonial South Africa," *Journal of Natal and Zulu History* (2004). Recent publications include "Experiments with Truth and Justice in South Africa: Stockenström, Gandhi and the TRC," *Journal of Southern African Studies* (2005); "The Owl of Minerva and the Ironic Fate of the Progressive Praxis of Radical Historiography in Post-apartheid South Africa," *History and Theory* 49 (2010); and "The 'Dark Sides' of Humanism in South African History," in *The Humanist Imperative in South Africa*, ed. J. W. de Gruchy (2011). He is currently preparing a work on the genealogy of the South African Truth and Reconciliation Commission process that focuses on (the lack of) an underlying amnesty settlement during the postapartheid transition to democracy.

Bhagavad Gita, 167n20; Gandhi's engagement with, 162–164

BhagvadGoMandal (lexicon), civilization in, 158

Bharati Bhavan (reform institution), 172; Bharati Granth Mala Series, 177–178; publication of *Fiji Mein Mere Ekkis Varsh*, 174, 177, 179

Bharat Mitra (newspaper, Calcutta): indentured labor in, 171, 179; readers in Fiji, 176

Bhave, Vinoba, 157

Bible, King James, imperial role of, 1

Bibles, bound, 27n32

Birbalsingh, Frank, 197

Birmingham Political Union, 83

Black, John, 35

black inferiority: stereotypes of, 194; stigmatization of Indians, 170, 171; theories of, 193

Boehmer, Elleke, 6, 17, 22–23

Boer republics: Dutch histories of, 118; war with Britain, 113. *See also* pro-Boer movements; South African Republic

Boissevain, Charles, 116

bookbinding industry, effect of empire on, 27n32

book industry, British, overseas markets of, 53, 65, 81

books: affective power of, 11–12, 63; materiality of, 9, 21; as object agents, 133; plasticity of form, 9; for railway travelers, 53; resilience of, 23; role in historical change, 20–21. *See also* bound volumes; printing, imperial; printing, Indian; texts

books, imperial: American reprints of, 4, 26n13; anticolonial, 3–4, 11; authority in, 1, 2, 16, 65; in British culture, 7; charismatic, 6–10; cheap editions, 75, 134; circulation of, 16, 22; classics, 3; in commodity chains, 7; in creation of doubt, 9; defiance of power, 20; as democratizing medium, 134; depiction

of change, 20; dispersed/dispersing, 12–13, 21; embodiment of authority, 1, 2; in everyday life, 2; geopolitical influence of, 2; and imperial sovereignty, 10–16; materiality of, 2, 7, 22; mobility of, 7, 9, 53; monumental, 1, 3, 11; as multiform commodity, 23; pamphlet material in, 2, 3; processes of, 7; as proxy for autonomy, 11; reception of, 7–8; recycling of, 39; role in civilizational progress, 16; social entities of, 9; source material of, 2, 3, 12; uncopyrighted, 4–5

Boomplaats, battle of, 121, 125

bound volumes: affective power of, 11–12; in Christian tradition, 11; market share of, 13; monumentality of, 12; privileged reading of, 64; in *Wide Sargasso Sea*, 52

Boy's Own (journal), 136–137

brahmacharya, Gandhi's vow of, 163, 164

Braithwaite, Lloyd, 208

Brathwaite, Kamau, 209

British Empire: Boer political struggle with, 120; capital in, 33; *A Century of Wrong* on, 20–21, 114, 120, 121, 122, 124–126, 128, 129; communication networks of, 51, 143, 145, 146, 147; disaggregated networks of, 2; dispersal of, 2; effect of *Scouting for Boys* on, 150; as free trade area, 139; geographic mobility within, 29; historical novels about, 20; James's opposition to, 191; labor supply of, 32; land disposal in, 32, 40, 41, 44; legitimating structures of, 196; market for books in, 53, 65, 81; masculine bonding in, 134; Mau Mau detention camps of, 216, 217, 221–231; mobile subjects of, 2; polemics about, 20; racial segregation in, 90–91; racism of, 193; rise-and-fall narrative of, 23; role of books in, 2–3, 9, 20; role of law in, 16; Scouting in, 131, 134, 147, 148; slavery in, 85–86; sociocultural policy throughout, 139; textual economy of, 4;

British Empire (*continued*)
Whig thinking on, 82; white men's
countries of, 99, 105–106. *See also*
commons, imperial; empires; Great
Britain; printing, imperial
British Indian Association of Fiji, 175
broadsheets, 3
Brontë, Charlotte: death of, 57; on inner/
outer value, 64–65
—*Jane Eyre*, 3; autonomous self in, 60–
61; books and reading in, 63–64, 66;
canonical status of, 66; charisma of,
51; circulation routes of, 8, 22, 51, 52,
53–54, 57–58, 65; colonial encounters
in, 8; as colonial formation medium,
58; composition of, 85; critique of
male authority, 60; dedication of,
52; defiant character of, 58; editor
figure of, 17, 39, 52; empire in, 51, 65,
66; Englishness of, 57, 65, 66; film
adaptations of, 67n4; injustice in,
20–21; materiality of, 66; mobility of,
51, 61; national culture in, 57; novel and
tract in, 64; popularity of, 50–51, 60;
publishing history of, 50–51; readers
of, 8, 51, 53–60, 66; reception of, 56, 57,
60; resistance in, 60–61; sale at auction, 66, 70n60; self-formation in, 65;
sovereignty in, 51, 58, 60–61, 66; travel
with Scott expedition, 58; use in South
African education, 58–60; and *Wide
Sargasso Sea*, 51–52, 61–63, 65, 67
Brontë family, legend of, 69n26
Burton, Antoinette, 51, 102

Canada: colonization of, 29, 34; White
Canada policy of, 106
capitalism: colonial, 33, 43–44; print, 15
capitalist reproduction, serialization in, 148
Caribbean: Black Power in, 205; dependency school (social science),
201; Haitian influence on, 208–209;
historiography of, 191, 197–198; independence throughout, 200; meaning

of freedom in, 208; neocolonialism in,
207; as site of modernity, 206; social
theory of, 208; in twenty-first century,
207–208, 215n81. *See also* Haiti; James,
C. L. R.: *The Black Jacobins*
Caribbean people: exiles, 205; identity
of, 205; impact of Haitian Revolution
on, 190–191; making of, 204–208;
response to colonialism, 206
Carlyle, Thomas, fictional editor device
of, 38
Carpentier, Alejo, 209
Catholic emancipation, 83; Macaulay
on, 80
censorship: imperial, 5; by U.P. government, 179, 183
Century of Wrong, A (Smuts and Roos),
4, 112–129; Afrikaner nationalism in,
121; audience of, 116; authorship of,
114–115; battle of Boomplaats in, 125;
Boer cause in, 6; British injustice in,
20–21, 114, 120, 121, 122, 124–126, 128,
129; core narrative of, 121; distribution
networks of, 115, 116, 117; editing of,
17, 18; and GRA *History*, 119; influence
of, 112; legacy of, 117, 127, 128; national
victimization in, 121–122; publishing
history of, 114; racial superiority in,
115; reception of, 117; republican independence in, 120; and SAR manifesto,
119, 120; secular approach of, 122;
Slagtersnek in, 122, 127; slavery in, 115;
subject matter of, 118, 121; Thomas
Dreyer in, 125; title of, 113, 117–118;
translations of, 117
Césaire, Aimé, 209
Chalmers, Thomas, 41
Chamberlain, Joseph, 113; imperialist
agenda of, 116, 138–139
change, historical: objectivist standards
of, 22; role of books in, 20–21, 23–24;
technologies of, 21; ubiquitous, 23
Chartist movement, 60, 77, 83; on
Macaulay, 78

Chaturvedi, Benarsidas, 15; at ashram Sabarmati, 20; collaboration with Sanadhya, 172, 173, 177; exposé on indentured labor, 184; literary ideal of, 19–20

Cheong, Cheok Hong, 97, 105; "Address to the Representatives of the Australian Governments," 101

China: as Asiatic power, 94, 99–102; civilization of, 98, 101; growth of power, 103; international respect for, 94–95, 99; Japanese defeat of (1895), 106; population of, 97, 98, 105; relations with Australia, 97–100; treaties with Britain, 98

Chinese: in Australia, 8, 94, 95, 96–102, 105–106; immigration restrictions on, 98; labor exploitation of, 98; migration across Asia, 94; poll tax on, 95, 98, 99, 100, 101; prejudice against, 98; rights in Australia, 100. See also immigration, Chinese

Chinese Question in Australia, The (Meng, Cheong, Ah Mouy), 97–99

Ch'ing imperial commissioners, tour of Australia, 94–95, 99–100, 101

Chirol, Valentine. See Viator

Christian Boys' Brigade, 135

Christianity: Gandhi on, 161; among Gikuyu, 224

Christian National Boer Committee, 116

civilization: Chinese, 98, 101; as disease, 159; self-understanding in, 160; transient nature of, 158. See also Sudhar/ Sudharo

civilization, English: in Macaulay's history, 72; morality in, 162; in Scouting for Boys, 137

civilization, modern: Gandhi and, 156, 157–158, 160–163, 166; self-destructive, 158–159

civilization, white: decline of, 90–92, 93, 94; threats to, 108–109. See also whiteness

Clark, William George, 56

Cloete, Henry, "Emigration of the Dutch Farmers," 123

colonial formation: gendered, 59; Jane Eyre in, 58

Colonial Gazette, Wakefield's writings in, 41

colonialism, settler, 30, 45, 46; children of, 137; immigration restrictions in, 101; market for books in, 53

Colonial Office, British, land grant policies of, 44

colonization: English liberals on, 45; intellectual traditions of, 30; legal foundations for, 41; Marx on, 43–44; modernity through, 86; political agitation for, 40; public debate over, 46; systematic, 29, 43, 45–46, 48n43, 54; Wakefield's theory of, 29, 30–35, 41, 54

commons: pedagogical, 58; textual, 55

commons, imperial, 25n12; access to property rights in, 5–6; books in, 7, 13, 16, 62; deterritorialized sovereignty in, 4; epistemological frames of, 23; Gikuyu cultural system in, 224; A Letter from Sydney in, 30; literary property of, 4; mobile, 5; newspapers in, 5; printers in, 13, 14, 27n33; temporal fluidity of, 63; Wakefield's theories in, 45, 46

communication, materiality of, 9

concentration camps, British, in South African war, 126–128. See also detention camps, Mau Mau

Cooper, Frederick, 203

Cooper, James Fenimore, influence on Baden-Powell, 140

copyright, 4–6, 14; in artisanal printing, 15; colonized elites' use of, 4–5; Gandhi's rejection of, 19; legislation for, 4; national models of, 19; ownership of, 18

Cox, Horace, 141

cultures, transfer of, 96

Dangarembga, Tsitsi, *Nervous Conditions*, 59–60, 65
Darnton, Robert, 31
Darwin, John, 25n8
Davies, Llewellyn, "Are All Men Equal?," 103–104
decolonization: James's anticipation of, 191; Kenyan, 217
Dedan Kimathi, 220
Deleuze, Gilles, 186n4
democracies, white self-governing, 107
Desmond, Cosmas, 128
detainees, Mau Mau: advice for, 228–230; anxiety over wives, 218, 222, 228, 229, 231; correspondence with families, 230; discipline standards of, 221–222; ethnographic work of, 218, 223, 226, 227, 231, 233; moral project of, 218, 221; organizations of, 227–228; threats to property of, 222; trial of cooperators, 227–228. *See also* Gikuyu (Kenyan people)
detention camps, Mau Mau, 216; cultural work in, 217, 221–231; inhumanity of, 217; moral order at, 221–222
determinism, racial, 103, 108; Pearson's refusal of, 92
Dev, Satya, anti-indenture activism of, 182
Devji, Faisal, 153–154
dharma, nondenominational idea of, 165
diaspora, African: intellectual traditions of, 210n5; literary-cultural figures of, 209; theater of, 194; vindicationism concerning, 192
Dickens, Charles: *David Copperfield*, 57; fictional editor device of, 38; *Morning Chronicle* contributions, 35
Dilke, Charles, 134; *Greater Britain*, 103, 138
Dingaan's Day commemoration, 122
discourse, imperial, influence of books on, 3
Dreyer, Thomas, 125

Dubois, Laurent, 197, 201
Duffy, Charles Gavan, narrative of Ireland, 80–81
Dundas, Henry, 195
Dutch–South African Society (NZAV), 116
du Toit, S. J., *Geskiedenis van Ons Land in die Taal van Ons Volk* (GRA History), 118, 119, 125

East Africa, British, Indian homeland proposal for, 107
Edgeworth, Maria, 74
editors: authors as, 17–18; fictional, 38–39
Education Act (1870), 137
Een Eeuw van Onrecht. See Century of Wrong, A
Elkins, Caroline, *Britain's Gulag*, 217
Elliot, T. F., 39
Empire (weekly), 84
empires: Christian, 1; communicative histories of, 7; end of, 3, 23; formation of, 3; of free market, 28n45; land disposal in, 44, 46; nineteenth-century, 26n25; paper, 2, 24n6, 62; transition to nations, 186; vertical/horizontal grids of, 10. *See also* British Empire
English literature, names memorializing, 1
Englishness: of *Jane Eyre*, 65, 66; stories of, 57; worldwide, 138–139
equality, human, conditions for, 156
Esty, Jed, 57
ethnography, Gikuyu, 224–225; by detainees, 218, 223, 226, 227, 231, 233; purpose of, 228, 231

Fawcett, Millicent, 74
Fick, Carolyn, 203; *The Making of Haiti*, 201–202
Fiji: British Indian Association of, 175; Hindi newspapers in, 174–175; indentured labor in, 169, 171, 174–175; Ramlila performances in, 182–183.

Gandhi, Mohandas K. (*continued*)
Sudharo in, 157–159, 161; textual fluidity of, 155; as theory of salvation, 161; in twenty-first century, 153; use of Gujarati, 155, 156, 158, 159, 167n16; on violence, 154, 16
—other works: *Dakshin Africa Na Satyagraha No Itihas*, 164; *Mangal Prabhat*, 165; *My Experiments with Truth*, 164; *Satyagraha Ashram No Itihas*, 165
Garrett, Elizabeth, 74–75
Gaskell, Mrs., 52; *Life of Charlotte Brontë*, 57
Gathigira, Stanley Kiama, *Mĩkarĩre ya Agĩkũyũ*, 226
Gaunson, David, 102
Geggus, David, 197, 201, 211n26
General Dutch Union (ANV), 116
Genootskap vir Regte Afrikaners (GRA), history of, 118, 119, 125
Gikuyu (Kenyan people): agriculture of, 224, 225; as autochthon, 225, 226; Christian converts, 224; complaints about British, 224–225; ethnography of, 216, 223–224; intellectuals, 225; marriage among, 218, 220, 221, 222, 228, 229, 231; matriarchal tyranny of, 230, 237n90; migration to Kenya, 225; moral project of, 218, 231; origin stories of, 224–226; poverty among, 218–219. *See also* detainees, Mau Mau
Gikuyu clans: in *Mĩhĩrĩga ya Agĩkũyũ*, 217, 223, 226–227, 228, 231, 232; multicultural genealogies of, 225; multilingual histories of, 227; number of, 223; origins of, 223–224, 236n57; role in detainee organization, 228; stereotypes of, 223, 226–227, 228, 231, 232
Gikuyu language: adulteration of, 233; cultural/intellectual innovation in, 232; readers in, 224
Gikuyu literature, 233
Gillies, Dunan, 101
Gilroy, Paul, 214n74; *The Black Atlantic*, 206

Girl Guides, 134, 148
Girl Guiding (1918), 134–135
Girvan, Norman, 205
Glencoe Massacre, 79
Glorious Revolution (1688), in Macaulay's *History*, 72–73, 76
Gluck, Carol, 45, 133
Gokhale, G. K.: in anti-indenture movement, 170; on *Hind Swaraj*, 153
Gordon, Lewis, 208
Gouger, Robert, 30, 37; and *A Letter from Sydney*, 38–39; support for colonization, 40
Goveia, Elsa, 197, 208
Great Britain: Afrikaner concentration camps of, 126–128; annexation of Natal, 123; annexation of Transvaal, 115, 118, 120; anti-indenture movement in, 169; emigration from, 32, 37, 44–45, 46; liberty in, 82; mass literacy in, 79; New Left of, 203; pro-Boer movements in, 115, 116–117, 128; role in abolition, 193, 195; social problems of, 31, 32, 34–35, 40, 41, 45; treaties with China, 98; unrest in, 77. *See also* British Empire; commons, imperial
Greater Britain, 139; Baden-Powell's vision of, 146; Chamberlain's concept of, 138
Great Trek, 119, 120, 123; Centennial of (1938), 127
Gucu wa Gikoyo, 220
Gujarati language: essay form in, 155; folk discourse in, 156; in *Hind Swaraj*, 155, 156, 158, 159
Gupta, Maithili Sharan, *Kisan*, 183

Hague Peace Conference (1899), 112–113
Haiti: earthquake (2010), 208; influence on Caribbean, 208–209; intellectual tradition of, 208; Pearson on, 93–94; tropes of inferiority concerning, 209; in Western imagination, 191

Indian Opinion (newspaper), 14–15; *Hind Swaraj* in, 155; Pearson in, 106; Sanadhya's work in, 175

Indians, racial stigmatization of, 170, 171. *See also* indentured workers, Indian

Indian Settler (Fiji newspaper), 175

individualism, feminist, 51

Inikori, Joseph, *Africans and the Industrial Revolution in England*, 201

injustice, British: in *A Century of Wrong*, 20–21, 121, 122, 124–126, 128, 129; in *Jane Eyre*, 20–21; in South African war, 126–129

intellectual property: disregard for, 14; imperial, 19, 26n19; international law on, 4, 26n15; textual practices of, 6

International African Service Bureau (London), 196

International Friends of Abyssinia, 199

International Printing Press (Durban), 14–15

Ireland: famine in, 80; Macaulay on, 73, 79–80, 81, 85; populations pressures in, 37

Irish Free State, Scouting in, 149

Irish Quarterly Review, on *History of England*, 80

Iriye, Akira, 92

Jain, Lala Chiranji Lal, 172

James, C. L. R., 61; anticipation of decolonization, 191; autobiography of, 200; circulation of ideas, 17; contribution to Caribbean historiography, 197–198; critique of *The Negro in the Caribbean*, 199–200; education in Trinidad, 58; formation of Workers and Farmers Party, 198; on future of Caribbean, 207; ghostwriting by, 210n7; intellectual life of, 192; Marxism of, 191, 202; as mentor, 205; opposition to empire, 191; optimism of, 207–208; Pan-Africanism of, 191; and People's National Movement, 198–199; post-colonial studies on, 197; radicalism of, 202; relationship with Williams, 197–201, 211n29, 212n42; residence in England, 192, 193, 198, 211n29; residence in U.S., 196; return to Trinidad, 198, 200, 204; split from PNM, 198–199; transnational community of, 205; at University of the West Indies, 204, 205, 214n63; vindicationism of, 192–193; and West Indian Federal Labour Party, 204; writings on Caribbean, 205

—*The Black Jacobins*, 4, 190–209; audience of, 196; availability of, 204–205; black agency in, 87, 195; black radical tradition in, 191; Caribbean freedom in, 206; causative effects of, 22; censorship of, 196; class in, 195; connection to *Capitalism and Slavery*, 200–201; contribution to historiography, 201–202; dramatization of, 205; educational role of, 191; format of, 11; influence of, 8, 190–191, 196–197, 208; James's critique of, 202; James's lectures on, 192, 199, 202; legacy of, 191, 197, 207; Marxism of, 202; metropole and colony in, 190; motivations for composition, 195; publishing history of, 194, 204–205; race in, 195, 203; reception of, 191, 196, 197, 210n21, 211n22; rejection of vindicationism, 195; revisions to, 191–192, 207; scholarship on, 192; slavery in, 194–195, 203, 214n74; Toussaint L'Ouverture in, 195, 202; translations of, 196, 211n22; use of the tragic, 207

—other works: *Beyond a Boundary*, 200, 207, 215n80; *A History of Negro Revolt*, 193; "How I Wrote *The Black Jacobins*," 192; "The Intelligence of the Negro," 192, 193; *Party Politics in the West Indies*, 199, 207; *Toussaint Louverture*, 191, 193–194, 205; *World Revolution 1917–1936*, 191

Jameson Raid (1896), 116, 118, 120, 121; convictions following, 123

Japan: military victories of, 106, 107; responsibility in, 9

Jeffrey, Lord, 74

Jones, Lloyd, *Progress of the Working Class*, 78

Jorissen, E. J. P., 120

Joubert, Piet, letter to Queen Victoria, 121–122

justice, imperial, questioning of, 21. *See also* injustice, British

Kabetu, M. N., *Kīrīra kīa Ūgīkūyū*, 225–226

Kago, Fred, 237n93

Kallenbach, Hermann, 155

Kamiti detention camp (Kenya), women at, 223

Karirikania (Gikuyu reading primer), 224, 225, 226

Kenya: consolidation of land in, 222; cost of marriage in, 219; decolonization in, 217; ethnic associations of, 219; postcolonial literature of, 233, 237n99; prison population of, 221; prostitution in, 219–220; Protestant schools of, 224; State of Emergency (1950s), 60, 231. *See also* detention camps, Mau Mau; Gikuyu (Kenyan people)

Kenyatta, Jomo, *Facing Mount Kenya*, 225, 226, 237n90

Kidd, Benjamin, *Social Evolution*, 103, 108

Kikuyu (Gikuyu ancestor), 225

Kipling, Rudyard, 23; Baden-Powell's use of, 131, 132–133, 135, 139–140, 152n32; Boer War stories of, 146; imperialism of, 134, 139, 144–145; planetary reputation of, 145

—works: *The Jungle Book*, 132, 152n32; *Kim*, 134, 139, 145–148; "A Song of the English," 144

Kitchener, Herbert, 113

Kochrab, Gandhi's ashram at, 165

Kruger, Paul, and Jameson Raid, 123

Kshatriya Upkarni Maha Sabha (Society for the Welfare of Kshatriyas), 177

Kudhar/Kudharo (wrong path), in *Hind Swaraj*, 159, 161

Kumaun region (U.P.), forced labor in, 180

Kunti (Charmar woman), account of indenture, 176, 179

Kuyper, Abraham, "La Crise Sud-Africaine," 116

labor supply, British, 32

Lake, Marilyn, 22

Lamming, George, 214n64; "Caliban Orders History," 204

land, imperial, disposal of, 32, 40, 41, 44

Langenhoven, C. J., nationalist writings of, 127

language, political, transplantation of, 49n55

law, British: on immigration, 105, 107; role in empire, 16

League of Nations, 150

Legislative Council (India), anti-indenture resolution, 170–171

legitimacy, imperial, pluralism of, 2

Leibbrandt, H. C. V., 119, 123

Lewis, Arthur, 198

Leyds, Willem, 116

liberalism, and anticolonialism, 86

Liberal Party, British, pro-Boers in, 116

liberty, English, 82

Linebaugh, Peter, 203

literacy, British, 79

literary studies, diverse methods for, 12

Livesey, Ruth, 57

Lloyd, David, 80–81

Loch, Sir Henry, 100

London, reading classes of, 54

L'Ouverture, Toussaint, 193; in *The Black Jacobins*, 195, 202

Ludlow, J. M., 78

Macaulay, Thomas Babington: on "blue-stockings," 75; on Catholic emancipation, 80; celebrity of, 72; early life

modernity: and amodernity, 160; black presence in, 195; in Caribbean identity, 205; European, 156; Gandhi's critique of, 166; of plantation slavery, 206; in postcolonial studies, 191; through colonization, 86; warnings against, 156. *See also* civilization, modern

Molema, Setseele, 90

Moodie, Dunbar, *The Rise of Afrikaner-dom*, 127

Morning Chronicle: Dickens's contributions to, 35; serialization of *A Letter from Sydney* in, 33–35, 39, 41; treatment of social problems, 34–35

Morocco, secularism in, 9

Moses, Wilson, 192, 210n5

Moya, Lila, 59; reading of *Jane Eyre*, 58

Mugikuyu (Gikuyu ancestor), 225

Mungai, John, 227

Mureithi, Anderson, 222

Muumbi (Gikuyu ancestor), 225

Mwariama, General, 220

Mwigwithania (Gikuyu-language journal), 225

Narayan, Jayaprakash, 174

Natal: British annexation of, 123; indentured workers strike in, 169

National Colonization Society, 37, 42

nationalism: association with imperialism, 149; colonial, 84–85; constructive cooperation in, 149; Indian, 6; oppositional identity in, 81; racially based, 86; spread of ideas in, 148

nationalism, Afrikaner, 114; commemoration of concentration camps, 128; narratives of, 118–121, 127; postwar development of, 121; victim-based solidarity of, 126–129

nationalism, Irish, 80; appreciation of Scouting, 143, 149, 152n38

nation-states, hegemony of, 19

Nawal Kishore Press (Lucknow), 13

Neame, L. E., *The Asiatic Danger in the Colonies*, 106

Nehru, Jawaharlal: on *Hind Swaraj*, 153; monumental books of, 11

Neill, J. S., 184

Newgate Prison: resources for prisoners, 31; Wakefield in, 29–30, 31–32

New Left, British, "May Day Manifesto," 203

New South Wales: colonial liberalism of, 86; land grants in, 44; readers of Macaulay in, 82

newspapers, imperial: cut-and-paste genres of, 14, 17; dissemination of *A Letter from Sydney*, 39, 41; exchange system for, 28n37; *Fiji Mein Mere Ekkis Varsh* in, 168; in imperial commons, 5; in print culture, 39–40; source material of, 5

newspapers, Indian-language, 14–15; *Fiji Mein Mere Ekkis Varsh* in, 168; in Hindi, 174–175, 177; on indentured labor, 16, 171, 178; for indentured workers, 175–176

New World: omission from Macaulay's *History*, 85–86; societal regression in, 36

New Zealand: British settlement of, 29; colonization of, 40–41; land conflict in, 54; readers of Macaulay in, 81–82; Wakefield's influence in, 45; White New Zealand policy of, 106

"New Zealand crisis," 40–41

Ngũgĩ wa Thiong'o, 232

Nicholas II (tsar of Russia), on arms race, 113

Nkrumah, Kwame, 196

Normanby, Lord, 41

novels: coming-of-age, 65; in postcolonial literature, 11; relationship to tracts, 18; Victorian, 12, 51

Nyeri (Kenya), migrant workers from, 219

Obrecht, Téa, *The Tiger's Wife*, 132, 133

O'Connell, Daniel, 83

Preller, Gustav, 127
Pretorius, Henning, 123
Pretty, Graeme, 48n31
Price, Leah, 11–12, 18, 63, 64; on reading, 67n6
Prinsloo, Joachim, 125
print: commoditization of, 15; as empire, 15
print capitalism, 15
print culture, imperial: apparatuses of, 40; charismatic texts of, 6; communication circuit of, 31; formative processes of, 3; informality of, 15; innovations in, 13–14; *Jane Eyre* in, 66; lack of copyright in, 14; newspapers in, 39–40; plurality of, 14, 16; recycling in, 39; serialization in, 148
printing, imperial: artisanal, 6, 14–15, 27n33; diasporic printers of, 13, 27n33; expansion of, 13–14, 52–53, 55; mass, 137
printing, Indian, 14–15; of anti-indenture propaganda, 181–182; democratization of, 174; in Hindi, 174–175, 176–177, 180; for indentured workers, 174–175; under Press Act of 1910, 177
pro-Boer movements, 129; British, 115, 116–117, 128; *A Century of Wrong*'s aid to, 116; global, 117
property rights, imperial, 5–6. *See also* intellectual property
public spheres, virtual, 7
purushartha (principal human endeavors), 161

race war, East–West, 106
racism: *The Black Jacobins* on, 203; of British Empire, 90–91, 193; of early twentieth century, 192; stigmatization of Indians, 170, 171
Ramlilas, 182; use in anti-indenture movement, 183
Ray, Karen A., 187n5
readers: as accomplices of authors, 26n20; autonomous self of, 56–57; effect of books on, 12, 55–57; expanded

choices for, 55–56; growth in number of, 75; indentured workers, 174–175; nineteenth-century, 52–56; relationship to cultural property, 5
reading: in ashrams, 20; hegemonic modes of, 18; international circuits for, 17; as measure of worth, 56; pick-and-mix format for, 17; privileged style of, 64; tempos of, 19, 56; Victorian mode of, 18
Rediker, Marcus, 203
Reitz, F. W., 122
religion: in colonial civilization, 44; effect on movement of words, 49n54
Report on Indentured Labour in Fiji (Andrews and Pearson), 170, 184
Retief, Piet, 125
Rhodes, Cecil John: Baden-Powell's use of, 131, 135; imperialism of, 134
Rhys, Jean, *Wide Sargasso Sea*, 8, 22; bound volumes in, 52, 62–63; imperial setting of, 62; *Jane Eyre* and, 51–52, 61–63, 65, 67
Richmond, Jane Maria, 54–55, 68n20, 74
Richmond, William, 55
Rift Valley Agikuyu Union (ethnic association, Kenya), 219
Rintoul, Robert, 41
Roberts, General, 113
Roberts, Lord Frederick, 135
Robeson, Paul, 193, 194
Robinson, Cedric, 201
Rodney, Walter, 204
Roos, J. de V.: authorship of *A Century of Wrong*, 114; "Dingaan's Day," 119; government positions of, 126; interest in Afrikaner history, 118–119. *See also Century of Wrong, A*
Roosevelt, Theodore, 8; on *National Life and Character*, 104
Royal Africa Company, 86
Rudder, David, 209
Rudé, George, 202
Ruskin, John, *Unto This Last*, 164
Ryan, Selwyn, 201

Sabarmati ashram, 20, 172

sabhyata (civilization), Gandhi on, 158

Said, Edward, *Orientalism*, 146

Sanadhya, Totaram, 19; access to Hindi press, 176–177; and Andrews, 172; anti-indenture activism, 173, 181, 182–183, 186; at ashram Sabarmati, 20, 172; collaboration with Chaturvedi, 172, 173, 177; education of, 174; experience of indenture, 170, 171, 174; and Gandhi, 172; Hindi writings of, 172; importing of Hindi books, 174–175; at Indian National Congress, 181; newspaper contributions of, 176; public curiosity about, 173; public speaking engagements, 181

—*Fiji Mein Mere Ekkis Varsh*, 4, 168–186; audience for, 173, 180; Criminal Investigation Department inquiry into, 179; distribution of, 178–179; following abolition of indenture, 186; Hindi language of, 173–174; indenture in, 6, 168, 171; influence of, 21, 183–184; labor contracts in, 173; legal strategy of, 181; literary offspring of, 182–183; manuscript of, 177; mass-based politics and, 185; minor status of, 170, 186n4; movement through imperial system, 22; newspapers' promulgation of, 178–179; novelty of, 174; origins of, 172; parochial reputation of, 168; personal stories in, 170, 171; preface to, 178; publishing history of, 15, 168–169, 172–173, 177–180; resistance in, 21; success of, 168; translations of, 168, 184, 188n30; U. P. government on, 177–178; U. P. police on, 173

—other works: *Kuli-Pratha*, 181; "Prastavna," 189n63

San Domingo, competition with Britain, 195. *See also* Haiti

sanskriti (civilization), 158

Satyagraha: communities of, 165; Gandhi's practice of, 163, 164–165, 183, 185

Satyagraha Ashram, 164; vows at, 165, 167n27

Schwarz, Bill, 137

Scotland, Macaulay's narrative of, 79

Scott, David, 215n80; *Conscripts of Modernity*, 207, 208

Scott, Robert Falcon, 58

Scott, Sir Walter, fictional editor device of, 38

Scottish Enlightenment, 35

Scouting: appeal to other movements, 144; breaking of class barriers, 143; in British Empire, 131, 134, 147, 148; circulation of principles, 148; core values of, 137–138; crosscultural interconnections of, 147; Cub, 152n32; as democratizing force, 138, 139; endurance of, 131; Fourth Law of, 141, 147; for girls, 134–135, 136; global, 131, 134, 142, 143–144, 149–150; homosexual associations with, 140–141; imperialist framework of, 146, 147; in India, 135; as life lesson, 147; national unity through, 143; for nonwhites, 139; popularity of, 141–142; same-sex bonding in, 133–134, 140; serialization of ideas, 148; team building in, 131; training in, 143. *See also* Baden-Powell, Robert: *Scouting for Boys*

Seeley, J. R., 134; *The Expansion of England*, 103, 138

segregation, racial: in British Empire, 90–91; global policies of, 108

Select Committee on Secondary Punishments, Wakefield's evidence before, 32

self, autonomous, 11; in *Jane Eyre*, 60–61; of readers, 56–57

self, imperial, gendered, 8

serialization: in capitalist reproduction, 148; in print culture, 148

Seton, Ernest Thompson, influence on Baden-Powell, 140

Sharma, Ram Narain, 176

Sharma, Suresh, 158

Shiel, M. P., *The Yellow Danger*, 104

Shiels, William, 101

Shifra Wairire, detention of, 223

Singapore, progress in, 94